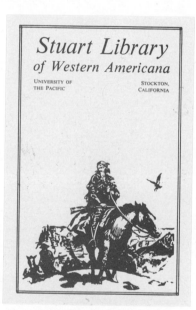

Author, Mark Fiester's interest in Breckenridge dates back to his first visit to the town in the Summer of 1939. Fascinated by the history of Breckenridge, he began to research old newspapers, books and reports. The result is a unique book about a unique community. A United Methodist Minister, Mark Fiester and his wife Roberta live in Frisco, Colorado.

Author, Mark Fiester holding Tom's Baby. Spread out on the table before him are almost two hundred glittering crystalized gold nuggets from the John F. Campion collection—United Bank of Denver, February 8, 1972

To the other half of the team—my wife—Roberta

BLASTED
BELOVED
BRECKENRIDGE

Mark Fiester

BLASTED
BELOVED
BRECKENRIDGE

Mark Fiester

Pruett Publishing Company
Boulder, Colorado 80302

ISBN: 0-87108-059-1

Library of Congress Card Catalog Number: 72-87818

First Edition

Pruett Publishing Company
Boulder, Colorado 80302

Printed in the United States of America
by
Pruett Press, Incorporated

ACKNOWLEDGMENTS

A Book's An Inn
A book's an Inn whose patrons' praise
Depends on seasons and on days,
On dispositions, and——in fine——
Not wholly on the landlord's wine.
(Richard R. Kirk)

We trust the inn-keeper's proffered cup—*Blasted Beloved Breckenridge*—is to your enjoyment, and that your day and disposition are favorably inclined to receive it as extended.

To adequately thank all who have contributed to *Blasted Beloved Breckenridge* would mean "parting the veil" and sending an echoing "thank-you" down silent corridors of long-gone years. In Breckenridge Valley Brook Cemetery one moves slowly from gravestone to gravestone —from friend to friend. Faces "come smiling through" and anecdotes come to mind of yesteryear. They speak of the cares, the foibles, the ordinary round of life—troubles, tears, joys— striving, gaining, losing. It was life, filled with events and episodes, intensely meaningful. Now all is locked in the halls of history and the timelessness of the tomb. The writer is forever grateful to those who lived that once-vibrant life and shared it with us. Many of the hitherto unknowns have become cherished friends. I thank them all.

There are some who were vitally interested in the writing of *Blasted Beloved Breckenridge*, but the call "from the other side" came and they departed before the book was finished—Minnie Thomas, Belle Turnbull, Helen Rich. Helen Rich's deep interest, her esteemed criticism, her lively encouragement were sources of inspiration to a struggling writer. How we wish we might have had her valued stamp of approval on final chapters. Life's endeavors are enriched by the friendship and assistance of such as these.

PICTURES

A Chinese proverb states, "One picture is worth more than ten thousand words." If true,

Blasted Beloved Breckenridge is in debt to the tune of two million. The following have generously shared pictures to enliven pages of this book:

Denver Public Library Western Collection, Library State Historical Society of Colorado, Denver Museum of Natural History, Denver *Post* Library, Summit County Historical Society, Summit County *Journal* Library, State Library of Victoria-Australia, Mitchell Library Sidney-Australia, New York Public Library, Chicago Public Library;

E. Bruce Schock (Arvada)-Architect's drawing of Father Dyer Church when first built, Continental Engineers, Inc. (Denver)-Planimetric Map of Blue River Valley 1860-1900, U. S. Geological Survey-Breckenridge Mining District-1911, Patterson Distributing Company (Denver)-F. G. Brandenburg and C. C. Patterson-Photographers, *Famous Gold Nuggets of the World*-Thomas Jefferson Hurley, Photo-Graphics Internationale (Arvada), King's Photography (Denver);

Cal Queal (formerly-Denver *Post Empire Magazine*), John Topolnicki-Photographer, Melvin Gaymon, Carl Enyeart-Jr., L. G. McKee, Rev. Robert John Stewart, Jack Caubin;

Mrs. Ray McGinnis, Mrs. Ted Fletcher, Mrs. H. G. Culbreath, Mrs. Minnie Thomas, Mrs. Marion Griffin.

RESEARCH

Writers of Western history are abundantly blessed by access to Denver Public Library, State Historical Society of Colorado, Denver Museum of Natural History. Western History Department of Denver Public Library is a bonanza for the prospector. Staff members are not only capable and qualified to assist the researcher, but, in addition, give individual consideration and attention as though you were the only person seeking help. No word of praise or gratitude could adequately express my appreciation for the personal attention offered so willingly by these wonderful co-workers in Colorado history.

Words of appreciation are due Summit County *Journal* for permitting files to be available to the searcher of historical items. "Tom's Baby" chapter required verification of many interest items. Information was sought from Bureaus of Mines and Geology of California, Montana, Nevada, Alaska, North Carolina and help was forthcoming quickly. Australia's Department of National Development was generous in assistance. James Keough, Topographic Division of the U. S. Geological Survey, provided altitude statistics of Ten-Mile Range peaks (and other high mountains)—information that will be appearing in the new 1972 maps of Rocky Mountain areas. Again, the writer is deeply indebted.

SPECIAL ASSISTANCE

Blasted Beloved Breckenridge needed help from many sources, and the response was gratifying. Mrs. Louisa Arps, co-searcher for "Tom's Baby," was especially helpful. Jack Brockman, Vice-President of Security Title Guaranty Company, allowed the writer to see Archie Willson's fake "Tom's Baby." Allan R. Phipps, President-Board of Trustees, Denver Museum of Natural History, was exceptionally generous in permitting the writer to be present when the Campion Gold Collection was opened and on display, providing opportunity for the writer to see and hold "Tom's Baby." Jack Murphy, Curator of Geology, Denver Museum of Natural History, took a lively interest in "Tom's Baby" from the time first approached by the writer. Much credit is due him for opening doors—and the safety-deposit box— to the Campion Collection. Then, too, one must mention introduction to a very interesting person (through correspondence)—Archie Willson, the creator of the fake "Tom's Baby." Archie thoroughly researched "Tom's Baby" and provided much corroborating information. All shared in the solving of "Maddening Mystery" and added thrills to the search.

Mrs. H. G. Culbreath's father was administrator of the Edwin Carter estate. Through the kindness of Mrs. Culbreath, estate papers were made available to the writer, providing many of the interesting and moving incidents in the Edwin Carter story. Daughter of Banker George Engle, plus a life-time in Breckenridge, ranks Mrs. Cul-

breath as one of our most qualified providers of historical information.

Mrs. Zoe Perrin and Mrs. "Frankie" Wilson shared stories that had been handed down of Breckenridge White Gloves and Wallpaper days. Their stories of early social life were delightful.

A special thank-you goes to Mrs. James Vasilka for sharing the historical record of Breckenridge's Fire Department beginnings. The record dove-tailed beautifully with historical items gleaned here and there, verifying the research.

The history of the Catholic Church would have been meager, had it not been for interesting and detailed information from three sources: Mother Jean Marie, O. S. B., Prioress St. Scholastica Convent, Chicago; Father Francis Hornung, Holy Cross Abbey, Canon City, Colorado; Father John Slattery, former priest at Breckenridge St. Mary's Church. A visit with Father Hornung was an unforgettable experience. A painful arm ailment did not deter him from typing and sending a number of letters, filled with interesting and informative items. How can one say adequate thanks for such gracious assistance?

The story of St. John the Baptist Episcopal Church was enriched through the sharing of Parish Records. This, too, was a kindness extended to the writer.

Then there is the one who has almost the last word to say—after having said many helpful words—Gerald Keenan of Pruett Press—publisher of *Blasted Beloved Breckenridge*. A writer has great need of a friendly, helpful editor. This writer found one.

And last, but not least by any means, much gratitude is due the congregation of Father Dyer United Methodist Church for patient indulgence and generous consideration during the writing of *Blasted Beloved Breckenridge*. It has been an honor to be pastor of such an historic church and wonderful people.

The list is long, but far from complete. Words of approval and encouragement came from many, expressing kindly interest and goodwill. We borrow from William Shakespeare, and say to all kind friends:

"I can no other answer make but thanks,
And thanks, and ever thanks."

(*Twelfth-Night*, Act III, Scene 3)

Bernard Kelly — *Denver Post Empire Magazine*

My first memory of Mark L. Fiester is a pleasant one; but it hardly held any hint of what was to come.

I was sitting at my desk on the third floor of *The Denver Post* building, writing—as I remember it—some cutlines for the weekly food column of *Empire*, the Sunday magazine of *The Post*. Somewhere between "pour batter into pan" and "bake at 350 degrees (Fahr.) until done," this man with pleasant face and disarming smile introduced himself.

Mark Fiester is an enthusiast, and as I too am an enthusiast, we got along well right from the start. *Empire* did a story on an Easter pageant he had written and produced. (He also wrote and produced a religious Pageant of Christmas that drew overflow crowds to Denver Auditorium Theatre.) But what was more important, we hit it off, Mark Fiester and I, and from that time on we met here and there, talked about whatever was current, and saw our acquaintance expand.

I remember feeling concern when he decided to give up the security of a city church for what seemed to me a remote and quiet backwater— a town called Breckenridge—where he was going to continue his ministry in an old, old church. This church had been established by a famous Colorado Methodist minister, the Rev. John Lewis Dyer, a man so widely known and revered that he's usually referred to only as Father Dyer. Father Dyer, who took to the steep, snowy trails on skis or snowshoes to carry The Word, called himself *The Snowshoe Itinerant.*

"I'm going to write a book about Father Dyer someday," Mark Fiester told me.

When you work with authors as I do you hear a lot of this kind of talk: "I'm going to write a book about. . . ."

Mark came to Denver now and then, and because our acquaintance now had grown to genuine friendship, he often came up to see me when he was in town.

"How's the book coming?" I asked him once.

"Which book?" he asked.

"The Father Dyer book."

He smiled.

"I'm afraid I kind of got sidetracked on that," he said. "Mind, I'm still going to write the Father Dyer book—but right now I'm researching a book about Breckenridge."

Breckenridge! Well, yes, I could understand that. A fascinating town. I was doing some research myself about then, and I would encounter Mark Fiester at the State Museum or among the cozy tables of the Western History Department of the Denver Public Library.

There's a register there, and when I wrote my own name, I often saw his. Once I saw him staring at a microfilm reader, typing notes on a portable typewriter. I was about to tap him on the shoulder, but decided not to. I'm glad now I didn't. I might have held up publication for a few days of the book you now hold in your hands.

Mark paid me a great compliment when he

asked me if I'd write a foreword to his book. Sure, I said.

"Write whatever you feel," he said.

I feel this: I had the privilege of reading some of the chapters of this book in manuscript, and the equal privilege of knowing its author. I'll try to tell you a little about him.

He was born and reared in Williamsport, Pa., and is a minister of the Evangelical Church. Unions have now changed that to the Evangelical United Brethren, then United Methodist Church.

In 1937 he married Roberta Dexheimer, daughter of the Rev. and Mrs. R. D. Dexheimer of Denver. It was 1965 when he decided to take that Breckenridge pastorate, for a $1,200-a-year salary, meanwhile providing his own parsonage and paying all the utilities. He did it because he wanted to lay a foundation for the future growth of the Father Dyer church.

Fortunately for them both Roberta Fiester had a job teaching in the Jefferson County School System (Paul C. Stevens elementary school, where she's a resource teacher) otherwise the work couldn't have been undertaken and a livelihood provided.

Roberta Fiester completed two years of theological seminary toward a Bachelor of Divinity degree, and this has been a fortunate thing. She was an A-student and is a good sermonizer, Mark says.

Mark is a good utility man, too. He can and does play organ and piano. If for some reason the organist is absent, he takes over at the keyboard while his wife opens the service. Once on a stormy day Mark opened the service, walked back to the organ to play a hymn, then stoked the huge stove with billets of pine, returned to the organ, and wound up at the pulpit.

Carrying out the needs of his ministry and trying to work on the book, meanwhile going back and forth from Breckenridge to Denver, has made Mark Fiester a good driver. He has made more than 500 round trips over the spectacular mountain road with no accidents.

During the weeks of the school year while Mark and Roberta are separated (except on weekends), the telephone connects them and whopping big bills are run up, but all for the good of this close-knit team.

For it is a team. Roberta Fiester is a good typist and editor. Mark types his pages and she retypes them for the printer. He's an early riser, she's night people.

"When she turns out the lights it's time for me to get up," he says.

Masses of notes accumulated. He used clothing boxes to store them, two boxes to a chapter. There are 24 chapters. A big kitchen table was moved out into the living room of the Fiester home in Frisco, and boxes and boxes of miscellaneous stuff were piled about the room. No one dared move them. If someone did the relatively mild Fiester let out a roar.

When he had written something, Mark would stretch out on a cot, close his eyes, and listen to Roberta read it back to him.

"We would often stop to argue over a word," she says.

"Like what word?" I asked.

"Mark likes the word *alas*," she says. "I took out a lot of *alases*. But I left one in, for his sake."

Driving down from Breckenridge after a weekend of work in Frisco and Breckenridge to return Roberta to her teaching duties, Mark sings hymns to pass the time. He knows the hymnal from front to back, all the verses.

In 1969 it looked like there might be no more singing and no book. On Good Friday night after the service in Breckenridge, Mark Fiester suffered a heart attack.

Roberta accompanied him to a Denver hospital, but not until she promised to return to Breckenridge to hold a cherished Easter service. She carried out her word.

Mark returned to Breckenridge the following June 7 to perform a wedding he had promised, but Roberta conducted services the rest of that summer.

As you see, it has not been easy. There were dark times, seemingly dead ends.

"We've been through lots of depths," Roberta Fiester says. "But the sun *does* shine again."

And it shines now for Mark Fiester in this big and fascinating book about *Blasted Beloved Breckenridge*.

Bernard Kelly

TABLE OF CONTENTS

	Introduction	*xiii*
I	Softly Beautiful Valley	3
II	Breckenridge 1859-1860	15
III	Pegasus	25
IV	Trumpet of Zion	41
V	Bayard and Breckenridge	49
VI	Marshall Silverthorn	57
VII	Skiing	67
VIII	Breckenridge Navy	79
IX	Ye Editor	87
X	Churches	97
XI	Schools	121
XII	Court Houses	129
XIII	Hospitals	139
XIV	Broncho Dave	143
XV	Indiana Gulch	151
XVI	Fireman's Hall	163
XVII	Sister's Mustard Seeds	175
XVIII	Dynamiting the Church Bell	185
XIX	Pug Ryan	201
XX	Boreas-Storm King	205
XXI	White Gloves and Wallpaper	219
XXII	Rough and Shady	237
XXIII	Maddening Mystery—Tom's Baby	243
	Addendum	293
XXIV	Edwin Carter: Miniature to Magnificent	303
	Epilogue	325
	Notes	335
	Bibliography	339
	Index	343
	Planimetric Map—Early Breckenridge—Blue River Valley Area	Map Pocket

Pruett Publishing Company
Boulder, Colorado

INTRODUCTION

BLASTED
("mild expletive for damned")

BELOVED
("greatly loved")

BRECKENRIDGE
("damned and loved")

May, 1860, a disgruntled prospector, fretting and puffing his way up the range from embryonic Breckenridge, Colorado, to Hoosier Summit, Rocky Mountain Continental Divide, paused long enough to take a final look at the Valley of the Blue and crudely print a retaliation sign. He fastened the placard to a tree, with an arrow pointing to Breckenridge. The caustic message read:

"TWENTY MILES TO HELL AND BACK!"

Dame Fortune didn't smile on all gold prospectors, especially the ones hastily looking for easily-gained wealth. The comment of unruffled Breckenridge was, "the loss of such customers is not regretted."

Nor did Breckenridge rank highly in the estimation of some of her visitors. An 1877 diary of the Princeton Scientific Expedition had a bizarre entry for Sunday, July 22nd:

We heartily recommend Breckenridge as being the most fiendish place we ever wish to see. We were forced to spend the morning and afternoon in the company of men whose language was vile. In the morning there was a series of dog-fights. A ring of yelling demoniacs was gathered around two poor curs. Upon the success or defeat of one or the other large sums of gold-dust were freely wagered. Old Judge Silverthorn innocently remarked that "the men would soon commence," and sure enough they did commence very quick, quarreling about the slightest thing, and fighting like devils while their breath lasted, which, on account of the rarity of the air at this altitude, was not more than ten minutes. Finally Breckenridge seemed satisfied and grew quiet outside in the streets, but the men only adjourned to the saloons (almost every other house was one), where their carousing kept up till late in the night.

Living in Breckenridge was not a pleasant experience for everyone. One gentleman, venting his spleen at a later date, expressed himself: "I was born and raised in Breckenridge, and I don't care to ever see the gol-darned place again."

Many a dissatisfied, disappointed, dejected, disgruntled one crossed the range for other parts, defiantly grumbling — *blasted Breckenridge!* Some drank deeply of failure, hardship, heartache, disappointment. Breckenridge hasn't been kind to everyone.

And, of course, there were some not disposed toward making a success of life in Breckenridge, or anywhere else:

"Some it pays, and others not,
So it is the world around;
Many would not make a cent,
Were it heaped upon the ground."

Far outnumbering the disappointed and displeased are the many who have found Breckenridge delightful and kindly-disposed. These go into ecstasy in their praise. For them there is but one degree—the superlative. Climate and scenery evoke the greatest vaunting.

The weather of the Rocky Mountain region has ever been a source of marvel. Dire predictions accompanied the foolhardy, rushing to the Rocky Mountain wilderness; they couldn't hope to survive the blasting heat of summer or the bitter cold of winter. 1858 pioneers found summer days hot at the base of the mountains, but the nights were delightfully cool, requiring a blanket or two. The winter of 1858-1859 was a big surprise; it was unusually mild ("so much so that the inhabitants of Denver and Auraria never stopped to do outdoor work, and that with their coats off. They hardly kept up a fire during midday hours.") At the end of the first year and a half, in this newly-settled area, Henry Villard ventured a definition of the climate which has been proved accurate through succeeding years:

1st. That, contrary to general belief, the winters are no more severe than in any of the States north of the Ohio.
2nd. That the spring is the most unpleasant of the seasons. (March and April can be boisterous and disagreeable—much more so than any portion of the winter months.)
3rd. That summer sets in late.
4th. That during the summer months hardly any rain falls, and that heat, although not as intense as in the States, is at times very great.
5th. That the fall months are the most agreeable time of the year.

First winter in the mountains held similar surprise and like pattern. First snows of the fall season vanished quickly, and glorious weather followed. Winter snows were not extremely heavy until spring had a right to be in evidence—then came the heaviest and most dangerous snows. Early summer had its rainy season, followed by incomparable summer and fall seasons. In general, this is the usual weather pattern of foothills and mountains.

Bayard Taylor, noted world-traveler and lecturer, joined in adulation and praise:

The air is at once a tonic, a stimulant, and a flavor. Whatever effect the climate of the Rocky Mountain regions may have upon the permanent settlers, there is no doubt that for travelers it is one of the most favorable in the world. It takes fat from the corpulent, and gives to the lean; it strengthens delicate lungs, and paints pallid faces with color; and in spite of "thin air and alkali water," it invigorates every function of the system. Two things are hardly to be surpassed,—water and sleep. The water is like crystal, icy cold, and so agreeable to the palate that I am tempted to drink it when not thirsty. It is said to contain a slight proportion of alkali, and a common phrase among the people attributes their irregularities to the "thin air and alkali water." The properties of the latter, however, are said to be anaphrodisiac, which is rather an advantage than otherwise, in a new country. As for sleep, I don't know when I have found it so easy to obtain, or so difficult to relinquish. When I awake in the morning the half-conscious sense that I have been asleep is so luxurious that I immediately sleep again, and each permitted nap is sweeter than the last.

The residents of this place (Breckenridge) profess to be delighted with the climate, although there is no month of the year without frost, and the winter snow is frequently three or four feet in depth. They have little sickness of any kind, and recover from wounds or hardship with a rapidity unknown elsewhere. I do not wonder at the attachment of the inhabitants of the territory for their home. These mountains and this atmosphere insensibly become a portion of their lives. I foresee that they will henceforth be among the clearest and most vivid episodes of mine.

Early morning was especially beautiful to Bayard Taylor, with mountain peaks flashing in rosy splendor, the first rays of the sun putting a golden glitter on snow-capped pinnacles. At one's feet silver sage was diamond-sprinkled with dew. Taylor wrote, "Among the Alps, such a morning is a rare godsend; here it is almost a matter of course."

Mornings and evenings in the mountains are softly beautiful in alpenglow, reds, purples and soft pinks, preceding sunrise and following sunset. Springtime garbs the aspen in shimmering chartreuse; fall season transforms the leaves to glistening gold, displaying all the undiscovered treasure-trove of the mountains.

A quaintness and charm sets Breckenridge apart from the ordinary mountain town. Long ago, "Ye Editor" of Breckenridge newspaper proudly prophesied, "from Deacon Huntress' cottage (at the south end of town) to the lower end of Main Street will one day be the prettiest half-mile of street in the mountains." To many it already *was* the prettiest. Breckenridge, however, never had the mansions and ornateness of the Colorado towns of Leadville, Central City or Georgetown. It was a charm designed for those of more moderate circumstances.

Breckenridge was proud. It possessed a generous measure of New England aloofness and independence. On one occasion, it defiantly proclaimed that some of the laws of the State were "alright for musty Denver, but they didn't apply to Breckenridge and couldn't be enforced." Could it have been Breckenridge that Helen Rich was describing in her book, *The Spring Begins*, when she wrote of Buckbush? (Helen Rich, a Breckenridge author, wrote novels that have Breckenridge area background.)

> Buckbush had a sort of law about the matter of outside people coming there to live. Anyone who wanted to come to Buckbush to live was welcome if that's what he called being welcome. He was welcome to buy property, to vote, to lease a mine or open a store, or just live there and do nothing if he was that well fixed. But he couldn't expect to be called by his first name, or be asked to join the firemen, and he wouldn't be nominated for office. Not for about twenty years. Up to about twenty years he was a stranger. After that he belonged to Buckbush as much as anybody else.

If not born in Breckenridge, you didn't belong until you had served an apprenticeship. Once you belonged, you belonged. Then came a loyalty that bound together. You really didn't belong until you had found your secret patch of wild raspberries, black or red currants, huckleberries, gooseberries, chokecherries or rare mushrooms—and, heaven forbid! you didn't expect anyone to reveal a favorite, secret patch.

Breckenridge is Breckenridge—unloved and beloved. It has known the explosive gold-mining booms of 1860 and 1880. It had the 1900 high expectation of the gold boat. It is now experiencing the boom of skiing and mountain recreation. Through it all it maintains its individualistic identity.

The author, a minister, had his first visit to Breckenridge area, summer of 1939. His father-in-law, another minister, owned a small cabin at Frisco, Colorado. It was worth driving day and night from New Jersey to spend a two weeks' vacation in the Rocky Mountains. In 1965 came the opportunity to pastor the Father Dyer Church in Breckenridge.

From the first visit to Breckenridge there has been a never-ending, never-failing fascination. Climbing the gold boat's mountains of stones, exploring wide-open deserted buildings, shading eyes and squinting through cracks of "boarded up" buildings—one's desire was whetted to know the stories represented in these relics of the past.

The few stories narrated were varied and widened in the telling. Sometimes they didn't actually concur. Little or nothing was available in printed form to tell the stories. Helen Rich's and Belle Turnbull's novels came later; their concern was the novel more than historical presentation. Later, Miss Rich was to explain—"You are endeavoring to do in historical presentation what we were seeking to do through the novel—preserve the idiom of the area—but in different periods of time. While you are primarily concerned about the period of time from the founding of Breckenridge to the end of the 19th century, we were seeking to preserve the way of life prevalent in the second quarter of the 20th century. Ours is a composite of not only Breckenridge but nearby, surrounding places during the last days of the gold boat era."

The author's desire to know Breckenridge lore and legend directed him to research. Old newspapers were avidly studied, as well as early-written books and reports. Some details have come from far-away sources, some direct from old-timers. The more one reads and learns of Breckenridge the more fascinating this "gem of the mountains" becomes. The difficulty is narrowing the stories to book form.

The intention was to center the stories around Breckenridge between 1859 and 1900. History has been described as an ever-flowing stream—it cannot be confined to certain specific brackets of time or to one area. It has the brooks and rivulets feeding the main stream and continually flows onward. Stories of Breckenridge enlarged to stories of the Breckenridge area, and sometimes the time element lapped over into the 20th century. We granted ourselves permission to glance a number of times over Hoosier Pass into South Park, for the history of South Park and Blue River Valley are inseparably related.

The plan of the writer is to present historical stories. Sometimes the historical is not what is desired for the story. Whenever fact and fancy came into conflict, fancy bowed to the historical fact. Poetic license has been employed rarely; where used, it is clearly evident to the reader. We consider the work ninety per-cent historical fact.

Much of the presentation is in quotation form. We could have re-written, abbreviated, put into modern writing-form, but the delicious "flavor" and feeling of "being there at the time" would be sacrificed. You read what was seen and interpreted by those present at the time—written in their own unique style. Occasionally, for clarity, punctuation marks were inserted and long sentences shortened into two or three.

The writer of books is forewarned—"expect frustration and crisis periods; they will come." They do! A crisis period came in the writing of this book—whether or not to include lengthy quotations—the oft-given admonition is, "abbreviate and relate in your own words." The concluding paragraph of an article in *Empire Magazine*, Sunday, May 23, 1971, by Joanne Ditmer, Denver *Post* writer, resolved the matter. The article concerned Mrs. Crawford Hill's mansion, now used as a social club. (Mrs. Hill reigned as Denver's early-day social queen.) The comment of a club member was: "It's a constant question of whether to tear down and build new, because we could have lots of extra services without the costly maintenance. But we'd never have all the charm and history this house has . . . and that's what we prefer."

The re-writing of Breckenridge stories presented the same alternatives—but a treasure of charm, history and documentation would have been sacrificed in the reconstruction. We prefer the charm, the history, the documentation preserved in the writing of those present at the time. Rightly termed, then, this book should be called *Breckenridge Stories* by many authors.

Chronological order is not followed. Instead, one particular story is developed at a time. It is hoped that you find yourself living the life of early Breckenridge, learning to know Bronco Dave, Jerry Krigbaum (the old "he-angel"), Marshall Silverthorn, "Ye Editor" of the newspaper, Father Dyer of the Methodist Church, Father Chapius of the Catholic Church, and a host of others. In the future, when roaming Breckenridge country, perhaps the old and almost forgotten will come to life again—Braddockville, U-B-Dam Flats, Buffalo Flats, Delaware Flats, Georgia Gulch, Parkville, Wapiti, Lincoln City, pre-1900 Breckenridge, Argentine, Dyerville, Dickey, Naomi, Lakeside—and one-cabin Eldorado West. If you gain a more familiar acquaintance with the life, the people, the places that made *Blasted Beloved Breckenridge*, the purpose of the writing will be fulfilled.

An early textbook defined history as a "record of all that man has ever hoped, done, thought or felt." We make a transmigration into the Breckenridge life of 1860-1900, into its happenings, hopes, thoughts and feelings. It is this kind of history we present.

Mark Fiester
Look Up Lodge
Frisco, Colorado

"SOFTLY BEAUTIFUL VALLEY"

Summer view, looking down into "Softly Beautiful Valley" from near top of Hoosier Pass. Frederick Leslie Ransome, *(Geology And Ore Deposits Of The Breckenridge District*—page 17), contributed the phrase "softly beautiful valley." In its context, it applied to the "verdant meadowland" of Snake River, describing a valley that eventuates in Blue River Valley. It is descriptive of the entire Valley of Blue River.

Winter view — "Softly Beautiful Valley"

Ruins of Hall's Historic South Park
(Valle Salade) Salt Works
—Courtesy Cal. Queal, *Denver Post*

SOFTLY BEAUTIFUL VALLEY

Rocky Mountain Continental Divide makes the decision for Colorado rivers, whether to go to the Pacific or Atlantic Ocean. Atop the Continental Divide, at Hoosier Pass, timberline, 11,542 feet above sea level, facing north, one looks down upon the "softly beautiful valley" of Blue River, Colorado. Right, left, and far ahead pinnacles — (pointed mountain peaks) — and aretes—(sharp narrow serrated ridges)—rise another two thousand feet toward the sky. These are the rocky ramparts defending the peaceful valley of the Blue. Erosion, excavating almost impregnable mountains, formed cirques—(steep circular amphitheatres)—surrounded by pinnacle and arete. Pocketing snow of many winters, pinnacles, aretes and cirques gain for themselves the name of "never-summer" heights—the snowy dome of the Continent.

In summer's softness, fleecy white clouds drift lazily in bright-blue sky, playfully permitting sunshine and shadow to caress mountain peak and valley. An ever-changing mood passes lightly and quickly across the vast panorama. In winter's harshness, turbulent clouds boil around summits and cast gray-black shadows over towering slopes, then slowly creep into the valley three and four thousand feet below. Storms come quickly and furiously—summer and winter. When the passion and fury subside, the softly beautiful again mantles mountain and valley.

Hoosier Pass is a gateway between South Park and Blue Valley-Middle Park. The huge, lush basin, South Park, is believed to be the remains of a sea that filled the basin fifty million years ago. Salt springs gush forth, indicating millions of gallons of strong brine deep in the earth. Spanish explorers called it Valle Salade, the salt valley. Numerous springs and freshets provide an abundance of sweet water, making South Park a veritable Garden of Eden.

The valley of the Blue slopes gently northward from Hoosier Pass, through heavy growths of pine and spruce, to the flat-floored valley that merges into Middle Park. Where forest surrenders to open valley Breckenridge took her commanding location as "gem of the mountain" and "queen of the valley."

Blue River has its headwaters near Hoosier Pass. In the first twenty miles, French Creek, Swan River and Snake River join the Blue from the east; Ten Mile Creek, from the west, enters at almost the same point as Snake River. (In recent years Dillon Reservoir changed the picture; the meeting point of Snake, Ten Mile and the Blue disappeared in the depths of "Dillon Lake." Denver Water Board accepted the reservoir as completed December 17, 1963. Estimations were that it would take five years to fill; an exceptionally good run-off "spilled" the lake in the summer of 1965.)

Upper Blue Valley, the ten miles from Breckenridge to Hoosier Pass, shows the residue of two glacial periods. Advances and retreats of the ice left their record in moraines and hummocks. Moraine deposits account for the mass of rocks, gravel and sand composing the floor of the valley; hummock deposits formed the small ridges and rounded knolls. Lateral moraine was the deposit on the sides of the glacier; terminal moraine marked the end of glacier movement. Terminal moraine is found south of Breckenridge, and smaller moraines are found in French Gulch and the three forks of Swan Valley.

South Park lays claim to sea basin origin

fifty million years ago; Blue Valley also has signs of ancient origin, other than the glacial. During the Pleistocene ice age the giant mastodon—an elephant-type, bulky proboscidean — roamed throughout North America. In 1861 two men, Barry and Kirkpatric, unearthed remains supposed to be of a mastodon in a gulch near Breckenridge. The *Rocky Mountain News*, June 22, 1861, reported:

ANTEDILUVIAN RELIC

We have in our possession—thanks to Mr. Silverthorn of Breckenridge—a portion of the tusk of a Mastodon or some other monster of remote ages. The tusk was found by some miners near Breckenridge, who were digging a ditch. It lay about five feet below the surface of the ground, in a gulch. The dimensions are, length a little over four feet, diameter at base eight inches and at the point a little more than four inches. The latter was broken off by a blow with a pick, before its character was suspected. Upon exposure to the air it crumbled somewhat and had to be wrapped with strips of cloth to preserve it. Two smaller teeth were found in the same vicinity. One of them, which we saw, had been split, but is still two and a half by three and a half inches in diameter and five inches in length, with roots and general outlines plainly distinguishable.

This we believe is the first discovery of the remains of Antediluvian monsters being found west of the Mississippi Valley.

Another revelation of ancient origin of Blue River Valley was reported in first issue of Summit County's first newspaper—Kokomo's *Summit County Times*. It told of a finding at Lincoln, French Gulch, four miles east of Breckenridge:

Over at Lincoln City (near Breckenridge), a few days since, the petrified body of an unusually large man was unearthed. It was discovered by a prospector while digging at the foot of the mountain. Its body was seven feet in length, and breadth across the chest thirty inches. In the immediate vicinity were also found several large iron and copper balls and a huge death-dealing war club of bone. The giant's body was not disturbed. These items are gleaned from Mr. D. C. Benard, a miner of the Eagle district, who was personally present when the excavation and discovery was made.

Four tribes of Ute Indians were numbered among the inhabitants of Colorado—the White River or Middle Park Utes, the Uncompahgre Utes, the Uintahs and the Los Pinos tribe. Utes were mountain Indians, nomadic hunters. For the most part, all were peace-loving, but Chief Ouray's band of Los Pinos and Uncompahgres were the most peaceable.

Before advent of the white man, White River-Middle Park Utes claimed South Park, Blue River Valley, Middle Park as their hunting grounds. The Indian trail, from one park to the other, traversed Hoosier Pass. In passage to and from parks sometimes the Utes camped at the entrance to Ten Mile Canyon, Frisco; other times at the mouth of Swan Valley on Blue River. Only an occasional explorer, trapper or hostile Indian invaded their domains. Utes lived a peaceful life in their hunting grounds, except for periodic raids from plains Indians, Arapahoes and Cheyennes, who delighted in capturing, humiliating and torturing Ute braves.

To the peaceful valley of Blue River the Indians gave the name Nah-oon-ka-ra. (Various spellings of the name are given—Nah-oon-kara, Nah-oon-ka-ra, Nah-un-kah-rea and Na-un-ka-ra. Correspondence with three Ute Indian Agencies brought similar reply—the word is not familiar and no adequate English translation can be made.)

Wildlife abounded in the park, valley and mountain — buffalo, elk, antelope, mountain sheep, deer, beaver, bear, rabbit, squirrel, grouse. Streams were filled with trout. Indian needs made small dent in the supply of animal, fish and fowl. Mountain lions, cougars, and other predatory animals and birds, had little effect on nature's abundant supply. Wild currants, gooseberries, strawberries and raspberries, in great abundance, tickled the palate of epicurean bears. Nature was prolific and generous.

Into this idyllic setting and life came the invasion of the white man, seeking wealth. The softly beautiful valley of the Blue must yield its treasures to gold-grasping man. Of the many Upper Blue mining camps—along river, in gulch and valley, on hill and mountainside—one was destined to rise above the others and remain—Breckenridge—"a proud little place, and well she may be, for she rests on a bed of gold, and has running by her doors a beautiful river whose waters fall into the broad Pacific."

Turn back the pages of American history to the beginning of the year 1858:

January, 1858, the only inhabitants of

what is now Colorado were Indians, a few French and American trappers, and a few soldiers at Bent's Fort, on the Arkansas, and Fort Massachusetts, in San Luis Valley. The excitement over gold discoveries had not yet begun; but before the close of the year 1858 it was under full sway, and the country gained four or five hundred inhabitants. They were living in Denver, Boulder and Golden. A little gold mining with pans and rockers and short sluice boxes was done in West Denver and at the mouth of Clear Creek and Boulder canyons. Gold had not yet been found in the mountains.

The conditions in the United States favored the rapid settlement of the country. The great financial panic of 1857 had swept away thousands of fortunes and impoverished hundreds of thousands. People were in the right frame to mind to emigrate to any region whose hope held out promise of bettering their condition. When the word went out that the yellow god been found at Pike's Peak the rush came. California, North Carolina and Georgia were the only gold-producing states. Silver was not mined anywhere in the United States.

A wonderful change has come over the world since that day. No railroad then reached farther than eastern Iowa. Minnesota, Wisconsin, Kansas and Nebraska were among the territories and but little settled. The entire population of the United States was only 30,000,000. Tallow candles and sperm oil furnished light for houses and cities. Kerosene had not been discovered, and gas was used in only a few cities in the world. The stage coach was the commonest means of travel, even in New England and New York. Ocean travel was largely in sailing vessels, and what steamers existed were side-wheelers. Rich men were few, and $10,000 was considered a competency. Millionaires were scarcer than kings. There were only five in the United States. Trusts and great corporations had not changed the business methods or life of the people. Wagons, and shoes, and homespun goods, and things now made by trusts, were manufactured in every town. The lives of the people were simple, and tramps were as scarce as millionaires.

In a political way the slavery question was the absorbing topic, and rumblings of the civil war were in the air.

1858 was the year of change for "America" and the "West." Previously, the Rocky Mountain West held little attraction for those who enjoyed the comfort and security of the civilized East. The severe panic of 1857, and rumors of gold in Pike's Peak country, gave a new aspect to the West.

People knew little about the far West. It was land that belonged to the Indian, aborigines of unknown origin. Spanish adventurers, in the sixteenth century, invaded the rugged vastness, foraging for gold. Face to face with austerities, they retreated. A few fur traders penetrated the region, bartering with the Indian for pelts and trinkets. Major Zebulon Pike, 1805, undertook an exploration expedition and viewed, from a distance, the towering peak that bears his name. Colonel Fremont, 1843-1844, on his way to and from the Pacific coast, "explored the headwaters of Green and Grand Rivers and the three Parks—a country heretofore known only to Indians and a few white hunters. His was the first regular exploring party that is known to have visited the Western Slope."

Except for the Spaniards, gold was not the main purpose of the early invasion of the mountains. Vague rumors of gold were not strong enough to incite action to seek possible treasure in the vast and feared wilderness. Green Russell, the Georgia miner, destined to play an important part in Rocky Mountain gold mining, on his overland trip to California in 1849, found traces of gold. Circumstances prevented his returning until 1858. In his 1858 summer expedition Russell found "color" in Cherry Creek and in the streams of South Park. When he returned to Cherry Creek in September he found many gold hunters had arrived at the settlement of Auraria and Denver—the two sides of Cherry Creek.

Green Russell's return to the border towns of Kansas, on his winter visit to the hometown Auraria, Georgia, set afire the imagination and desire of those suffering hardships of the depression. He reported his gold endeavor was only fairly successful and that he planned to return in the spring of 1859 for further exploration. That, along with the meager reports forthcoming, set the stage for the gold rush. Russell maintained "that nothing very encouraging had as yet been discovered, and a large emigration was hardly warranted." The poverty-stricken interpreted otherwise; the "haves" were concealing the truth; easy wealth was in the mountains merely to be picked up from the ground.

Pike's Peak excitement, 1859, was at fever point. Newspapers heralded extravagant claims. Common sense was abandoned. Green Russell

Softly Beautiful Valley

carried to the East only twenty-five ounces of gold for the labor of twelve men for an entire summer. Regardless, the emigration of 1859 was in progress before winter released its grasp. Many could not afford teams, wagons, adequate food and clothing for the hundreds of miles to be traveled. Some hitched themselves to hand-carts, loaded with scanty provisions of food and clothing. Others walked with simple provision loaded on their backs. Suffering and death were the fate of many.

Gold was not found in abundance in Cherry Creek at Auraria and Denver. "Stampeders"— "the go-backers"—started returning to "America" in disappointment. Others pushed into the mountains. Then came the Gregory discovery up the north fork of Clear Creek—yielding $1.50 to $4.00 a pan. The exodus from Auraria and Denver was on. Green Russell discovered a gulch three miles south of Gregory's and washed out over a hundred pounds of gold in four months. Central City and Idaho Springs were born. Deeper and deeper into the mountains, and higher and higher, climbed the gold seeker. At last he stood on the crest of Continental Divide and before him lay the softly beautiful valley.

The remainder of the 19th century saw the Valley of the Blue transformed. Pleasant valleys and gulches were gouged and torn, seemingly beyond nature's redemption. Verdant hillsides were creviced and washed away by powerful hydraulic stream, leaving unhealed, naked wounds. Mountainsides became pitted and pock-marked, spewing forth mounds of foreign-colored tailings like festering carbuncles. The gold boat, dredging valley bedrock, heaped mountains of stones and boulders in its wake where nature had planted willow and sagebrush. Forest fires, carelessly and purposely set, ravaged dense growths and valiant giants. Need for lumber and firewood toppled countless pine and spruce. Hindrances to man's whim, or work, fell before the steady blows of axe or biting of the saw. Slowly, but surely, nature's delicate masterpiece became inharmonious, discordant.

Wildlife, abundant in mountain and valley, was not spared. Buffalo harvesters, getting two to three dollars for a hide, succeeded in reducing the millions of buffalo roaming plain and mountain valley, almost to the point of total extinction. The years 1871 to 1878 accomplished the feat. Buffalo was the Indian's primary meat supply. Killing off the buffalo was one of the best means of subjugating the Indian. Today buffalo meat is considered by many to be superior to beef in tastiness and it is lower in cholesterol and higher in polyunsaturated fats. This may explain why the Indians and mountain men of the past century were so hardy and long-lived.

The professional hunter came to the forefront, providing a supply of wild meat for the mining camps. In 1879, Kokomo's first newspaper reported: "Three wagon loads of elk came in from Green Mountain yesterday and were offered for sale at five and ten cents a pound." Wagon loads of wild game were a frequent sight in the mining camp. Freighters were busy hauling loads of elk, deer, antelope, mountain sheep and bear from Middle Park-Grand River to Leadville in its boom days. It was a highly profitable business with elk, deer and antelope at 12¢ per lb., mountain sheep 12½¢, bear 15¢. All mining camps welcomed this supply of meat; a miner couldn't spare time from his gold-digging to go hunting—and beef prices were exorbitant. Breckenridge, 1881, patronized the professional hunter:

Jack Burns brought in on Saturday a load of deer and elk from the Middle Park and leaves tomorrow for another load. He expects to be back in ten days. Jack is one of the best hunters on the western slope and never misses when he goes for game.

L. G. Johnson and Joseph Prest brought in this morning fifteen deer, two dozen grouse, an elk and one range bear, the largest ever brought into market. They have in camp, three bears, five elk and a large number of deer which will be delivered on order. Johnson can be found at Finding & Co's this evening and to-morrow morning.

What was happening in field and mountain was also happening in stream and river: "Messrs. Ford and Maynard recently went on a fishing excursion near Bergen's Ranch, and succeeded in capturing twenty-five hundred trout in a few hours." "The Tarryall delegation to the Buckskin Joe Convention, on their return, stopped at Trout Creek and amused themselves fishing for a time with extraordinary success. They caught about two hundred pounds."

Ute Indians were not faring much better. Villard, in *The Past and Present of the Pike's Peak Gold Regions*, denounced the Ute Indians as the "bloody Utahs"—a "bloodthirsty, wily tribe who steal and murder whenever they can do so with impunity." Villard did condescend to say: "During the winter several hundred of them were, however, reported to have camped for three weeks near the Blue River diggings without giving the miners any trouble." Wallace Stegner, *Beyond the Hundredth Meridian*, has the explorer, Major John Powell presenting a different picture of the Utes. He acknowledged that they were "incorrigible beggars," but he spent weeks with the Utes, learning their language and ways, "granting to the Indian the rights of his own habits and attitudes, and he was safe with the Utes and his possessions untouched."

Utes removed scalps when the white man started taking possession of South Park. When stakes were driven into the ground, the Indian knew that surveys, land parceling and settling would follow. Sometimes scalping was the price. The Meeker Massacre came when Nathan Meeker plowed the Indian's favorite race course, fenced the land, attempted to make farmers of them and observers of the Sabbath. Utes massacred the men at White River Agency and carried the women into captivity. Chief Ouray interceded with White River chiefs for the release of the prisoners.

Only once were Blue River miners greatly alarmed by the Utes. The big scare came October, 1879, following the Meeker Massacre, when reports came that Utes were on the warpath and headed up South Park to Fairplay, Alma, Montgomery and over the mountain to Breckenridge. Montgomery was reported "burned to the ground;" Breckenridge was "in ashes." Excitement ran high the night Breckenridge was reported endangered; women and children were started on their way to Denver. Governor Pitkin stood ready to send troops when verified word was forthcoming. Father John Dyer wrote: "The Indians were not within a hundred miles. All the while the Indians were keeping themselves as far off in the southwest as possible."

By 1880 the Ute Indians were treated away to reservations. The happy hunting grounds of South Park, Blue River and Middle Park now belonged to the white man. The idyllic had ended.

Today the Valley of the Blue has its charm and loveliness—but not as "softly beautiful" as when gold-glazed eyes first looked upon it from Continental heights.

Courtesy—Denver Public Library Western Collection—From *Mining Reporter,* Vol. 40, #23, Dec. 7, 1899, p. 343.

Breckenridge—"Gem of the Mountains"—shortly after turn of the century. Courtesy—Library State Historical Society of Colorado.

Courtesy—Carl Enyeart, Jr.—From *Goldfields of Summit County, Colorado*—Summit County Mining Exchange.

Courtesy—Denver Public Library Western Collection—*Mining and Industrial Reporter*, July, 1887. p. 23.

Mining "carbuncles" on mountainside east and north of Breckenridge. Foreground: Hills of stones left in the wake of goldboat dredging.

Gold Boat entering Breckenridge from the north. Courtesy—Denver Public Library Western Collection.

"Gulch Mining, Near Breckenridge, Colorado." — (*Crofutt's Grip-Sack Guide of Colorado* — 1881—Vol. 1, p. 79). Courtesy— Denver Public Library Western Collection. (Old-timers of Breckenridge area claim this sketch can only be entrance to Ten Mile Canyon, Frisco. Frisco is "near Breckenridge"—nine miles. Ute Indians camped near this location.)

Railroad to Frisco Station—entrance Ten Mile Canyon.
Courtesy—Mrs. Ted Fletcher

Softly Beautiful Valley

Ten Mile Canyon view from writer's cabin home—"Look-Up Lodge."

Main Street, Frisco, 1889-1890, showing popular Leyner's Hotel.
Courtesy—Mr. L. G. McKee.

Denver—when gold was discovered in Blue River Valley—Breckenridge.
Courtesy—Library State Historical Society of Colorado.

BRECKINRIDGE

August 10, 1859 - August 10, 1860

Breck*i*nridge. It is not a misspelling. For about a year the little mining camp on Blue River, Western Slope of the Continental Divide, was Breck*i*nridge. Even in that short history it was sometimes spelled Breck*e*nridge. As late as 1880 it was Breck*i*nridge to some people. Sometimes both spellings were used interchangeably, as we read in the *Miners' Record*: "FROM BRECK*I*NRIDGE — Breck*e*nridge, July 6, 1861." The new-born town wasn't exactly sure how to spell its name.

For eight months the camp wasn't officially named or recognized as a town. There were, however, three mining districts on the Blue: Pollard at the south end of present Breckenridge, Spaulding at the north end, and Independent in the middle.

Accounts of founding the town of Breckenridge are not entirely clear. One report claims that General George E. Spencer came into the area in August, 1859, building cabins with intention of laying out a townsite. In the spring of 1860 Spencer & Co. claimed 320 acres of land, under the townsite law of Congress.

A second story is that nothing definite had been done in 1859 regarding a town site, but Spencer had intended his town to be located near Fort Mary B in the Spaulding district. A second group desired to found a town a mile farther south, but that could await spring. Felix Poznansky headed the latter group.

When, in the early spring of 1860, Spencer discovered that the site of his proposed town had been taken up as a ranch, he decided to move up the Blue to a different location. The other group was not of a mind to have Spencer jump its site, so they quickly laid out a townsite and named it Independent, after their mining District.

It is related that a meeting of the two proponents occurred later in the spring at a camping spot four miles from Tarryall, South Park. Spencer was on his way to Blue River to establish his town; Poznansky was going in the other direction to Tarryall for supplies. Spencer accused Poznansky of jumping his townsite. Poznansky countered with, "You told me your townsite would be at the Fort." "I changed my mind," Spencer replied. Poznansky's answer was, "You can't have our townsite." Spencer replied that he would get it. Asked how, he said, "By first improvement." ("First improvement" was equivalent to right of possession; a building eight logs high constituted a "first improvement.")

Poznansky continued to Tarryall where he wrote a letter to his son, instructing him to get help and start building a house at once. The letter was carried by a messenger during the night. When Spencer arrived on the Blue next day, there was Poznansky's house eight logs high, and laid on six feet of snow in the town of Independent.

Independent was a name not wholly inappropriate to the mind and spirit of the town about to rise on the banks of the Blue. It was not, however, to remain Independent; it was to become Breckinridge. Spencer & Co. offered to survey the town and give twelve choice lots to all of the Independent group, excepting Poznansky. Spencer insisted that he have the townsite and the right of naming it. The Independent group, excepting Poznansky, acquiesed.

The survey consisted of only one street. In 1864 Judge Bissel wrote to Poznansky, "Whereas, the Breckenridge townsite never lived up to their agreement made with the Independent Townsite company, we therefore have jumped the townsite and included you in the jumping, and you are entitled to one-twelfth of it."

One great desire of the camp was for a post office and a regularly-established postal route from Denver. A politician offered the thinly-disguised suggestion: "If the residents would consent to name the town for the Vice-President the chances for getting a post office would be enhanced. The office was established and Gen. George E. Spencer appointed postmaster, but before his commission arrived he left the country, turning the office over to Mr. O. A. Whittemore."

John Cabell Breckinridge was Vice-President of the United States during Buchanan's Presidency. In the 1860 presidential election there was a split-ticket in the Democratic Party— Douglas and the pro-slavery Breckinridge. Lincoln polled 1,866,452 votes; Douglas, 1,376,957; and Breckinridge, 849,781. The Constitutional Union Party's candidate, John Bell, polled 588,879. Had not the Democratic Party been split, its total vote would have been 2,226,738. The electoral vote was: Lincoln 180, Breckinridge 72, Bell 39 and Douglas 12.

Breckinridge was elected to the Senate, where he opposed Lincoln's war policy. He resigned and joined the Confederate Army as a brigadier general, and later advanced to major general.

The little town on the Blue asserted its independence and loyalty by promptly changing its name from Breckinridge to Breckenridge.

The National Archives and Records Service of Washington replied, in answer to a request about the Breckenridge post office, "The records of the Post Office Department in the National Archives show that a post office was established at Breckinridge, Summit County, Colorado. The postal records do not show the exact date the name of the office was changed to Breckenridge, nor do they include an application for the post office at Breckinridge."

Hall's *History of Colorado* gives Ruben J. Spalding credit for first gold mining on Blue River. (The name "Spalding" often appears "Spaulding." "Independent" and "Independence" are also used interchangeably, as one and the same; also "Pollard" and "Pollack" are used to designate the one mining district. Hall uses "Spalding" consistently.) Mr. Spalding wrote his account for Hall thirty years later. Hall wrote the story from incidents reported by Spalding:

Spalding arrived in Denver from Missouri in July, 1859. At the time there were only a few log cabins on the townsite. After prospecting about the country for a time, toward the last of July he was invited to join a company then forming to prospect the western slopes of the Rocky Mountains. The party of about thirty men started from Denver the morning of August 2, 1859. On the night of the 3rd they camped at Manitou Springs, on the 4th took the Ute Indian trail into the mountains. Soon afterward the company divided. Fourteen, including Spalding, continued through South Park to where the town of Fairplay was subsequently located; thence up to the base of Mount Lincoln, where Montgomery was established a year later. Here they crossed to the western slope, on to Blue River. Continuing down the Blue, to a point about one-fourth of a mile below the present Breckenridge, they halted. It was here that the first stakes were driven into the ground to mark the spot where it was their purpose to prospect for gold. The instinct which prompted this determination seems prophetic of after results. The exact date was mid-afternoon of August 10, 1859.

"We sunk a hole three feet deep on a bar," writes Mr. Spalding, "and I, having mined in California, was selected, as the most experienced man in the company, to do the panning. The result of the first pan of dirt was thirteen cents of gold, the largest grain about the size and shape of a flax seed. The second panful gave twenty-seven cents, both yields being weighed in gold scales brought for the purpose. This was the first recorded discovery of gold on Blue River. Our little party now felt jubilant over the strike thus made and began to realize that here lay the fulfillment of their most ardent hopes." The company united in according to Mr. Spalding the honor of the first discovery, an event of great importance in the subsequent history of the territory and state. He was by unanimous vote given possession of the claim wherein the gold was found, which he occupied and worked with satisfactory returns. His associates, now fully convinced that a great precious metal-bearing region had been fairly hit upon, proceeded to stake off claims, each 100 feet along the river and across it, to include both banks. Mr. Spalding, by right of discovery and miner's usage, was allowed 200 feet. Realizing the jealousy of the Ute Indians, to whom all the mountain region belonged, their warlike spirit and their hostility to the intrusion of the white men, and to provide against attack, the miners erected a block house or fortification, which was afterward christened "Fort Mabery," in honor of the first white woman who crossed the range to French Gulch. It was situated on the main highway, on the west side of the river, a little southwesterly of the present Breckenridge stamp mill and concentrators. A few traces of the foundation still remain.

The first log dwelling in the new camp was erected by Mr. Ruben Spalding. Soon afterward the miners set to work to turn the course of the river by digging a large canal, the head being very near the present town of Breckenridge. This accomplished, they were prepared for the more earnest business of placer mining. About this time some men came in, bringing a whip-saw and began cutting lumber for sluices and other purposes.

Says Mr. Spalding: "I don't recollect their cash price for boards, but distinctly remember that I gave my mule, that cost me $140, for 175 feet of lumber and two sacks of musty flour. With the lumber I made three 'toms' and went to mining in water ankle deep, and having nothing better to wear on my feet I roped them with pieces of a saddle blanket, which answered the purpose of boots very well. The first day's work netted me ten dollars and a bad cold. I remained on Blue River during the winter of 1859-60 in company with nine others, only a few of whose names are now remembered. One was James Mitchell, another a Mr. Eaton, Balce Weaver, two Norwegians and a man named Ogden. Snow fell to great depth—six to eight feet. We made each man a pair of snowshoes of white pine, nine to thirteen feet in length; breadth in front four inches, and at the rear end three and three-fourths inches.

"In January or February, 1860 (I can't remember which), we all mounted our snow-shoes, taking blankets, tools and provisions, and went down Blue river about six miles, where we built a cabin of small pine logs and claimed a town site, calling it Eldorado West. It was from this cabin that Mr. Balce Weaver went prospecting and discovered Gold Run diggings beneath snow eight feet deep. French Gulch was discovered, I believe, by a French Canadian known as 'French Pete.' In 1861 I was elected sheriff of Blue River and at once appointed Dr. P. H. Boyd my chief deputy."

Hall recorded additional items from various sources, mainly the recollections and correspondence of pioneers:

Directly opposite the Spalding discovery,

on the east bank of the river, William H. Iliff and an associate found a pocket of auriferous gravel of limited extent, which yielded two dollars per pan of dirt. Afterward nearly $7,000 was extracted from a space 40 feet square, with a depth of less than 10 feet, which illustrates the richness of certain parts of this gulch. Provisions becoming scarce, Messrs. Iliff, James Mitchell, one called "Cucumber," and another whose name can not be ascertained, late in August started out with pack animals en route to Denver, the nearest depot for such supplies. ("Cucumber" probably gave his name to Cucumber Creek and Cucumber Gulch.) The arrival of this party in town, coupled with the stories they told and the amount of yellow metal exhibited, created much excitement, and, as a natural sequence, a general stampede of the unemployed men on its streets toward the scene of those wonderful revelations occurred. By the middle of September, following, (1860), about two thousand people had settled in Spalding and contiguous camps.

William Byers, editor of the *Rocky Mountain News,* wrote an article for the *Miners' Record* regarding a trip to mines in Blue River Basin, 1861. He had the following to say about the fort at Breckenridge:

Less than a mile below Breckinridge, is Fort Mary B. built for, and occupied as winter quarters in the winter of '59 and '60 by the few settlers who were on the Blue then. They were uncertain as to the feelings of their Indian neighbors, and to provide against contingencies, very wisely prepared themselves for defense. A number of block houses, sufficient to accommodate all, were planned and built in a hollow square—all facing inward. The walls were of green logs and the roofs of earth, so that while almost impregnable to arms from without; they could not easily be fired. Two openings to the court, or enclosure, were easily guarded, and they were really well situated for defense. On one side is the old channel, and on the other, the new one, of Blue River. All the buildings are now deserted and falling to ruin.

The building of a fort at Spalding's diggings is reality; the proper appellation is ambiguous. According to Spalding the name was Fort Mabery, named for the "first white woman who crossed the range to French Gulch." Byers, and many others, called it Fort Mary B. "in honor of Mary Bigelow the first woman quartered at the fort." In addition, one can choose from the names

Meriby, Fort Meribeh or Fort Maribeh. The list can be extended to include Fort Independence and Jones Fort. The most common terminology is Fort Mary B. (Denver Post Office, 1861, advertised a list of unclaimed mail; the name of N. Bigelow was listed. It was supposed that he was mining somewhere in the mountains.) Whatever the name, the fort was never needed for protection against the Indian.

Although Blue River diggings were discovered in late summer, the lateness of the season didn't deter others from rushing to the western slope. A number prospected and staked claims before winter became too ominous. A few, having a fair amount of provisions, decided to risk the unknown austerities of winter in the mountains. The number who wintered at the Fort was twenty-five. Some were members of Spalding's original group; others were latecomers. Social life was at a minimum. Many whiled away winter hours by writing news letters to Denver's *Rocky Mountain News* and Golden's *Western Mountaineer*. These writers were reporters of exceptional ability. Through their eyes we re-live the first year of the little community of Breckinridge. Other correspondents visited Blue River Diggings; we also glean from their writings.

Rocky Mountain News   September 10, 1859
Having this day returned from a prospecting tour, and thinking a brief statement might be of some interest to your numerous readers, I enclose the following:

I left Mountain City, Gregory's Diggings, about the tenth of August, in the company of C. G. Russell and others—twelve in number. We traveled through South Park for two or three days, finding gold everywhere. After resting a few days at "Tarry All Diggings," (since known as "Grab All Diggings") we started over the divide, determined to prospect Middle Park, and the Blue and Grand rivers. We arrived at the Spaulding Diggings, discovered by Mr. Spaulding and party. Here we found old friends, Messrs. Jones and Fenton, and many others all appearing to be well satisfied with their prospects as a mining country in this particular location. Our company prospected very little in that location.

From this point we started down that branch of the Blue occasionally prospecting, and finding gold in every pan. At a distance of seventy-five miles from Spaulding's Diggings the small stream we had followed had grown to be a considerable size and formed a junction with another large stream running east to west. It was the opinion of our company that we then were on the Grand River, one of the main branches of the Colorado.

J. Casto

FORT INDEPENDENCE, on Blue River
October 4, 1859
Thinking you would be pleased to hear from your friends who, perchance, have wandered over the Snowy Range, I now write you about our new diggings, on the river.

We have been here near two months, the weather has been, and is, very fine. We have found the bed of the stream very rich (for, mind you, we have dammed the river) and I have no hesitancy in crying out "Eureka." We are able to pan out from three to eight grains of the precious metal, to the pan, on an average, within six inches of the top of the ground. We are all "O.K.," except for one thing, namely, flour and bacon is scarce, and we dislike to go after it. Many of us expect to winter here if we can get provisions. There is plenty of game, such as black bear, elk, moose, deer, black and grey wolves, rabbits, beaver, and better than all, the finest fish I ever saw, and "I haven't always been at home." Will not some of your provision merchants send out some hundred sacks of flour? There is no difficulty in reaching here, the road is good and plain. My opinion is that four wagon-loads of provisions could be sold here in one day, and *that* at figures which would *pay*.

We have seen no Indians, and the old mountain boys say they seldom come this way. We are having quite a good time at present, and the health of the miners is excellent.

We all want news badly, and if you will send us papers by any chance, we will send in return as fine specimens of gold as the Rocky Mountains can afford.

Yours truly,
E. H. Boyd M.D.

BLUE FORK OF THE COLORADO
October 9, 1859
Thinking you would be glad to hear from an old fellow miner, I take this opportunity of informing you and the public generally through your valuable paper, in regard to our prospects, and what we are doing in the newly discovered mines. We have constructed a dam across the stream and turned the water for about two miles, and although we have been very much hindered by our dam leaking through and preventing us from digging in the bed of the stream, yet wherever we have been able to get

down to the bedrock, we have so far been liberally rewarded for our labor, taking out on an average ten dollars a day to the man. Illinois Gulch is paying about sixteen dollars a day to the hand and French Gulch is paying from ten to twelve dollars a day to the man. In Pollard district they are taking out about one ounce a day to the man. We have water in great abundance and never failing.

The gold discoveries, in this country, are only in their infancy: leads, gulches, and bars, beat California out and out.

S. G. Jones

Rocky Mountain News   November 17, 1859

Messrs. Ming and Solomon, who recently sent a train loaded with goods for South Park and Little Blue diggings, have received orders for additional supplies. They report the mines exceedingly rich, the miners all making money, and every man with a good supply of the needful on hand.

Some gentlemen who arrived from Little Blue on Sunday evening last, say they have found their claims much richer than they at first supposed. They have made over a thousand dollars apiece in the short time they have been able to work since the discovery, which all will remember, was made late in the season.

The Western Mountaineer November 25, 1859

A Trip to the Blue

Jones Fort is located near the center of this mining country, and about twenty-five persons intend wintering there—rather a desperate undertaking, knowing as they do, that they are surrounded by hostile Indians, although they have shown themselves friendly as yet, I could not but fear for their safety. I hope in another year to see a good military post established at this point; when this is done the miner in that vicinity will be as safe as he is in "America," (as the miners say).   Lew.

Not much news came out of the mountains in December, January and February, but the *Rocky Mountain News* reported, that "companies are daily leaving Denver for diggings in South Park, Blue River, Gregory's and all points in the mountains." (During this time, we remember, an exploring party went out from the Fort on snow-shoes, down the Blue a few miles, founded Eldorado West and discovered the rich Gold Run diggings.)

Blue River, Jefferson Territory March 5, 1860

According to promise I now purpose to give you a brief sketch of the business of young Jefferson Territory. We arrived here on the last day of February, and crossed over the Snowy Range, from Tarryall to this place on snow shoes; that being the only practicable mode of traveling in this region of country at present. The snow is from one to six feet deep.

On arriving here, we found twenty men, one woman, and four children, who came in last fall, and have remained ever since as permanent citizens. We find them not in a suffering condition by any means, but rather short of provisions, though all seem to be in fine spirits, and sanguine of soon being amply rewarded, out of their rich claims, for the many inconveniences and privations they have undergone the past winter.

There have been no recent discoveries of gold in this vicinity, except in a gulch six miles below the Fort, in which there have been good prospects found. News to that effect, going back to Tarryall, there were no less than fifty men set out immediately for the Blue, to satisfy themselves in regard to the report. All came on snow shoes, and on their arrival pitched into the new gulch, staking off and prospecting claims.

Successful mining is impossible as yet, owing to the great depth of snow and frost. The belief prevails that spring is near at hand, and all manifest a desire to be at something which will eventually—if not immediately—pay them. They are branching out in every direction; some prospecting by shoveling off the snow, and building fires to thaw the ground, where they wished to prospect. Some are looking out for ranches, some mill sites, some for town sites; while others are chopping and whip-sawing sluice lumber. Thus you see preparation has fairly commenced for a summer's operation.

But, alas! there is nothing in the line of provisions for sale in this country, except a little flour, which is retailing at forty-five cents per pound; consequently a good many of the snow shoe emigrants are returning to Tarryall, for more grub. If any of your merchants want a store house built in this vicinity, let them give us the dimensions, we have inexhaustible quantities of good building timber.

But the question may arise in the merchant's mind, "have you Blue River Boys any money to pay us for our goods?" Try us, with some good old bacon, flour, coffee, and tobacco —especially smoking tobacco—but Toas lightning and tangleleg whiskey, etc., we can get along very well without as yet.

Wm. A. Smith

Rocky Mountain News   March 21, 1860
J. H. Ming, Esq., returned a few days since from the Blue River and Tarryall. He does not bring very encouraging reports from that region. The snow still covers most of the country, and in many places is very deep. The ground is hard frozen, snow falls frequently, and little work can be done to advantage. Excellent prospects have been found, and a few miners are making money.

Whilst some have every faith in the mines of that region of the country, we cannot but advise everyone to wait awhile before starting. We are of the opinion that the heaviest snows of the winter have yet to fall in most of the mountain country, and that nothing can be done to advantage in the Park or on the Blue, until late in May.

Breckenridge, Jefferson Territory

April 2nd, 1860

As I have been a steady resident of the Blue River diggings since the last of February, I again write you concerning the weather, the mines and other business. The weather is quite mild and pleasant and has been the greater portion of March. We have had decidedly less wind during the month of March than I have witnessed for several years. We have had frequent showers of snow, though invariably followed with a bright, warm sunshine, melting it off about as fast as it falls. Were it not for the deep snows, it would be much more pleasant spending the winter here than out on the plains, for this reason: we are located in a beautiful valley, surrounded by lofty mountains, covered with immense forests of tall pine timber, forming a complete harbor against all such high gales and storms as you have on the plains. Men are strung along the river for forty or fifty miles, prospecting, but no recent discoveries of importance have been made.

Wm. A. Smith

Rocky Mountain News   April 7, 1860
The writer crossed the range on the afternoon of the third inst. There is no snow of note between Denver and Tarryall diggings. Breckenridge is no longer a paper town, but is in actual existence, in the vicinity of the best mining region yet discovered in the Rocky Mountains. Many houses are under contract to be built as soon as the disappearance of snow will permit. It must, at least, be an important trading post, being a central point for the mining region, as now discovered and opened up.

Respectfully yours, L. A. O.

Breckenridge, Blue River, J. T.   May 17, 1860

As there were many during my recent visit to your city, making inquiries, and no doubt are still, in regard to the Blue River mines, their extent, value, etc., permit me through your columns, to make the following statement:

It is a well known fact to the most of your readers, that these mines were discovered late last fall, by parties who had not means nor time to prospect the country to any extent before winter set in with its usual snows, falling and drifting from two to ten feet deep; consequently the most of them left the mountains for want of supplies, fearing too that the approaching winter in this locality would be too cold for endurance. A small party who were fortunate enough to have a winter's supply on hand, notwithstanding the many reports, that if they attempted to winter here, they would not live to see another summer's sunshine, that they would either be massacred by the Utes, or wild beasts, or perish under deep snows, or sicken and die for want of medical aid; determined to take up their residence here, regardless of consequences, undergoing the many privations, and braving the hardships of a remote and snowy wilderness; men who are now by their daily labor reaping the reward of an energetic, persevering and judicious people, accumulating from ten to forty dollars per day to the man. The Blue River mines, though in their infancy, yet bid fair to become one of the richest points for mining in the Rocky Mountains. As the snow disappears better and richer diggings are found.

We have three store houses under way, two in Breckenridge, and one in Fort Mary B., which will be stocked with a variety of miners goods soon. Lumber is being sold at twenty dollars per hundred feet. Beef at fourteen and sixteen cents per pound. Emigrants are pouring in at the rate of about fifty a day, with occasionally one returning.

W. A. S.

M. B. Ogden sent a day-by-day report of the snowfalls during the winter months for publication in the *Rocky Mountain News*. The complete report was published; we include only excerpts.

Fort Mary B., Blue River   May 18th, 1860
Ute Territory

We arrived at this point on the 18th day of August last, and have kept a statistical record of the fall of snow during the winter, which we send you for publication.

From the 18th to the 30th of August it rained

more or less every day, but not so much as to stop work.

The total snowfall was 154½ inches, making twelve feet, ten inches in all, but none of the snows that fell before the 7th of November, remained on the ground more than one day, and during that time we had the most beautiful weather possible to conceive. Pleasant, warm and clear during the day; cool but not cold or changeable until the 7th of November, when snow commenced falling in earnest. (The big snows were 20 inches—November 7-8-9; 14 inches December 24th; 10 inches April 18-19; and 11 inches May 1-2.) Although twelve feet, ten inches have fallen, there never was more than three feet, eight inches at any one time, on the ground near the fort. At this date the snow has almost entirely disappeared from the valley of the Blue, though the Range is still impassable for animals, but cannot be so for another week if this weather continues. Extensive preparations are being made for mining. Some rich gulches have been found the past week.

M. B. Ogden

Breckenridge   May 30, 1860

Since the disappearance of the snow in the valleys of the streams west of the snowy range, this portion of the gold mines assumes an entirely different appearance from that previous to the last week. Large numbers of wagons are arriving daily from the States and Denver, with provisions and tools. Pack trains come in daily, and from one hundred to two hundred emigrants are daily coming in to operate the mines or follow other avocations. Some return, disgusted with the prospects, denouncing the country as a humbug, but a majority start out immediately prospecting or preparing their claims for summer's work.

The mines, Independent and Spaulding, are located on Blue River, but as yet, little sluicing has been done. The owners of claims here have been busily engaged in turning the River from its bed, and draining their claims. Since the disappearance of the snow, the river has become so swollen, that the ditches prepared for it, are found too small, and the claims are badly drained.

The town is full of begging Utes, who are very friendly, and are much more agreeable than the Cheyennes or Arapahoes, as they are cleanly and noble in appearance. There are about twelve hundred Utes camped at the mouth of Swan River and Ten Mile Creek. We have no fear of them whatever, as they are positively friendly. Four new stores are being built

in this new city, which will soon be filled with the necessary supplies for a large mining population.

We have one lady living in Breckenridge and one on Gold Run; we would be glad to welcome many arrivals of "gentler" portion of gold-seeking humanity, and can offer a pleasant country, good locations, and very peaceable neighbors as an inducement. The people are very orderly, and quiet here, except an occasional lawsuit. There is no liquor used on this side of the range yet, and generally the people mind their own business.

We had preaching by the Rev. Mr. Parker last Sunday. Mr. George Spencer is the acting agent for the town of Breckenridge, and is practicing law successfully.

I will write you occasionally giving hereafter statistics, and a more definite summary of news, as I can by taking some pains offer more interesting correspondence.

Yours very respectfully,
Sea Pea

From Blue River Mines   June 3, 1860
Breckenridge

Since my last, but little of interest has transpired in this portion of the country, except the discovery of new diggings, which to us is expected as a "matter of course."

Breckenridge is improving rapidly and promises to be a place of importance. In all probability we will have a population of five thousand within a month, one third that number being in this vicinity now.

The Utes have left us for the South Park, where they have encamped since Tuesday last. They have their squaws and children with them. I wonder if the Arapahoes and Cheyennes would not like to know of their whereabouts.

A new saline bank has been discovered in Plunketts Gulch, which yields very pure salt. The importance of that article hereafter will be unnecessary. Messrs. Spencer & Plunkett have invested largely in the property, and will soon be prepared to furnish customers with any amount. More next week.

Sea Pea

Breckenridge, Blue River   June 9, 1860

Allow me to inform you that business of all kinds on and near Blue River is becoming more lively every day and the prospects for better times more flattering. We can now buy anything in the line of provisions or clothing, either at the Fort or in Breckenridge. Messrs. Iddings and Co. are now selling in Fort Mary B; Messrs. Schollkaph, Whittemore & Co. have opened their large and newly furnished store house in the city of Breckenridge.

Breckenridge has just cleverly commenced improving. Quite a number of dwellings are finished and under way. Some five or six business houses are also under way, besides two that are already finished. The valleys, gulches and hill sides are alive with men.

On Thursday last, a very destructive and dangerous fire was seen, passing up through a heavy body of timber just below the Fort, near French Gulch, which is supposed to have been set on purpose, by some maliciously disposed fellow who has escaped justice as yet, but will not much longer, if he is not very careful, as there are shrewd miners and prospectors watching for him, who will, if they catch him, or them, in the act of starting another fire in the mountains, deal out a little of old Judge Lynch to them and give them their free papers to leave the mountains.

Some five or six hundred Utah Indians visited us a few days ago; they manifested no ill will towards the whites, but passed off towards Tarryall very quietly and friendly.

A few very respectable looking ladies have ventured over to see us. Send us a few more, as we need several boarding houses started in this country.

W. A. S.

The summer of 1860 saw vast change in Blue River Diggings. Sea Pea, writing to the Golden *Western Mountaineer* on June 10th, said:

French Gulch is being opened and is richer than anticipated. One month ago you could scarcely see a human being away from the fort; now I can hardly look in any direction without seeing herds of stock and scores of wagons, tents, cabins and bower houses. For twelve miles on the river, and from mouth to source of every gulch the skirts of timber are lined with the canvas of wagons and tents. Breckenridge is improving very rapidly. After an absence of one week I hardly knew the place. Many new buildings of substantial character are going up, and what was a few weeks ago a forest, with the exception of eight houses, is now a clearing with streets extending each way, and built along with stores, dwellings, shops and saloons.

Five miles north of Breckenridge, Swan River enters Blue River from the east. In late June, Georgia, American and Humbug Gulches were discovered about eight miles up the range. According to Hall's *History of Colorado*, (Vol. IV, p. 328), "Georgia Gulch was discovered by a Mr. Highfield, a Georgia miner, who gave it the name of his native state." For some time after its discovery it was thought "only to be passably good," but soon it was reported: "The richness of Georgia Gulch is almost fabulous." William A. Smith reported to the Rocky Mountain *News*, (July 1, 1860): "The latest discoveries were made about ten days ago. They are on Swan Creek. Three gulches are not only rich, but *very* rich. One of them, discovered by a party of Georgians, has yielded as high as twelve dollars to the single pan of dirt. The gold is coarse and bright." Swan Valley was BIG news in July, 1860, "and Georgia takes the premium." And forest fires were big news.

From Blue River Mines   June 16, 1860

During the past week raging fires, which have either been set accidentally by some reckless parties, or on purpose by some unprincipled specimen of mankind, have caused great disturbance throughout this country. If there is any crime, aside from murder, that deserves hanging, it is that of firing timber in the mountains. We warn the persons who are in the habit of setting fires to run at large in this vicinity, that the general disposition of the miners, so far as I have heard them express themselves, is to hang them if caught in the act; so if they are not unusually careful they will be called on at an unexpected hour to visit a foreign country, called Eternity, where they will, I fear, not only see, but feel, the effects of hotter fires than they ever experienced in the Rocky Mountains.

W. A. S.

Blue River   June 23, 1860

Since my last, we have witnessed one of the most destructive fires that has ever passed through the Blue River country. On Tuesday last, about 3 o'clock, a fire broke out somewhere near the junction of French Gulch and the river, taking its course up French Gulch on the south side, through one of the thickest bodies of timber in the country. It continued its course, with increasing flames at least one hundred and fifty, if not two hundred feet above the ground. It reached Negro Gulch, crowning directly over it, where over one hundred men were at work. As soon as they saw the great danger they were in, they began with all possible haste to save their supplies by pitching them into prospect holes, and shoveling dirt over them; but the flames approached with such speed, that all were compelled to fly, with their things not more than half secured, in order to save their lives; some barely escaping. Edwin A. Webber, Addison Bail, myself, and three others who delayed a little more time than the rest of them, trying to save our property, were overtaken by the fire, before getting out of the timber. The only way we could, and did escape, was by jumping down into a deep hole in the gulch, where some men had been sluicing, and where there was a little stream of water running, in which we were obliged to lay down and roll over and over, wetting our clothes to keep them from taking fire. While in the act of rolling in the water, the flames were rolling over us, from one bank of the gulch to the other, heating and smoking us almost beyond endurance, and had it not been for kind providence bringing about a sudden change of wind, turning the smoke and blaze down the gulch, making a way for our escape up the gulch, what would have been our condition today is unknown. One man by the name of P. B. Sisler, who remained in a deep hole just below us, all the time of the fire, got the crown of his hat burned out, his shirt burned through on the back, and his back badly burned and blistered all over. The loss of property is eight wagons burned to ashes, some of them loaded with valuable clothing, provisions, etc., one mule, valued at two hundred dollars, burned to death, and several other head of stock lost supposed to be burned, three hundred feet of lumber, several ready made sluices, tents, cabins and other contents, and many mining tools. Total loss estimated at about three thousand dollars.

A few days ago two men were seen in the act of setting out fire purposely. They were pursued, but were lost sight of in the thick brush. Had they been overtaken and shot down in their tracks, it would have been nothing more than justice and a benefit to the people generally.

W. A. S.

From Blue River Mines   July 29, 1860
Breckenridge

Since my last I have spent a few days in passing around through the various mining districts. I find the older mines are paying their usual amount as heretofore represented, and the new mines, which are on Swan River, some eight miles east of this place, are yielding gold both in quality and quantity almost unreasonable to state. They consist of the following name gulches: Galena, Brown's, Virginia, American, Humbug and Georgia, all of which are situated close together.

The Georgia Gulch as yet takes the premium, though Humbug is near its equal; the rest are just being opened out and promise quite flattering. There is now in the Georgia and Humbug Gulches some forty sluices and toms running daily, which yield on an average $20 a day to the man. Two men took out in one day last week $316; another claim presented its proprietors with a $53 nugget of pure gold. Taking out of nuggets weighing from two to ten dollars is of a daily occurrence. Claims are selling at from $1000 to $3000 each, while others are asking from $5000 to $7000.

There are more than fifty gulches on the head waters of the Swan not yet tested. A few faint hearts have sold their claims on the Blue for a song and left, while others with undaunted courage are taking out $3 to $8 per day to the man. But the time will come when the sluice brush will sweep the bed rock from bank to bank. That is my honest opinion. We have a scope of country about sixteen miles up and down the river, and about six or eight miles wide, in which successful mining is going on in almost every direction; the most of which has been developed within the last three months. Look at the present and imagine the future, and the "blues" are nowhere.

I see men every few days from the headwaters of the Blue, from the celebrated Silver Lode, who unanimously report a good thing, bringing specimens with them which are supposed to be from thirty to eighty per cent silver; time will tell.

Uncle Sohns, who wintered here last winter with his family, took a great deal of pains in preparing a very nice garden this spring, putting out seeds of all kinds. He now has a variety of vegetables on hand, which are a little the *finest* of any I have seen in any country—were they a little *finer* he would have to use a telescope to gather a mess. Had you the cool evenings and frosty mornings that we have you might have *fine* vegetables too.

In traveling through the mines, I was surprised to see so many women and children. I believe there are children enough in this country to support two or three good schools, were they all together. Families should not hesitate to emigrate to Blue River, fearing that we are all a lazy set of uncivilized beings—for such is not the case. During the whole spring and summer I have heard of no shooting or stabbing affrays in all the Blue River country. The people, generally, know their own business and attend to it promptly—letting others alone.

I frequently hear the question asked, "Why do the Editors of the *News* not pay us a visit?" Why don't you, Messrs. Editors? We are as good looking as others, and can show as fine looking gold as any of them whom you have visited at other places. Please give us a call soon.

W. A. S.

August, 1860, completes full-cycle since Ruben J. Spalding made his debut on Blue River, mid-afternoon August 10, 1859. In August, 1860, the miners of Breckenridge were "all excited about the silver leads just discovered about five miles from here. Hundreds of claims have been staked out. It is said that it assays $1700 to the cord."

The winter of 1859-1860 at Fort Mary B. proved a good instructor as to the difficulties of mining and prospecting during winter months. It also proved that winter in the mountains could be fairly delightful. As August, 1860, drew to an end there were many returning again to "America." There were also many staying in the mountains.

The stage was already set for the next spring and summer season. The mines of Swan River Valley had been opened and would be coming front-stage—Delaware Flats, Galena, American, Humbug and Georgia Gulches. Blue River would still be in the act, but Swan River would be providing the excitement.

Mr. Editor of the *Rocky Mountain News*, "why not pay us a visit?"

PEGASUS
and the
GOLDEN HORSESHOE

Greek mythology has many delightful stories and none is more enchanting than Pegasus, the winged horse.

Poseidon, lord of the seas, kept a stable of magnificent horses, the finest and the fleetest, with brazen hoofs and golden manes. To Poseidon, the horse was sacred and a symbol of power. Pegasus was the noblest of his steeds.

Ancient Greeks believed Pegasus flew to the heavens, taking his place among the stars as the Flying Horse constellation. Before he left the earth, it is said, that wherever ground had been struck by Pegasus' hoof, fountains of pure water sprang forth. A stamp of his hoof caused a spring to emerge on Mount Helicon, home of the nine goddesses of literature, art and the sciences.

Undoubtedly, Pegasus' brazen hoof struck the eastern slope of the Valley of the Blue at Breckenridge. Imprint of the golden horseshoe is unmistakable. Glittering gold, teeming springs, gushing rivulets marked an easily discernible hoof-print of the winged horse. The golden horseshoe, at Breckenridge, was indeed the treasure chest of "Blue River Diggings."

Dramatically the golden horseshoe took form and shape. Prospectors, with pick and pan, penetrated the gulches, scratching earth and finding gold. Unexpected, unlikely places suddenly became towns and "cities"—Delaware Flats, Parkville, Lincoln City, Paige City. More were to come later—Tiger, Swan City, Rexford, Swandyke, Preston, Braddockville.

In the 1880s Braddockville came into existence near the junction of Swan River and Blue River, forming part of the heel of the golden horseshoe. It was not a large town. It hardly had right to be called a town; it was only a sparse, sprawling settlement. Dave Braddock's ranch buildings, a few cabins, a railroad station and a post office were Braddock-Braddocks-Braddockville. The post office was established January 18, 1884, and discontinued December 27, 1890.) The railroad station and post office were granted largely as a concession to the population of nearby mining camps. Braddockville itself didn't warrant a railroad station or a post office. Twenty years earlier, January or February of 1860, some of the Spaulding party came down the Blue from

Fort Mary B., erected one cabin in this same general vicinity, and called the place "Eldorado West." One-cabin Eldorado West was a still-birth, but mid-winter prospecting out of Eldorado West opened Gold Run diggings to the south and east. The forty years, 1860-1900, would show how generously Pegasus had favored the locality of the golden horseshoe.

In bonanza years the heel of the golden horseshoe was Braddockville at the north and Breckenridge at the south. One flange of the horseshoe extended up Swan Valley to Humbug-Georgia-American Gulches; the other flange went up French Gulch to Lincoln City, Paige City and Farncomb Hill. The Wapiti Group formed the toe of the horseshoe. All along the flanges, toe and heel of the golden horseshoe came the discoveries destined to be the richest gold producers in Breckenridge Mining District.

Summer of 1860 had been a time of discoveries and beginnings along the flanges of the golden horseshoe. Summer of 1861 saw a mass emigration to Blue River diggings. As early as March and April prospectors struggled into the mountains through deep snows, multiplying the number who had wintered at the camps. Swan River Valley received the greatest influx. The invitation to "Messrs. Editors of the *Rocky Mountain News* to visit Blue River Mines" was about to be accepted. On-the-spot reporting would be forthcoming.

William N. Byers, founder and editor of the *Rocky Mountain News*, was one of the best qualified in this kind of reporting. One of his colleagues wrote of him: "Mr. Byers is the best statistical writer—the closest observer of mining matters—and the most successful collector of items in relation to the prospects and developments of mining interests—in this Territory. He can travel over a larger extent of mining district in a stated time, and give a better and more truthful account of what falls under his observation, than any person connected with the Press in this Territory. It is a peculiarity of his which defies all efforts to excel." Byers was noted for his many expeditions and explorations that took him to the activity of the times.

Almost all Colorado people know the story of William N. Byers rushing into Pike's Peak country, April 23, 1859, and establishing the first newspaper in the area, the *Rocky Mountain News*. In order not to show favoritism, he erected

his printing establishment in the dry stream bed of Cherry Creek, midway between Auraria on the west bank and struggling Denver on the east bank. A few years later the location was liquidated by one of the now-famous Cherry Creek floodings.

What is not generally known is that William N. Byers established another newspaper in 1861, nurturing the belief that the center of Western activity could be elsewhere than Denver. July 4, 1861, William N. Byers, Editor, published the first issue of the *Miners' Record* at Tarryall Mines, South Park, Colorado Territory. John L. Dailey, Edward Bliss and H. R. Rounds were associated with him, but Byers personally supervised the new project. While serving as editor of the *Miners' Record*, Byers traveled into the nearby mining camps of South Park and Blue River, printing firsthand stories in the *Miners' Record*. We read in the first issue:

Thursday Morning   July 4, 1861
GREETING

We begin to-day what we hope will prove a long and pleasant intercourse with the people of the Great Central mining region. In launching our little barque upon the sea of journalism, at this time of wars and rumor of wars; in this season of unprecedented depression in all departments of business, trade, commerce and manufactures; we venture more than ordinary risks, but knowing and appreciating the character and wants of the intelligent and enterprising people by whom we are surrounded, and to whose gratification we hope to cater; we set out with a confidence that our labors will be both pleasant and well rewarded. In choosing a location we have sought to establish our paper where it will best and most conveniently subserve the interests of all the mining districts surrounding the great heart of the mineral region.

Having defined our position, and with our tripod firmly established here upon the highest spot at which a newspaper was ever printed in North America, or—we believe—in the world; with the click of the type already ringing in our ears, we enter cheerfully and earnestly upon our task.

The *Miners' Record* had a brief life-span, July 4, 1861, to September 14, 1861. It was an exceptionally fine newspaper and gave intimate accounts of happenings of the mining towns of South Park and over the range into Blue River Valley. But on September 14th the announcement came:

SUSPENSION

With this number, we find it necessary to temporarily suspend the *Miners' Record*. The reason for so doing is simply because we find that the receipts of the office will not pay the current expenses from week to week. For three weeks past they have been barely sufficient to defray board and paper bills—leaving scarce anything left to pay for the labor of our compositors; and we could scarcely hope for any material improvement during the late fall and winter months. Such being the case we do not feel like trying to keep up the publication during the winter at a cost of over one hundred dollars per week. A majority of the subscribers who began with beginning of the volume paid for three months, and though our list is now quite large, it would in two weeks more, which closes the first quarter, be considerably reduced and the season is too far advanced to expect many renewals or new subscribers.

We find that we rather anticipated the country in the establishment of a printing office in the Western mines. Of subscriptions we have but little cause of complaint, but the people have manifested but little disposition to advertise, and there has been scarce any call for job-work. These last arc what kccps a newspaper office alive, and without it, not a single newspaper ever published in Colorado, has ever paid for its cost of publication.

It is with feelings of profound regret that we have consented to succumb to necessity, and even temporarily dissolve our connection, and break off our intercourse with the miners of the Snowy Range, where we have made many friends whom we shall long remember and esteem.

Upon the opening of another season, the publication will be resumed, should the country prove prosperous. With thanks for the many kindnesses received, and the wish that each and every reader of the *Record* may prosper, we bid them all adieu for a time.

It was final adieu as far as the *Miners' Record* was concerned; it did not revive. It is fortunate that a complete set of the newspapers has been preserved and is available to the public on microfilm at the State Historical Society. The *Miners' Record* is one of the best research sources of early South Park mining camps—Buckskin Joe, Lauret (Lauret City), Brushwood Park, Fairplay, Alma City, Tarryall, Hamilton, Montgomery—as well as camps across the range in the Valley of the Blue. Of particular interest is Byers' tour of "The Mines In The Blue River Basin," recorded in the July 20, 1861, issue of *Miners' Record*. It was Editor Byers' acceptance of the invitation to personally visit the Blue River Mines and give an on-the-scene report.

Miners' Record   July 20, 1861

Having recently made a tour, and given a brief description, of the Western mines, on the head waters of the Platte, Blue and Arkansas; we shall proceed now to describe in the same manner, those in the Blue River Basin. To enable us to do properly and understandingly, we set out on the 16th inst., to travel over the ground.

The summit of the Snowy Range is reached in about seven miles, without any steep ascent, and the pass is over a grassy ridge or opening half a mile wide, with timber along the foot of the higher mountains on each side. The descent on the opposite side is equally as good as the ascent from the Park.

Passing down the Blue, none of the gulches has been found rich until Illinois is reached, a mile and a half above Breckenridge. The discovery was made in the fall of '59 by a man named Glick who is a disciple of necromancy, and, we are told, believes firmly that he made his great discovery by the practice of magic. He was one of the pioneers on the Blue, and had a claim among others in its bed, but when most of them set to work to turn the river; he looked on awhile and predicting a failure, set out alone to hunt easier diggings. Passing up the valley he kept tossing his tincup before him. It piloted him through the timber, across the little park or delta of the gulch, and up the mountain side into it, where it would hardly be suspected from below that a gulch existed. The faithful coffee-cup however was a true pilot, and led him forward through brush and over rocks, for a third of a mile, and then stopped, and in language which he understood, said "dig." He dug and found good pay; but winter came on and he had to leave for Denver. In the spring he gave half of his claim to a man for bringing him up from the plains, and has been working ever since, with varying fortunes. He showed us one nugget of $26.68, and a number of smaller ones, taken from his claim. Quite a number of claims on the gulch are paying well—as near as we could learn from four to ten dollars per day to the man—mostly in coarse gold.

"The Patch" is a timbered ridge, or tongue of the mountain, between Illinois and French gulches. Gold is found here all over the surface and the pick and shovel are steadily uprooting the forest. Some hundreds of acres are partially dug over, but not one-fourth of the ground has yet been touched. The pay dirt is on the surface, from six to eighteen inches deep, overlaying a bed of clay, creased and seamed with slight depressions, in which most gold is found.

Breckenridge is the first point of importance, reached by the traveler over this road, and until recently the most town-like of any settlement in the Blue River country. The population is probably between seventy-five and one hundred persons—embracing quite a number of families. There are several stores, hotels, meat markets, saloons and a U. S. Post Office —the only one west of the Range.

A mile below Breckinridge, French Gulch heads far up in the Snowy Range. It is full ten miles in length, and from fifty to two hundred yards in width. About midway of its length is the principal mining district, and some very heavy work has been done in it. Some claims pay very largely, but like in most large gulches, the pay streak is hard to find, and a vast amount of work has been done without yielding any remuneration. The principal settlement has received the name of Lincoln City, and is already a very respectable sized village, with it shops, hotels and business houses. Near the mouth of French, very good pay is obtained in the left bank, or what is in reality the foot of the hill on which the "Patch" is situated.

We left Breckinridge on the morning of the 17th, and crossing the old channel of the Blue on the dam, followed down the wagon road, recrossing to the east side again in two and a half miles. A number of small gulches come in from the east, and on some of them, work is being done. On the west side there are five or six gulches, that are now being well prospected, with good promise. One of them, the Iowa, is quite extensively worked near its mouth, and good pay is obtained, but we were unable to learn particulars.

The turning of the Blue was a herculean task, performed by the little band of pioneers who first wandered over onto its waters in '59. A dam was built which has stood the floods of two summers; and the entire river then conducted for two and a half miles—part of the way through deep cuts, to where it again enters its natural bed. When the water was out of the way however, the work seems to have been abandoned, and but few ever realized anything

from their claims. If they had continued their joint labors, and put a bed-rock flume in the old channel, we believe every man of the company, might have long 'ere this, enjoyed the fortune for which he sought.

About six miles below Breckinridge, and nearly opposite the mouth of the Swan, is Gold Hill on the west bank of the Blue. It is a new, and as yet untried, mining district, and is properly bank or hill diggings. A ditch is being brought in, to supply water for hydraulic operations, which will begin work in a few days.

Turning up the Swan the first mines are found upon Gold Run, which comes in from the South. Gold was first discovered in it, in June '60, about a mile above its mouth. From seventy-five to one hundred claims pay steadily, from four to ten dollars per day to the man.

Buffalo Flats, at the mouth of Gold Run, is the widening out of the deposit of that stream, where it reaches the valley of the Swan. The formation is principally clay, intermixed more or less with sand and gravel. Some claims are paying well, but many are not, and the general feeling seems to be among the miners, that as one of them expressed—"Buffalo Flats is a failure." With plenty of water—which there is not—they can doubtless be made to pay well. Gold Run is almost devoid of boulders and heavy rocks.

A mile above, Delaware Gulch enters the Swan, coming down almost parallel with Gold Run, and forming the same kind of delta, or "flats," at its mouth. No good pay has yet been found in it—though it prospects well. It has but little water, and hence is not more worked.

Delaware Flats are just now the most noted of mines. A smooth grassy slope is being rapidly dug over and washed away, and with wonderful results. Everybody is busy, lumber is snapped up as fast as sawed, speculation runs high, and prosperity smiles. A town of twenty or thirty houses occupies the site, where a week ago there were but three or four cabins, and tents and white topped wagons dot the hills on every side. Claims yield from eighty to two hundred and twenty dollars per day to the sluice, working eight men, four at a time. One company worked here last season, but nobody can tell what they did, and their operations on the naked prairie seem to have attracted but little attention at the time.

Galena Gulch enters Swan, from the southwest, two miles above Delaware. The gulch has but few people in it, and many of the claims are idle. A few are paying very largely, and the prospect is that it will rival the famous Georgia, which it much resembles. Its history is yet in its infancy.

Excelsior Gulch comes next above Galena —is very similar in appearance—runs parallel with, and is a mile and a half distant from the latter. It was first claimed up last week, and a dozen or more men are now prospecting it.

From Galena we followed up the Swan, six miles to the mouth of Georgia. In the park, near its mouth, quite a town has sprung up. It is becoming the center of a large trade and gives every evidence of prosperity. Georgia Gulch is short of water, and many claims are idle and will remain so until the new ditch is finished— which will be in a few days. The claims that have water, are doing well, both in Georgia and in Humbug. Several gulches enter the Swan above Georgia, from the same side.

The American Gulch is worked with considerable success, but we had not time to visit it, and cannot speak more particularly.

All the area described in this article is doubtless exceeding rich, and we shall expect, before another year passes, to see every one of its gulches worked, and hundreds of rich quartz leads opened in its hills and mountains.

Byers' predictions for the area were modest; it was to become a fabulous region. Within a few weeks, summer of 1861, the *Miners' Record* was reporting amazing growth in many of the camps. Humbug and Georgia Gulches were paying best returns of any of the mines.

Merchandizing, saloon-keeping, auctioneering and peddling are overdone for the present. Loafing, gambling and spreeing are assiduously patronized, particularly in the north wing of the lower town. Delaware Flats, like Buckskin Joe, is all the excitement of these days. Claims are pretended to be bought and sold for hundreds and thousands, and new log buildings, shanties and tents spring up into existence by dozens every few days. They have a theatre in Delaware Flats already, and as soon as a billiard table arrives, it is prognosticated the city will be "finished." There is a great deal of mining going on in the Flats, and with many very successfully. Several tents are located on the plaza, to which reinforcements of the "fancy" are constantly arriving from the columns of the bummer grand army of Georgia Gulch and Denver.

There are no less than three or four different theatres of "shows" at present in the Georgia Gulch mines. The "Colorado Minstrels," assisted by Md'lle Haydee, give concerts every night nowadays in Gayosa Hall, Georgia Gulch. The "Pioneer Theatre Company" gives entertainments nightly in their big tent at the lower end of the same gulch; Prof. Barton, the "great Magician and Wizard of the Mountains" gives exhibitions alternate nights in Georgia and Delaware Flats. A big dance is given almost nightly in the Georgia Hall, and a half dozen of sporting saloons are regularly open, day and night, to furnish professional sports with the needful and to fleece the verdant miners of their hard earned dust and highly prized nuggets. Verily the people of these mines are singularly blessed or cursed, as the case may be, compared with us quiet, forsaken folks in South Park cities. There are not as many loafers, idlers or bummers in Buckskin Joe as in some other parts of these mines.

Langrishe & Dougherty's large theatre in Parkville, Georgia Gulch, is nearly completed, and will be ready for occupancy by the middle of next week, when their distinguished and talented troupe are expected to arrive from Central City. With two large theatres in full blast, and the numerous other places of amusement, Parkville may be set down as a "fast" locality, and the popular place of resort for those in search of amusement.

The rapid development of Swan Valley was almost unbelievable. According to the Spalding account, Gold Run was discovered in January or February of 1860 by Balce Weaver. Mining began in the early summer. The *Rocky Mountain News*, July 11, 1860, reported discovery of Georgia Gulch in mid-June, by a party of Georgians. By April of 1861 an extensive building program was under way:

Rocky Mountain News
April 30, 1861

Breckinridge, April 24th
In Georgia and Humbug gulches, with the increased supply of water, a corresponding increase of work is being done, and I do not know of a claim being worked but what is paying well. A good deal of building is going on here at present. The Masons are putting up a two-story building in the Park at the foot of the gulch. The upper story is to be devoted exclusively to the Order, and the lower to be occupied by Mr. O. A. Whittemore, as a storeroom. The Order of O. H. M. are also putting up a fine two-story building, adjoining Gayosa Hall, at the junction of Georgia and Humbug. Like the other buildings, their upper story to

be for the exclusive use of the Order, and the lower to be occupied by P. Valiten, as a storeroom. The character of the buildings through this entire section, that are at present being erected, is highly creditable, considering that there is not a sawmill in operation this side of the range.

Yours,
Pettenes

In late summer there was another report to the *Rocky Mountain News* of feverish building activity:

August 21, 1861

Humbug and Georgia Gulches lie between two little ranges, and run into one another, something like the Gregory and Central City gulches. In the Humbug part of the gulch, there are several stores, saloons, etc., of course,— among which the "Bed Rock," "Gayosa" and "Metropolitan" are the most prominent. (Gayosa was named after a miner's home town, Gayosa, Missouri.) In the lower part of the gulch, (Georgia) there is a snug little collection of stores, hotels, mechanic's shops and houses, citified under the cognomen of "Parkville." The best hotel there is the Chapin House, kept by J. B. Chapin, from Leavenworth, and if not the "best hotel this side of sunset," is assuredly the best in this section of the mines. Some fifty persons sat down to meals, morning, noon and night, while we were there.

There is a mint in Georgia Gulch, by J. J. Conway & Co.—Jewelers and bankers. Their machinery seems to be as fine as that of Clark, Gruber & Co.'s, and their $5 and $10 gold pieces look as nice and rich as Uncle Sam himself could get up at his establishment.

Our young friend Tom Wanless, is completing a large theatre building here for Langrishe & Dougherty's Dramatic Troupe, who are expected here in a few weeks to present the legitimate drama for the delectation of hundreds of gold diggers in these various gulches and cities adjoining.

There is another large theatre building almost completed here, with a large storeroom underneath, suitable for carrying on a general merchandising storage or commission business. The large hall above will be for balls, amusements, public meetings and everything of that kind. It is within a few yards of Langrishe & Co.'s, owned by Messrs. Willand & Co., who deserve credit for their enterprise in getting their large building up. There is a theatre here now nightly, in a big tent, under the management of Messrs. Caven, Gooding & Pardse.

They are doing a fair business. The "Colorado troupe," assisted by M'lle Haydee give entertainments nightly in Gayosa Hall. One or two men minstrel and dramatic troupes are still said to be en route here, presuming it to be the "land of Ophir" certain. We privately believe they will not make much over "cost and freight" by the time they get through. The majority of successful miners know full well how to take care of every grain they get out,—they intend to soon leave for the States to winter.

Great numbers throughout all these places, nevertheless, are loafing and idling away their time—neither owning claims nor wishing to work if claims were donated to them.

There is an excellent lager beer brewery established here in Parkville, by Henry Weiss, in company with Endlich and Goode of Denver—and its manager is making lots of money out of it, as much as he could out of a "discovery" claim.

There are but few ladies or families throughout these places, and but few of the amenities of social life, such as are to be found in Denver or in the cities of Gregory mines. Theatres and concerts, are principally attended by the male sex alone, and the balls are chiefly no more than "stag dances" throughout. They have in Georgia Gulch almost every night, among the bummers and "fancy" of both sexes, what they call "free and easy" dances, in a large hall, at which from fifty to a hundred, including about a score of "females" were generally in attendance,—and the way they carry on, irrespective of the loss of money or manners, is a caution to a looker-on. It would seem as if some of those disciples of Esculapius at Denver had given the city a mammoth emetic, and Vesuvius like, your town had thrown up here among us, *all* of the gamblers, bummers and roughs, whose familiar faces were for the past year discernible in Denver. Sunday is observed here commendably—although we believe there is no officiating Clergyman here to blow the trumpet of Zion among these erring multitudes. Brother Billingsley or Father Kehler (Denver clergymen) can find here a wide field of labor, in the winning of souls from the ways of wickedness, by the time they get through regenerating the downfallen of Denver, and have cleaned out the tares from among the mildewed wheat throughout that aforesaid immoral granary, from which barbarism, on the sly, seems to be bursting out.

The *Miners' Record*, of the same time, September 14, 1861, reported, "Humbug Gulch, by means of hydraulic and otherwise, is tearing up 'Mother Nature' at a fearful rate, undermining houses and removing every obstacle in their progress in searching for the precious ore."

During the same time, Lieutenant W. T. Roath, Company D, first regiment Colorado Volunteers, enrolled recruits at Georgia Gulch. Volunteers encamped a short distance below town where they drilled daily and trained in Zouave tactics. Lieutenant Roath received this special training from Ellsworth's Chicago Zouaves.

Lieutenant Roath raised the first American flag that was ever raised in Georgia Gulch, and when first hoisted, it was the subject of many curses and threats from noisy secessionists, who are located in certain quarters of Parkville, who boasted that it must come down immediately, but who did not discover what they considered favorable opportunity of carrying out their threats; so the stars and stripes still float proudly over Camp Downing and a company of men who are able and willing to defend them.

Brother Billingsley and Father Kehler did not come from Denver to rescue the wayward in Georgia Gulch and the Valley of the Swan. But come next spring, April, 1862, one was to trudge over Georgia Pass in the deep snow to blow the "trumpet of Zion" in the camps of Swan Valley, French Gulch and the Blue River Basin. His name, and his ministry in "the true riches," was destined to be remembered as long as the gold of Breckenridge. He would learn to ski on the slopes of Gold Run and the hills of the Swan, and become known as the beloved "Snow-Shoe Itinerant."

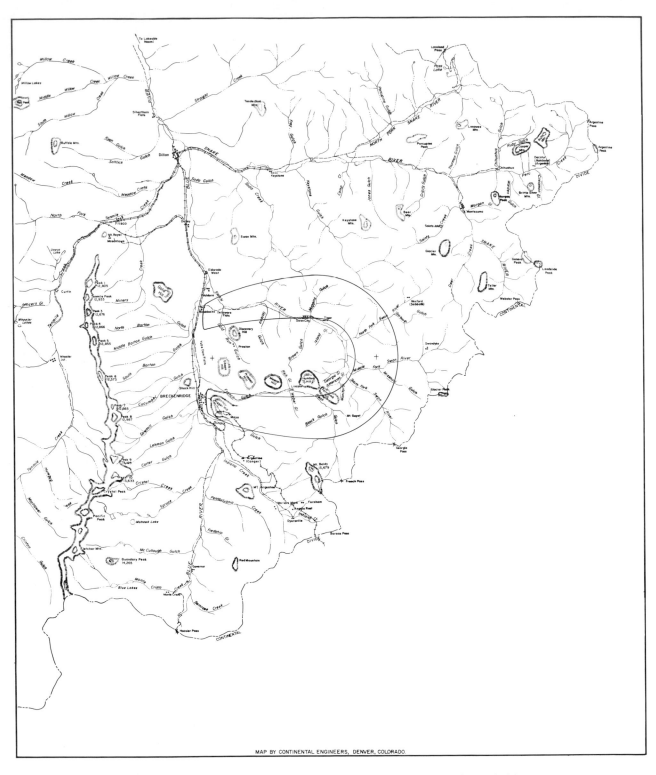

Planimetric Map of Breckenridge Area—1860-1900—Showing "Golden Horseshoe." Map: Continental Engineers, Inc., Denver.

William Newton Byers
Editor: *Rocky Mountain News* and *Miner's Record*.
Courtesy—Denver Public Library Western Collection.

33

1971 Ruins of Gold Run Diggings.

Preston—south of Gold Run Diggings, at top of Gibson Hill. Postoffice established July 13, 1875—John Shock, postmaster; remained as postmaster to a date later than October, 1887 (probably to demise of Braddock postoffice, December 27, 1890). Preston postoffice sub-station established October, 1887, at Jumbo Mine (2,000 feet distant from Preston), serving Jumbo Mine, Quartzite Ridge and Gibson Hill. An "air line wagon road" was built between Breckenridge and Gold Run, via Preston, 1880. Dave Braddock's daughter carried mail on horseback from Braddock Station to Gold Run and Preston when snow permitted.

Wapiti—toe of golden horseshoe. Victoria Company purchased Ware-Carpenter holdings, 1888; known as Victoria for a short time; 1894 name Wapiti given and postoffice granted. Large center building—office, postoffice, living quarters; right—stable barn. Picture: Courtesy—Library State Historical Society of Colorado.

Interior of Wapiti office-postoffice, showing Johnson-Ware ornate safe. Courtesy—Library State Historical Society of Colorado.

Aerial view of gouged Georgia Gulch (foreground) and surrounding mountains and mines. Courtesy—Denver Public Library Western Collection.

Mountain park at the mouth of Georgia Gulch. In this park, and mouth of the gulch, was Parkville, with a reported population of 7,000-8,000. Parkville aspired to be seat of Summit County and Colorado State Capitol. Habitations have completely disappeared from park and gulch.

A sturdy, lone cabin stands sentinel at the head of Georgia Gulch,
quietly surveying the havoc of man's feverish grasping for gold.

Rock-strewn Georgia Gulch in wake of gold-digging.

One of the first Masonic Lodges in Colorado was built at Parkville.
Nothing remains of the building. A Masonic Monument marks the site.

SITE OF

Summit Lodge #2 A. F. & A. M.

1861—1864

Colorado Territory

One of the Three Original Lodges

which formed

THE FIRST GRAND LODGE OF COLORADO

In 1861

Erected In Humble Commemoration

By

Breckenridge Lodge #47

1940

Across the road from Parkville's park, a path leads into a virginal, shadowed pine growth. A sign requests, "Please walk; do not enter on vehicles." Down this short path Parkville funeral processions carried their dead. In a small clearing, surrounded by pine trees, the dead went to their last resting-place. No markers record names; only mountain stones border grave sites.

A stone-marked grave (foreground). In the shadow ahead is the Masonic Monument to the Unknown Pioneers.

Masonic Monument in Parkville's Cemetery

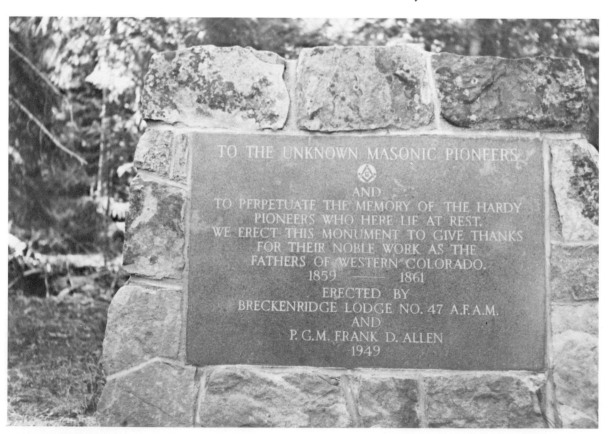

TO THE UNKNOWN MASONIC PIONEERS
AND
TO PERPETUATE THE MEMORY OF THE HARDY
PIONEERS WHO HERE LIE AT REST.
WE ERECT THIS MONUMENT TO GIVE THANKS
FOR THEIR NOBLE WORK AS THE
FATHERS OF WESTERN COLORADO.
1859 ——— 1861
ERECTED BY
BRECKENRIDGE LODGE NO. 47 A.F.A.M.
AND
P. G.M. FRANK D. ALLEN
1949

TRUMPET OF ZION

Blow ye the trumpet in Zion,
and sound an alarm in my holy mountain:
(Bible—Old Testament—Joel 2:1)

The "trumpet of Zion" sounds "the message of the Lord;" but the "message of the Lord" wasn't the most urgent concern in the mining camp.

The composition and employment of the average mining camp was described by a writer of the times: "It is surprising what few are really workers on claims to the proportion of other pursuits. The regular average per centum might be classified as follows: Thirty active miners, ten merchants and saloon keepers, five mechanics, fifty loafers, gamblers and fancy men. Lousy with lawyers, pettifoggers and scrub doctors—six married men with their own wives—ten grass widows, three antiquated females desirous of permanent homes and partners for life—one ossified old maid, two that are hastening to ossification—single and married men—and a few pups, cats and chickens. Most of the men are sitting in their houses or tents, watching the weather, and as a *'general business'* playing 'high low jack' or 'seven up' for whiskey. This is the *chief* employment of almost half the population of Georgia and other gulches, from daylight to dark, throughout the week, Sunday not excepted." Night time had the ball, the dance, the theatre, the saloon, billiards, gambling. The "message of the Lord" wasn't the greatest concern in the mining camp. But the trumpet would sound.

Rev. William Howbert of the then-named "Methodist Episcopal" Church, is credited with conducting the first religious services in South Park. Friday, July 6th, 1860, Howbert crossed the range at Boreas Pass into Blue River country, spending the night at Breckenridge. He stayed at Gold Run Diggings Saturday night. Sunday morning, July 8th, Howbert preached at Blue River (probably at Spaulding diggings, Fort Mary B.) and organized a class of six members. In the afternoon he preached at Breckenridge and organized a class of seven members.

Other churches were mindful of their flocks scattered throughout the mountains. In August, 1861, the Right Reverend Bishop Talbot of the Protestant Episcopal Church visited Tarryall in the interest of mining camp ministries. September, 1861, the Catholic Church sent a priest from Denver on a tour through the mountains, visiting members of the Church.

August 11th and 12th, 1860, Presiding Elder of the Kansas Conference of the Methodist Episcopal Church—John Milton Chivington—held a quarterly meeting on Blue River. "This was Chivington's first visit to this region, and was the first meeting of the kind held beyond the range." (Chivington lost his relationship to the M. E. Church when he became active in the army. He was the Colonel Chivington of the notorious Sand Creek Indian massacre, for which he has been both blessed and cursed.)

Religious services in the mining camps were held outdoors, or in private homes, tents, saloons, storerooms, or any available public building. Marshall Silverthorn's Breckenridge hotel was used on many occasions. Church buildings, for the most part, were slow in coming. Howbert started a 30x40 log church at Hamilton in midsummer, 1860, but by the time it was two-thirds completed his congregation had vanished to another scene of mining excitement. The church was never finished. Central City and California Gulch (Leadville) built churches in the fall of 1860. The rapid depopulation of mining camps worked havoc both in the building of congregations and the erecting of church edifices.

South Park was without a Methodist house of worship as late as 1867. A former hotel, from deserted Montgomery, was moved to Fairplay and reconstructed as the South Park Father Dyer Chapel. Blue River didn't get a place of worship until the erection of the Breckenridge Father Dyer Church in 1880.

John Lewis Dyer, previous to his coming to the Pike's Peak region, had been an ordained minister, serving in the expanding work of Methodism in Illinois, Wisconsin and Minnesota. The financial collapse of 1857 swept away his meager possessions; his sole extravagance had been going security for struggling churches. The final reckoning stripped him of everything and left him in debt $750—an obligation to be paid at a later date.

Two things determined Dyer's trek to Pike's Peak gold country—the financial depression had not eased by 1861, and a serious eye ailment prognosticated approaching blindness. If he were to see the glowingly-reported Pike's Peak gold region, the trip could not be delayed.

The journey started from Lenora, Minnesota, with Dyer riding a fine horse; his possessions were in a carpet bag—his Bible, hymnbook, Church Discipline, copy of Lorain's *Sea Sermons,* and a change of linen. At Newton, Iowa, the horse was stabled where a peck of corn was within reach; the animal almost foundered. After leading it a few miles the next day, he sold it for a gun, an old watch, and $15. Then followed a hundred-mile walk to Omaha, Nebraska, where Dyer hoped to join a wagon-train crossing the "great American Desert." At Omaha he joined a train, paying $15 for board, carrying of his gun and carpet bag, and the privilege of walking the 750 miles. The last night on the plains his pocketknife, watch and cash ($2.50) were stolen. He arrived in Denver, June 20, 1861, and after a few days' visit with his son, Elias, started another hundred mile walk to Buckskin Joe mining camp. Remarkably the eye ailment completely healed and he lived a long life without aid of eye glasses.

Although he was not under church appointment, Dyer immediately started preaching at South Park camps, California Gulch (Leadville)

and the camps along the Arkansas River. Dyer was under a Divine commission: "Woe is unto me, if I preach not the gospel!" (I Cor. 9: 16.) Dyer's ministry at the Blue River Mission, the golden horseshoe, is related in his autobiography, *Snow-Shoe Itinerant*:

About the 1st of February (1862) I started on foot for Denver. We had a stage once a week to Buckskin Joe. Fare, ten dollars each way. I could walk the hundred miles in two days and a half. If I did not make money, I could save some.

In the latter part of March, 1862, I received a letter from the presiding elder of the Rocky Mountain District, Kansas Conference, asking me to take charge of Blue River Mission, Summit County, Colorado. The next day I started on foot. I went by Central City, and the first day out it snowed four inches, which made it bad walking. The second day reached Kenosha Hill, remarkably tired. My purse of gold-dust was so light that I feared there would not be enough to pay my bill. I told the landlord that it was possible that my means would not meet my expenses, but wished to stay, and that I would remit to him. He said that it would be all right, and the call for supper soon came. When I sat down, I saw that the food was all cold, except a weak cup of tea. After a few mouthfuls, I became sick and left the table, and lay down on a bench in the bar-room and rested, for I was almost given out. After half an hour, another man came in for supper, and while he was eating, I went in for a drink of water, and saw hot coffee, ham, and eggs. I thought I would never say anything about pay again until after breakfast. I rested all night, and in the morning ate a hearty breakfast, and gave the host my purse. He weighed out my bill, and I had some left. There were at least twenty-five miles to walk, and but one house. I took dinner at that house and handed my purse to the landlord, and he weighed out my bill and I crossed the range on a snow-path; for, although it was April, the snow was from five to fifteen feet deep.

I reached Georgia Gulch on the second day of April, (1862) and was received kindly. There were about one hundred and fifty people in the Gulch, and I found some few that had been members of some Church. I gave out preaching for the next Sunday at ten and a half o'clock, and at French Gulch in the afternoon. The hall was well-filled in the morning, and there were about forty hearers in the afternoon.

There was a friendly Jew at Georgia Gulch, who proposed to raise the preacher something, and took a paper and collected $22.50 in dust; for that was all the currency then. This amount was quite a help, as there were only ten cents in my purse when I got there. We had at first five preaching-places for two weeks, and afterwards more.

I saw that what I was likely to get in the new wild country would not board me, as common board was seven dollars a week, and a man had to find his own bed, and do his own washing. I had a chance to buy a cabin in French Gulch or what was then called Lincoln City, and I set up in a humble way keeping bachelor's hall. My bedstead was made of pine poles, even to the springs. The bed was hay, with blankets for coverings. I slept well, and rested as well as though I had been in a fine parlor-chamber. My furniture was primitive and limited—a table, and a couple of boards against the side of the wall for a cupboard, six tin plates, half a set of knives and forks, with a few other indispensables; a coffee-pot, a tin cup, and a pot for boiling vegetables—when I had them—and a frying-pan. I had a few books to read—the Bible, hymn-book, and Methodist Discipline, with two of our weekly *Advocates* and *Rocky Mountain News*. I tried to keep up with the times.

The compass of my circuit was not large. The farthest appointment was six miles; and I preached about seven times in two weeks. I formed one class, and then discovered that there was little profit in it, as the people stopped so short a time in one place. I concluded to get everybody out, and then preach the truth burning hot, whether my hearers were in the house or around the camp-fire, or, at other times, under the shade of a pine-tree. We generally had good congregations. The way we got them out was to go along the gulches and tell the people in their cabins and saloons where the preaching would be at night, and then, just before the time, to step to the door where they were at cards, and say: "My friends, can't you close your game in ten minutes, and come and hear preaching?" I tried to adapt myself to the situation, neither showing that I felt above anyone, nor ever compromising with sin or with transgressions, and being always ready to speak for the Lord Jesus Christ.

We cooked by a fire-place, generally baking our bread in a frying-pan set up before the fire. I must not forget to say that we had stools and benches in place of chairs. There was one

chair left in my house, made by some one out of crooked pine-limbs, with the seat of ropes. It was so comical that if I had it now, I would certainly place it in an exposition. It was easy enough for an editor.

I tried to make my cabin useful. It was about eighteen feet square, and, taken every way, the best place to hold our meetings. The floor was hard ground. I got gunny-sacks and made carpet, and covered the table with two copies of the *Northwestern Christian Advocate.* And thus I preached to the people in my own house, not in a hired house, as the Apostle Paul did.

My appointments were Park City (Georgia Gulch), American Gulch, Galena Gulch, Delaware Flats, Gold Run, Lincoln City, Mayo Gulch, and Breckenridge. It was a two weeks' circuit. I preached once at least in Gibson Gulch, and I must say that we had, without an exception, good behavior and good attention. Although we all looked rough, the miners treated me and the cause of Christ with respect. Often after preaching I was greeted warmly, and some of them would say the service reminded them of home. They were generally liberal, although it was not the custom always to pass the hat, and sometimes the preacher, when his pants began to wear out, would think the boys rather long between collections. It was common to give a dollar all around; and to this day I would as soon ask miners for help, with assurance of receiving, as any class of men I have ever found. They were always ready to divide, although at times they would take exceptions to a man that wore a plug hat or noticeably fine clothes.

This was the regular round on the circuit. We had a new field, one that gave a good chance to read human nature, in the fastness of the Rocky Mountains, where moral and religious restraints were absent. The most of the men would go to the bar and drink, and play at cards, and the Sabbath was a high day for wickedness. Balls were the common amusement, especially in winter. The women were as fond of this as the men. Although far in the minority, they were accosted like this: "Now, Miss, or Mistress, you must surely come, as we can't have a set or cotillion without you." Often the father was left with the children at home; at other times both went and took the children; and then the old bachelors would hold the baby so that the mother could dance every set.

I will give an instance at Lincoln City, at our hotel. They must give a Christmas dinner, and, of course, a dance at night. I concluded to take dinner with them. The host made me no charge, as it would be what we old bachelors called a square meal. As I was about to leave, the ladies pleasantly invited me to stay to the dance. Of course I could not accept the invitation. But they said: "You visit at our houses, and you ought to show us respect and stay." At the last came the lady of the house, and said: "This is an extra occasion, and it will be no harm for you to dance with me; why can't you accept my offer?" The reply was: "You're a lady, but not quite handsome enough for me to dance with." She was taken back at that, and the others laughed, and I got out, as my cabin was only two hundred feet away. They soon fiddled me to sleep. But they danced till daylight, and often drank at the bar. Being full, and having no place to sleep, they went up to Walker's saloon. He made some hot sling, and that set them off. They declared that every man in town must get up, and the preacher should treat the company or make a temperance speech. It was just daylight when we heard them on the street, and as they had always passed me before, I turned the key and hoped they would do so again. But when they found the door fast they said: "If you don't open it we will break it in." I threw it open and invited them in; but they said: "We have come to take you up to Walker's, and you either treat or make a temperance speech." I requested them to let me eat breakfast first; but they said: "You must go now." I slipped out, leaving the door open, and went ahead of the company.

Soon there were over forty men, and they called a chairman or moderator; but they were too drunk to be moderated. I got upon a box and stated my arrest, and proposed to make the speech. They said: "Go on." I said: "Gentlemen, first I will tell you what I think! There is not a man here but would be ashamed for his father, mother, sisters, or brothers, to know just our condition here this morning." They stamped and roared out, "That's so," all over the house. "And next," I continued, "if we were not so drunk, we would not be here." (Cheers, "That's so, too!" all over the house.) "And if we were a little drunker, we could not do as we are now doing." (Cheers and "That's so!" all over the house.) I wound up and was about to take leave, but the judge said: "I move that we vote that everything Mr. Dyer has said is true;" and they gave a rousing vote. He said, "The ayes have it," but that I must not go yet; and made and put a motion that they all give Mr. Dyer

one dollar apiece; and that was also carried. They took the hat, got twenty dollars, and I thanked them and went home to breakfast.

As all the mining was gulch or placer diggings, a great part of the people left in the fall to winter—some for Denver, some to other points. Only a few would come back in the spring; for men did not come to Pike's Peak—as it was called—to stay, but to make a raise, and then go back.

In the summer a troupe of theatrical performers came across to Summit County, and played all the camps—Sunday morning at one place, and in the evening at another. I thought the devil was traveling the circuit as well as myself. I have thought less of theaters ever since. There is little about them but evil.

In March, 1863, I received my appointment from Kansas Conference. My work up to this time had been as a supply. I was readmitted to my former church relationship. It was a surprise, for I had not made up my mind to stay in the mountains. This decided me to stand the storms and leave the events with God, and do the best I could to build up the Church in this wilderness country. I was put down for South Park and on the third day of April left Lincoln City.

John Lewis Dyer—forty-nine years of age when he made the long trek across the "American Desert"—fifty years of age when he crossed Georgia Pass to begin his Blue River Mission ministry—was destined for fame and remembrance. His 1862 ministry on Blue River Circuit was the first regularly conducted services in the Valley. Later, 1879-1880, he was again assigned to Breckenridge. It was then that he built the church bearing his name, Father Dyer Methodist Church. As a "father" to the far-from-home miner and miner's family, the people of the mountains lovingly bestowed the name *Father* Dyer. No greater ordination can be given than that by the flock. When Colorado built its capitol building in Denver, sixteen founders of Colorado were chosen to have their likenesses appear in stained glass at the top of the gold-gilted dome. The people of Colorado unanimously chose Father Dyer to represent the spiritual. The trumpet of Zion had been sounded in the mountains.

It is almost weird to contemplate that the barren flats and gulches of present-day Swan Valley were once fair-sized towns, vibrant with the theatre, the dance hall, and all the raucous life of the mining camp—mecca of the bummer, the gambler, the "fancy." Now one searches for a ruin, a scrap of wood, a building foundation to mark the spot of that throbbing life. Hardly a shred of habitation remains. Lonely quietness hangs heavily where once life resounded from valley, gulch and mountain top. Delaware Flats is nothingness. Georgia Gulch is a jagged, unhealed wound. Parkville totally disappeared—only a monument stands, marking the site of the Masonic Lodge. Another Masonic monument, one-fourth mile distant, marks the cemetery where some of the pioneers lay down for eternal sleep. Their graves, outlined with pebbles and stones, are nameless. Chattering squirrels and scolding bluejays protest human invasion, berating you for disturbing the solitude. One feels himself trespassing on the past. Over all could be written, "and the place thereof shall know it no more." (Psalm 103:16)

"The Miner's Recreation"—Appeared in The Summit County *Journal* and Breckenridge *Bulletin*, May 13, 1911. Courtesy—L. G. McKee.

Rev. John Lewis Dyer

Rocky Mountain *News* August 25, 1932—Sec. 2, Page 11.
Courtesy—Denver Public Library Western Collection.

Trumpet of Zion

Father John Lewis Dyer

State Capitol Dome   Denver, Colorado
The Denver *Post* Library

BAYARD AND BRECKENRIDGE

1866

Breckenridge area gold boom, early 1860s, tapered off after the summer of 1862. Placer mining was not as easy and rewarding as at first. Hydraulic mining was in its infancy. The day of big machinery and heavily-financed companies was in the future. Only the energetic and richly-favored stayed to work claims. Population of Parkville, Delaware Flats and Breckenridge plummeted as rapidly as it had skyrocketed. Gay life depended on a generous flow of gold dust; tightened pouch strings sent the "bummers" and "fancy" to more lucrative camps. The Methodist Church didn't send another "to blow the trumpet of Zion," following Dyer's one-year appointment; Blue River Mission was "to be supplied"—which meant occasional preaching, whenever a preacher was available. Camps of the Upper Blue River settled down to a plodding, hard-working pace. Gone was the delusion of effortlessly picking up buckets of gold.

Topography of Upper Blue River (from present-day Dillon to Breckenridge) hadn't been greatly changed by placer mining; the great change of surface features came with hydraulic washing and gold boat digging. (Much later, Dillon Reservoir would submerge vast acreage, considerably changing the appearance of the valley.)

One hundred years ago Upper Blue River Valley was marshy bottom land, covered primarily with willows, sagebrush and occasional pine, spruce and aspen. Through this pleasant valley Blue River flowed rapidly. Henry Villard described the river in 1860: "Blue River is about three rods in width and several feet deep. It is a beautiful, clear, swift stream. Its banks are wide and bordered by high, sloping hills, covered with tall pine trees. The scenery in the vicinity of the Blue diggings is possessed of every charm of an Alpine landscape." Early summer melting snows made Blue River difficult to ford. Indian trails along the river were the best routes to travel.

BAYARD TAYLOR

Bayard Taylor, American author, world traveler and lecturer, made a summer tour of Colorado in 1866. He sent reports to the *New York Tribune* for publication. The articles appeared in book form the following year.

Bayard Taylor was a brilliant, artistic and highly perceptive individual. He was courteous, appreciative and complimentary in his tour through the newly-settled West. He found the way of life uninhibited. Of the miners he said, "people are so crowded together, live in so primitive a fashion for the most part, and are, perhaps, so glad to escape the restraint, that they are more natural, and hence more interesting than in the older States. It is hard to recognize the staid New Englander. He has simply cast off his assumed shell and is himself; and I must confess I like him all the better. Men of culture and education are plenty, yet not always to be distinguished by their dress or appearance. Society is still agreeably free and unconventional."

One practice was anathema to him—"I only wish that the vulgar, snobbish custom of attaching *City* to every place of more than three houses, could be stopped. It has become a general nuisance, telling only of swagger and want of taste, not of growth. In Colorado, if one talks much about the mining towns, he must add one seventh of his speech in repeating the useless word *City*."

We might expect a "looking down the nose" from this gentleman crossing the "great American Desert" in 1866, enduring all its hardships, crudities and inconveniences, arriving at a seven-year-old struggling settlement on the plains, Denver.

Instead, Taylor was convinced "the American Desert" was a myth; almost all the territory had possibility of productive reclamation. "I am fast inclining toward the opinion that there is *no* American Desert on the east side of the Rocky Mountains." Of Denver, he said, "the views which have appeared in the illustrated Eastern papers are simply caricatures. Denver is as well built as any town of equal size in the Mississippi Valley—and some of the buildings are of considerable architectural beauty. There is no part of the town which does not afford a view of the great range." "I find myself constantly returning to the point which my eyes seek, with unwearied interest, whenever I lift them from the paper. Ever since my arrival I have been studying the mountains. Their beauty and grandeur grow upon me with every hour of my stay—nowhere grotesque in outline, never monotonous, lovely in color and atmospheric effect. I may recall some mountain chains which equal, but none which surpass them." "Business of all kinds is extraordinarily dull at present, and the people are therefore as much dispirited as Colorado nature will admit. Denver seems to me to have a very brisk and lively air, and the people one meets are brimful of cheerful energy." "I was interested in noticing how attached the inhabitants are to the place. Nearly everyone who had recently been East seemed rejoiced to return. Even ladies forget the greater luxuries of the Atlantic Coast, when they see the Rocky Mountains once more. The people look upon this glorious Alpine view as one of the properties of the town."

Most of Taylor's observations on Colorado were praise—generous, glowing and sincere. He was pleasantly surprised at the "degree of refinement" and "graces of life" so often in evidence. His conclusion was "it is only the half-cultivated who relapse toward barbarism. Mountain life soon rubs off the veneering, and we know of what wood men are made."

At the little mining town of Empire, Taylor was joined by six others for the expedition over Berthoud Pass into Middle Park—McCandless and Davis (from Pittsburg), Beard (an artist), Byers (editor of *Rocky Mountain News*), Sumner (Byers' brother-in-law) and White (in charge of animals and camp duty). Empire natives considered it foolhardy to attempt crossing little-known Berthoud Pass at such an early part of the summer, but the venture succeeded in shorter time than considered possible. After exploring the lower part of Middle Park the group headed for Breckenridge where Taylor had scheduled a lecture for July 2nd.

Jack Sumner, experienced trader and mountain man, and William Byers, editor of the *Rocky Mountain News*, served as guides for the expedition. It was an opportunity for Byers to get away from the editor's desk and make another visit to the mining country. June 5th there appeared a farewell note in the *Rocky Mountain News*:

Off To The Mountains

Disgusted with the persistent failures of the telegraph, and consequently disappointed in getting the much-wished-for-news of the admission to statehood, we are off today for the mountains, and shall hope that a contemplation of their stupendous grandeur will give us an additional zest for editorial labor, as well as inspire us with an increased love for this our adopted country. We shall keep our readers posted of our movements, and what we see and hear on the way—as we make the trip "over the range."

We expect to have a good time, and in so far as our capacity will allow, will make a display of the same through these columns. Should the State of Colorado be admitted during our absence, we hereby deputize and appoint every reader of the *News,* to give three cheers for the new State as our proxy, and when we learn the fact, we will re-echo the same from the summit of the grandest old peak we can find on our travels. *Au revoir.*

Byers could have extended his trip ten years, awaiting Colorado Statehood—August 1, 1876. The reports, however, of Taylor and Byers give us the picture of Breckenridge and area in 1866.

TAYLOR'S 1866 REPORT

A ride of three miles up the valley brought us to another river, foaming down through a wild gap in the mountains on our left. This was the Snake which we had now reached. At this place the Blue receives a considerable affluent on the opposite side—(the confluence of Blue, Ten Mile and Snake.) We forded it (the Snake) with some difficulty, the water rushing over our saddles, and followed a barely discernible trail along the foot of the mountains. The Valley of the Blue became narrow, hemmed in by the feet of spurs from the main chain. The bottom land was marshy and full of pools, and we were sometimes forced to climb around quagmires and fallen timber, at points of threatening steepness. Sometimes, also, a slide of rocks had come down from above, leaving piles over which the animals must slowly and cautiously be led. The little gray coneys sat on the stones above, and barked at us as we passed.

It is rather difficult to measure distance during travel of this kind; but I suppose we had made about three miles after fording Snake River, when the trail—or, rather, what was left of it—terminated at the Blue. There were signs that the stream had been crossed here, and as we had been looking with longing eyes at the pleasant open bottoms on the other side, we imagined our troubles at an end. Mr. McCandless plunged in, his mule breasting the impetuous current, and, after being carried down some yards, succeeded in getting out on the other bank. Mr. Byers followed, and then the pack-mule, Peter; but, on reaching the centre of the stream both were carried away. I was watching the horse, madly endeavoring to swim against the current, when there was a sudden call for help. The drift-timber had made a raft just below, the force of the stream set directly toward it, and horse and rider were being drawn, as it appeared, to inevitable destruction. Mr. Sumner sprang into the water and caught Mr. Byers' hand; but the next moment he was out of his depth, and barely succeeded in swimming ashore.

All of this seemed to take place in a second. The river made a short curve around a little tongue of land, across which we sprang, in time to see Mr. Byers catch at and hold the branch of a drifted tree, in passing. In another moment he had extricated himself from the saddle. White rushed into the water with a lariat, and the danger was over. Horse and rider got out separately, without much trouble, although the latter was already chilled to the bones and nearly benumbed. The pack-mule, with all our luggage, was completely submerged, and we should probably have lost everything, had not White grasped the mule's ear at the turn of the river, and thus assisted the beast to recover his footing. It was all over before we were clearly aware of the full extent of the danger and of our own fears.

When the wet clothes had been wrung out, and the wet pistols fired, we set forward, compelled to follow the east bank of the Blue, with *no* trail. We had the choice of between mud-holes and fallen timber, or a steep of loose gravel and sliding stones, which defied us to get a firm foothold. Thus we worked our way along, with almost incredible labor, for an hour or more, when we reached an overhanging

rocky wall, at the foot of which the river foamed and roared in a narrow channel. When we had climbed around the rocks and reached the mountain side above, a fearful-looking slant of disintegrated shale, through which a few stunted aspen bushes grew, lay before us. The crumbled rock slid from under our feet, and rattled in showers from the brink of the precipice into the water below; and but for the help which the bushes gave us in the worst places, we should probably have followed. Messrs. Byers and Davis, who were in advance, seemed at times to be hanging in the air.

While resting among the roots of a pine-tree, which enabled me also to support my pony, I descried Mr. McCandless riding up the meadows beyond the river with a mounted Indian on each side of him. As they were Utes, there was no trouble to be feared, and we supposed they were guiding him toward Breckenridge. Beyond this perilous corner of the mountain we found a faint trail, with a promise of better travel ahead.

A mile or two more, and a broad valley opened on our left. A very muddy stream—which could be none other than Swan River—came down it to join the Blue. Mr. McCandless and one of the Indians here rode down to the opposite bank and hailed us. The latter was the famous Ute chief, Colorado; he said we could now either ford the Blue, or take a good trail to Breckenridge on our side of the river. We chose the latter, and presently came in sight of Delaware Flats—a collection of log-cabins, across the open valley. Leaving them to the left, we struck toward another settlement called Buffalo Flats; both places are inhabited by miners engaged in gulch washing. The cattle pasturing on the grassy bottoms were a welcome sight, after five days of savage Nature.

Being now but four miles from Breckenridge, we spurred our weary animals forward, taking a trail which led for a long distance through a burned forest. It was scenery of the most hideous character. Tens of thousands of charred black poles, striped with white where the bark had sprung off, made a wilderness of desolation which was worse than a desert. The boughs had been almost entirely consumed; the sunshine and the blue of the sky were split into a myriad of parallel slices, which fatigued and distracted the eye, until one almost became giddy in riding through. I cannot recall any phase of mundane scenery so disagreeable as this.

Finally the wood came to an end, and

green meadows and snowy peaks refreshed our eyes. Over ditches, heaps of stone and gravel, and all the usual debris of gulch-mining, we rode toward some cabins which beckoned to us through scattered clumps of pine. A flag-staff, with something white at half-mast (a flag of truce—the bully of Breckenridge had been whipped the day before by the bully of Buffalo Flats); canvas-covered wagons in the shade; a long street of log-houses; signs of "Boarding," "Miner's Home," and "Saloon," and a motley group of rough individuals, among whom we detected the beard of our parted comrade and the blanket of the chief—such was Brecken-ridge!

The place dates from 1860—yet, of the five thousand miners who flocked to this part of the Middle Park in that year, probably not more than five hundred remain. At present there is a slight increase of life. Some new cabins are going up, and for some distance beyond the limits of building one sees lots staked out, and signs displayed,—"Preempted by ————————." At the first house we reached, we found a long table set for dinner, and a barrel of beer on tap, which had come over the snowy range from Montgomery the previous day. The host, Mr. Sutherland, sus-pected our impatient hunger, and only delayed the meal long enough to add the unexpected delicacy of oyster soup. Then, taking the bugle with which he blew the signal for the immortal Light Brigade to charge at Balaklava, he made the notes of "Peas upon a trencher" ring over the shanties of Breckenridge. Since that splen-did Crimean episode, Mr. Sutherland and his bugle have done loyal service in a Colorado regiment. I was glad of the chance which made us almost the first guests of his new establish-ment—especially as his bounty in providing equals his gallantry in fighting.

In strolling up the street, after dinner, I noticed two individuals entering a building. One was middle-aged, and carried a book un-der his arm; he wore "store clothes." The other, a lively young fellow, with a moustache, sported a flannel shirt. The latter reappeared on the bal-cony, in a moment and proclaimed in a loud voice,—" Oh yes! Oh yes! The Honorable Pro-bate Court is now in session!" Thereupon he withdrew. The announcement produced no ef-fect, for he immediately came forth again, and cried,—"Oh yes! Oh yes! The Honorable Pro-bate Court is now adjourned!" I waited to see the Honorable Probate Court come forth, with the book under his arm; but instead of that,

the lively young man made his appearance for the third time, with a new announcement,—"Oh yes! Oh yes! The Honorable Commission-ers' Court is now in session!"

How many other courts were represented by these two individuals, I am unable to say; but the rapidity and ease with which the sessions were held gave me a cheerful impression of the primitive simplicity and peace of the popula-tion.

We discovered a hotel—or its equivalent —kept by Mr. and Mrs. Silverthorn, who wel-comed us like old friends. The walls of their large cabin were covered with newspapers, and presented a variety of advertisements and local news, from New Hampshire to Salt Lake. If the colored lithographs on the wall were doubt-ful specimens of art, there were good indica-tions of literature on the table. The kind host-ess promised us beds,—real beds, with sheets and pillows.

In the evening, the court-house, to my sur-prise, was filled with an attentive and intelligent audience. Mrs. Silverthorn kept her promise. When the artist and myself found ourselves stretched out in a broad feather-bed, with some-thing softer than boots under our heads, we lay awake for a long time in delicious rest, unable to sleep from the luxury of knowing what a per-fect sleep awaited us. Every jarred bone and bruised muscle claimed its own particular sen-sation of relief, and I doubted, at last, whether unconsciousness was better than such wide-awake fulness of rest.

I shall always retain a very pleasant recol-lection of Breckenridge, and shall henceforth associate its name with the loyal divine, not the traitor politician.

(Breckinridge family lineage included prom-inent statesmen and clergymen. Bayard Taylor's comment referred to Robert Jefferson Breckin-ridge, "the loyal divine" and John Cabell Breck-inridge, "the traitor politician.")

BYERS' 1866 REPORT

July 2d was delightfully pleasant, and noon found us at Breckenridge which is looking quite prosperous. Several new houses have gone up this spring, and more are to be built. Sev-eral camps, and a number of white-topped wagons in the vicinity, indicated newcomers, who had not yet secured more permanent homes.

There is a good supply of provisions and goods in Breckenridge. Also good accommodations for travelers or boarders. Mr. Silverthorn has remodeled and refitted his old and well-known house, and is feeding his guests with the best the country affords. Alex Sutherland, late of Denver, has also built and fitted up an excellent boarding house, which for a "square meal," can't be beat anywhere. Alex calls his guests to their meals by a tune on the bugle; the same with which he sounded the charge of the immortal six hundred at Balaklava.

(Balaklava is a small seaport village on the southwestern tip of the Crimean Peninsula, guarding the entrance to a small valley surrounded by mountains. In the Crimean War the British, French and Russians fought the Battle of Balaklava on October 25, 1854. The report in the London *Times* said, "some one had blundered," ordering battle at such a strategically, easily-defended battleground. Tennyson, reading the report, in a few moments immortalized the blunder and the battle in a ballad. Sutherland, and his bugle, it is claimed, sounded the order for the charge of the Light Brigade. Twelve years later Sutherland and his bugle were in Breckenridge.

Alex Sutherland, and bugle, have disputed claim to Balaklava fame. An Englishman, William Brittain, and his bugle, have vied for the honor. April, 1964, Ed Sullivan, television personality and actor Laurence Harvey paid $4,480 for a battered bugle supposedly owned by Brittain and used to sound the charge of the Light Brigade. Descendants of Sutherland refute the claim, saying that Sutherland was the bugler of Balaklava, and that he, and his bugle, are buried in Denver's Fairmount Cemetery. Sutherland was buried in Mount Olivet, but a daughter, for religious purposes, had the body disinterred and buried May 10, 1909, in Fairmount.

Sutherland's sojourn in Breckenridge was brief—summer and fall of 1866. January, 1867, he was in Denver presenting and directing concerts. Sutherland was a leader in Denver music circles until the time of his death, November 10, 1904.)

Editor Byers continues:

From Mr. Silverthorn we learned that an excellent school has recently been started in Breckenridge. It is well attended and will be kept running. In the evening of our stay there was a large audience to hear Mr. Taylor lecture, and it is needless to say that they were well pleased.

(Editor Byers' appraisals of mining conditions at Oro City, Buckskin Joe and Breckenridge in 1866 were practically the same—"the prospecting mania has subsided, and men have settled down to regular work again.")

Another gold boom, shorter-lived than the 1860, would take place at Breckenridge in 1880.

Bayard Taylor
Courtesy—Denver Public Library Western Collection

ALEXANDER SUTHERLAND, BUGLER OF THE LIGHT BRIGADE.
Died November 10, 1904.

Courtesy—Denver Public Library Western Collection

Bayard and Breckenridge

MARSHALL SILVERTHORN

and

THE OLD SILVERTHORN HOTEL

Rocky Mountain News   September 15, 1887

JUDGE SILVERTHORN DEAD

HE WOULD HAVE BEEN SEVENTY-NINE YEARS OF
AGE TODAY

HE TELLS SOME FRIENDS OF IT, AND FALLS TO
THE FLOOR DEAD

A PROMINENT AND POPULAR CITIZEN EXPIRES
SUDDENLY LAST NIGHT

"If I live until tomorrow," said Judge Marshall Silverthorn, one of the pioneers, and best known men in Colorado, to a party of friends in the Walbrach Block last night, "I shall be 79 years of age."

Half an hour later, the county coroner was notified that Marshall Silverthorn was dead. In the parlor of Mr. C. F. Leimer, on the third floor of the Walbrach Block, lay Judge Silverthorn's body. He had called on some friends living in the building early in the evening, and up to 8:30 o'clock, when he died, was in the best of spirits, and was the life of the party, singing and romping about as gay as the youngest young lady in the party. After an hour's romp with the children, he approached the sofa, upon which was seated a couple of friends, one of whom was Mrs. Leimer, and said, "I'm feeling as young as any one of you, and if I see tomorrow, will be 79 years of age." One of the party started to congratulate him, but he warned them to wait twenty-four hours.

He then walked towards one of the windows, stood looking out for an instant, and fell to the floor with a groan, his head striking a table against the wall. The ladies and gentlemen in the room rushed to his side and lifted him. He was unconscious, and a messenger was dispatched for a physician. Dr. Lyman responded,

but before he arrived Judge Silverthorn was dead. His body was laid out on the floor and a messenger sent for his daughter, Mrs. Joseph C. Wilson, who lives at 1247 South Fifteenth Street, and with whom Judge Silverthorn resided. The lady came at once, and was frantic with grief at the death of her father, who had left home in the best of health and spirits only a few hours previous.

Judge Silverthorn's other daughter, Mrs. C. A. Finding of Breckenridge, was notified by telegraph of her father's death, and will be here today. The body will be taken to his late residence this morning.

(An error appears in reporting Silverthorn's age. His tombstone, Denver Riverside Cemetery, reads 1811-1887. Other records concur as to the birth year. Death, September 14, 1887, indicates an age of 75 years, 11 months, 29 days—one day short of his 76th birthday.)

(Another confusion is in the spelling of "Silverthorn." The sign on the early hotel read, "Silverthorns Hotel;" the family tombstone is marked, "Silverthorn." Deeds and records in Summit County Courthouse have "Silverthorn" spelling. "Silverthorn" and "Silverthorne" are used interchangeably in some writings.)

News of Silverthorn's death saddened Breckenridge:

*Breckenridge
Daily Journal*   September 15, 1887

MARSHALL SILVERTHORN DEAD

At about ten o'clock last night, those of this community who were still afoot were surprised to learn that Mr. Charles Finding had received a telegraphic dispatch announcing the death of his father-in-law, the Honorable Marshall Silverthorn, at nine o'clock last evening in Denver. The news passed through the camp to every house where the occupants were not abed.

Judge Silverthorn came from his native state, Pennsylvania, to Colorado in 1859; in 1860 he came from Denver to Breckenridge and has been a constant resident ever since. At times, in the early days, he was the principal, and sometimes the only, business man in the camp. He was storekeeper, postmaster, justice of the peace, blacksmith and landlord by turns of all combined. Mrs. Silverthorn, who died here several years ago, as well as the "old judge," as the old timers always called him, by hundreds of kindly acts were entitled to and have ever received from men of all classes in this country the most kindly remembrance. Scarcely a man ever spent a season on the upper waters of the Blue, or its branches, from 1860 to 1880, but has the remembrance of some kindly act by the deceased couple graven upon the tablets of his heart to be effaced only when that organ ceases in life-giving beats.

Mr. and Mrs. Silverthorn, during their long residence here, accumulated considerable means and were prominent in all matters of public interest. The Judge was proud of his adopted State and loyal to Summit County when the darkest clouds overshadowed it, and the direct road of his sympathies was by the way of Summit County. Many a man has approached him with that talamistic word to obtain relief when meeting the Judge abroad, and at home he was ever ready to assist in any public work or to aid his neighbors who had become permanent residents of this gem of the mountains.

Marshall Silverthorn was a prominent man in the section of his native state which he left before he came west. He had served his county in the legislature and his party in several state conventions, but the financial crash of 1857 caught him and his business with the thousands of others, and he came with what was left him to Colorado and started fresh on a second successful career.

Judge Silverthorn was old in years and full of honors. He first saw light in Columbia County, Pennsylvania, in the year 1811, consequently was 76 years of age at his death. He leaves two daughters to mourn his loss, Mrs. Charles A. Finding and Mrs. Joseph Wilson of Denver.

It is safe to say no other citizen in Summit County, suddenly removed, would have touched so many vibrating chords in the hearts of the people of this County as has the sudden death of Judge Marshall Silverthorn.

In former days the number of floral tributes gave the funeral director an idea of the size of the crowd to anticipate at a funeral service. The number of people attending is often an indication of the esteem of the deceased among friends and fellowmen. Marshall Silverthorn's funeral was unusually large both in attendance and floral tributes.

Breckenridge Daily Journal   Sept. 20, 1887
From the *Rocky Mountain News,*
19th inst.

HONOR TO THE DEAD

The funeral services of one of Denver's oldest and most respected citizens, Marshall Silverthorn, took place yesterday at 2 p.m. at the residence of his daughter, Mrs. Joseph C. Wilson at 1247 South Fifteenth Street. Shortly before 2 o'clock about one hundred and fifty members of the Colorado Pioneers, to which Judge Silverthorn belonged, not only by membership but also by virtue of his early settlement in this country, formed in line at city hall, headed by Titus' cornet band. The Patriotic Order of the Sons of America, of which Mr. Silverthorn was an enthusiastic member, having united with the order when it was first founded in this city, were out in equal numbers in all their regalia, and together they marched to the solemn music of the band to the home of their deceased brother.

At the conclusion of the exercises it was found necessary, in order that all might take a farewell look at their sleeping brother, to bring the casket out onto the lawn, where all the hundreds present filed by it in impressive silence. The casket, which was of black broadcloth and velvet, was loaded with handsome floral tributes, the finest that could be obtained in the city. The remains had been partially embalmed and looked as life-like and natural as if in the repose of sleep. The completeness of all the funeral arrangements reflected much credit on C. H. McHatton & Co., who had the matter in charge. The remains of Judge Silverthorn were escorted to their last resting place in Riverside Cemetery by one of the longest burial processions that has taken place in this city for a long time and included fully five hundred people.

Only occasional glimpses are given of Marshall Silverthorn and the early days of the Silverthorn Hotel. By the time the local newspaper came into existence, 1880, Silverthorn Hotel was near the end of its heyday. Mrs. Silverthorn died in 1883, and the "Judge" spent his remaining years in Denver, with only infrequent visits to Breckenridge. Earlier writers give a snapshot picture of Silverthorn and his hotel. Editor Byers of Tarryall's *Miners' Record*, August 1861, reported: "The Breckenridge Hotel, Store and Post Office, three in one and one in three, kept by mine host Silverthorn, is the best place to stop on the Blue." Samuel Bowles, eminent journalist of the *Springfield Republican* and author of *The Switzerland of America*, 1869, wrote: "There is a good hotel here (Breckenridge), of logs to be sure, with a broad buxom matron, and black-eyed beauties of daughters, to whom, after dinner, we consigned Governor Bross, with warning against his fascinations."

Attaching ourselves to the Princeton Scientific Expedition, 1877, we get another glimpse of Silverthorn, his hotel and life of the times in Breckenridge. The Princeton Diary reported:

After leaving the summit of the pass we descended into the valley of the Blue River, which we followed to the little town of Breckenridge, twenty-six miles from Fairplay. Judge Silverthorn, who was the owner of the hotel, said that the house was full, but if we could sleep in the "corral" we might stay. We examined it and accepted the offer. It was in the upper story of the establishment, under the roof. While we were ridding ourselves of our numerous packages, the Judge disappeared. We found on going down that a drunken fellow had been behaving unseemly in the street, and that our little shrivelled-up judicial authority had made out a warrant, served it himself, and seizing the prisoner by the back of the neck, had kicked him up the side of a hill to the calaboose, although he had complained of being very ill a few minutes before.

This little affair gave rise to a trial, which of course we attended. Judge Rieland read from a large and formidable-looking document, "Gibbs, you are charged with disturbing the peace." (Aside) "I'm in a hurry, so plead guilty. If you take one of them lawyer fellows, I'll stick you." Gibbs asked how much the fine was, and the Judge announced very formally that he should be fined $1.50 and costs. Whereupon Gibbs asked, in tones that made the "visitors" look around to see where the door was, "Where's my revolver?" He only wanted to

pawn it, however. After this the court adjourned for drinks all around.

Alice (Polk) Hill, 1884, in her *Tales of Colorado Pioneers*, enlarges the picture of "our little shrivelled-up judicial authority" and recounts Silverthorn's first venture into the Wild West:

You must see Judge Silverthorn; he loves to talk of the old times. He came here in '59, and was judge of the Miner's court. He is a diminutive man, almost dried to a crackling, and has such a strange, weird look that you couldn't help wondering to what age or order of human beings he belongs. His hair and beard are grizzly gray, and he chews continually. When he tells a border tale his little keen eyes twinkle with humor and intelligence; then he goes into convulsions of laughter and kicks up his feet until he resembles a jack-knife, half-open—forming a picture altogether grotesque. But he is the soul of honor and goodness, with a heart so large that it is continually running over with kind deeds and comforting words.

His wife was called the mother of the camp, the good Samaritan to all in trouble and distress. How the boys loved her! She always spent her winters in Denver, and in the spring when they heard Mrs. Silverthorn was coming, they put on their snow-shoes, met her at the top of the range and brought her down on a sled. With loud hurrahs, and hats tossing in the air, they heralded her arrival.

Silverthorn has looked just as he does now for the last twenty-five years. It is said that when he was on the way to this country he stopped at some town on the Missouri River and looked around for a party who were *en route* to the Blue, but they shook their heads deprecatingly and said they did not want any graveyard deserters; wouldn't have time for funeral services on the road.

He at last succeeded in closing a bargain with one party, and the first night out, when they had gone into camp, and the old gentleman was reconnoitering for buffalo chips, there arose a discussion among the campers about "that old man;" they thought he was likely to die on the way, and they decided then and there to eject him. When he returned they informed him of their decision.

He pulled off his coat, and like another David, challenged the biggest man in the camp to fight him, declaring he could lick any of them. He was so plucky they concluded to take him, but they slipped a few boards in the bottom of the wagon in case they might have need of a coffin on the way. (There was no need of the coffin boards for thirty years.)

Agnes (Finding) Miner tells the experiences of her grandparents (the Silverthorns) coming to Denver and of the early days of Breckenridge and the Silverthorn Hotel. The story is related as coming from the lips of her mother—Martha (Silverthorn) Finding. Possibly the story had been written by Martha Silverthorn at an earlier date.

Early in the year 1859 my father, Marshall Silverthorn, decided to come to Colorado for his health, arriving in Denver, May 17, 1859. Improving rapidly in health, he returned to Pennsylvania to bring back his family. With his wife and three children, he started on his return trip to Denver early in March, 1860. (The family consisted of two daughters, Matilda M. and Martha S., and a son, James R. who was born in 1858 and died in 1863.)

In Council Bluffs we outfitted for the trip across the plains. We did not travel on Sundays. Mother devoted this day to washing, baking and cooking for the following week. Twice during the trip the Indians were determined that my father should trade my mother for some of their ponies. The last time they were inclined to be rather ugly about it and Father had quite a time with them.

We arrived in Denver May 18th, 1860, just a year and a day after my father's first arrival. We rented a house, for eighty-five dollars, at what is now Fourteenth and Lawrence Streets. This house was built of rough boards, with no paint and most of the windows covered with white muslin. It was called the Denver House after General Denver. Soon some friends of Father's wanted to board with us. With so many extra, Mother had more than she could do, so hired a daughter of old Left Hand, an Indian Chief of the Arapahoes.

In the latter part of May, 1861, we started for Georgia Gulch, but stopped in Breckenridge. Here we rented a house that had been a store owned by O. A. Whittemore and C. P. Elder. There was one very large front room and a smaller room in the back which we used for a bedroom and kitchen. The floor of the kitchen was made of very old sluice boxes that had been worn until the knots stood out, caused by constant washing of water and gravel. As a rule these boxes were burned and the ashes panned for gold that would collect in the knots and crevices. The front room had a dirt floor

with shelves and a counter running along one side. Father took a team and hauled sawdust from an old mill above town and covered this dirt floor to the depth of six inches. Mother sewed burlap sacks together and made a carpet. Then Father made pins such as are used for fastening tents down and nailed the burlap down with these. All dust sifted through so it was easy to keep clean. In this room, we made three beds, end to end, on the floor, by placing two logs one on top of the other. The enclosure was filled with hay, then feather beds that had been brought from Pennsylvania were placed on this.

This room was a dining room during the day to accommodate those who came to Breckenridge and had no placc to go. The Postoffice was in the front part of the room and a pigeon-holed box, of about three by five feet, held all the mail.

Saturday was the general eastern mail day and the miners all came down to get their mail. There were two other arrivals of mail during the week, but Saturday's mail was the principal one. The letters were distributed by calling out the names, the men answering "Here." And the letters were tossed to them.

In a few months Mother was asked to bake bread, pies and cake to sell the day the men came down for the mail. This meant forty or fifty pies alone and a hundred pound sack of flour was very often used in the day's baking. A quart of milk was included and this was paid for in gold dust which I weighed out. I would take in between thirty and forty dollars.

One summer I was sent down to the placer mine to take Father's lunch to him. I walked along slowly picking strawberries and wild flowers on my return and had been home only a few minutes when one of the men came running up and asked Mother if I was home. A large buffalo had come along, and in his excitement or anger, had torn up all the sluice boxes and followed my trail, crossing the river just before he reached town, which was all that saved me.

In the spring of 1862 we bought another house and moved into it. Here I helped Father build a fireplace and a cellar, bringing up the dirt from the cellar in a bucket. We then papered the walls of the house with newspapers.

In the fall of 1863 we went to Denver so that my sister and I might enter school. Each year, early in June, we would drive to Breckenridge, taking about four days for the trip. All provisions had to be hauled from Denver.

Leaving Hamilton about eleven o'clock at night, we would start over Boreas Pass when there was a crust on the snow so that we might walk on it. In January 1873, I was married to Charles A. Finding and the next year was the last we were compelled to walk over the Range. We carried our little baby in our arms a distance of fifteen miles.

Agnes (Finding) Miner provided additional information in another story, *Founding and Early History of Breckenridge, Colorado*:

After the great mining epoch between 1859 and 1862, the population slowly dwindled, until only a few hundred remained. Breckenridge was the County Seat after 1862. There was a hotel built by my grandparents (where the County records were kept) and not more than a dozen other cabins along what is now known as Main Street. There was a good wagon road all the way from Breckenridge to the summit of Boreas Pass.

A court session was held once a year and was called Court Week; a dance was always held for this occasion, the music being furnished by fiddlers, accompanied by an organ. Every Sunday evening, services were held in the hotel dining room, a printed sermon was read by someone and the old Moody and Sankey hymns sung, into which everyone entered wholeheartedly.

As I said before, the court records were kept in the hotel. Georgia Gulch, or Park City, wanted the county seat and an attempt was made to change it over there. My Grandmother noticed the County Clerk, busily packing his records in a burlap sack, and when he had been called out for a while she hid the sack and in so doing saved the county seat for Breckenridge.

It took plenty of gold to pay for provisions in those days. Flour was $42.00 a barrel, and not the white flour that we have now, but a gray Mexican mixture. My grandmother mixed up a 100 pound sack at a baking. Butter was $2.50 a pound and eggs were $2.50 a dozen. Muslin was used in place of window glass, and a dirt floor covered with many inches of sawdust and burlap sacks served as a floor covering, and the rooms were papered with newspapers.

1880 was known as the "boom" year, and it is estimated that there were 8,000 people in the county. The sound of carpenters' hammers never stopped day or night. It was a wide open town with eighteen saloons and three dance halls adding to the gaiety of life in a mining camp.

The first unit of the Silverthorn Hotel was the Whittemore supply store, built in the early spring of 1860. Silverthorns rented this property, 1861, and converted it into a small hotel. (Mr. O. A. Whittemore moved to Parkville, summer of 1861, and operated a store in the first floor of the Mason's new two-story Lodge building.) The two-story Silverthorn Hotel annex, to the south, probably was an addition by the Silverthorns in 1862.

Mrs. Silverthorn's death was death-knell for Silverthorn Hotel as a famous hostelry. She had been the spark that made it a profitable business. After her death, Marshall Silverthorn lived with a daughter in Denver, occasionally visiting Breckenridge. Through the years the building was rented for various business ventures — Evans Pharmacy, G. C. Smith Jewelry, doctor office, cafe, barber shop—and numerous other uses. It stood on the west side of Main Street, midway between Washington and Lincoln Avenues. A distinguishing feature was that it was the only building with a roof running north and south; all others in the block ran east and west.

In 1940 a warranty deed was executed between Agnes Miner and Jay Cooper for possession of the property. For a short time Mr. Cooper operated a barber shop at the location. He also used the property for storage of furniture and possessions, expecting to renovate and make living quarters.

Demise of the historic Silverthorn Hotel came in the summer of 1957. Cooper had part-time residence in Salida and Breckenridge. While away, the property was vandalized numerous times and many of its relics disappeared. He finally decided to raze the property.

Summit County has perpetuated the name Silverthorn in a newly-formed town, Silverthorne, two miles north of old Dillon. A substation post office was established January 8, 1962. Formerly the area was designated "Silverthorn Flats." The opening of Straight Creek Tunnel, through Continental Divide, and construction of Interstate 70 will, undoubtedly, greatly enhance the development of the town.

For almost a century Silverthorn Hotel was an historic landmark in Breckenridge. It is sad that it ended so ignominiously. Perhaps some day an enterprising entrepreneur will perpetuate the historic stopping-place in Silverthorn (Silverthorne) or Breckenridge and a "Marshall Silverthorn Hotel" will again play host to visitors in the Valley of the Blue.

Early 1860 Breckenridge — Main Street — Between Washington and Lincoln Avenues (looking north). Silverthorn Hotel in center — roof running north and south. (Note stream flowing from east hillside.) Courtesy — Library State Historical Society of Colorado.

Sawmill on east side of Main Street; Silverthorn Hotel on west side. Courtesy—Library State Historical Society of Colorado.

Silverthorn Hotel, showing original and annex. Date of picture—possibly 1870s. Martha (Silverthorn) Findings' daughters were born 1873, 1875, 1877. Two infants appear in the picture. (Note Winglee Laundry at left). Courtesy—Library State Historical Society of Colorado.

"Diminuative" — "Wizened" — "Dried to a crackling" — "Old Judge Silverthorn." Courtesy — Library State Historical Society of Colorado.

Marshall Silverthorn

Silverthorn Hotel in the 1900s. Courtesy—Denver Public Library Western Collection.

OLD LANDMARK TO BE RAZED

Above: THE SILVERTHORNE HOTEL on Main Street, Breckenridge. The popular stopping place in early gold mining days, this hotel was owned and operated by Mr. and Mrs. Marshall Silverthorne, grandparents of the late Mrs. Agnes Miner. A well-built log cabin, the hotel boasted real sheets and pillow cases. In more recent years it was a barber shop. It is now owned by Mr. Jay Cooper of Salida. It has been burglarized frequently in recent years with not even a suspect's being apprehended. Hence, Mr. Cooper's decision to have it torn down. It is sad to contemplate that one of the few remaining edifices in Breckenridge must fall a victim to the unlawful acts of thieves and vandals.

Summit County Journal, June 21, 1957.

Breckenridge—1867. Silverthorn Hotel, center. Directly opposite, east side of street, is pump and trough provided by Silverthorn for thirsty horses and oxen. Pump removed October, 1881. According to Mrs. Ted Fletcher (Breckenridge), picture is dated 1867 and the little boy sitting on the tree stump (foreground) was Eli Fletcher. Courtesy—Mrs. Ted Fletcher. (Others have dated the picture earlier—1864.)

SKIING

Skiing became centennial "Gold Boom" of Breckenridge. Gold put Breckenridge on the map in the 1860s; skis started another "gold rush" in the 1960s. Gold dust or white powder, it all added up to the same thing—gaiety, hilarity, prosperity in the old mining camp. Something new? Breckenridge has *always* been on skis!

WHO WAS THE FIRST SKIER IN THE UNITED STATES?

THE FIRST SKIER IN AMERICA WAS A COLORADO

METHODIST PREACHER

The above caption appeared on an article in the Canon City *Record*, February 3, 1938. The article continued:

Who was the first skier in the United States? Some woodsman who hailed from some Scandinavian country or whose forefathers did? Did the Indian know of skis, or invent them? Where and how did they become known and used in this country?

In the January 13, 1936, issue of *Time*, there was an article on skiing, and it gave Father John L. Dyer, a Methodist itinerant preacher of the early days of this section of the country, the credit for being the one who introduced skis to this nation:

In the United States the first skier on authentic record was the Reverend John L. Dyer, a Colorado Methodist preacher, who used skis to carry mail to his parishioners in the early 1850's.

His work among the trappers and Indians and miners took him all over this section of the country—up and down the Arkansas valley,

over into the San Luis valley, down the Rio Grande into northern New Mexico—preaching the gospel he believed in, and ministering to all.

No doubt it was necessity that caused him to turn to the ski. In winter, with snow such as covered much of the territory he traveled, it was at times pretty difficult going.

The snow shoe was a great help, for on skis he could make much better time—(down hills great speed could be made)—and so one can imagine how much of a help they were to him. Where did he hear of them and how to secure them? Well, we don't know that, but hope to find out and tell you.

Research confirmed the report. *Time Magazine* did have the item in its sports column. It would have been a "feather in the cap" of Breckenridge if one of their pioneers (the builder of Father Dyer Church in Breckenridge) could be claimed as "First United States Skier." Alas, 'tis not true. Father Dyer did not introduce skiing in this country, nor was he the first skier in the Breckenridge area. Neither did Father Dyer carry mail in the early 1850s—or just to parishioners. His mail-carrying took place during the winter of 1863-1864 and included everyone on the route.

John Lewis Dyer accepted a Methodist appointment to Blue River Mission, Summit County, April, 1862. This brought him to the Swan River and Breckenridge area. It is here that we have first mention of his skiing—and he was a novice at the art.

I made me a pair of snow-shoes, and, of course, was not an expert. Sometimes I would fall; and, on one occasion, as I was going down the mountain to Gold Run, my shoes got crossed in front as I was going very fast. A little pine-tree was right in my course, and I could not turn, and dare not encounter the tree with the shoes crossed; and so threw myself into the snow, and went in out of sight.

Snow-shoeing was the most satisfactory method of winter traveling in the mountains. The winter previous to Dyer's crossing Georgia Pass to Georgia Gulch the snowshoe was in use. Hall's *History of Colorado* records: "All provisions received by the miners of Georgia Gulch in the winter of 1860-61 were packed over the range from South Park by men on snowshoes." Dyer used "shoes" for traveling to his preaching places in Swan Valley, French Gulch and along the Blue River. A winter's practice on "shoes" made him thoroughly skilled in the art. His appointment at Blue River Mission was only a year's duration; the following year was at South Park:

On the third day of April (1863) I left Lincoln City (French Gulch) and stopped at Mr. Silverthorn's in Breckenridge until about two o'clock in the morning, when I took my carpet-sack, well-filled, got on my snow-shoes, and went up Blue River. The snow was five feet deep. It might be asked, "Why start at two o'clock?" Because the snow would not bear a man in daytime, even with snow-shoes. From about two o'clock until nine or ten in the morning was the only time a man could go; and a horse could not go at all. When about three miles up the Blue River, back of Mc-Cloud's, the wolves set up a tremendous howling quite near. I was not alarmed, but passed quietly along, and was not disturbed. It was not likely, I thought, that the good Lord would let anything disturb a man going in the night to his appointment, although wolves and bears with some Rocky Mountain lions, were numerous.

Father Dyer's ability on snow-shoes provided an opportunity to augment the meager remuneration he received in his ministerial work.

About midwinter I found myself without means, and so sought work, but could get none, unless I would work on Sundays, which was out of the question except to prevent actual starvation. In the forepart of February, 1864, a man came to me who had the contract to carry the mail from Buckskin Joe to Cache Creek by Oro, California Gulch, a distance of thirty-seven miles. It was once a week, and he offered me eighteen dollars a week to carry it on snow-shoes. I thought at once: "I can preach about as often as I have been doing, and am not obliged to go on Sunday." So I

took the mail, and crossed the Mosquito Range every week, and preached three times a week.

The mail's weight was from twenty-three to twenty-six pounds, with from five to seven pounds of express matter. The carriage was on snow-shoes, over an Indian trail that was covered from three to twenty feet with snow. My snow-shoes were of the Norway style, from nine to eleven feet in length, and ran well when the snow was just right, but very heavy when they gathered snow. I carried a pole to jar the sticking snow off. Suffice to say that the winter of 1863-1864 was a remarkably hard one, and the spring held on until June, with terrible snow-storms. I was the first one to cross the Mosquito Range with a horse. That was the third day of July. The mail-bags went the trip across and back every week.

Early February to August, 1864, was the extent of Father Dyer's snow-shoe mail-carrying. The designation "Snow-Shoe Itinerant" came from years of meeting preaching appointments in the mountains by this means of travel.

Father Dyer was not the first United States Skier. Nor was he the first in the Breckenridge area. First winter travel in the Breckenridge area was on snow-shoes or Norway skis. In fact, before Breckenridge had its name, the inhabitants were on skis. William A. Smith, one of the twenty-five at Fort Mary B that first winter, wrote: "The snows are not as objectionable as some would imagine, from the fact that when men become accustomed to traveling on snow shoes, they can travel further in a day, and with greater ease, than they can walk on bare ground." He also added: "The present mode of immigrating to this country brings to mind the Indian's remark, when he said, 'when white man sets his head, no river, no mountain, no weather, no devil, stop him.'"

Editor Byers of Denver's *Rocky Mountain News* was a man not content to spend all his time at a desk; he wanted to be familiar with the big, new West where the action was. February 8, 1860, he and a small party set out for Blue River mines.

Seventeen days later—February 25th—they arrived at Tarryall and made preparations to cross the range to Blue River. "Some were doubtful of success, but all our company seemed inspired with the spirit of determination." There was but one way to cross the deep patches of snow on the mountain—snow-shoes. It was a fairly new mode of travel so the editor felt obliged to describe "shoes" and the art of skiing.

The preparation first and mostly needed was the snow-shoe, which is a board eight or nine feet long, four or five inches wide, and an inch and a quarter thick in the middle, tapering to half an inch at each end, steamed and turned like a sleigh shoe in front; the foot resting under a strap in the middle of the shoe, by which the shoe is moved. Thus equipped, with a balancing pole in hand and a pack from twenty-five to fifty pounds each, four of us started to cross the snowy range to the Blue River mines.

Untutored in the art of snow-shoeing, we expected a weary trip and were not disappointed. Such a continued succession of miscalculation as our feet made on arriving at the foot of the range, and on attempting to ascend, we never experienced since our first introduction to skating on our own native rivers. One great difference we found to be in measuring our length on, or in the snow, the other on the ice. While crawling out of the snow we recollected that we might have been rubbing a sore head if sporting on the ice, and I believe, that anyone following our company that day might have seen pictured along our path, characters enough for a Chinese alphabet. Arriving at the top of the range, we found ourselves panting in the high air like hunted deer, and the wind a little too cool to be salubrious. Here we were compelled to act our boyish sport again, as we could not go down on our snow shoes perpendicularly as man standeth; we therefore tied our shoes together and seated upon our packs made our way down the mountain at the rate of about fifteen knots per hour, for about a mile and a half, when we again erected ourselves and at an easy downhill grade pursued our way for about six or seven miles, when we reached the first sight of human habitation after leaving Tarryall, in the vicinity of the Blue River Mines—having performed a weary day's journey of thirteen or fourteen miles with five days' provision in our packs. The snow was about three to three and a half feet deep.

Father Dyer, or Breckenridge, cannot lay claim to first skiing on this continent. "Snow-Shoe Thompson" is sometimes given credit for initiating the art. (Thompson, however, does not have a clear claim. Reportedly, there were midwestern Norwegians and Canadians enjoying and employing this means of travel much earlier.)

When the 1849 gold rush struck California, almost all mining was done at lower altitudes.

Gold discoveries in the uplands led to mountain settlements. Winter snows created travel and transportation problems. Front Stage—Snow-Shoe Thompson. The Alta, California *Daily*, February 20, 1876, told the story of Snow-Shoe Thompson:

"SNOW-SHOE THOMPSON"

The Adventures and Exploits of a Famous California Mountaineer—The Most Remarkable Mail-Carrier in the World—Twenty Winters on Snow Shoes in the Wilds of the Sierras—A Man Who Laughs at Storms and Avalanches and Safely Walks Where Others Fall and Perish.

During the winter of 1856, while at work on his Pootah Creek ranch, Thompson heard of the trouble experienced in getting the mails across the snowy summit of the Sierra Nevada Mountains. At the time that he heard of the difficulties encountered in the mountains on account of the great depth of snow he was engaged in cutting wood on his ranch. One day while he was splitting the trunk of an oak tree he thought of the snow-shoes he had seen in use in his native country when a boy. Though he was but ten years of age when he left Norway he still remembered something of the appearance of the snow-shoes he had seen in that country. He determined to try to make a pair out of the wood of the oak he was splitting. His recollections of the shoes he had seen when a child were in the main correct, yet those he made were rather heavy and clumsy— that is, they would be so considered at the present time. They were ten feet long, four inches wide behind the place where the feet rested, and were four inches and a quarter wide in front. They weighed twenty-five pounds. Mounted on the shoes, with his long guide-pole in his hands, he dashed down the sides of the hills at a fearful rate of speed.

His first trip over the Sierras was made in January, 1856. He went from Placerville to Carson Valley, a distance of 90 miles, carrying the mail-bags strapped upon his back and gliding over fields of snow in places from thirty to fifty feet in depth, his long Norwegian snow-shoes bearing him safely and swiftly along upon the surface of the snow. Having successfully made the trip to Carson Valley and back to Placerville, he continued to carry the mails between the two points all that winter. The weight of the bags was generally from sixty to eighty pounds; but one winter, when he carried the overland mail for Chorpenning, his load often weighed over one hundred pounds.

Thompson's adventures, carrying the mail over this "Siberia of snow," are thrilling reading. He carried no gun, because of the additional weight—no blanket for the same reason. Camp was at the stump of a dead pine tree, which he set afire for the night's warmth. His pillow was one of Uncle Sam's mail-bags—his mattress a depth of fifteen to thirty feet of snow. As many as thirty-one trips were made during a winter.

Father Dyer's harrowing mail-carrying experiences parallel some of Snow-Shoe Thompson's adventures—eight winters later. In his book, *Snow-Shoe Itinerant*, Father Dyer relates an especially hazardous crossing of the mountain:

I left California Gulch about the middle of March. It was thawing, with alternate snow and sunshine, until about one o'clock. The snow stuck to my shoes so that traveling was very heavy. None but those who have tried snow-shoes when the snow sticks to them can understand how soon it will tire a man down, knocking the snow off at every step. It was so this time. When within a few hundred feet of the pass at the head of Evans Gulch, I looked to the north and saw a black cloud just coming over. The wind that preceded it gave evidence of its terror. No pen or tongue can describe its awful appearance. I fastened and tied up my neck and ears, and took bearings with reference to my course up the mountain, about how it would strike me, so that I might keep my course in the snow. But when the storm struck me, I could not have stood up had I not braced against my snow-shoes, which I had taken off and held in position for that purpose. I had thought I could keep my course by the bearings of the storm, but when it struck me, it was a perfect whirl, and I had nothing left but the shape of the mountains, and by this time the snow was so dense that it appeared to be a white wall within ten feet in any direction.

I found myself unable to make more than fifty yards before resting, and had to hold my hand over my mouth and nose to keep the snow out so that I could breathe, bracing with my snow-shoes in order to stand. On the west side the snow all blew off, so that I had to carry my shoes. About the third stop, I came to a large rock, and braced against it; and in the midst of the awful surroundings, poured out my soul to God for help, and felt encouraged to try, in His name, to make the trip. I could not travel against the wind, so I had to bear to the right, which brought me on the range south of the old Indian trail, where there was no way to get down without going over a precipice. I hoped that the wind would abate, so that I might make the trail. But I could not see anything in the whirling snow. It took my breath, and I concluded to retrace my steps; for I felt that to stay there or go forward was equally to perish. I made a desperate effort, but started east instead of west. I had gone scarcely three rods when my foot slipped off the precipice. I threw myself back in the snow. The air was so thick with snow that I could not see how it was. I could not tell whether the pitch was ten or fifty. The cold wind seemed to be feeling for my heart-strings, and my only chance for life was to let myself go over. I took my long snow-shoes, one under each arm, holding the crooked end in each hand for rudders, and believed that if I could thus keep my feet foremost, I could go down alive. I said, "O God, into thy hands I commit my soul, my life, my all; my faith looks up to thee;" and then, with composure, I let go; and, as might be expected, there was a great body of new, soft snow for me to fall in. I have never been certain how far it was. It was soon over, and I was buried in six or eight feet of new snow that had just blown over. My heels struck the old snow, which must have pitched at an angle of more than forty-five degrees, and my weight carried me, and according to former desires, my feet were foremost, and I went at railroad speed. My snow-shoes must keep me straight. I was covered with snow from the start. I raised my head so that I could breathe, and when I had got near one-half mile, I began to slack up, as I had passed the steepest part, and soon stopped.

When I was within one mile of my cabin, I saw a pool of water in the creek; and as I had been fearful for some time that my feet were frozen, I went in over my boots in order to draw the frost out, when I still had hopes that my feet were not frozen. I reached my lonely cabin, started a fire, and my feet began to hurt. For two weeks I was confined to the house, doctoring my feet. I sent to H.A.W. Tabor, our Fairplay storekeeper and paid him sixteen cents a pound for corn to make hominy, which I considered a luxury. The third week I was able to carry the mail again.

"Gold-Rush miners fostered the birth of American skiing." Bill Berry, Reno, Nevada, wrtier said: "But for this hardy race of snow-shoers the early conquest of the West might not have been possible. Eastward (from California) they wended in one prodigious leap, for their strange trail was known to the mining camps of the Colorado Rockies, then north to the mountains of Montana and Yellowstone." From the practical issued the pleasure aspect of "snow-shoeing," and Breckenridge has long shared the pleasure. Snow-shoeing and the winter sports have been the delight of Breckenridge "when the days begin to lengthen and the cold begins to strengthen."

Winter in the mountains had its gay social aspect, mellowing frigid harshness. Community social life sparkled during snow months. Tinkle of sleigh bells sounded day and night. The "one-horse open sleigh" provided business transportation and pleasure. More elegant sleighs were fashionable for social calling and proper for courting "Miss Fannie Bright." East Lincoln Avenue, after a community project had cleared it of stumps and boulders, was the hill for snow-shoeing, sledding and bob-sledding. Box-sleds, filled with straw and noisy merrymakers, drawn by two teams of spirited horses, were vehicles of many a lively party. Winter days and nights were filled with unforgetable memories.

Coasting, with all its thrills, perils and squeals of delight, was popular in Breckenridge on snappy cold winter nights. Watson's advertisements held the answer: "Blow, blow, thou winter wind. What care we when clad in one of Watson's suits of fleece-lined underwear."

COASTING—1880

The right royal sport of coasting is assuming a dangerous form of late. Last evening a freighting sleigh was procured and at one trip had forty-seven persons on board. It was guided by a gentleman named Mark Decker, on skates, who proved himself a master at the art of skating, but the great weight on the sleigh and the boulders in the street render such trips dangerous with the most skillful managers.

We suggest to the coasters that the crown of the hill opposite Fletcher's saloon be graded off about a foot and the hollow just below be filled up with snow. Then an even grade will carry sleds across the bridge.

Nearly two hundred people were out sleighriding and coasting last Saturday evening.

COASTING ON LINCOLN AVENUE—1881

Dave Elder, John Mahon and others connected with the smelter have been beguiling the tedium by constructing a coasting sled. It is ten feet long, with two sets of runners and holds about a dozen. The hearts of the children are made happy as they take possession of it at recess, before and after school, receiving help from the willing hands of bystanders. The merry laughter of the children, the mishaps of beginners on snow shoes make Lincoln Avenue lively. Truly winter in the mountains is not without its pleasures.

Work slackened during the snow months, giving more time for pleasure—and for inventive minds and hands. E. C. Peabody wrote of Breckenridge, anticipating the era of snow-mobiles, ski-bobs and various forms of snow transportation. The greatest spurt of activity occurred during the snow blockade, winter of 1898-1899.

INVENTIVE MINDS TRIED TO IMPROVE TRANSPORTATION

The problem of getting places confronted everyone; and, since "necessity is the mother of invention," some one was going to try to improve skis, skis being the best and easiest way to move about. Previous to the opening of the road several parties made the trip back and forth to Como on skis or webs. The only person using webs that I recall, was one Felix Martin, a French Canadian. When I saw him go up Ridge Street on a pair of webs, I got a thin board and fashioned some shoes. My tools were a saw and hammer, that was all I had to work with. I went out after dark to try them out, so no one could see me struggling with them. I still have them and believe they could be used by putting on some foot straps. The one difficulty I found with them was the snow gathered on top of them and did not fall through, as it does with webs.

Where the Court House now stands was a row of houses that extended so far as the tree, which still stands near the corner of the Treasurer's office. George Engle owned a building at the northeast corner of Ridge and Lincoln. This was used by a contractor named Mitchell. Since there was little carpenter work to do, his men had plenty of time to work on their ideas, which ran to Snow Bikes. This was what was wanted the most. The first attempt was an idea of Walter Henderson. His idea was a pair of skis with a frame built on them with a pair of pedals, a sprocket wheel made of wood with nails driven at regular intervals with the heads sawed off. The belt was of leather about one and a half inches wide, with holes punched and spaced to engage the nails in the sprocket. The belt went back to a wooden shaft on which was another wooden sprocket with nails driven in for sprocket teeth that were supposed to engage the holes in this leather belt. On this shaft were placed four or six wooden paddles that were to push this sled as they rested on the snow, a little below the bottom of the sled runners. To steer this bike was a third and shorter shoe placed between the runners and a little ahead. This operated by a pair of handles, like bike handles. The power? That was derived by leg power the same as a regular bike; gas and small engines were not much in use in those days, fifty-three years ago. The day this snow bike was taken out for its trial run was a Sunday, just after noon. It was moved out of the shop and given a start at Ridge Street on Lincoln Avenue and was headed for Main Street; Henderson was unable to steer it in a straight line. By the time he got to Main Street, the power plant was exhausted. With the help of five or six men it was pulled back in the shop for future use as kindling wood.

At the same time two other Mitchell men began building a sled, however they used the frame of an old tandem bike, mounted on runners, using the regular sprockets and chains to the rear wheel hub. On the rim of this wheel were placed triangular pieces of metal with the point outside, which was much better than the Henderson sled, but on trial, was no more of a success. Two men could not furnish enough power to drive it on a level road, and in soft snow it would not move at all. That venture ended any ideas of making skiing easier.

The demand for skis was great that year, as that was the only outdoor sport to be had, as well as the only means of travel; bob-sledding wasn't good, as snow fell so regularly the hills could not be kept open for sliding.

The only skis any one saw those days were made locally. They were made with just a strap across the instep and a bridge or block placed under the arch of the foot. Skis were never fastened to the feet, as that was considered too dangerous. One might get a leg broken on a fall, but many a ski took off alone down the hill, sometimes to be lost or broken.

The best skis were made by Eli Fletcher; the kind of wood used was native spruce or pine, ash, oak or Texas pine. Texas pine, quartered and sawed, were the fastest skis made and needed no waxing; the more they were used the better and faster they became. The usual length of the ski at that time was ten and twelve feet.

Father Dyer did not introduce skiing in the United States; nor Snow-Shoe Thompson; nor mid-west Norwegians on their "flat-boards." History hints at Leif Erickson.

Way back in time man sought a means of travel to conquer winter snows. Skiing is not an innovation. Much research has been done into the history of skiing, but there is still some doubt as to its origin. The Swedish Hoting Ski, dug up in a peat bog, is the oldest known example of prehistoric ski and dates back to between 3000 B. C. and 2000 B. C.

"Vanity of vanities; all is vanity. The thing that hath been, it is that which shall be; and that which is done is that which shall be done; there is no new thing under the sun. Is there any thing whereof it may be said, See, this is new? it hath been already of old time, which was before us."   (Ecclesiastes 1: 9-10)

CROSSING THE RANGE ON SNOW SKATES.

Snowshoe Thompson crossing the Sierras on snowshoes, carrying the mail. Reproduced from an engraving by Charles Christian Nahl (San Francisco 1818-1878). ("Who Was Who In America" Vol. 1). Courtesy —Denver Public Library Western Collection.

Snowshoe Thompson's grave — Genoa, Nevada — (name often spelled Thomson). Picture supplied by former Geona postmaster. (Note snowshoes on tombstone).

ON SNOW-SHOES.

Snow-shoeing in the 1860s—Breckenridge and nearby areas. Picture from Father Dyer's autobiography, *Snow-Shoe Itinerant*. Courtesy—Denver Public Library Western Collection.

CABIN AT MOSQUITO.

Father Dyer's cabin and skis on Mosquito Pass.
Courtesy—Denver Public Library Western Collection

A FEARFUL DESCENT.

Artist's drawing of Father Dyer plunging over a precipice. (Picture from his autobiography *Snow-Shoe Itinerant*). Courtesy — Denver Public Library Western History.

Mrs. Minnie Thomas and friends travelling on a sleigh between old Dillon and Frisco. Courtesy—Mrs. Minnie Thomas.

A Breckenridge sleighing party. Courtesy—Mrs. Ray McGinnis.

Breckenridge ladies snowshoeing. Agnes (Finding) Miner—4th from left.
Courtesy—Denver Public Library Western Collection.

Agnes and "Tonnie" Finding snow-shoeing.
Courtesy—Mrs. Ray McGinnis

Skiing

Men Skiers, Irwin, Colorado, 1883.
Courtesy—Library State Historical Society of Colorado.

Summit County *Journal*—August 31, 1907): "Twenty-five years ago yesterday, August 30, 1882, was a great day in the history of Summit County. Snow fell to the depth of two feet and light sleighs were run on the streets. The first and only real August snowstorm in history. The next day the snow disappeared and roads were dry." Courtesy—Library State Historical Society of Colorado.

BRECKENRIDGE NAVY

Breckenridge is a pretty site for a city, with the Blue River running by, suggestive of a spacious wharf and a line of piers to ape the institutions of New York, Boston and those other little down east towns.

That's the way a reporter from the *Rocky Mountain News* saw Breckenridge in 1861 and reported it for his newspaper. The August 10, 1861, *Miners' Record* reprinted the article "From Denver to the Blue." It's been hard ever since for Breckenridge and Summit County to give up the idea of a navy.

In fairly recent years Dillon, Summit County, Colorado, had its "Dillon Navy Days." Summit County's first organized river boat races were held on the Blue River June 30th and July 1st, 1956. The classes included kayaks, canoes, and anything seaworthy. The first year of Dillon Navy Days was a "smashing success."

Saturday events were in heavy rainfall. A goof race opened the festivities. Hud Prestrud won the event in a boat made of innertubes, held together by a triangular board. He was closely followed by his brother Dick, in the same kind of boat, which shows that skilled seamanship was the deciding factor in this brotherly competition. Earl and Eleanor Ganong took third in a leaky skiff which was gaily decorated with pennants. Earl rowed while Eleanor bailed. A close contest developed for fourth and fifth places, with Tink Bailey, in a one man rubber life raft sailboat, finally edging out Dick Ryman and his bravely painted rectangular cement mixing trough, which foundered shortly after it passed the finish line at the Public Service bridge north of (old) Dillon.

The stellar event of Saturday was the two run slalom which was held on the Blue River from the old dump (east of old Dillon) to the Public Service bridge, with twenty-two boats participating in the event. Eric Seidel of Salida made the outstanding run of the day, followed by Xavier Weurfmansdobler, also of Salida.

The downriver race started Sunday afternoon with thirteen boats entered. The race started at the Blue River bridge, east of Dillon on Highway 6, and ended just above Mark Pritchard's bridge, over about a nine mile course. Salida racers took the first five places. John Bailey came in sixth.

Thus was instituted the annual Dillon Navy Days. It provided exciting amusement and competition for the next three years.

Vice Admiral Richard Ryman directed the 1957 Navy Days. World Champion Walter Kirschbaum placed first on the Blue River slalom, followed by Xavier Weurfmansdobler of Salida. In the team race the Boulder team won; Blue River Navy flipped and was unable to finish.

In 1958 Henri Kadrinka, Swiss national white water champion, was the winner of Saturday's slalom event and Sunday's downriver race at the 3rd annual Dillon Navy Days celebration. Willi Gertsgrasser of Germany took second in both events and Karl Schroeder of Italy placed third in the slalom, while Roger Paris of Orleans, France, placed 3rd in the downriver race.

Dillon Navy Days were rescheduled a week previous to the famous Arkansas River events. World-famous contestants entered Dillon Navy Days as a "warm-up" to the Arkansas River contests.

Salida captured six of the seven trophies awarded at Dillon Navy Days, 1959. Blue River

Navy entrants came in fifth, sixth and twenty-seventh in the slalom events. Earl Ganong of the Blue River Navy, who was running an exceptionally good race, made a spectacular finish in last place. He flipped while going under a low footbridge and lost his paddle. After beaching and draining his boat, he found a long pole from a dead tree nearby, and finished the race using the pole as a paddle amid the cheers of spectators.

Construction of Dillon Reservoir sank the Dillon Navy.

Summit County was not to remain long without a navy. December 3, 1966, through the promotional activity of Frank F. Brown, Jr., Editor and Publisher of the *Summit County Journal*, the U S S Summit County was officially designated as the U S S Summit County, Colorado—a coup won over Summit County, Ohio and Summit County, Utah. Listed as L S T—1146 (Land Ship, Tank), "its primary purpose is to land fully equipped tanks, and other battle-ready vehicles, on shores held by the enemy. The L S T may also be called upon to transport tanks, crews and equipment over long distances at sea before the actual landing takes place."

With appropriate ceremonies outside Summit County Court House, "Summit County, Colorado" became the official name of the ship. Summit County commissioners and dignitaries joined naval officers in re-christening the vessel. Commissioners presented a large copper plaque—USS SUMMIT COUNTY—COLORADO—1966; Lt. Judis, Commanding Officer, in appreciation, presented the ship's flag to the County.

Again, Summit County navy was of short duration. After a notable record in the service of our country the ship was de-commissioned October 31, 1969.

Of all the valiant attempts to promote a Summit County navy none equaled "Captain" Samuel Adams' expedition in the summer of 1869. It was Breckenridge Navy par excellence.

Explorers, opening the vast western regions, were possessed with wishful thinking—a navigable route to the Pacific Ocean must exist. This was a motivating consideration in Major John Wesley Powell's expedition, 1869, "to explore the upper Colorado River and solve the mysteries of its three hundred mile canyon." Others had theories, dreams and imaginations of the same kind.

Captain Samuel Adams was one of the most colorful explorers seeking a waterway route to the Pacific. Wallace Stegner wrote of him, "Of all the makers of fantasy who touched the history of Colorado, few approached Samuel Adams. His career is a demonstration of how far a man could get in a new country on nothing but gall and the gift of gab, so long as what he said was what people wanted to believe."

Adams presented himself at the Powell camp and offered his services, representing himself as an authority on the Colorado River. Furthermore, he claimed authorization from ex-Secretary of War, Stanton, to accompany the Rocky Mountain Scientific Exploring Expedition. After examining references, Powell sent the "impressive, fast-tongue" scientific authority on his way. "It would take more than a rebuff from Powell to discourage Adams from leading the nation into Canaan."

On July 12, 1869, Sam Adams was raising the curtain on a new scene of his low-comedy subplot. At Breckenridge, a mining camp on the Blue, on Colorado's western slope, he had made himself solid with a congenial group, of a mentality to suit his own. They were predisposed for the spiel he gave them, eager for the news he brought of riches and opportunities along the river, willing to play a long shot—or as they appeared to conceive it, a sure thing.

They fitted Sam Adams out with four boats, built on the spot out of green lumber, undecked and with no air compartments, and they enlisted in his expetition to the number of ten men. Captain Sam Adams, Ricker, O'Connor, Decker, Foment, Frazier, Waddle, Day, Lovell, Twible, Lillis. They equipped themselves (for there is no reason to believe that Adams could have equipped them) with Spencer muzzle-loading rifles and two hundred rounds of ammunition apiece, and with a good many hundredweight of assorted supplies. For the flagship the ladies of Breckenridge made a flag upon which was inscribed, "Western Colorado to California, Greeting."

Adams' purpose was to descend the Blue to its junction with the Grand a few miles southwest of Gore Pass, and from there to float on down this unobstructed waterway to California. It was not quite clear how far away California was horizontally, but it was a cinch that from Breckenridge, at an altitude of ten thousand feet, it was almost two miles vertically.

Breckenridge gave him a large sendoff, with speeches and cheers, at the launching place two and a half miles below town where two of the boats pushed off. (The other two were hauled down twelve miles by wagon, and launched there.) So full was Adams' heart that in his journal that day he recorded a long paragraph in praise of Summit County, where "upon the extreme limits of civilization, enterprise and moral worth were superior to that of any other I had ever met."

Down a creek which Adams describes as falling 80 to 120 feet per mile, they ran nine miles. With scientific care Adams noted the width and depth of the river, leaving blanks for the figures to be filled in later, and that night in a jovial camp they dined upon homemade bread of the wife of Judge Silverthorn, presented to them at parting. There had been no difficulty that day, Adams says, though his boat was twice upset.

Next day there was a new launching, after the wagoners who had brought the other boats had left. Judge Silverthorn made a speech and presented Adams with a dog. What ever happened to that miserable animal in the next month is one of the dark and tantalizing silences of history.

The experiences of the next day, July 14, might have given Adams a hint of what was coming. In what his journal calls Rocky Canyon they bounced around a corner full upon a bad rapid. Within seconds Adams, Waddle, Day, O'Connor, Twible, Lillis, Decker, and everybody else in the expedition except the occupants of the last boat were hanging onto rocks in midstream, trying to make themselves heard above the roar of water. Their "instruments," whatever those were, as well as Adams' box of papers, including his letters of "authorization" from the Secretary of War, went down the Blue. The fall in Rocky Canyon Adams estimated at over 250 feet in a mile and half.

On Sunday, July 18, somewhat quenched by the ducking, and in need of repairs, they sent Mr. Lovell by land back to Breckenridge for more "instruments" and matches. Adams does not state what instruments would be available in the mining camp of Breckenridge; it is allowable to believe that it was the matches he really needed. As the rest of the group hung around Pacific Park waiting for Lovell's return they began to show the first signs of failing enthusiasm. On Tuesday, July 19, Adams' diary notes that they raised thirty dollars and gave it to Mr. Ricker and sent him back home as a "common nuisance."

Others had also begun to doubt, but Adams talked them into going on, saying that he would proceed though no one accompanied him. Heartened and with dry matches, they pushed off again, but had gone only a short distance when the boat of Lillis and Decker hit a rock and was demolished. Somewhat forlornly they stopped for the rest of the day to fish out of the rock downstream whatever could be salvaged. Minus his instruments, Adams remained at a scientific disadvantage, and again had to leave a blank in his diary: "Distance by water from Breckenridge, ——miles."

By Thursday, July 22, dissension had begun to rend the little group of explorers to its foundations. O'Connor, Foment, Decker, and Frazier gave up and started back, as Adams' diary says contemptuously, "to tell of their heroic actions, etc."

The day after the great desertion, Mr. Waddle showed up temporarily missing, so that Adams had to run his boat alone. He swamped only once, when he drove under a fallen tree. For eight miles, according to his record, he had smooth and easy sailing to the junction with the Grand. There the party camped, fifty-five miles and twelve days out of Breckenridge, and one boat and five members fewer than they had started with.

Here for a week there is a gap in Adams' journal, perhaps because he was too busy to write, perhaps because his pencil floated off to join his instruments. Presumably they rested. Not impossibly, in this week the unhappy dog met his fate, whatever it was. At last on July 30 they started again and ran five miles, stopping at the mouth of what Adams calls the Grand Cannon (sic). It appears to have been Cedar Canyon. Camped here for two and a half days, the party washed clothes, cleaned guns, brought journals up to date, and waited for Twible and Lillis to carry out dispatches to Hot Sulphur Springs and bring back newspapers and more matches. Adams totted up the river he had run and estimated the fall as 3500 feet.

Next day, when the boats entered the "Grand Cannon" through a slot "fifty feet in breadth," they had had to line over several very bad stretches where Adams said he leveled and found the fall to be thirty-four feet in four hundred yards. Never on the Colorado had he seen such water, he said. Undoubtedly he hadn't.

Only a few hundred yards into the canyon

one of the boats being lined swung out of control over a fall, filled with water, and was badly damaged. They lost a hundred pounds of bacon, a sack of flour, an axe, a saw, an oven, two canteens of salt, thirty-five pounds of coffee, and other articles. When they took stock after laboring past the bad spot they found that they had left two hundred twenty-five pounds of lumpy flour, fifty of bacon, and fifteen of coffee and salt.

Undaunted, they persevered. On August 3 they made paddles and repaired their boats and lined down an additional three hundred yards. Next day, lining with great difficulty through a roaring rapid, they found a slab of their lost bacon lying unhurt among the rocks, and were cheered as by an omen. It was the only good thing that had happened to them since they left Breckenridge.

By now they were deep in the gorge, with a huge domed mountain before them as if to stop the river, and the walls overhanging them so alarmingly that they began to wonder what they would do if Indians ambushed them from above. It was impossible to run, all but impossible to line or portage, difficult even to go back. The fall, Adams estimated, was fifty feet in five hundred yards, about the slope of a good coasting hill.

On August 5 one of the boats filled and swamped and was caught by its line among rocks. They worked all morning to free it, only to see the line part in the afternoon and boat and load rush down into the falls and disappear forever. They had been four days of panting work making three quarters of a mile, and now, with one damaged boat remaining, they were faced with a seemingly impassable chute. But whatever Sam Adams lacked—ability to see, willingness to tell the truth, capacity to think straight—he lacked neither courage nor persistence. It gave him enormous satisfaction to assume that they were descending at the rate of one hundred twenty feet to the mile, for though the descent caused them great difficulty, they approached that much more swiftly the near-sea-level reaches that would give them smooth sailing. On August 6, stiffening their courage for trouble ahead, the members of the party threw away all extra clothing and equipment and stripped down for passage in the one boat. Adams says that he gave the waves his box of papers (lost once already, on the second day out) and abandoned his instruments (which except perhaps for a hand level and a thermometer he had never had and wouldn't have

known how to use) and on the seventh day they struggled from difficult portage to difficult portage until after the fourth round the boat swamped, broke its line, and rushed in disintegrating wreckage to join the other three.

Other men might by this time have begun to entertain doubts about the water route to California. By now the brave flag with its greeting from the ladies of Breckenridge was snagged in some rapid or driftwood pile, and all four inadequate boats were on their way to the Gulf of California in splinters. But Captain Samuel Adams was a dedicated man. With his five companions he built a raft and floated the skimpy remains of their provisions around a perpendicular corner, where on August 9 they sifted and dried their flour, of which they had one hundred twenty pounds left, along with twenty of bacon. Waddle, Lovell, and Day, musing over the stores and contemplating the river ahead, decided that day to start back by land. It was like the nursery rhyme of the ten little nine little eight little Indians. Adams now had left, besides himself, only two little Indian boys. The three indomitables went on, packing their stuff three miles down the canyon, passing en route the rocks strewn and plastered with discarded clothes that they had tossed overboard higher up. On August 10, square-jawed, they built a raft five by fourteen feet out of drift logs and took to the water again.

At the end of three miles the raft hit a rock and spilled overboard all their salt, all but ten days' ration of flour, and all their knives and forks, which were becoming fairly unnecessary anyway. They still had a camp kettle and a frying pan, but the raft was a wreck. When they had dried out they reconnoitered down the river. As far as they could see the water roared and pounded through one rapid after another. Reluctantly, on August 13, they decided to give it up and start back. The water-level route to the Pacific would have to wait a little while.

But to the eye of Sam Adams what he and his light-witted companions had come through had the look of a hard-won success. From the first to the last he demonstrated a mastery of things that were not there. The 4500 feet of fall which he thought he had navigated were actually between 2000 and 3000.

The sequence of Adams' navigation exploit was a $20,000 compensation claim tendered the United States Government "for services in exploring and opening the Colorado River." After many rejections a recommendation was suggested that $3750 be granted. This, too, was rejected "on the ground that whatever services Adams might have rendered had been unauthorized."

Poor Sam Adams was doomed never to reap the rewards whether for patents or exploration. He was a preposterous, twelve-gauge, hundred-proof, kiln-dried, officially notarized fool, or else he was one of the most wildly incompetent scoundrels who ever lived. But fool or scoundrel, he was a symptom. In his resistance to fact and logic he had many allies who were neither so foolish in their folly nor so witless in their rascality as he, but whose justification and platform was the same incorrigible insistence upon a West that did not exist.

Gold boats were Summit County's most ambitious attempt at a "navy." It all began in 1898 with Ben Stanley Revett's grandiose idea of dredging the gold from Swan and Blue River rockbed. The fleet was launched with a mixture of hope and hilarity.

Breckenridge Boom of '98   March 19, 1898
Building Of Two Gunboats Up Swan River By
B. S. Revett
Bombardment On The Nuggets Will Begin In
The Spring
B. S. Revett, Commander, Will Lead The Fray

But little anxiety has been felt concerning Breckenridge on the Blue should war be declared against Spain. Should the word be received that any Spanish flotilla was coming up the Blue the boats over on the Swan could soon be prepared to act as gunboats and rams and would vanquish any fleet that may be sent this way. Dillon, being more exposed, might suffer some damage. (April 2, 1898—Revett's North American Gold Dredging Company has the scows nearly completed and will soon be in operation.)

Summit County Journal   June 18, 1898
From the top of each of Revett's dredges will float a beautiful silk pennant with a hand work representation of a swan, the design being made by Mr. Revett. Each dredge will be numbered, a plan which will do away with the necessity of naming.

December 9, 1899, had a comment not appreciated or shared by nature lovers:

A debt of gratitude we will never be able to pay, transformed Swan River from a worthless barren wilderness to scenes of commercial and industrial activity, the like of which was never dreamed of, three years ago.

Ben Stanley Revett introduced gold dredging boats to Summit County. Nine dredges composed the gold boat fleet on Swan River, French Gulch and Blue River, operating from 1898 to 1942 at various times and by several companies. Navigating Blue River, from Swan River to south end of Breckenridge, was almost a thirty-five year voyage, counting anchored and sailing years.

The gold boat was the only Blue River upstream navigation to reach Breckenridge's "spacious wharf." It ended its journey midnight, October 15, 1942. Boulders too large for the operation lay just ahead. Behind were miles of rock tailings blocking a retreat. World War II signed the death certificate for gold dredging. Collection of scrap metal for the war effort, fire and sinking left only a shattered hulk of the gold boat.

The Four Seasons Development Center, with its bell-tower, is now rising at the site of the gold boat's last anchoring, but the "beautiful swift stream" is dissipated and seeps through miles of stones. Hope of a Breckenridge Navy has faded.

Breckenridge is a pretty site for a city, with the Blue River running by, suggestive of a spacious wharf and a line of piers to ape the institutions of New York, Boston and those other down east towns.

COUNTY HAILS NAVY NAMESAKE

The USS Summit County, Colorado
Courtesy—Summit County *Journal*

Lt. Judis holds plaque presented to his ship by Summit County Commissioners. Courtesy—Summit County *Journal*.

Only boat of Breckenridge Navy to dock at Breckenridge piers. Gold boat was operating in the summer of 1939. Temporarily stopped operating August, 1939, and resumed operations May-June, 1942. Completely ceased operations October 15th, 1942, midnight, and was dismantled. Picutre taken by writer, summer of 1939.

"YE EDITOR"

"The pen is mightier than the sword"—and often it is used with rapier thrust. The newspaper was a motivating implement in Breckenridge early days. In addition to bringing news, it was used to cut, jab, prod and goad, thereby putting "dynamite" under citizens and civic officials. "Ye Editor" wielded strong influence and power, second to no other in the community.

Breckenridge had a twenty-year history before it had a newspaper of its own. Denver Rocky Mountain *News* reached the mining community, subject to irregular mail delivery. Items concerning Breckenridge and Blue River Diggings appeared frequently in the *News* columns, contributions of local writers. These items provide us with many historical records of the first twenty years of Breckenridge. Editor William Byers, Rocky Mountain *News*, made his second western-area newspaper venture by publishing the *Miners' Record*, 1861. *Miners' Record* was printed at Tarryall, Park County, across Hoosier Pass from Breckenridge. It was of short duration, July 4, 1861, to September 14, 1861. Three months of the *Miners' Record* gave historical data and interesting reading of Breckenridge-South Park area. We regret that its life-span was so short, for it was newsy, and reported on-the-scene activity of the area. Shifting population, lack of advertising and job printing made *Miners' Record* an unprofitable venture.

The first newspaper to be published in Summit County was Kokomo's The Summit County *Times,* September 27, 1879. Kokomo and Robinson were booming towns mid-way between Frisco and Leadville.

Summit County *Journal*　　　January 5, 1907

A GLIMPSE INTO HISTORY

The other day in looking through the archives of the *Journal* office, we unearthed a copy of the first newspaper ever printed in Summit County, Colorado, viz: The Summit County *Times,* bearing date of September 27, 1879, published at Kokomo. In 1879, Kokomo, Robinson, and other towns located near the summit of Fremont Pass were the scenes of an exciting mining boom. There were from three to five thousand people in that small district and everything in general was sizzling hot. Kokomo was the metropolis and Breckenridge a mere village. Mail and transportation was by stage route, the principal line running between Leadville and Georgetown, via Dillon, in those days.

The second gold boom came to Breckenridge in 1880, and Thursday, July 22, 1880, the Breckenridge *Daily Journal* made its debut, Jonathan Cooper Fincher, Editor. It was ambitious for a newspaper to publsh a daily in a small mining community, yet daily newsy happenings were reported. Another Breckenridge newspaper followed quickly, the Summit County *Leader.* Its first issue was dated Saturday, July 31, 1880, and was sold on the streets of Breckenridge the next day, Sunday, August 1st. Other nearby communities provided in quick succession the Robinson *Tribune* (Dec. 1880-1883), Eagle River *Shaft,* Ten Mile *News,* (1881-1883), Dillon *Enterprise* (April 14, 1882-1899) and last, but not least in any respect, the Montezuma *Millrun* (June 24, 1882-May 26, 1888).

A *weekly* Summit County *Journal* was

added to the *Daily Journal* by our ambitious journalist, J. C. Fincher. Its first issue was Saturday, April 4, 1883. The *Daily Journal* reminded its readers: "First Year; No. 1, August 4, 1883. Don't forget this is the day the Summit County *Journal* makes its first appearance. All desiring to see a first class home paper should get a copy."

"Ye Editor," as Jonathan Cooper Fincher liked to call himself, was a colorful newspaper man, unsurpassed by nearby editors, and probably unequaled in the long, unbroken life of the newspaper he established—*Daily Journal*—Summit County *Journal*—July 22, 1880, to the present time.

Jonathan Cooper Fincher was born in Berwick, Pennsylvania, March 11, 1829. In 1857 he was married to Miss Hattie Blankman of Philadelphia. Twelve children were born to this union, nine surviving at the time of his death, June 16, 1911. In early life Fincher learned the machinist's trade, but being of a literary turn of mind took up newspaper work, writing for eastern papers in different capacities. For twelve years, 1880-1892, he continued his newspaper publishing in Summit County. He then sold to James W. Swisher and retired from active public life. His last nineteen years were lived in Denver. In the twelve years of editorship, no better known resident lived in Summit County.

Publishing a newspaper in Breckenridge was not without handicaps. At the beginning of the third year of the *Daily Journal* Ye Editor gave a brief summary:

Daily Journal   July 22, 1882

To-day the *Journal* enters its third year of publication. Its first year was one of continued doubt and fear; its friends were uncertain as to its future. They were fearful lest the uncertainties of business connections would leave the little barque stranded during the dull seasons; as it grew older stronger confidence was established until doubts have been dispelled and even dud seasons are now looked upon as not the worst calamities. Let it suffice to say that the third year is entered with very few and comparatively light drawbacks as compared with those of the first and second. For past favors in the line of legitimate business the *Journal* remembers its friends and hopes in the future to be of even more service than in the past.

At the ending of the third year the *Daily Journal* gave a more complete narration of first hectic years:

Daily Journal   July 21, 1883

This issue completes the third year of the publication of the *Journal*. When the first copy of the little sheet was placed upon the streets what a difference between the camp then and since. The boom of '80 was on the town. Town lots were ready-selling commodity. "Ten foot holes" sold readily as mines, "vest pocket specimens" drew crowds of observers, the "future great" was undoubtedly Breckenridge. Already sanguine locators saw in the near future the glory of Leadville eclipsed and all eyes were turned to Breckenridge. A bank had been started, a fire company was being organized, smelters were being built, dance houses abounded, gambling houses were numerous, bars were well patronized, hotels and lodging houses were crowded, restaurants could scarcely feed the crowds that demanded attention, shells, called by compliment, houses, were being built in all parts of the town, all and everything bore the evidence of excitement. Each man owning an interest in a partly developed claim acted as if he felt sure he was in fact a bonanza king and not merely a prospective one. Thus set the sun of '80. As truth flashed upon the excited crowd that their expectations were premature Breckenridge awakened from her unwarranted dreams to facts more in keeping with her reality. Breckenridge had but one unfailing memento of the boom of '80 and that was the daily appearance of the *Journal*. During all these changing phases the *Journal* continued its visits noting the decline as mildly as possible, still noting the changes. To those who, like the *Journal*, have stayed with the town in its gloomy days we have but this to say, "tarry yet a little while and see the town enter upon its true existence!" We are satisfied that ere another anniversary passes the public will demand, and its patronage will support, a daily with direct telegraphic news, news gatherers that will make a daily desirable to people abroad as well as at home. We have established our faith by our works.

This closes the third year of the *Daily*.

The weekly Summit County *Journal* encountered the same difficulties. It gave its accounting at the end of the first year.

Our Second Year

This issue commences the second year of the publication of The Summit County *Journal* and we take pride in scattering a few extra copies among non-subscribers in town as well as elsewhere in the county.

It has been our aim to present each week during the past year to our patrons a sheet in which all of local interest to Summit County readers and to all parties abroad who might be interested in Summit County matters might be found. If we have been reasonably successful we ought to feel content, for with the exception of the last month the year has been the dullest the county has known since the boom of '80. We have endeavored to give the readers of the *Journal* the plain unvarnished truth, steadily curbing the reports of wealth until there could be no question of its extent and value, until we think the character of the paper is established for truth and reliability the equal of any sheet in the state.

The *Daily Journal* for over four years and the Summit County *Journal* for one year have been published in your midst and have never annoyed any person with importunate appeals for advertising, job work or subscriptions, and neither has ever been the recipient of charity aid.

Thankful for past business favors the publisher begs leave to assure his patrons that he will strive to merit their continuance of the same during the coming years.

The *Daily Journal* and the Summit County *Journal* continued side-by-side existence until the end of July, 1888, when the Summit County *Journal* became the only Jonathan Fincher publication. "Ye Editor" kept at the helm another four years. It was a marvel to many journalists. On September 19, 1887, the National Editorial Association, passing through Breckenridge to Leadville, "expressed surprise that the little *Daily* was so tenacious of life and admitted that its equal under all circumstances was not published in the United States."

The *Journal* printing establishment was a bee-hive of activity, and a most interesting place. October 21, 1887, an item, "As Others See Us," appeared in the *Daily Journal*:

A few weeks ago the editorial excursion train stopped at our mountain gem of a town an hour or two, during which time the *Journal* office was visited and this is the way it struck the visitor and appeared in the Red Wing *Republican:*

In this city of the mountains, with a population of 957 inhabitants, two papers are published, and one, the *Journal,* both daily and weekly. A visit to the office of the *Daily Journal* and a conversation with the gentlemanly editor and publisher, Col. J. C. Fincher, who has passed his sixtieth year at least, (actually 58 years of age) revealed the rather interesting fact that the paper and office are run by himself and his three daughters, editing the paper, doing the type setting, proof reading, press work and job printing. During our visit the forms were locked up and put on the press, a Washington hand press, by the young ladies, and then one inked the forms and fed, while the other worked the press, pulling the lever with as much ease, and better nature, than many men, who often refuse to work one of these "man killers." But then these are mountaineers. The Colonel is a splendid specimen of a man, large, straight and strong, and the girls partake of the father's characteristics.

"Ye Editor's" customary generosity wasn't always extended to rival newspapers and editors. At first he welcomed the "newspaper front" that emerged in the early 1880s. In fact, he proposed a County association; "there are many points in business which might be made mutually beneficial by an occasional conference." But as competition increased belligerency replaced generosity. Libel suits seemed not a serious threat, and name-calling and accusations were far from flattering; sometimes they were crude and brutal. Even physical encounters occurred to enliven matters.

The Summit County *Leader* made its appearance in Breckenridge only a week later than the *Daily Journal.* The *Daily Journal* was Democratic; the *Leader* was Republican. For two years the *Leader* was headed by Bishop as editor, Caswell as publisher. In 1883 Frank Smith was editor and publisher. By this time the *Leader* was in real difficulties. The Summit County *Journal,* August 2, 1884, reported:

Our neighbor on the hill, whose lamp of life went glimmering on the 19th inst. commenced life as a solicitor of public help. The first appeal was to furnish it a place to call its home. By circular of date July 23rd, '80, the proprietors Bishop and Caswell, announcing that they were ready for job work, and would issue their first paper at the latter end of the following week, and for the help received from liberal citizens they would afford them advertising space in the *Leader* for the pittance of five dollars per inch per month. When the spark of life went out on the 19th of July many Republicans breathed freer than they had done for months.

What the Republicans want in the shape of a newspaper here, is a first class paper conducted by a man of brains, a gentleman and withal honest. Beggars, fools and knaves should be given a wide berth.

The *Leader* was established to fleece the people of Summit County and it did its work well; it knifed its friends worse than its enemies.

With the liberal support given by the merchants of this city and its official patronage, the *Leader* should have paid had ability, business tact and, above all, honesty marked its conduct. Its whole course was a disgrace upon the profession and it died unhonored and unsung.

As a contrast allow us to call attention to the difference, the *Leader* started to charge $5.00 per inch per month where the *Daily Journal* at the same time charged but $2.00 for the same space and the Summit County *Journal* charges but seventy-five cents per month for the same space.

We are often asked how in the world we get along and keep up? A question easily answered: By hard work and attending to our business, and on that line if our patrons would pay what is due us, instead of keeping us out of it, we could to-day pay all we owe and be able to pay cash for a power press and make the interests of Breckenridge just hump themselves, and we wouldn't have to pass a hat or take up a camptown collection.

The *Journal* to-day is poor only because of the backwardness of men to pay what they owe the office. That is the difference between hard work, attention to business and no putting on of style and snobbery, brass and airs.

The *Leader* was taken over by Charles E. Hardy in 1884 and operated until 1892. Summit County *Journal* and Summit County *Leader* were not on friendly relations. October 3, 1887, "Ye Editor" of the *Daily Journal* commented: "Our attention has been called to a copy of last week's issue of the breech-clout from the cesspool on Lincoln Avenue. The editorial force has been increased. It now consists of a fool and a liar, both

cowards, that's all." March 10, 1888, reported another incident:

Thursday afternoon the corners of Main Street and Lincoln Avenue were made a little lively by a rather unfriendly interview between the editors of the *Journal* and the *Leader*. Some very uncomplimentary remarks on both sides resulted in the *Journal* planting a light right hander among the whiskers of the *Leader*. The latter returned the compliment with a clip over the head from his cane. A second followed and a third on the side of the neck when the old one then applied the cane dodge and one blow on the *Leader*'s mug settled the business. The city funds were improved a little thereby.

Breckenridge was favored with another newspaper 1888-1889 — the Summit County *Democrat*. The news brought an offended exclamation from "Ye Editor."

Daily Journal   January 11, 1888

GAWL!

Under the date of January 9th the Denver papers published the following telegram: "Breckenridge is to have a new Democratic paper. It will be called the Summit County *Democrat*, and will make its first appearance on Saturday, 28. It is understood that W. S. Montgomery, formerly of the Leadville *Journal*, is behind the new enterprise, which is a guarantee that it will be 'Simon pure' in its news and editorial departments. It will indeed fill 'a long felt want,' as the democracy of Summit has never had a newspaper exponent that could be depended upon in case of emergency."

Summit County *Journal*   January 21, 1888

A street rumor was started Thursday that one of the editors in the Lincoln Avenue kennel had suicided. It turned out that it was only the shooting of Dr. Stephenson's spitz dog in front of the den that started the report. A passer-by remarked that the carcass was a fair intimation of what the *Leader* would be after the new paper started—a dead dog. (Hardys' paper outlasted Montgomery's three years.)

Oren K. Gaymon established the Dillon *Enterprise* beginning Friday, April 14, 1882. His printing press was brought into Summit County over Boreas Pass, down Indiana Gulch, by sled and horses. His Republican politics added fuel to Fincher's vituperations.

James W. Swisher, formerly editor of the Montezuma *Millrun*, October 1, 1887 to May 26, 1888, succeeded Fincher as editor of Summit County *Journal* in 1892. In 1897 (horror of horrors!) the Republican O. K. Gaymon became editor and publisher of the Summit County *Journal*, continuing until September 25, 1909. On this date Gaymon printed his "Adieu and Thank You." "Failing health and business considerations have induced us to part with the *Journal*. This is a day of consolidations, and hereafter the *Journal* will issue from the same office under a combination name, with J. W. Swisher as publisher." (Swisher, after retiring from the *Journal*, had purchased the Breckenridge *Bulletin* with A. L. Wood as editor and manager. September, 1908, Wood was ushered out of his job and Breckenridge as "a disgrace to the town.") The consolidated paper was published October 2, 1909, to August 14, 1914, under the combined name of Summit County *Journal* and Breckenridge *Bulletin*. James W. Swisher died August 21, 1910, and was buried in Breckenridge Cemetery. Mrs. Mary Swisher published the paper for a short time and then it went into other hands.

It was O. K. Gaymon and the Republican Dillon *Enterprise* that irked "Ye Editor" the most. We follow the antagonists through the columns of the *Journal*, regretting that the *Enterprise* hasn't also been preserved for posterity. Here, again, "Ye Editor's" first generous impulses changed to name-calling and ridicule:

March, 1882: "It is reported that C. W. Craighead and O. K. Gaymon have purchased type, etc., from the *Register Call* with which they propose starting a new paper in Dillon, Summit County, to be known as the Dillon *Enterprise*." April 15, 1882: "Last night's mail brought to our table a copy of the first issue of The Dillon *Enterprise*, published at Dillon, ten miles north of this city. The *Enterprise* is a six-column folio, very neatly gotten up, well filled with selections and original matter. The first number as a sample promises that the *Enterprise* will rank A-1 in the list of weeklies in the County. Breckenridge merchants will find it to their advantage to use its columns in extending their business. We extend to the new *Enterprise* a hearty welcome believing that Summit County

is large enough for all that are here and more that may come." May, 1882: "The Dillon *Enterprise* has already had a change of ownership—Craighead withdrawing, the present proprietors being Chandler, Spaulding and Gaymon. The crew is certainly large enough to properly manage a larger craft." July 18, 1882: "Yesterday during a visit to Dillon we called at the *Enterprise* office and found neighbor Gaymon in one of his characteristic moods of good humored hopefulness, and although his present office might not keep out a November zephyr he expects to have a better shop of his own before September snows fly."

By July, 1887, "Ye Editor" was willing to grant progress to the Dillon paper. "The Dillon crossing foghorn, known as the *Enterprise*, is becoming really a readable county paper." Now the ridicule accelerates:

Daily Journal   October 8, 1887

Every town has its feist; we all know what pestiferous little cusses they are. Sedate old watch dogs take no notice of them; passers-by, if they come too near, kick them into the gutter; only kittens and children hold them in awe. Dillon has its feist; it answers to the name of Gaymon. It is the meanest of its kind and is composed of fleas and barks—get out you cur.

Daily Journal   November 14, 1887

Now after the election is over comes the Dillon Crossing Foghorn into court and by the pen of its assinine editor delivers its opinion of Breckenridge people and papers after the following manner:

There are a number of nice, respectable people living in Breckenridge, but viewing the place from political standpoint, we believe we but voice the sentiment of the balance of the county in pronouncing it nothing more nor less than a rotten borough, of the rottenest kind. Not only that but it tolerates, from day to day, the circulation of the rottenest Democratic paper published in the known world.

Rivalry continued into 1891 and 1892—until the end of "Ye Editor's" days with the Journal:

September 12, 1891: Dillon has reached its

level, a road side station where pitching quoits, running horse races, jumping, etc., etc., is the highest position the denizens hope to reach. What a pity some directing mind is not among them to develop the town in the direction that Providence has marked out and surroundings so rich qualify it for. September 19, 1891: Poor Dillon has got down to a wayside horse race town. What a pity, but that is about Gaymon's size. October 10, 1891: Gaymon tried hard in his last blast in his foghorn to reach the level of decency in his editorial notices of the Democratic ticket; the strain however was so great that it nearly broke his straddle string. October 24, 1891: The press of the Republican party in this county is the object of scorn and contempt. One is managed by a fool and the other by an ass. The one publisher (Hardy of the *Leader*) ought to be pensioned by the party and retired to a woodpile with a saw and sawbuck for the balance of his life, the other (Gaymon of the *Enterprise*) spanked and put to bed until he learns to open his mouth without putting his foot in it. October 28, 1891: The irresponsible idiot in charge of the leading Republican organ of the county in his mental dribble last week insinuated things that he dare not charge, against men infinitely his superior in moral worth that every decent Republican in this city was profoundly disgusted with the paper in which his foul rot was printed.

May 28, 1892: Mr. Oscar D. Bryan, a former newspaper man, has been visiting our county in the interest of the Keeley Institute for the cure of Alcoholic and morphine appetites. He has been paying particular attention to the Republican editors of the county. July 9, 1892: Gaymon of the squawk was at the county seat on the fourth trying to get on a penny-pitching match. The editor for the squawk at the crossing carries the belt as being able to pitch ten pennies into a three inch circle at ten paces. Some of the by-standers must invariably furnish the coppers.

The *Bi-Metallic* was published in Breckenridge, 1892-1893, editor, George H. Clark and publisher, Sam W. Jones. The Breckenridge *Bulletin* began March 5, 1898, and continued to September 25, 1909. Coming after "Ye Editor's" retirement they were spared his editorial barbs.

Many fine things could justifiably be said of "Ye Editor" and his *Daily Journal* and Summit County *Journal*. Furthermore, the "human" aspect of the man, revealed so interestingly in his writings, makes the reading of his newspapers highly entertaining. His petulant idiosyncrasies are a delight, especially when it came to politics and close-at-hand newspaper competition. One smiles, sometimes laughs aloud, at the tirades made on Rev. Passmore for closing Breckenridge saloons on Sunday and enforcing gambling laws. "Ye Editor's" verbal attacks were transferred from pastor to the church, with snide remarks elevating the Episcopal Church and thereby down-grading the Methodist: "Anyone wanting to hear a good sermon, go to the Episcopal Church; all who enjoy a good sermon are requested to attend the Episcopal Church." "Come to the cosy church at the corner of French and Lincoln and hear a good sermon." "Services at the Episcopal Church are largely attended by the better class of our citizens."

One could almost weep with "Ye Editor" that "as usual, the *Journal* didn't receive an invitation and was left out" when Breckenridge "select fourteen" had another gathering. He bewailed, "the utterly utts are getting too-too-too." We rejoice with him that "Thanksgiving passed off very pleasantly, and much to our surprise, even the editoral table was graced with an elegant sample of the American bird, well-filled and roasted to a turn. The bird was a Thanksgiving remembrance from a thoughtful friend who does not reside on the east side of the Blue. We trust his shadow may never grow less, and that all his geese may be swans." The butcher, residing on the east side of the Blue, duly responded at Christmas time: "We know many of our people realize that we are in the holidays. Chris Kaiser, the princely meat market man of Lincoln Avenue, remembered the *Journal* in the shape of a fine, plump, fat turkey. Thanks." We felt truly sorrowful when "Col. J. C. Fincher, ye editor, was taken to the train Wednesday in an almost helpless state to go to Cottonwood Hot Springs, to get relief from an acute attack of rheumatism." His lament a month later evoked sympathy: "George Goodier has been growing fat on an attack of rheumatism which lasted four weeks, while our faber fell away from the same cause during the same time, but some people will be contrary." But the law of retribution evened the score: "Our esteemed townsman, whose illness we noted last week, ventured out too early after his first illness and is now suffering a relapse."

Cruel Breckenridge! "The *Journal* has just cause of complaint. George Hammerslag, at the last election, carried the town by a nice majority, while we tried it twice and slipped up both times. It ain't fair." "Sam Richards declares he thinks the boys who went prospecting with him have absquatulated with the big golden bowlder they found a few weks ago." (Dictionary of American English says "absquatulated" means "to depart—go away—decamp . . . especially in a surreptitious or hurried manner. It is somewhat being replaced with "skedaddle.")

Yes, "Ye Editor" was colorful and he added spice to daily doings in Breckenridge, but in 1892 he absquatulated—skedaddled—to Denver.

It has been said of the Finchers that they brought up their children a credit to their parents and themselves. Later records show that the sons and daughters made names for themselves in the professions of politics, journalism and teaching. The youngest of the family, Arlington, ("Arl"), remained longest in Breckenridge. He learned the trade of blacksmithing, and was also a popular member of Breckenridge's dance orchestra. "Arl" was long and kindly remembered for his gentle escorting of his mother on the streets of Breckenridge.

For some unpublished reason, "Ye Editor" and wife parted company; she continued to live in Breckenridge; he in Denver. The death notice mentions that six of his children were at the deathbed of "Ye Editor," but no mention is made of Mrs. Fincher being present. She was listed as a survivor. Burial took place in Denver Fairmount Cemetery. Newspaper advertisements announced that Mrs. Fincher had furnished rooms to rent in Breckenridge. For a while she had a novelty shop. In 1895 she opened an ice cream parlor; it was a popular place to go for cake and ice cream, following the dances.

INTERESTING ITEMS FROM THE PEN OF YE EDITOR

1881: The lake on Main Street still attracts attention. The town trustees ought to look after it or somebody will be drowned." A week later: "And still that mud puddle continues an eye-sore at Main Street and Washington Avenue." 1882: "Where! Oh, Where! is the street committee of our city dads? South Main Street is in a deplorable condition. The creek makes its channel alternately in the street and on the sidewalk and zig-zags down for a quarter of a mile. Some of the residences have to be approached by circulatory routes after the manner of approaching a Mississippi planter's residence during inundation. The condition of that portion of Main Street is a disgrace to the town as well as a serious inconvenience to the residents thereon."

1882: The town trustees should direct the new street commissioners to have the glass, tin cans and bale wire cleared off the streets before the town is brought in as defendant in a suit for injury of valuable stock. There should be an ordinance against making our Main Street a general receptacle for refuse, glassware, empty tins cans or bunches of bale wire. Their removal would be an improvement to the public highways." 1882: "This morning a couple of fast riders were before Police Justice Tippett, and for fast riding were fined three dollars and cost. Too many of our riders think the clear streets the proper place to speed their horse. Such is not the case and it will be well for the marshal to bear in mind that all fast drivers are liable to a fine and it should be imposed and collected no matter who the offender is." 1882: "The musical bray of the burro is heard at all hours in the vicinity of town. May his voice never become silent in this vicinity." (In 1909 it was a different story: "On and after July 17 the practice of allowing jacks or burros to run at large in the town of Breckenridge will be in violation of law. Owners of such animals will take due notice hereof and govern themselves accordingly. Such animals, if found at large, will be taken up and impounded. By order of the board of trustees.) 1882: "A California earthquake or something of the kind to break the long drawn out monotony of this section would be cheerfully welcomed."

1886: "The city trustees should pass an ordinance, or rather a resolution, ordering the arrest of all calithumpians. Whether large or small, the practice is a nuisance and should be abated." 1886: "Fine bologna sausage and odorous limberger cheese, the latter extra strong-scented, at Mrs. Mueller's.

1888: "The surveyors who originally laid out the plat of this town must have been knock-kneed, cross-eyed, left-handed and stuttered like sin, for there are no four blocks in the town on the same lines." 1888: "Painting artists are at work on the M.E. Church. Ditto on the Catholic Church. When will the Congregationalists do likewise?" "The marshal should follow up the war upon dogs; the orders should be tags or death. If we must run the risk of dog bite let it be at least a licensed dog. The practice of throwing dishwater, carcasses, manure, etc. in yards should be stopped."

1891: "Just received from California a barrel of orange cider, a delicious temperance drink, call and sample, at Gus Fox's." "If you wish to see a very fine lot of furniture, the best ever in Summit County, drop in and look at Deacon Huntress' stock. He has some daisies." "Mr. George Engle went and perpetrated matrimony on Monday last. He returned with his bride, of course the boys didn't fail to compliment him during the evening." "There are two hefties in our village whose united weights aggregate 518 pounds avoirdupois, and then our two most extended men measure together 12 feet, 9½ inches." "Go and try the bath at W. L. Marks. All new and fresh and sweet, Marks' Tonsorial parlors on Lincoln Avenue. The popular tonsorial artist, W. L. Marks, has put in two fine bath tubs so that his customers may, if they so desire, enjoy a general renovation."

1892: "At the Trustee Meeting last evening, having talked themselves dry the board adjourned to the Nugget Saloon to irrigate." "Mat Brewer, who has been sojourning in this vicinity for the last two years, departed for Denver this week. Ta, Ta."

And we say "Ta, Ta" to "Ye Editor." Had it not been for him much of the color and history of early Breckenridge would have been lost. Ta, Ta! Jonathan Cooper Fincher.

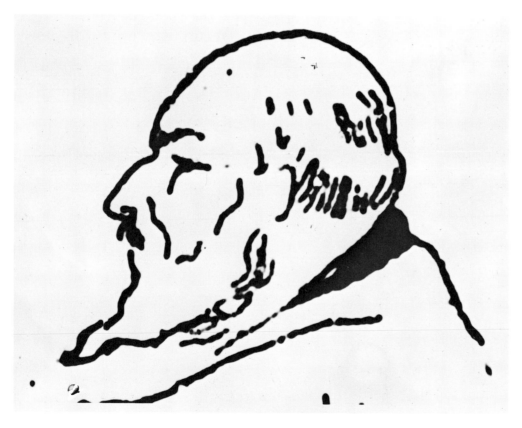

Sketch of "Ye Editor" (Jonathan Cooper Fincher), Editor and Publisher of The Summit County *Journal*. Sketch appeared in Denver *Republican*, December 7, 1895.

O. K. Gaymon, Editor Dillon *Enterprise,* wife Augusta, baby Alva, at the printing office and home at Dillon, Colorado. Another son, Melvin, has been a life-long resident of Breckenridge. Courtesy—Mr. Melvin Gaymon.

BRECKENRIDGE CHURCHES

In 1971 a member of the Catholic persuasion remarked, "I could name you fifty families in the Breckenridge area, born and raised in the Catholic faith, who seldom ever attend church. Now we have four masses and the church is filled —but they are mostly visitors and newcomers to the community." The informer added, "And I could name an equal number of Protestants who attend in the same manner." There is truth in that comment.

In 1909 Ye Editor of the newspaper observed: "Rev. William Walder will hold services in the M. E. Church. According to present arrangements services will be held in the Methodist Church once in about three weeks, and that is oftener than a great many of our good people will attend." Episcopal and Catholic services were held less frequently.

Back in 1881 the picture was somewhat different. "The church going bells of yesterday made the day seem like a Sabbath in the East. Three services in the one Church and regular service in the other. Verily, we are becoming a civilized community."

Sometimes the political, the social, or unusual happenings of the times served as motivating factors for church attendance:

One good effect of the coming political convention is that candidates who seldom visited church are now found among the faithful. Last evening, at one of the congregations in the city, there was noticed a very sedate-looking young man with a strongly marked countenance who is said to be an aspirant for clerk; a black-haired, small-sized man, dressed in blue; another one who once sported locks of light auburn color, somewhat scarce now—both candidates for judge. A tall, sycamore-like individ-

ual, said to be a candidate for sheriff, was there also. How many more aspirants were there our reporter failed to discover. The political world is excited to boiling heat; the Breckenridge churches have been well-attended.

And sometimes the unusual motivated toward church:

Yesterday there was considerable electric disturbance during a short shower. The lightning struck at several places on the hills, and on Gibson, where prospectors are thick, it created some commotion. The deputy sheriff was prostrated and considerably stunned by a shock, while his partner was knocked off his pins, and, being on the incline running into their prospect, he rolled into the workings like a ball of clay. Fortunately, aside from shock, neither of the men was injured, but they felt it was a close shave, and doubtless both will take seats near the front of the sanctuary next Sunday.

Gold-seekers opened the Valley of the Blue in the fall of 1859. Emigrant prospectors poured into the valley before winter-spring snows had fully disappeared. Itinerant preachers moved from one mining camp to another. Rev. William Howbert, Methodist preacher, came to Denver, June 14, 1860, and was immediately assigned to South Park Mission, July 6, 1860. Promptly he made a trip across the range to Blue River country. Beardsley, the Methodist historian, writes of William Howbert:

With an extra shirt in one pocket, a Testament and hymnal in another, bread and beef in a third, I started about one o'clock on foot for Blue River, crossing the Snowy Range at what is now called Boreas Pass, arriving at Breckenridge at night, stopping with Brother Oldham. I left an appointment to preach on Sunday at 4 P. M., then went on to Gold Run, where I put up with Brother Onis for the night. Sunday morning I preached at Blue River, (Spaulding Diggings—Fort Mary B.), organizing a class of six members, and at Breckenridge in the afternoon, (July 8, 1860), forming a class of seven. The Lord was with us to bless.

This was the beginning of Methodism on the Pacific Slope in Colorado. To William Howbert belongs the honor of preaching the first gospels sermons in each of the above-mentioned localities so far as is now known.

Methodism was getting a foothold in the mining camps, and we read: "The 2nd Quarterly Meeting of the M. E. Church will be held at Masonic Hall in Parksville, Georgia Gulch, on Saturday and Sunday, September seventh and eighth, 1861."

In April, 1862, John Lewis Dyer, Methodist preacher, later to become known as Father Dyer, the Snow-Shoe Itinerant, was assigned to the Blue River Mission, Summit County, for a year's ministry. This was the first full-time ministry in the Valley of the Blue.

Various religious denominations carried on spasmodic ministries in the mining camps around Breckenridge, but it was not until the 1880s that houses of worship were erected and denominational congregations formally established. In 1892 Brother Ballinger of the Como *Record* came to Breckenridge on a Sunday and was surprised "to find all the saloons open and running full blast. The church ditto." But Brother Ballinger thought the churches had the best of it as they had the biggest crowd. Exact records are not available, so the story is pieced together largely through newspaper items. The Summit County *Journal*, coming into existence 1880, presented much of the picture.

Building of church edifices did not take place in Breckenridge until the mining town had a twenty-year history. At first the type of architecture was as simple in design as country school houses that dotted mid-western plains—four walls, roof and attic space. Steeples, bells, vestibules, gothic windows were later innovations. Benches and chairs provided seating. A center chandelier of kerosene lamps, lowered and raised by chain, furnished lighting. Heating, if it could be properly termed such, was by wood-burning stove. Near the stove one blistered; farther away the worshiper shivered and snuggled deeper into his heavy coat. Watson's "fleece-lined underwear" was a winter necessity. Little change was necessary to convert church buildings into storerooms, barn or blacksmith shop, if necessity arose.

Private homes, storerooms, or a grove of trees served as preaching places before 1880. Father Dyer often preached in saloons. Lack of an imposing church edifice didn't hinder proclamation of the gospel message.

THE METHODIST CHURCH

Methodism dates its beginning to John Wesley's religious experience at Aldersgate Street, London, May 24, 1738. This experience of the "heart strangely warmed" became a motivating religious experience characteristic of Methodism.

Episcopal Methodism began in America with episcopals (bishops) considered the chief administrative officers. Thus the nomenclature, Methodist Episcopal Church. It continued under this name until the unification of the various branches of Methodism into The Methodist Church, 1939. Union with the Evangelical United Brethren Church, 1969, changed the name to The United Methodist Church. Father Dyer built the first church in Breckenridge, the Methodist Episcopal Church—often abbreviated to the "M. E. Church."

John Lewis Dyer was born March 16, 1812, in Madison County, Ohio. As a young man in Illinois he went through a soul-shattering Aldersgate experience which led to acceptance of a religious "call" into the ministry of the Methodist Episcopal Church. Ministries in Illinois, Wisconsin and Minnesota preceded his Rocky Mountain ministry.

The prospect of approaching blindness, 1861, determined a visit to Pike's Peak country before it was too late to see the wonders of this newly-opened territory. Walking from Omaha, Nebraska, to Denver, a distance of 750 miles, Dyer arrived in Denver, June 20, 1861. July 9th he completed another one hundred mile walk through the mountains and South Park to the rip-snorting mining town, Buckskin Joe, at the foot of Continental Divide. Here began a Rocky Mountain ministry of forty years, extending over much of Colorado and New Mexico.

Breckenridge was included in Dyer's 1862 Blue River Mission appointment. There was another appointment to Breckenridge in 1879 that extended to August, 1880. The second gold boom of the area began in 1880. It was during this pastorate that the historic Father Dyer Methodist Church was built. Father Dyer tells the story:

In 1879 I was appointed to the Breckenridge Circuit. I had spoken of that county, and its need of a preacher, but when I heard my name read out, with no missionary appropriation, to an entirely outside and new work, I felt hurt. To be sent to the hardest circuit at my time of life, (67 years) and not on an equal footing with other preachers of the conference, was rough on me, and unfeeling in those who sent me. But my old-time loyalty stood me in hand, and I concluded to go and do the best I could for a year.

The cabinet named the circuit after the county, and the presiding elder did not know where to address a letter to me. Probably he did not know the size of the county, which, beginning forty-five miles west of Denver, extends to Utah, and north to Wyoming. Since then seven counties have been made out of it; and in all of them there are, at this writing, only two preachers of our Church, and they are supplies.

The preacher thought it time to secure a lot for a church. He canvassed all the town; but none had a lot to give. One was offered away out, but was refused. Giving a back-lot for a church had played out with me.

In the fall, 1879, I bought a lot and a cabin. It was about one hundred and fifty feet deep by fifty wide. The Town Company undertook to change the survey and take two-thirds of it from me under pretense that the county had a claim on it. They even undertook to fence it up; but when they began, I began too. I hired men to put in posts; but as soon as I turned my back they came to my men, within forty feet of my house, and told them they would send an officer and arrest them. My hands quit. After dinner I went to digging postholes myself. The Town Company's representative came with two witnesses, and warned me to stop work. I never laid down my pick, but told them I was a man, and a law-abiding man at that, and his were as good witnesses as I wanted; and I warned him before them to keep off my lot and to leave. By this time the witnesses started, and he followed. He was the company's commissioner; and was very good when he found he could not bulldoze me.

I gave half my lot to the trustees to build a church on. We carried a subscription paper till I got enough to start on; and went to the saw-mills, got all the lumber I could, and we went to work and put up a house twenty-five by fifty feet, posts sixteen feet high, and inclosed it. I nailed the first shingle, and did more work on it than any other man.

While I went to conference. August 12-15, at Georgetown, the friends finished the roof and put the floor down; and the next Sunday we had service in the first church on the Western Slope in our conference, with a good organ. We had no aid as yet from the Church Extension Society, which gave two hundred and fifty dollars after I left. This was a year of toil, and no pay to speak of—about two hundred dollars was all; and I paid traveling expenses, and did more hard work than I ever did before, take it altogether. I left about thirty-five members. Including the lot, the church cost me all of three hundred and fifty dollars.

Rev. J. F. Coffman finished the church and built the small log parsonage north of the church building. Conference gave him $300 toward salary, "and having the office of school superintendent, made out to live. The unsettled condition of mining-camps is unfavorable to the keeping up of religious societies." At the end of Rev. Coffman's three-year pastorate the report was as follows: "present roll of members—28; the church building cost nearly $1,200 in money. Considerable labor was donated. The log parsonage cost about $400. All has been paid. The estimated salaries of the pastor the last three years were as follows: First year, $950; second year, $1,000; third year, $1,000. The amount received was: First year, $900; second year, $860; third year, $740. At the present date, July 21, 1883, there is a deficit of $450."

Much of the history of Breckenridge's Methodist Church is centered around its builder, Father John L. Dyer. In the spring of 1880, while the church was in the process of being built, Father Dyer aided two young prospectors "whom fortune had used roughly." He helped them build a small, hand-hewn log cabin on his property— "a log pen, ten or twelve feet square, just large enough for them to stand up in and make a stopping-place." (Later the 12x12 cabin was used by the church for storage of coal and wood. When threatened with demolition in 1968 it was moved to the writer's property at Frisco, Colorado; restored, and now serves as the writing studio of these Breckenridge historical stories.)

January, 1881, Father Dyer started building

a cabin up Indiana Gulch near his mining claims, making the six mile trip from Breckenridge and returning each day. February 19th he moved his wife, and the last of his goods, into the new cabin home. In the vicinity of Dyer's cabin the little town of Dyerville (Dyersville) sprang up. Rubble and remains of Warrior's Mark and Dyerville are still in evidence.

But Breckenridge and the little church he had built had strong drawing power on Father Dyer. Coming down to Breckenridge from Dyerville Father Dyer preached on numerous occasions. It was said, "The mere mention of his name is all the recommendation necessary in order to insure a full house."

In the spring (1886) I went to Breckenridge to look after some interests. I found our Church without a preacher, and told them I would stop and preach for them till the presiding elder would supply them. It resulted in my staying the year out. The Church people were few in number, and hardly any well-to-do. Such a place, I am sorry to say, has few friends with the preachers. I tried to do what I could for them.

It was two years before I was relieved. I preached at Breckenridge twice on each Sunday, and at Lincoln about once in two weeks; and on week evenings at Montezuma, Dillon, Kokomo, and Robinson, preaching an average of four times a week.

There were three or four hundred people at Breckenridge, and the offices were well sprinkled with gamblers and saloon-keepers. There were about nine saloons, and all had card-tables. They had been in the habit of taking the organ out of the church to their balls. About dark one night I heard something in the church, and ran out. A wagon was backed up to the door, and the organ was almost loaded. I objected, and was told that they had leave from the officers of the Church. But I was firm, and they left without it. I speak of these things to show how little regard people had for sacred things, and what a preacher had to contend with, and the material he had to work on. Some would say that such should not have the gospel preached to them. But I think they ought to have both love and the gospel. O, may God send men after his own heart, who can thunder his wrath as well as display the glories of his great salvation!

This last two-years' term in Summit County was commenced in my seventy-third year, and closed in my seventy-sixth. At this age I felt it a tax too heavy to bear. But where can rest be found? For an old man who has always kept going, to stop is distressing, and time hangs heavy on his mind. Only the grace of God can keep him in a cheerful mood.

News items during this two years' voluntary ministry in Breckenridge spoke of Father Dyer as "the old veteran"—"the old stalwart"—"the pioneer Methodist preacher"—"Father Dyer, the venerable preacher of the Methodist Church." In November, 1886, Father Dyer was in a ruction with the town trustees regarding ringing the fire alarm bell for church purposes. When the privilege was withdrawn, Father Dyer, undaunted, rang the bell next Sunday morning. Father Dyer made later visits to Breckenridge—1891-1892 and 1899. The 1899 visit was probably the last; his death occurred June 16, 1901.

Breckenridge *Bulletin*   September 22, 1899

Rev. Father Dyer made one of his itinerant preaching tours during the week to some of the mining towns. The reverend gentleman bears his many years well in spite of the accident a few years ago which compels him to get around on crutches. He has known and visited Breckenridge for thirty-seven years.

Rev. G. E. Tuttle came to the Breckenridge pulpit, following Father Dyer's last pastorate. The pattern of problems to plague the church for years was already established—rapid-changing population in the mining town, difficulty of financing a ministry, lack of interest in church attendance and activity, little willingness of a minister to sacrifice time and energy. Rev. Tuttle's ministry was of a year's duration:

Daily Journal   July 14, 1888

Everybody should attend the M. E. Church tomorrow evening and hear brother Tuttle's farewell sermon, and they should remember to take something along to put into the contribution basket, not a nickel or a dime, but a good full-faced iron dollar. There is not a man or woman in the congregation but could afford to drop the biggest silver coin made and very many could and should make the color of gold show in the basket. Remember the collection is not to buy candles or wood, but to pay a year's salary, remember that.

Breckenridge Methodist Church, for the most part, followed old-time Methodism. Father

Dyer was concerned primarily about "soul-saving." His practice was to preach the Word burning hot—the wrath of God as well as the love of God. Mining camp population shifted rapidly; preach for a decision while there was an opportunity! Dancing, card-playing, salooning, the social ball, and many forms of recreation were taboo. Sabbath observance was strictly regimented. Such a policy provoked criticism; sometimes it erupted into open opposition. The pastorate of Rev. Florida Passmore provoked a dynamiting of the church bell and burning of the preacher in effigy. Rev. William M. Dye came later to Breckenridge, hailed as "by far the ablest minister Breckenridge ever had." His was another one-year ministry. Rev. Dye preached a series of sermons—The Five Great Sins of Breckenridge: Sabbath Desecration—Indifference—The Dance—Card-Playing—The Licensed Saloon. On the matter of Indifference he pointed out that there was "but one resident minister in Summit County." Sermon topics were not announced beforehand. Somehow or other "Sin No. 4"—Card playing—leaked out. "Someone circulated a report—no church Sunday evening—with the result the audience was much smaller. The minister alluded to the nature of this report in not very pleasant terms." (Breckenridge had its afternoon and evening Euchre Clubs and also the 500 Clubs.) Closing the saloons on Sunday was a hard blow; Rev. Dye was the instigator. The Breckenridge *Bulletin* reported after the Sunday closing: " 'Twas a Dry One!" "No place to go, except to church, and to go to his church is to go to Dye." The "moulder of morality" made up his mind not to return to Breckenridge for a second year:

Breckenridge *Bulletin*   August 22, 1908

During the term of Rev. Dye's pastorate he has done more to build up the Methodist church than had been accomplished since the days of Rev. Passmore. His action in closing the saloons according to law made him some enemies, but few will question that he thought it to be his duty as a minister of the gospel. The community will be the loser by virtue of his removal from this place.

Revival and temperance meetings at the Methodist Church were attended with mixed purposes—some for soul-searching, others for entertainment. One couldn't be sure who was coming for what. The Widow Van Cott conducted a week of services in 1886; Father Dyer considered the meetings highly successful; the church was packed to overflowing for every service. Ye Editor encouraged Breckenridgians to attend and spoke complimentary words about Widow Van Cott and her efforts. But he couldn't resist reporting items in lighter vein:

Last night at Mrs. Van Cott's services many shed tears whom it was thought were past that period of sensibility. Think of a cadaver crying over his sins, but it is said such was the case, not but what there were sins enough, nevertheless the crying reminded one of the traditional crocodile.

Sheriff Sam Blair broke over his usual custom and last night went to church—did anybody see a star fall?

Mrs. Van Cott's meeting at the M. E. Church last evening was well attended and very interesting. The church-goers of Breckenridge are not very emotional and sensational services are not likely to add to the sheaves of the harvester.

Tomorrow afternoon Mrs. Van Cott purposes addressing the men of the congregation alone. Now the women all wonder what in the world she is going to say to them, several stalwart married daughters of Eve are taking lessons as to tacking their hair up short, and squirting tobacco juice so as to pass as masculines on that occasion, moderate sized mens suits will be in demand for a few hours.

The Como *Record* jibed the editor of Breckenridge *Journal*: "Mrs. Van Cott was very successful in her revival meetings at Breckenridge until Col. Fincher of the *Journal* put in appearance. Then the portly revivalist gathered her skirts about her, jumped out the back window and broke for the woods."

Father Dyer's report was:

There could not have been a more general interest awakened among miners and citizens than there was in Breckenridge. Every meeting was well attended, and deep interest was shown from the start. Twenty joined; some were reclaimed and some converted, and the little society was revived. If she could have stayed another week, from all appearances, much more good could have been accomplished. She held services twice each day, and worked incessantly.

Another revivalist, Miss L. M. White, followed the temperance theme. In her two weeks of meetings 113 signed the pledge.

Social life, within accepted boundaries, was permitted in the Methodist Church—strawberry socials, oyster suppers, musicals and programs. The Christmas Tree program and party was a community affair, held in the M. E. Church. All children were invited to participate and receive the Christmas goodies and gifts from Santa Claus. But when a Methodist strawberry social ended in the G. A. R. Hall, and the gay blades tried to take over for the regular Friday night dance, opposition was forthcoming. Father Dyer insisted they were dancing direct to hell. The hassle finally ended with "the dancists withdrawing at a late hour, and lighting up the Fireman's Hall and enjoying themselves until the 'wee sma hours.' "

The two decades, 1880 to 1900, were the boom years for Breckenridge churches. Attendance and interest were at highest peaks during these years. The 20th century saw many short-term ministries and frequent use of supply pastors. Not many of the denominations offered regularly scheduled services. The 1930 "depression years" brought a severe slump in church activity. Breckenridge Methodist Church became a "Community Church" under Methodist sponsorship. Later it became a "Federated Church" —Presbyterians and Methodists uniting forces in Breckenridge and Leadville. (Four years were under Presbyterian leadership; four years under Methodist.) In 1965 the Breckenridge church became self-supporting with a resident ministry and the Leadville Church became full-time Presbyterian. The church at Breckenridge is now known as the Father Dyer United Methodist Church. Church ministries had difficult times in mountain mining towns.

ST. MARY'S CATHOLIC CHURCH

The early history of St. Mary's Church was not easy to uncover. Efforts have been partially rewarded through old newspapers and the generous assistance of Father Francis Hornung, Holy Cross Abbey, Canon City, Colorado. A few items of interest eluded research efforts.

We assume that the Catholic Church provided a ministry to the hundreds that flocked to Breckenridge Blue River Diggings during the gold rush of 1860-1861. The *Miners' Record*, published at Tarryall, Park County, mentioned, September 14, 1861, that the "minister of the Catholic Church in Denver is on a tour through the mountains, visiting members of his church who are so situated that they are unable to attend the regular service, and to establish points where occasional services may be held in different localities." Whether Breckenridge was included in the tour was not mentioned. Other than the three-month *Miners' Record* mountain newspapers did not come into existence until 1879-1880 and some of these early papers are not available to researchers.

The Breckenridge *Daily Journal*, Wednesday, October 12, 1881, provides the first substantiated report of the work of the Catholic Church in Breckenridge—a visit from Bishop Machebeuf:

Bishop Machebeuf

Among the arrivals in Breckenridge last evening was the venerable and well beloved head of the Catholic church in Colorado.

During the evening many of the prominent members of the church called on him at his rooms at the Denver House, and conferred with him in regard to their mutual interests in this section. This venerable prelate, one of the most profound scholars and logicians of the age, has given for years his best abilities, his vast powers of mind and education, to the building up and advancing the interests of the Catholic church in Colorado and New Mexico. He travels to the most insignificant parish, listens to the most trifling details, and with most lofty self-abnegation journeys over mountain passes and through the plains to reach the humblest and the lowest of his church. With his talents, his acquirements and reputation he might have taken high rank in populous and refined communities, but like the apostles of whom he is the follower, he has taken upon his shoulders the burden of building up and consolidating the missionary work in this diocese.

Our place is honored by his presence, and we trust that all Catholics, Protestants, Free-thinkers and No-thinkers will remember the presence of this noble soul, whose only aim is to purify, enlighten and improve the country.

Another item appeared in the same issue of the *Daily Journal*: "Father Thomas M. Cahill, who arrived last evening with the bishop, left at noon today for Como."

Notices appeared in the *Daily Journal* of a Catholic service to be held, October 23, 1881: Friday, October 21: "There will be services held in the Catholic Church on Sunday next, at which Father Cahill will officiate." Saturday, October 22: The attention of the members of the Catholic Church is called to the fact that services will be held in the church, corner of High Street and Washington Avenue, to-morrow morning. The Rev. Thomas M. Cahill will officiate."

It appears that a church building was quickly erected on the corner of High and Washington in the period between Bishop Machebeuf's visit, October 11-12, and Sunday, October 23rd. Further news items reveal that it was a shell construction, lacking finishing and furnishing. No news items appear regarding the actual construction of the building.

Father Cahill conducted services somewhat on a once-a-month basis. The next service, after October 23rd, was December 11th. A Christmas Service was held by Father Cahill on Sunday, December 25th. The *Daily Journal* gave another item, December 29th: "The performance at the Catholic Church at midnight on Christmas Eve is being highly spoken of by all who attended. For a first attempt and in a new camp the effort was highly commendable."

Father Cahill conducted services Sunday, February 19, 1882. The same newspaper that announced the February service included another item: "Rev. Father Cahill came over in the coach yesterday. His genial countenance beamed on us in our newspaper sanctum. The Catholics on his circuit are fortunate in having a pastor who combines sound learning and rare executive ability with remarkable suavity of manner." Thereafter, Father Cahill officiated March 12th, April 2nd, and May 6th. This is the last time Father Cahill's name is mentioned in the newspaper items. Enlarged activities start appearing in the newspaper columns, bespeaking not only a change of priests, but also the stationing of a priest in Breckenridge. An anouncement appeared in the Summit County *Journal*, May 30, 1930, telling of "The Good Old Days—May 24-29, 1882: "Rt. Rev. Bishop Machebeuf of Denver will be here on Thursday and will hold services on Friday in the Catholic Church. Rev. Father Chapuis is already here and will probably be stationed at this place."

Saturday, July 8, 1882: "There will be services at the Catholic Church to-morrow at 10 o'clock a.m. and mass at 8 o'clock Monday morning for the Altar Society." Thursday, July 13, 1882, there was announcement:

A FAIR

It will be with pleasure that our citizens will learn that the Catholic congregation of this city purpose holding a fair to raise funds to properly complete their pleasant little church on High Street.

The church has been used for holding services for a year, but is not properly finished; it needs lining, papering, painting and furnishing with seats, etc., and, the proposed fair will be held for the purpose of accomplishing these results. The exact date cannot yet be given but will be somewhere from the 20 to the 25 of August and will be continued for two or three days. Anyone wishing to co-operate with the ladies getting up this commendable fair will be thankfully welcomed. Apply to any lady or gentleman belonging to the church for further information.

It is proposed to close the fair with a grand ball which will, if possible, exceed any similar preceeding event given in the town.

The coming of the railroad to Breckenridge seemed to change plans for the Fair and Ball. The *Daily Journal*, Wednesday, July 26, gave a big announcement of the Sunday services of July 30, 1882: "Catholic church services for next Sunday will be as follows: at 8 o'clock a.m. mass and preaching in English. After the 10 o'clock services a meeting will be held to complete final arrangement for the railroad celebration ball for the benefit of the church. It will be seen in our advertising columns that our Catholic friends will give a railroad celebration ball in honor of the arrival of the iron-horse in the valley of the Blue. The event is well worthy of celebration and the purpose to which the proceeds is to be devoted is one worthy of general support. We trust they may meet with entire success." The announcement of the Sunday services was also printed in Italian for the benefit of the many Italian workers on the railroad. The large advertisement announced: "Railroad Celebration Ball—In Aid of the Catholic Church. A Grand Ball will be given at the Fireman's Hall on Tuesday evening, August 1, 1882, in celebration of the arrival of the locomotive and cars in Breckenridge. Preparations for a grand time are being made."

Father James E. Chapuis, a French Canadian, began his pastorate in Breckenridge mid-year, 1882 and continued until mid-December, 1886. Father Chapuis was both visionary and promoter; his plans for Catholicism in Breckenridge were large-scale. During his pastorate he asked for establishment of a hospital and school by the Benedictine Sisters; surprisingly to many the request was granted. Through his efforts Breckenridge had a Saint Joseph Hospital and Saint Gertrude Academy. Also the *Daily Journal* reported, "Father Chapuis expects an assistant, an old father, who will be able to officiate at the daily services required by the changes proposed. Hereafter a new and more efficient choir will be organized and perfected for regular services."

Father Chapuis received his assistant, but he was a young priest. *Daily Journal*, January 27, 1883, reported: "Bishop Machebeuf has appointed Father Carrigan, a young and newly ordained priest, as an assistant to Father Chapuis of this parish. The appointee will celebrate his first mass in the Catholic Church to-morrow morning. Father Carrigan hails from Auburn, New York, where his parents still reside." Church Calendar in the *Daily Journal* reported until August 18, 1883—Rev. J. E. Chapuis, Pastor and Rev. J. P. Carrigan, Assistant. August 18th it was reported, "Rev. J. P. Carrigan returned to Denver and will probably stay there." A Rev. Father Ley was the assistant in 1886, and the two —Chapuis and Ley—left Breckenridge in December, 1886. Father Chapuis' grandiose dream included a monastery and college in Breckenridge.

> Fathers Rhabanus Gutmann, O. S. B., and Eusebius Geiger, O. S. B., arrived at Breckenridge, December 18, 1886, at 6:00 A. M. The snow was three to four feet deep. Mr. John McNamara received them and conducted them to the St. Gertrude Academy where they celebrated the sacrifice of Mass, took breakfast and then took possession of Rev. Chapuis' house.

Father John Slattery, a recent priest at St. Mary's, researched its early days, relating Father Rhabanus' description of the rectory, the church and the people of Breckenridge:

> Our house is roomy enough, but cold as a dog-kennel. The house of the Sisters is not much better. On the outskirts of Breckenridge a church-like structure stands, a mere skeleton, which is a disgrace to the name of St. Mary. The church was put under roof six years ago and is still in *statu quo*. The location of the church is poor and the Bishop wants to move it. The church, in its present condition, cannot be used at all. (Father Rhabanus held first services in the Sisters' convent chapel.) Of the people, Father Rhabanus said: It seems as if all the roustabouts, rascals, loose women, adulterers, etc., etc., find their way to Breckenridge.

Father Francis Hornung, Holy Cross Abbey, Canon City, Colorado, supplied the following additional information of early endeavors in Breckenridge:

> The fathers related that the rectory was 1,000 feet from the church, so that it was often very hard, and in winter impossible, to get to the church on account of the deep snow. Also, the Sisters' hospital and school were in another part of town, with consequent difficulty in attending them in winter. The titles of some of the churches were as follows: Breckenridge, St. Mary's; Alma, St. Patrick's; Como, St. Benedict's; Montezuma, St. Edward's; and Robinson, Our Lady of Snow.
>
> These missionary priests and their successors, Fathers Rupert Tragesser, Boniface Wirtner and Modestus Wirtner, labored in this wild territory for four and a half years. But within a few months both Bishop Machebeuf and the Benedictines realized that a monastery and college would never flourish there."

The first winter was very hard for Fathers Rhabanus and Eusebius. The rectory was poor shelter against winter's coldness. Snows were deep and travel difficult. Both had to be hospitalized because of illness. Father Eusebius had a severe cold and tried to doctor himself while Father Rhabanus was in the hospital. He was supposed to stay in a warm bed and get rid of the cold by perspiration. But to do so he would have starved or frozen to death, for he had no one to take care of him. The fire almost went out; he had to get up and change perspired clothing in a cold room and tend the fire—result, the cold got worse instead of better. Second winter was better, for they insulated their house against stormy blasts. The summers were beautiful—but much too short; winters came soon and stayed long; temperature was cold, snows were deep.

St. Mary's Church knew hardship. At first planks on nail kegs provided the seating. There was little provision for warmth against winter's cold. Easter offering amounted to $2.27. Some of the offerings were in foodstuffs, otherwise the priests would have starved.

Father Chapuis had another project that did not reach fruition during his pastorate—the moving of the Catholic Church from High Street and Washington Avenue to a different location. The Church was picturesque against its mountain background of greenery, but it was too far out on the edge of town. There had been talk about moving the building, but it didn't materialize. The lots on the northeast corner of French and Lincoln, adjoining St. Gertrude's Academy, were under consideration. *Daily Journal*, November 12, 1886, mentioned it again: "The removal of the Catholic Church to the lots at the corner of French and Lincoln is again being talked about, perhaps it may be carried out this time." But 1886 was not to be the year, nor was French and Lincoln to be the new location.

1887 saw an important happening in the Breckenridge Catholic Church. Postulant Minnie Brandt took the veil as a full Sister in the Order of Saint Benedict. The occasion was reported in the Summit County *Journal*, October 22nd: "The ceremony of taking the veil at the Catholic Church Sunday drew to the little church as many observers as could find standing room. The services were more than usually impressive and the veteran Machebeuf never appeared to better advantage before this community. Since the *Journal's* last visit to the church the interior of the building has been lined and canvassed and papered and otherwise arranged so as to afford proper accommodations in which it was formerly deficient. The painting of the windows, while not particularly artistic, is a decided improvement and breaks the glare of the sun and gives a much more pleasant light throughout the room."

Easter, April 1, 1888, brought forth elaborate preparations in building appearance and worship service. "The Sisters and some of the male members of the Catholic Church have put in considerable time decorating the church for Easter services. The church is nicely papered, inside the altar is carpeted, and at the rear of the church a raised platform has been enclosed with curtains where the choir can be kept together and separate from the congregation. The choir

for Easter ceremonies will consist of Sister Anastasia, organist; Waldo Osgood, 1st violin; John Osgood, violincello. Sopranos—Sisters Adelaide and Pauline, Misses Brune and Spencer; Altos—Mrs. Montgomery and Miss Marshall; Tenors—Mr. C. B. Cramer and F. M. Conesny; Basses—W. S. Montgomery and John McNamara." (Sister Pauline made her perpetual vows at Breckenridge.)

"Ye Editor" had been prodding the Catholics about painting the church—"The Catholics have done pretty well, but their church would be a model of beauty with its background of a green hillside, if the church edifice was only painted white and then the surroundings and approach to the church should be graded and grassed, with proper walks. The church could be made the most inviting place in town with a little money and labor." July 11, 1888, the *Daily Journal* reported: "The Catholic church since its painting looks like another building. It seems strange that our Christian friends are so slack about making their little church edifices look cheerful and attractive."

1888 had another notable happening. All references in the Breckenridge newspapers spoke of "The Catholic Church" or "The Catholic Church of Breckenridge." Saturday, May 19th, contains the first mention of "St. Mary's Church." Thereafter announcements appeared in the Church Calendar: "St. Mary's Catholic Church of Breckenridge. Services 1st and 3rd Sunday of the month. Early Mass 7 a.m. in Sisters chapel. High Mass 10 a.m. Sunday School 3 p.m. Benediction 3:30 p.m.

July 26, 1890, the Catholics of Breckenridge purchased Lots 10 and 11 in Block 11, Abbett Placer, from Clara C. Westerman for $250. The instrument was filed August 22, 1890, and signed by Nicholas C. Matz, Bishop of Denver in trust for the Catholics. (County Clerk records, Book 55, page 330) This is the present location of St. Mary's Church. We assume that the moving of St. Mary's Church from its location at High Street and Washington Avenue to the present location on French Street, between Lincoln and Washington Avenues, took place shortly after the purchase of the lots. Newspapers of the time are missing, so no exact date can be determined. The move could have taken place during the pastorate of Boniface Wirtner or Modestus Wirtner (Wertner). The Summit County *Journal*, June 18,

1892, reported: "Father Wertner left Breckenridge for Pueblo. He has been parish priest in Breckenridge for the past two or three years. Rev. C. M. Algier succeeds him."

1899 was another noteworthy year for St. Mary's Church. The Summit County *Journal*, July 22nd, had an interesting item: "The priest and members of the Catholic Church at this place are endeavoring to raise sufficient funds to purchase a bell for their church. As they are sorely in need of a bell, their ambition is a laudable one, and we have no doubt but that they will readily gather the required amount. Procure a creditable one; one with a clear, religious tone. In fact, one whose sweet, melodious peals will tend to draw sinners as well as saints to the house of worship —in contrast to certain bells that we know of, the broken and blanky, blank, blank sounds of which often drive men to strong drink and detest the inside of a church." August 12th had good news: "Father Robinson, of St. Mary's Church, returned Tuesday from Denver, where he purchased a clear, sweet-toned bell for the Catholic Church. The bell has already arrived here and will be hung in proper place within a few days." September 29th: "The Catholic Church Society is building a belfry and cupola on the church, which will greatly improve the looks of the edifice." The blessing of the bell took place (according to the Breckenridge *Bulletin*) on Sunday, October 15th, in conjunction with a confirmation service, conducted by Bishop Matz. The Bishop also blessed a statute donated to St. Mary's by Mrs. McMannis. October 20th: (Breckenridge *Bulletin*) "The cupola for the new Catholic Church bell is now complete and the sweet-toned herald of holy worship will soon be pealing forth its musical notes of invitation. Father Robinson has worked with untiring energy to secure this necessary adjunct to St. Mary's and is entitled to much credit for its acquisition." November 18, 1899: "Father Robinson read out the receipts and expenditures for church repairs for the past two months. The amount collected was $210; the expenditures for the bell, bell tower, paint, etc., were $314; $90 is the amount still due for the construction of the belfry."

One additional item bears mentioning: Father J. C. McCourt followed Father Robinson as Breckenridge parish priest. Father McCourt was brother to the famous Elizabeth McCourt— "Baby Doe"—wife of H. A. W. Tabor, Colorado's never-to-be-forgotten gold and silver multi-millionaire.

The Catholic Church, like the sister Protestant Churches of Breckenridge, had its difficult years. It began under great handicaps; it has continued through the years in like manner.

....CONGREGATIONAL CHURCH

The Congregational denomination was the third to build a church in Breckenridge:—Father Dyer M. E. Church (spring and summer of 1880); St. Mary's Catholic Church (summer and early fall of 1881); and the Congregational Church (late fall of 1881). A church notice, Summit County *Leader*, dated September 11, 1880, indicated that Catholics and Congregationalists had been holding services somewhere in Breckenridge previous to the building of their houses of worship. The Congregationalists had services every Sabbath at 11 a.m., Rev. George F. Chipperfield, pastor; the Methodist Episcopal, regular services every Sabbath at 8 p.m., Rev. J. L. Dyer, pastor; and Catholic services were being held every fourth Sabbath, at 9:30 a.m., Rev. Father Thomas Cahill, priest.

In May, 1881, there was a house-warming party for the new Congregational minister, Rev. W. F. Bickford. It was a well-attended pleasant affair "at his residence on the apex of Nigger Hill." In June, Congregational services were being held "in the M. E. Church, French Street near Lincoln Avenue, on alternate Sundays— preaching at 11 a.m. and 7 p.m." Sunday School was in the M. E. Church every Sunday at 2 p.m.

Within a few months the Congregationalists were building their own church. In late August, 1881, it was reported: "The Congregational church building has been enclosed and the roof boards put on. It will require two weeks to complete the structure." October 5th: "The Congregational Church will be completed in a few days." The Congregational Society gratefully acknowledged the receipt of financial aid from friends at home and abroad. An oyster supper was planned by the ladies of the Society for October 27th— proceeds to be given to the building fund.

The Congregational structure was built on the corner of French Street and Lincoln Avenue —probably the north west corner, which is now lawn on the Court House property. First religious services were scheduled for Sunday, October 30, 1881. "Congregational Church, corner of French

Street and Lincoln Avenue, W. F. Bickford, pastor. Services at 11 a.m. All are cordially invited."

Services were held before the building was entirely completed. There was a December 12, 1881, newspaper notice: "Painters and paper hangers are at work on the new church this week. They expect to finish the house by Thursday night, when the Ladies Social Circle will at once begin preparations for the Fair to be held at the church. The Fair will continue two days and evenings, December 20 and 21. There will be singing by a select choir and entertainment provided." The following week had another newspaper article:

The new Congregational Church is rapidly approaching completion, Clark is putting on the paper which will be tastefully ornamental and when completed will make the size of the room appear much greater than it really is. The whole building is calculated to get the most service possible out of the room. The gallery over the reading room and the folding doors by which the reading room and auditorium of the church can be thrown into one gives a seating room of at least one-half more than appears at first sight, then the pulpit being recessed leaves the full size of the building partially duplicated for use of the audience. The interior of the church corresponds with the outside in tasty arrangement and when completed will be an inviting spot wherein to spend a few hours each week in devotional exercises. Mr. Nashold, the builder, deserves credit for the workmanlike manner in which every advantage has been taken to utilize and beautify the building. The congregation should receive the cordial support of the public for their worthy and acceptable contributions to the useful ornaments of the town.

Moving buildings seemed to be a popular pastime in old Breckenridge. Churches were not spared by the building mover either. September 2, 1882, church notices were reading: "Congregational Church on the corner of Harris Street, between Lincoln and Washington Avenues, Rev. W. F. Bickford, pastor." An application for a loan is recorded in Summit County Records "To buy on East side of Harris Street, Lot 4, Block 7. Also an organization of the Congregational Church is recorded by the 34 ft front by 36 ft deep church on Harris Street. In the organization of the church B. M. Newcomb and Dr. C. C. Velsey were elected trustees; J. N. Paisley, treasurer; deacon, J. N. Paisley; clerk, W. F. Bickford. In the early spring an organ was purchased, following a town canvass for donations, largely due to the efforts of Mrs. Charles E. Wood.

The Congregational Church was well attended at first and promoted an extensive social program. The July 22, 1887, *Daily Journal* reported:

The Congregational Church now has a full choir accompanied with a cornet and the music is excellent. Mr. C. B. Cramer is the chorister, Professor Fryer presides at the organ and Mr. Hart, of the telegraph office, plays the cornet. Those who love good music should attend the Congregational Church. Service every Sabbath morning at 11 o'clock and in the evening at 7:30.

Interest and attendance ebbed in 1887 and the Congregational Church was struggling. Then, October 1, 1887, Rev. William C. Gibbons became pastor and church life was invigorated. Dr. Gibbons was, undoubtedly, the outstanding minister of Breckenridge Congregational Church. He greeted the community through the columns of the *Daily Journal*:

A Card to the Public from Dr. Gibbons

Oct. 1, 1887

Friends of Breckenridge. I have come among you to preach the gospel of love and good works as I understand it from the teachings of Jesus Christ. I am not sent here by any association or superintendent, but by invitation of some of your citizens. I am not here to preach any especial church doctrine, theological exegesis or confession of faith. I have a simple creed. I believe in the fatherhood of one God, and the brotherhood of all men. A man's evil ways does not in the nature of things divorce me from this relationship. I would be pleased to have you attend the Congregational church providing you do not attend any other. To the boys working in the mines I would say: dust off your clothes, never mind your boots, but come to church. The seats are free, the gospel songs are good, and we will try and preach you into the kingdom of love and truth. An hour spent with us on Sunday evening will do you good, revive the memories of tender childhood, the dear old home, dearer because it is so far away, the ever blessed memory of mother will seem to hover over us in such a place at such a time.

On next Sunday evening, October 2nd, the subject of my lecture will be "Creation." Preaching in the morning as usual.

On the following Sunday evening, October 9th, I contemplate giving a temperance address in G. A. R. Hall. Subject, "My own experiences, or foot prints on the sands of time."

Dr. Gibbons made valiant effort, but the financial and spiritual results were not up to expectation. The town prodder, Ye Editor of the newspaper, 1888, reminded the worshipers on Harris Street—"a few dollars worth of paint would improve the looks of the cosy little Congregational Church."

Looking back to June 9, 1886, the Breckenridge *Daily Journal* sounded another note of church-building activity: "There is talk of buying lots and erecting an Episcopal church and parsonage. The more the merrier." Lots were purchased, but church and parsonage were delayed. The Congregational Church was used frequently for Episcopalian services as early as July, 1887. In September and October, 1891, the Episcopalians were using the Congregational Church for Sunday School, in addition to morning and evening worship services. November 28, 1891, the announcement appeared in the newspaper: "We are pleased to learn that our Episcopal friends have purchased the Congregational Church."

The Breckenridge Congregational Church apparently disbanded; all mention of it ceased with the selling of the church.

ST. JOHN THE BAPTIST EPISCOPAL CHURCH

Members of the Episcopalian faith were in Breckenridge area from its beginning. As early as August, 1861, the Right Reverend Bishop Talbot of the Episcopal Church visited Tarryall, South Park, and other mining camps of the region. Whether he crossed the range to Breckenridge is not known, but Silverthorns, and undoubtedly other Episcopalians were in the area. Religious services were often held in the Breckenridge Silverthorn Hotel, but were not under the auspices of any particular denomination. Whenever any itinerant minister came to town the hotel was available for religious services.

Episcopal services were being conducted in Breckenridge the summer of 1886. The Rev. Mr. Prentiss, of the Episcopal Church, Leadville, was scheduled to preach in the M. E. Church, Tuesday evening, May 24th. Bishop Spalding had ministered to his Episcopalian flock at an earlier date in the M. E. Church. Bishop Spalding was to hold morning and evening services in the G. A. R. Hall, Sunday, June 13th, at which time he administered baptism, confirmation and holy communion. June 27th, Episcopal Services were held, morning and evening, at Fireman's Hall. At this time there was considerable talk of buying lots and erecting an Episcopal church and rectory. In fact, a first step was taken in July, 1886:

The Episcopalian congregation of this city has purchased the frame building which has long stood unoccupied on the north east corner of Lincoln and French. It will be removed across the avenue and remodeled and fitted for a chapel.

The little chapel didn't materialize. July, 1887, there was more agitation for building a church. "It is decided by the friends of the Episcopal church to proceed at once to secure, by subscription and otherwise, sufficient money to erect a new church in this city." Rev. J. A. Antrim came and conducted services in the Congregational Church, July 21, 1887, having in mind a building program for the Episcopalians.

The little church was well filled and the hearers were well satisfied with the service. The ladies of the guild, who are exerting themselves to secure regular services, are entitled to the thanks of the community. Mrs. Laws, as president, and Mrs. Veene as an able assistant, have labored long and persistently to secure the establishment of a congregation here, and if finally successful, will be entitled to kindly remembrance.

Work was started on the erection of a Sunday School building on the lots, corner of French and Lincoln:

The Ladies Guild have decided to erect a small building on the rear of their lots on French Street, for the convenience of the Guild and also for Sunday School purposes. Next season they hope to be able to erect a nice little church upon the front portion of their lots. The present undertaking is in no way to be considered a church building.

By mid-November the building had been erected, enclosed and roofed. Ye Editor remarked the following summer: "The new building on Lincoln Street, opposite the sisters' school, should be finished. In its present condition, filled with shavings, it is an invitation for some incendiary to try the virtue of a match." The building program of the Episcopalian congregation remained at a standstill.

In the fall of 1891 Episcopalians were holding services quite regularly in the Congregational Church on Harris Street. The Reverend Francis Byrne conducted morning and evening services, September 20th. Sunday School was at 10:00 a.m. Rev. Charles W. Hodder conducted services Sundays, October 18 and November 1st. The announcement came November 28, 1891:

> We are pleased to learn that our Episcopal friends have purchased the Congregational Church and lot. The building will be removed to the lots corner of French and Lincoln Avenue where considerable additions thereto will be made. The station will be known as the Mission of St. John the Evangelist of Denver.

December 12, 1891, Summit County *Journal* brought additional news:

> The Congregational Church, lately purchased by the Episcopalians, has been removed to the fine lots belonging to that Society on the south east corner of French and Lincoln Avenue, where it is being refitted and added to so that when completed it will be a cozy and comfortable chapel and Sunday School room.

> Next Friday and Saturday evenings the ladies of the Episcopal Church will hold a fair, the object being to raise funds to defray the expense of the removal of the church to its new quarters.

The Fair was a huge success; everybody had a good time. The net proceeds were $225—an amount that far exceeded the anticipations of the ladies in charge. "The New England dinner was splendid and enjoyed by over one hundred; the dinner was more than palatable." "The Ladies of the Guild endeavored to make the Fair a festival of 'Peace and Good Will,' a festival that would be, to each and all, a happy, pleasant memory. Frowns and regrets have come only from those who did not participate, and who are, as usual, miserable because others are happy."

January, 1892, was a time of remodeling the former Congregational Church to meet the needs and desires of the Episcopalian congregation. "The new Episcopal Church, corner of French and Lincoln, is in place, and as soon as the carpenters, paper hangers and painters get through the cosy little chapel will be ready for services. Captain J. F. Sullivan is papering and painting the church; it will be a daisy when completed."

Dedication of the Episcopal Church was Sunday, March 13, 1892. The Summit County *Journal* gave advance coverage:

> The Church, henceforth to be known as St. John's, will be formally opened and dedicated tomorrow, the 13th of March. It is a little over five months since the Rev. C. W. Hodder first came to Breckenridge and the people who are members of the Episcopal Church determined to try and establish a church here. For years they had been trying to attain this object but up till this had failed to realize it. They have at last succeeded beyond, I venture to think, the wildest hopes of the most sanguine. All honour to them for their perseverance. The following list and description of presents and donations to the church will give some idea of the enthusiastic manner in which everybody has taken the matter up and brought it to its final issue, in the beautiful and complete little church at the corner of Lincoln Avenue and French Street.

> The altar, a beautiful piece of work in white and gold, is the gift of Mr. and Mrs. W. R. Forman and bears a plate with the inscription, In Memory of Deber Forman, died 10th of October, 1891.

> Upon the center of the altar, standing on what we are told is an imitation tabernacle, is a handsome solid brass cross, inscribed as follows: In Memory of Little Clinton, died Dec. 6th, 1882,—"Peace through the cross." This, as well as the elegant brass altar desk, is the gift of a friend, who wishes the name kept secret. On either side of the cross, but upon a slightly lower level, are two more memorial gifts in the shape of polished brass flower vases, given by Mrs. J. D. Roby and Miss Remine, one in memory of their mother, Maggie A. Remine, and the other in memory of their sister, Clara L. Wintermute. On the extreme right and left of the altar stand two very fine candle sticks (Eucharistic lights) these are the gift of the Rector in memory of his mother, father and two sisters.

> The Vesper lights (three branches) were given by Mrs. M. H. Huntress.

> One of the most beautiful of all the gifts, is a magnificent solid silver communion set, consisting of Chalice and Paten, the work of the Tiffany Glass and Decoration Co., N. Y., the inscription informs us that this elegant piece of work, was given by the Little Mustard Seeds in memory of Sister Finding.

> The handsome oak and plush sanctuary chair next claims our attention, which we find is the joint gift of Mr. and Mrs. M. H. Huntress. Opposite, there is a credence table the work and gift of Capt. J. C. Sullivan who has

done so much to beautify the little church. The handsomely worked hanging is the gift of an unknown friend.

The sanctuary carpet is the gift of the Ladies Guild. The altar rail is the result of collections taken up at private services.

Looking west from the sanctuary there stands a handsome wrought iron and brass lectern, the work of J. and R. Lamb of N. Y. (as also are all the altar ornaments.) This beautiful and costly piece of work was given by Mrs. C. A. Finding and Mrs. J. C. Wilson to perpetuate the memory of their mother and father, (the Marshall Silverthorns), who were among the first settlers in Breckenridge.

The stove, carpet in the body of the church, matting-chairs, etc. are the gift of Mr. Hodder and personal friends.

The plant for the electric light, consisting of two handsome chandeliers of four lights in the centre of the body of the church, one of two lights in the sanctuary and one light over the choir, was given by Judge Clark.

The flue, was the considerate gift of Mr. Chas. A. Finding.

The prayer desk was the gift of a personal friend of Mr. Hodder, who does not wish his name known.

There is also a large plain Latin cross to go outside the church, donated by a friend who wishes his name kept from the public eye. Lastly, though by no means least, thanks are due to Mr. Birr who kindly donated the work upon the foot walk outside. (Other gifts should have been listed—parament hangings—red, white, green, violet;—cruets by the Mustard Seeds; organ by the Ladies Guild; Communion linen by Rev. Hodder.)

In thanking the many friends in Breckenridge who have so kindly come to his help, the Rector wishes to state that he most emphatically desires all those who have by word or deed done so much to make his work pleasant and successful here to feel that at all times they will receive the heartiest of welcomes to the little church they have so very liberally helped him to build.

Rev. Charles W. Hodder is a graduate of the Church Theological Seminary in Reading, England and also of the Owens College of the Victoria University, Manchester, England.

He commenced his ministry in the West Indies, but was forced to abandon his work there through ill health, after less than a year's work in England. He came to this country in January, 1891, remaining east in N. Y. as a private tutor till last September when he came west to avoid the dampness of the eastern winters.

An account of the March 13 Dedication Services appeared in the following week's newspaper:

On last Sunday, pursuant to announcement, the beautiful little chapel at the corner of Lincoln and French was dedicated and the internal furnishings duly consecrated by Right Rev. Bishop Spalding. The church was filled to its utmost capacity, both morning and evening, even to all standing room being occupied. The sermon on both occasions being preached by the Bishop. At the evening service the rite of confirmation was conferred upon seven applicants. The solemn service was very reverently witnessed by all present.

The advice given by the Bishop when announcing the first officers of the church was very appropriate and was no doubt received in the spirit intended. The words of encouragement will long be remembered by the officers and members of the congregation, and should dull seasons overtake them the good advice given on Sunday will strengthen their hands for the increased work.

The new church starts out under very encouraging auspices and the Rev. Hodder has every reason to believe and hope that his congregation will not only be a permanent, but a growing one. The pastor himself has already secured a following of well wishers outside the church as well as within its borders. Every good citizen can but wish the new church, its pastor and congregation a God-Speed on their way.

The first vestry was formed March 14, 1892, and the parish was designated as St. John the Baptist. Rev. C. W. Hodder was engaged for a year at $100 per mensem (month).

Rev. Hodder was highly educated and often presented lectures of public interest in the G. A. R. Hall. One series of lectures was on Africa; another on the Necessity of a Personal God.

The Breckenridge electric light company was incorporated January 2, 1892. Electricity was turned on in Breckenridge, March 24, 1892. A grand ball was held on the 25th in honor of the occasion. "No longer will our dancing friends have to dance by the light of the moon, or a penny dip, but will be able to disport themselves in a flood of light equal in brightness to the rays of the noonday sun." Rev. Hodder gave a series of learned lectures explaining the marvels and mechanics of this new thing—electricity. St. John's Episcopal was the first Breckenridge Church to have electric lights—March 26, 1892.

Rev. Hodder attended the Diocesan Council, meeting in Denver, June 1st. "June 14 Rev. C. W. Hodder and bride returned from their bridal trip." The Ladies Guild of St. John's met June 23rd and elected Mrs. Hodder president.

Church squabbles were not long in coming to the newly-formed church that had started "under very encouraging auspices." In February, 1893, a unanimous resolution was passed, requesting the Rector to ask for the resignation of two Ladies Guild officials "on account of the position of antagonism they had taken up and the injury they were doing the church by their talking." They refused to resign and appealed to the Bishop. A new Bishop had been consecrated Missionary Bishop; he visited Breckenridge and "investigated the matter of the Ladies Guild and likewise charges or rumours against the Rector. Verdict never received." A Mr. Withers arrived to investigate the charges or rumours against the Rector. His verdict was that the rumours were utterly without foundation." A note was added—"Congregation falls off lamentably."

Rev. Hodder resigned, July 3, 1893, as Rector of the parish—"finding himself totally unable to overcome the prejudice by Mr. Wither's visit to this place." (A reconsideration must have occurred, for Rev. Hodder did not leave his Breckenridge parish until late September, 1894.)

A September 29, 1894, newspaper item reported: "The Rt. Rev. W. M. Barker, Bishop of Western Colorado, will not visit Breckenridge as formerly intended on the 3rd of October, and we are informed that St. John's Episcopal Church will be closed for an indefinite period." The Rev. Richard Mercer was appointed Nov. 17, 1895. He remained six months "under the most discouraging circumstances." Rev. Galway was a well-liked rector, serving in 1900. Rev. Chauncey Edgar Snowden was a popular rector for a two-year term—1908-1910. Reverend Robert John Stewart served from June 6, 1967 to May 23, 1968. His departing comment was, "There is an appalling lack of interest for this Mission. Consequently, I have resolved to move to Leadville at the earliest opportunity where the work of the Church may more profitably advance."

There have been a number of fine, short-

time ministries of parish rectors at Breckenridge St. John the Baptist's Episcopal Church. All experienced the hardships and difficulties common to the work of the church in mountain town-mining camps.

CHRISTIAN SCIENCE CHURCH

The Breckenridge *Bulletin*, August 13, 1904, had a brief notice: "Mrs. B. M. Chapman, a Christian Scientist from Denver, with her son and daughter, have rented the Hoopes' cottage on Ridge Street." The newspaper Church Directory, August 27th, had an addition to the church announcements regularly appearing: "First Church of Christ, Scientist. Sunday Services will be held at 8 p.m. Subject, 'Man.' Wednesday evening meeting 8 p.m. Until further notice, meetings of the Church will be held at 'The Hillocks,' the residence of Mr. and Mrs. Forsythe, to which all are cordially invited." October 1, 1904, meetings of First Church of Christ, Scientist, were scheduled at the Arbogast Building on Main Street.

Breckenridge *Bulletin*   Sat., Oct. 1, 1904

Mrs. W. H. Briggle, Mrs. Frank M. Goddard and Mssrs. Fincher, Fry, White and Godfrey will assist in the music to be furnished at the opening exercises of the First Church of Christ, Scientist, in the Arbogast building tomorrow evening.

The Church Directory of the week announced the subject for the Sunday meeting: "Are Sin, Disease and Death Real?" Sunday School would be at 3 p.m. and there would be a Wednesday 8 p.m. service. The Reading Room at the Arbogast building would be open week days from 10 a.m. to 8 p.m. In the summer of 1910 announcements ceased in the Church Directory, but occasional news items appeared in Summit County *Journal* as late as April, 1916. The exact ending of Christian Science Church effort in Breckenridge is another of the unknowns.

In 1909 and 1910 Church Directory announcements located First Church of Christ

Scientist services at Ridge Street, between Lincoln and Carter Avenues. The exact location is not designated. A large log building (formerly a rooming house—destroyed by fire in 1969) possibly could have been the location of First Church of Christ Scientist on Ridge Street. It is also possible that services were in a private home.

The scarcity of news items in the local newspaper would indicate that First Church of Christ Scientist did not get a strong foothold in Breckenridge life. Few of the old-timers remember that a Christian Science Church ever existed in Breckenridge.

CHURCHES—EPILOGUE

As "Ye Editor" saw the Churches of Breckenridge at the end of 1883 and 1884.

The *Daily Journal*   December 8, 1883

OUR CHURCHES

Strangers visiting our mountain hamlet seldom think of enquiring about or into our church facilities, and it being so common to find little communities in the mountains of a thousand or more souls who have no place of worship and no pastoral services, that unless their attention is called thereto come in to our town and go out without realizing that Breckenridge has three of the coziest churches in the mountains. The Methodist church on French Street, the first built, was erected in 1880. In addition to being in an obscure position it is overshadowed by the large Fireman's Hall beside it so that a stranger would have to come directly in front of it before he would realize that it was there. It has a seating capacity of a couple of hundred of a congregation. The Catholic church, the second erected in town at the corner of Washington avenue and High street, is so far to one side of town as to be missed by strangers coming into town. It is not yet completed although used for the last three years. It can seat a congregation numbering three hundred. The Congregational church on Harris street between Lincoln and Washington avenues, is a little gem of a chapel. It looks every inch the ideal of a neat little country church, tasty in design, simple in construction and furnishment. It suggests at first sight that it must be the resort of a happy and contented congregation. Its inside view is, if possible, more impressive than its outside appearance.

In these three churches every Sabbath there are services held, sometimes no preaching, but Sabbath schools, prayer meetings, etc., are always sure to be held—strangers are always welcome and truth compels us to add there is always room for all that come.
Summit County *Journal*   December 27, 1884

CHURCHES

Let a visitor to a town be a believer or a non-believer he is at once interested in the number and condition of the church edifices. It tells the observer at once what manner of people he has fallen in with. The stranger in Breckenridge could soon make up his mind on a Sunday that this people, although our lot is cast amid the clouds of heaven, that as a people we remembered the ways of our forefathers and on the Sabbath day visited the sanctuary.

The Methodist Episcopal church, a large roomy and comfortable edifice, built like the people of the denomination it represents, is for service rather than show. It is comfortably finished and furnished. Being located beside the Fireman's Hall rather detracts from its appearance from the street, but worshipers within its walls give no heed of so light a matter as outward appearances while they are enjoying comfort and contentment within.

The Congregational church on Harris street is a model of neat, quiet and unobstrusive comfort. Its outward appearance and internal finish at once conveys a pleasant, cheerful and hearty sense of worship peculiarly attractive to a thinking man. Its simplicity is its recommendation both without and within, in its internal arrangements it carries the idea of comfort and completeness in every feature.

The Catholic church, a much larger and more imposing edifice to look upon from without, is built upon a very prettily located lot at the corner of Washington avenue and High street. Although on the extreme eastern limit of the town it is none too far for the visitor to our town to note its commanding presence. The locality and outward presentment of the building commends itself at once, but we regret to add the comfort of the visitor is all in the outside observation, the edifice barely affords shelter to those within its walls, comfort during cold weather it has none. The church was designed for a complete chapel and could at a very moderate cost be made one the neatest places of worship in the state. The walls should be canvassed and papered. The auditorium should be supplied with seats or chairs and then worshipers and visitors could visit it and enjoy its services in comfort. Cannot our church going friends all join hands and before the winter passes make a visit to this pleasant church at least as comfortable as either of the others?

The three churches in our city we think will compare favorably with those of any town of the size of this in the state and we desire to see the inside compare favorably with the outside, for we believe good comfortable, pleasant edifices make good congregations or at least in-dicate good fellowship among the society, and good church communities are a great help to the community at large.

Breckenridge church history of the twentieth century was ably described and predicted in one of the speeches at the laying of the Court House cornerstone, July 31, 1909. While extoling the virtues of the County the speaker added: "Church Services are kept up wherever a few can be gathered to listen to the doctrine of religion and morality."

Methodist Episcopal, Breckenridge's first church building, built by Rev. John Lewis Dyer during spring and summer of 1880 on present site, north of Court House on French Street. First service held Sunday, August 22, 1880. Later known as Methodist Church, Community Church, and now Father Dyer United Methodist Church.

Catholic Church of Breckenridge, second church built in Breckenridge.
Built in early fall of 1881, corner of Washington Avenue and High
Street. Later named St. Mary's Church. (Lots for present location,
French Street between Lincoln and Washington Avenues, purchased
July 26, 1890. Move to present location followed shortly thereafter.

St. John The Baptist Episcopal Church, third church building erected in Breckenridge. Formerly the Congregational Church, it was built in the late fall and early winter of 1881. Building site, corner of Lincoln and French, (probably northwest corner)—(present Court House lawn.) Before September, 1882, moved to east side of Harris Street, between Lincoln and Washington Avenues. November 9, 1891, sold to Cathedral of St. John the Evangelist, Denver, for $350. Then became St. John The Baptist Episcopal Church of Breckenridge, mission of St. John The Evangelist. Moved from Harris Street to present location (southeast corner of French and Lincoln) early December, 1891.

Architect's drawing of Appearance of Father Dyer Methodist Church when erected. Catholic and Congregational churches were of same simple design and construction. (Drawing: Courtesy—E. Bruce Schock, Arvada, Colorado, architect.)

Arched windows, steeples, bells and vestibules were later additions: Methodist bell-belfry summer 1890, arched windows—June, 1892, vestibule—July, 1905; Catholic bell-belfry—October, 1899; Episcopal vestibule—November, 1905, bell-belfry—December, 1965.

Methodist Church-right-center; schoolhouse-left-foreground; Ware-Carpenter Concentrator-west-background. Date — sometime between 1892 and 1895. Courtesy—Denver Public Library Western Collection.

Interior of Methodist Church as restored and redecorated, 1966-1967.

Catholic Church of Breckenridge on its first site, corner of Washington Avenue and High Street—far left, foreground. Schoolhouse, far right, dates picture after 1882. Courtesy—Denver Public Library Western Collection.

Interior St. Mary's Church—1971.

Episcopal Church (formerly Congregational Church—Harris Street) moved to present site — Lincoln and French Street — December, 1891. School House (foreground) completed and occupied 1882. Electric light poles installed January-March, 1892. (Wires are not in evidence in picture.) Electricity turned on March 24, 1892. Dates picture February-March, 1892. Courtesy — Denver Public Library Western Collection.

Dedication St. John The Baptist Episcopal Church, Sunday, March 13, 1892, Right Reverend Bishop Spalding presiding. Courtesy—Reverend Robert John Stewart.

SCHOOLS

Breckenridge received wide publicity in the early 1960s when a consolidated school was proposed for Summit County. Many Breckenridge citizens were "boiling hot" on the issue. Cracks were appearing in the walls of the fifty-year old building in Breckenridge and it was no longer safe for school purposes. The advantages of a county school were advocated, but many wanted their own school in their own town. The forces for consolidation prevailed and today there is an excellent county school located at Frisco, Colorado. You may be sure it wasn't an easy victory. But Breckenridge was accustomed to school squabbles.

Until October, 1882, Breckenridge school pupils got their "larning" in a 20 x 25 foot, one-room schoolhouse, on the west side of north Main Street. (In 1887 the building was moved to the east side of Main Street, opposite its former location.) In 1880 there were 45 pupils—22 boys and 23 girls; 1882 had 33 pupils—16 boys and 17 girls. The school term was of three months' duration. Sometimes school dismissed for a few days "owing to the terrible conditions of roads and foot trails." On one occasion the teacher announced: "There can be no Public School for the ensuing term, therefore, in order to meet the demands of the people, I shall open a private school at the schoolhouse, October 17th. My terms will be as liberal as practical and tuition will be payable weekly. I promise the most earnest efforts to secure the best results in scholarship and deportment. Hoping to meet a felt need, and to have the patronage of all parents, I am very respectfully, A. J. Floyd." About this time "the marriage of Professor Floyd and Miss Woods was consummated . . . from the ladies who were present we learn that the bride was just lovely and the bridegroom looked just sweet."

Agitation for a new school building was rising toward the end of 1881. A Breckenridge resident wrote:

> It cannot be too strongly impressed upon our school trustees that the town demands greater school facilities. The present teacher is doing all one man can do to help the town out of the dilemma, but do his best there are some things he cannot overcome. One school room for a town with a population of two thousand is simply a burlesque upon school systems. There are today over one hundred children of proper age to attend school who are too small to travel a half or three-quarters of a mile to school and when the snows of winter are here it will be worse than now. There should be at least two more comfortable school rooms opened, one in the southern end and one in the eastern or north-eastern portion of the town. They would be filled with little urchins who cannot travel to the present school room, and if they could reach it there would be no accommodation for them.

> The largest town in the third county of the state can certainly more than fill one 20 x 25 foot room with scholars. If the town can afford to build and maintain a five thousand dollar edifice for the accommodation of fire apparatus, it certainly can invest five hundred dollars for the building of a couple of school houses.

The school issue was complicated; some wanted a large school built, others thought three or four small, inexpensive buildings, strategically located, would be better. To further complicate the matter some gave priority to a new water system and fire-fighting apparatus. The School Board called a public meeting in January, 1882:

The citizens of all classes are respectfully urged to be present at Fireman's Hall on next Saturday evening, there to discuss the question of building a NEW SCHOOL HOUSE. Every citizen is interested and every one is invited to participate in the discussion.

There was at least one who read the notice, and he was a citizen of Breckenridge:

Daily Journal   Feb. 1, 1882

In your paper of yesterday I read a notis of a meeting for to bild a new school house. Now sir there is a nigger in the wood pile in that thing. I aint no profit or anything but you can put it down as a sure thing that is a put up job for somebodys benafit. I shall be at that meeting and opose all skeams. We have enuff schools now, if the room is to small bild a shed wing adition to it like Adamsons grociry. I am opposed to ecstravaganz and me and my friends will be on hand you bet, you cant by us of for a glass of rot gut whisky neither.   R.

Another letter followed the next day:

Mr. Editor—I see in to days paper you printed my lyttel note and you printed a lot of mistaks in it. I was in a saloon to-night and heard a lot of men laffing at it. Now sire that was a mean trick and I will remember you for it you may know how to spell better me but I have more money in bank than you have and it wasent learning that made it. I am opposed to this hyflightin fashun of stuffing childrun with so much education that they dont want to work. A good warm log school house was good enough for me and will do for my naburs childrun as well.

Dont go and spell this letter rong as you did the one you printed to-day or you will be sorry for it. Ime as good a man as you are and Ile make you no ot. Ime oposed to this school house swinddel and Ile be there to meeting don't you forget it. if you shute of yure mouth you will find some body to stop it.   R.

The School Bonds carried in the March election, despite R's "oposing."

At the special election last Saturday, to vote for or against the issuing of bonds to build a graded school building, the bonds carried by a majority of three to one. The Board was very exact in scanning the qualifications of voters and rejected a large number of votes, representing taxable property. The question of progress has been decided and another forward move is made that will entitle Breckenridge to recognition among the foremost towns of the state.

The school house we will have; but water works not for some time.

Summit County *Journal*   October 5, 1882

The Breckenridge public school was opened yesterday in the new school building on Lincoln Avenue and Harris Street. The enterprise of the citizens has secured the finest school building in Summit County, costing upward of $5,000. The building is an elegant one, located in the central portion of the town, furnished and finished appropriately and artistically. Mr. E. Nashold drew the ground and elevation plans and was awarded the contract for building. The painting and papering was done by Clark and the stoves were furnished by Hartman Bros. The school is two stories high with four rooms, 29 x 48 ft., with 12 ft. ceiling.

Daily Journal   October 9, 1882

Our new School House is universally commended of the town and is the best public building in the county. The two rooms are fully furnished and equipped with desks, blackboards, etc. The finish of the rooms is as inviting as ever was schoolroom. The grounds surrounding the building are being cleared up and fenced so that all will be in keeping with the main building.

On Saturday last the fine large bell that will call the laggard to his lessons was placed in the belfry. It is a present to the school by the contractor, Mr. Nashold, and is emblematic of both his good judgment as well as his liberality. The bell can be heard in all parts of the town and from the mountain sides. Its peals re-echo to the distant and far off cliffs that ne'er heard the like before. Mr. Nashold deserves the thanks of scholars and parents for his forethought in making so useful a donation. The upper rooms of the building will not be finished this season, but as the demand is made for schools they can be finished.

Summit County *Journal*   May 7, 1892

The time for securing teachers for next school terms draws nigh. It behooves those interested in our schools to consider who shall be selected to teach the young mind of the scholar in the line wherein it should go. A rumor has been on the street that there would be no male teacher employed, but that all the schools would be under lady teachers. We trust this is incorrect, for quiet as our young people are and well behaved as our youths are as a whole, there are nevertheless some school children who will develop into incorrigibles if lady teachers alone are employed, the presence of reserved force always has a good effect upon ignorant, gross and evil natures. We must take children as we find them and not as we could wish them. The schools of this place have experimented quite enough to prove the non-success of all lady teachers and The JOURNAL hopes there will be no more of it. There should be at least one gentleman in charge of the higher room, if not one each for the two higher rooms. By no means make a step backward.

Twenty-five years later Breckenridge again clamored for a new school. "The present building is inadequate as to size and arrangement. We are in distress for room. A full high school course cannot be given. Our building is old, illy planned, lacking proper heating facilities, deficient in number of rooms, and in quantity and quality of paraphernalia, and altogether out of date." An election was held May, 1908, and Breckenridge was emphatic for a new $20,000 school building—for the bonds, 57; against the bonds, 2. The contract was awarded Messrs. Ladd & Sawyer, of Denver, and the building was under roof by mid-October. It was located on Harris Street, between Lincoln and Washington Avenues.

February 7, 1909, "the new school house was thrown open to visitors, preliminary to its final cleaning and preparation for occupancy by the impatient school."

Summit County *Journal*   March 27, 1909

At last, and after much deliberation, the board of education of School District No. One, consisting of R. W. Foote, Chris Kaiser and William Thomas, has concluded to make the Breckenridge high school a real and accredited high school, in fact as well as in name. Heretofore the Breckenridge high school has been such in name only, graduating the pupils from the tenth grade.

Hereafter the full modern high school branches will be taught here, thus placing the school on a par with the public schools of Leadville, Denver, Colorado Springs and other cities.

The reason that the full high school course, beyond the tenth grade, has not been taught here before was on account of expense and insufficient room. Now with our new and modern school building, the board has taken an advanced step and in the right direction, by ordering in the full course of study, depending upon the liberal support the tax-payers have prof-

fered, together with the substantial assistance the county commissioners will probably render, to support the additional departments, and thus make it not only a Breckenridge high school, but a Summit County high school, where the advanced pupils from the whole county can avail themselves of the eleventh and twelfth grade work without incurring the expense of attending schools in remote cities.

Besides the erection of the new school building, this resolution on the part of the board will prove the most popular official act of the present board's tenure of office. It will not only keep much money in the county, but pupils under the watchful eye of parents.

In this important public matter, the board of education has again given evidence of its wisdom, sagacious executive ability and keenness to keep pace with the general demand to place Summit County pupils on an equal footing with their neighbors, and at a minimum cost.

The Summit County *Journal*, February 21, 1920, noted: "Work on the new school house is under way. It will be in readiness for occupancy for the 1920-1921 year in September." This applied to the building of the auditorium-gymnasium annex. Breckenridge now had a praiseworthy school for fifty years.

ST. GERTRUDE'S SELECT SCHOOL

In the summer of 1884 Father Chapuis, of St. Mary's Catholic Church, looked at Breckenridge property in prospect of establishing a Sisters' School in the town. The particular lots in mind were on the north side of Lincoln Avenue above French Street. August, 1886, he purchased these lots. Father Chapuis' plan enlarged to a school and hospital. The plans unfolded in the spring of 1886.

Father Chapuis announced in May, 1886, that "the Sisters who are to take charge of the proposed hospital and school will arrive in Breckenridge about the first of June." In June the furniture for the Benedictine Sisters' School was arriving.

Daily Journal   July 3, 1886

The Benedictine Sisters will open school for the teaching of children in English on Tuesday next (6th) in the Catholic Church on the corner of Washington Avenue and High Street, school will open at the regular hour 9 A. M. The charge for tuition will be fifty cents per week for each scholar.

A select boarding school will be opened by the sisters in about two months at which children from the surrounding towns or elsewhere can board with the sisters while being schooled at a cost of twelve dollars per month, where music is added to the other studies three dollars additional will be charged.

The highest department will be under the direction of Sister Hilda who is now in charge of St. Joseph's Parochial School of Chicago, Illinois. Sister Anastasia will have charge of the lower department. Her record as a teacher antedates her life as a sister, she having been a teacher before she was admitted to the sisterhood.

The Benedictine Sisters opened school according to announcement and also took charge of the hospital. "The music of our various school bells would convey to strangers the idea that this is a school-going community." Pupils of St. Gertrude's Select School presented a program of music and readings at the G. A. R. Hall, in November, benefit of the school.

The Sisters' School, in 1887, was not in the church, but at the Lincoln Avenue location. The school was to open August 1st. "By that time all repairs, alterations and additions to the buildings will be complete." St. Gertrude's was now a boarding and day school. Our best information comes from the St. Scholastica Convent, Chicago, Illinois. Mother Jean Marie, O. S. B., Prioress, provided material from letters, reports and narrations of the pioneer Sisters of Breckenridge from files in St. Scholastica Convent, Chicago. The material is taken, mainly, from *Where There Was Need*—A History of the Chicago Benedictine Sisters from 1861 to 1965—a manuscript not published.

The Colorado Beginnings of the Chicago Benedictine Sisters

Breckenridge, Colorado, in the 1880's had need of a hospital to care for their sick and injured; the children had need of a school. In this breach the least likely were sent. To try to reason why Reverend E. J. Chapuis, the pastor of the little Catholic Church, would try to get religious for this pioneer work and even more so, why he was successful, a little background information is necessary. (Colorado public schools were rather slow in formation.)

The Breckenridge priest turned to the first bishop of Denver, Colorado, Bishop Joseph Projectus Machebeuf for assistance. The bishop, who had asked Archabbot Boniface Wimmer

for priests to help in the Denver diocese, suggested that Father Chapuis write to St. Vincent's Abbey, Latrobe, Pennsylvania. Since in 1885-1886 Archabbot Boniface was ill, his assistant, Reverend Augustine Schneider sent the request to the prioress of Sts. Benedict and Scholastica Convent, Chicago, Mother Luitgard Huber. Before Mother would accept the work so far away she sent two members of the community to investigate. Sister Theresa Krug and Mother Ottilia Hoeveler went out to Breckenridge in the spring of 1886 and returned with the information which won the consent of the Sisters to accept the new mission. Education was the principal work of the Sisters. In September, 1886, St. Gertrude's School was opened in Breckenridge in a remodeled frame house with a staff of three Sisters, and a small enrollment of boys and girls. Sister Anastasia was the only teacher. Mother Luitgard Huber, who had remained until the mission was permanently established, immediately began to make preparations for a boarding and day school. She bought three frame houses which she had moved to a more desirable location, where she had secured lots. (corporation minutes of Community.) According to the *Steamboat Pilot,* April 17, 1936, the buildings were located on the north-east corner of Lincoln Avenue and French Street, across from the Episcopal Church. The article notes that the Catholic convent had both boarders and day scholars from Leadville and other Colorado towns for many years.

Mother Luitgard wrote from Breckenridge to the Chicago motherhouse to request that Sisters Hilda Walzen, Valerie Theis, (a novice) and Miss Katie Rupp, (a postulant who received the habit at Breckenridge,) were to come to Breckenridge immediately. Sister Pauline, years later, recalled that trip and life in the little mountain town where she later made her perpetual vows.

Although by January, 1887, the school was functioning well, with "forty boarders and a larger number of day scholars;" the school was not destined to continue long. A severe decline in the price of silver and the consequent decrease in the population of Breckenridge caused the Sisters to consider moving their school to some other place. They first chose Boulder, but through the persuasion of Bishop Matz, decided to move to Canon City. Sister Rose Brehm, superior of St. Gertrude's School at the time, then purchased the grounds and buildings of the old military academy, located on the corner of Seventh and Pike Streets, Canon City, Colorado. The Benedictine Sisters still have a boarding and day school there—St. Scholastica Academy. (The Sisters moved to Canon City in June, 1890 to property purchased in May, 1890.)

St. Gertrude's Select School had only four years in Breckenridge. Father Chapuis' ambitious dream for Breckenridge did not materialize. Father Francis Hornung, of The Abbey School, Canon City, commenting on the Breckenridge endeavor of the Benedictines, said: "Mining camps, far up in the hills, did not have resources to start a livable monastery." So it proved to be in Breckenridge.

A rare picture showing both the 1882 and 1909 Breckenridge school-houses. Summit County *Journal*, Saturday, August 6, 1910, stated: "The cupola on the (1882) school was taken down Wednesday and the old school house will, in a week or two, be a memory only." Picture: (from the east)—Courtesy Mrs. Marion Griffin.

Picture (from the west) shows the 1882 and 1909 schools, and the new Court House. Courtesy—Mrs. Ted Fletcher.

Center (front)-1882 Public School; right—a short distance farther west—
St. Gertrude's Select Private School; left—St. Mary's Catholic Church on
French Street. Date of picture—between 1887 and Oct. 1899 (Catholic
Church doesn't have belfry.) Courtesy—Library State Historical Society
of Colorado.

"Blow-up" showing St. Gertrude's School—center. Courtesy — Denver
Public Library Western Collection.

COURT HOUSES

Summit County was large when boundaries were established by the First Legislative Assembly, 1861. Since that time seven counties have been formed from it and Summit is the smallest of the seven. At one time Summit County was about one-sixth of Colorado. Maps included show how Summit evolved from a large county to its present size.

Park City, Georgia Gulch, at the head of Swan Valley, vied with Breckenridge for the county seat in 1862. One story is that court records were held in the Marshall Silverthorn hotel, Breckenridge. An attempt, made by the County Clerk to transport the records to Park City, was thwarted by the resourceful Mrs. Silverthorn.

Other stories are related to the effect that the county seat was in Park City for a short time. At the time of the laying of the cornerstone of the present court house, Summit County *Journal* chronicled the history of Summit County courthouses:

The original county seat was located at Park City, near the mouth of Georgia Gulch, where in the days of rich gold diggings a city of 5,000 people arose—in a day, as it were. Thirty-eight years ago the county seat was moved to Breckenridge and located in a cabin on the ground where the Enterline King store now stands, on the west side of Main Street. Later the house of records and courts was established in the Rankin buildings, north of the *Journal* office. Next the county offices were moved to what is now the Engle bank building, and from there to their present quarters, east side of Main Street.

In October, 1908, the Taxpayers' Committee made an appeal for a new court house. At an election the following month court house bonds received a majority, favoring a proposition for creating a bonded indebtedness of $75,000. Next came a decision on location of the new building. Some favored a Main Street location; the board of county commissioners were strongly in favor of the Lincoln Avenue-French Street location. One speaker, favoring the Lincoln Avenue location waxed eloquently:

Summit County *Journal*   February 27, 1909

Let us locate the court house on the most beautiful spot in Summit County, where Old Sol directs his first rays of light in the early morning, before the tiny sparkles of dew have left the lips of the fragrant rose; and at night, when the myriads of stars in the vaulted space of heaven are twinkling in constant recognition of the vanities of man, the cold light of the moon will first kiss the walls of our building and send from its chimney tops softened shadows on a mansard roof. Put the court house on Lincoln Avenue, and sun, moon and stars will see your work and pronounce it good."

Where else could the court house be located after that fervent plea? "The commissioners decided to place the court house on the county's quarter block at Lincoln Avenue and French Street, having deeds in escrow to the row of buildings along Lincoln Avenue, at option for $1,814.60. The Merkle lot, on Ridge Street, 50 x 60, will be secured if it can be gotten at a reasonable figure. With this, the court house site will be 192 feet on Lincoln Avenue, 151 feet on French Street, and 150 feet on Ridge Street."

"Inasmuch as the question is now settled and we will have a court house, let's lay aside all differences as regards to location and feel that the commissioners have had the interest of the entire county at heart and have acted in good faith; and, furthermore, let's assist them in every way possible toward the building of a court house that will be a credit to the town and county."

Saturday, July 31, 1909, was a festive day in Breckenridge—the laying of the cornerstone for the new Summit County Court House. All business suspended for an afternoon holiday so that everybody could participate. The town was decorated lavishly, with banners and streamers hung across all streets. Ideal weather prevailed and the people turned out *en masse*.

Grand Masons, and other dignitaries, arrived by train. Visiting Masons came from Fairplay, Alma, Como and Jefferson. A parade formed with seventy-five Masons in regalia, followed by a brass band and the local firemen. A chorus of fifty voices added life and charm to the occasion.

Summit County *Journal*   August 7, 1909

Last Saturday was a big day in Breckenridge. Summit County is building a new court house, and it was fitting that public observation should be made of the laying of the cornerstone thereof. As per custom on such occasions, the corner stone of aforesaid building was laid, squared and plumbed by the grand officers of the order of Ancient Free and Accepted Masons.

The ancient custom of depositing a box of mementoes in the center of the stone was duly observed. A portion of the contents of said copper box consisted of a copy of the resolution passed by the board of the county commissioners authorizing the construction of the court house, samples of town and county bond issues, current coins, copies of local papers, gold nuggets, literature pertaining to the county, book of poems, "Sweet Summer Land," by Mrs. Florence Watson. Besides these, a copy of the constitution and by-laws of Blue River Lodge, No. 49 A. F. and A. M. The box contains other articles of historical value too numerous to mention. The stone was laid in due and ancient form, in cement, sealed with the wine, the corn and the oil. The cement had a quantity of gold dust emptied into it by the Grand Master when the mixture was prepared. Every-

thing was perfect, except that the initials of County Commissioner W. H. Hampton were transposed in the cutting of the stone, otherwise the piece of Colorado granite was a beautiful piece of work. In the evening there was a banquet for Masons and wives, also county and town officers and wives. A grand free ball at G. A. R. Hall concluded the festive day.

February 5, 1910, Summit County *Journal* wrote of an addition to the court house that had not been in the original planning:

Ladies Of County to Have Rest-Room

A long felt want in Breckenridge has been a retreat or rest-room for women—a place whither ladies who are in town on brief business or shopping visits may retire for a little privacy and rest, and where they may find the essential means of "touching up" their complexions and rectifying possible defections of the toilet, etc., etc. Such rest rooms for women are found in the public buildings of many eastern towns and have proven a boon to the fair sex wherever introduced.

Now that Breckenridge is about to enjoy the advantages of a commodious new county building, it has occurred to some of our public spirited matrons that it should contain a retreat for women such as above described. Encouraged by every county officer and influential citizen to whom they have confided their scheme, they have gone so far as to confer with the county commissioners in regard to the matter, and have been told that the large basement room in the south-east corner of the new court house would be cheerfully placed at the disposal of the ladies of the county.

The originators of the plan have now done all they can do unaided. For any further steps in the matter they need the co-operation of their sisters. A meeting of all ladies interested in such a project is therefore called for 2:30 o'clock Saturday afternoon, February 12, in the county court room, on Main Street. Plans will be formulated for properly furnishing and decorating the room; ways and means will be discussed of providing the necessary funds, and various committees appointed to carry out the wishes of the meeting.

It is proposed to make a real cozy nook out of that southeast room and to provide everything a woman needs for comfort, rest, privacy, and the restoration of neat appearance.

No one can question the propriety of choosing a room in the county building for this purpose. The beneficiaries will be principally visitors from outside points—women in attendance upon court or having business in the county offices, ranchmen's wives and daughters who need rest after a long ride, shoppers who come here between trains and so forth.

Summit County *Journal*   March 12, 1910

Rest-Room An Assured Fact

The members of the Rest-Room association met at the residence of the president, Mrs. J. F. Condon, to discuss ways and means for the accomplishment of their project.

The committee on decorating and furnishing had carefully looked over the ground and reported that the sum of $125 would be necessary to furnish the room in a manner befitting the name—a rest-room. Curtains, rockers, easy-chairs, a couch, a carpet, a library table and other small accessories can be secured for this modest sum.

Each and every member was full of enthusiasm, and all feel confident they will win. "In their bright lexicon there is no such word as fail." The rest-room is an assured fact.

> They are bound to have a rest-room,
> Why, of course, they'll have a rest-room,
>   That is what the smiling ladies state.
> Every one will do her duty—
> It is sure to be a beauty,
>   For Breckenridge is always up to date.

St. Patrick's Day, March 17, 1910, was dedication day of the new Summit County Court House, and it was "carried out in a manner becoming an occasion of this nature"—arrayed in splendor of beautiful flowers and a flood of light from basement to dome:

Summit County *Journal*   March 19, 1910

If any citizen of Summit had his doubts about the "taking qualities" of the proposed dedication ceremonies at the new court house, those doubts must have been most effectually dispelled by what transpired within the spacious halls of the magnificent building Thursday night, when the people, *en masse*, celebrated the acquisition of the most useful, attractive and satisfactory public improvement in the county's history.

Early in the evening the windows of the building and its dome began to light up and assume a festive appearance, until the whole building was alight and smiling out in all directions upon the community which it is destined to ably serve during the years to come. Proud citizens from every station in life, dressed in holiday attire, filed into the inviting doors in a growing and ever growing stream, until the town was practically depopulated and every room of the new building was teeming with intelligent life and reverberating with all the expressions of sociability and good cheer that emanate only from happy people. Every where were heard expressions of delight from those who inspected the county's new official home for the first time.

Shortly after 8 o'clock, music by the Breckenridge brass band, from the lofty dome, announced to the community the opening of the dedicatory exercises. Hon. J. W. Swisher, standing on the main stairway leading to the second floor, surrounded by a large group of school children holding tiny flags, made the opening remarks of reminiscent nature. The children, always gladly heard, sang "The Star-Spangled Banner." The Rev. C. E. Snowden invoked heaven's blessing. After another selection by the band the chairman of the meeting, Commissioner A. W. Philipps, was introduced and explained, in well chosen words, the case of the commissioners in the matter of the erection of the county house. The popular Breckenridge male quartet was heard to the delight of all. Hon. Caesar A. Roberts, of Denver, the main speaker of the evening, directed his masterly address toward showing the importance of the new edifice as a standard and example for the future building to be done in its vicinity, and predicted a period of architectural improvement for our town. The Breckenridge orchestra then added a liberal quota to the pleasures of the occasion. Rev. C. E. Snowden, the next speaker, dwelt upon the administration of justice that would befit and should be found in the new temple of the blindfolded goddess. In the district court room, Hon. C. L. Westerman inspired an attentive crowd with visions of future wealth and greatness by a talk on the mineral resources of Summit County. "America," by the children, closed the memorable event.

In every principal room there stood on a neatly linened table a huge bowl of punch, presided over by smiling ladies, generally the wife of the incumbent of the room. In these well patronized spots the several county officers received the hearty congratulations of their friends.

In many ways Summit County Court House remains the focal point in Breckenridge.

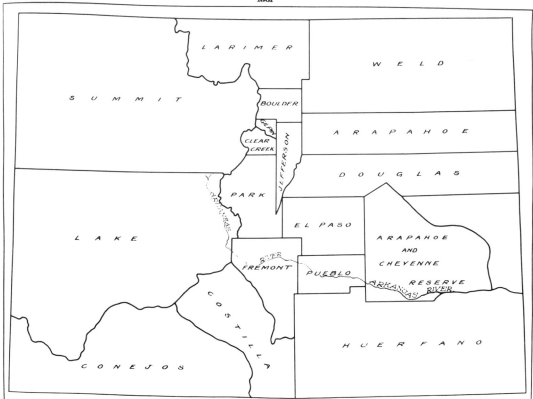

Original Size of Summit County — 1861

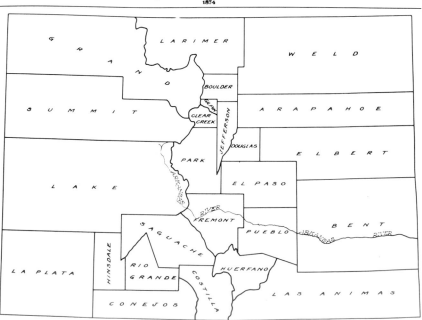

Original Summit divided into Summit and Grand Counties — 1874

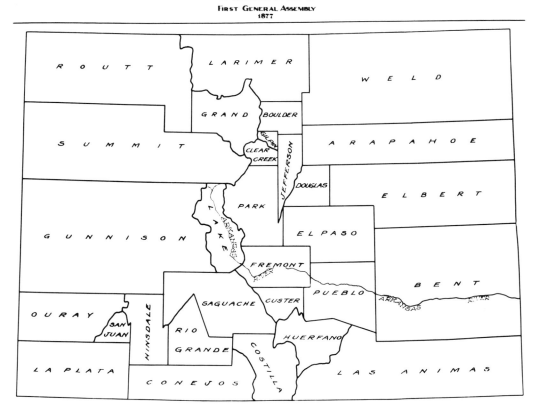

COLORADO
First General Assembly
1877

Original Summit County divided into Summit-Routt-Grand Counties—
1877

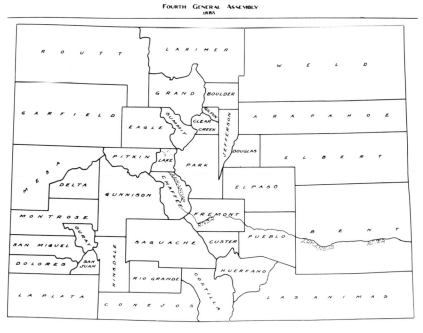

COLORADO
Fourth General Assembly
1883

Original Summit divided into Summit-Routt-Grand-Garfield-Eagle Counties—1883, giving Summit its present size.

Court Houses

COLORADO

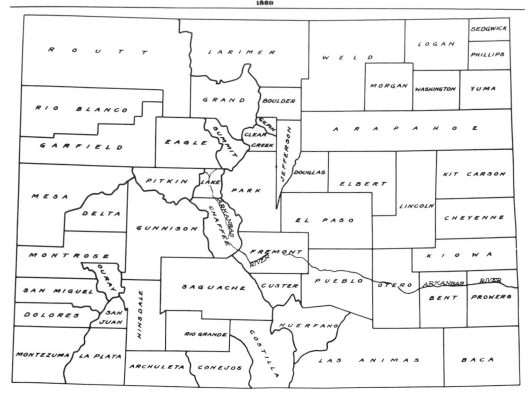

Original Summit divided into Routt-Rio Blanco-Garfield-Eagle-Grand-
Summit Counties — 1889.

COLORADO

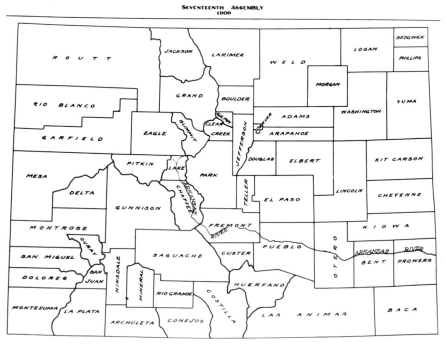

Original Larimer County divided into Jackson and Larimer Counties—
1909.

COLORADO

Eighteenth Assembly
1911

Original Summit divided into seven counties:
Moffat-Routt-Grand-Rio Blanco-Garfield-Eagle-Summit—1911.

COLORADO

Nineteenth Assembly
1913

Present Day Counties of Colorado — 1913—

Court Houses

Masonic Lodge Members marching to Court House Cornerstone
Laying Ceremony.

Court House Cornerstone Masonic Ceremony. Saturday, July 31, 1909.
Courtesy—Denver Public Library Western Collection.

Summit County Court House Flag-Raising Ceremony, August, 1936, Governor Ed Johnson officiating, when a disputed, supposedly unclaimed strip of land—"No Man's Land"—was formally annexed. Courtesy— Denver Public Library Western Collection.

HOSPITALS

Summit County *Journal*   January 6, 1900

William Merkle Horribly Maimed

Thursday afternoon William Merkle, a well-known and highly respected citizen of Breckenridge, was mining on one of his claims on U-Be-Dam Flats, (Yuba Dam Flats) below town. He will never mine again. Having the day before sank a drill hole, and loaded it with three sticks of giant powder, which when the fuse was ignited, missed fire. On the occasion above mentioned, he went down to pick or drill out the unexploded charge. While engaged in said hazardous act, the load "went off" with a terrific explosion. Mr. Merkle luckily escaped with his life, though he received bodily injuries that will cripple, maim and disfigure him for life—should he recover at all.

With the exception of the thumb, his right hand was completely severed; his left eye is shot out, a drill was driven through his left cheek, while the top of his head received several deep scalp wounds.

Being alone, the mangled man started to walk to town, but near the old Jones Mill he was overtaken by Miss Agnes Finding and carried in her sleigh to Dr. Scott's office where his wounds were dressed. Yesterday his friend Charles Merrill took him to the St. Joseph's hospital in Denver where it is hoped he will recover.

There were many gruesome accidents in the mines. It was not until the turn of the century that a mining inspector was appointed to the Breckenridge area. Previously, the mine owner, or worker, followed his own discretion. Injuries and fatalities were inevitable. Breckenridge had need of a hospital to care for the men hurt in the mines. Injuries and illnesses of the community at large also required medical attention.

The first hospital was a feeble attempt to meet this need. It was located near the northwest corner of Harris Street and Washington Avenue. Apparently it was a joint-endeavor on the part of the Miners Protective Association and the County. Breckenridge hospital needs were thereby administered until the coming of the Benedictine Sisters. Encouraging news was in the *Daily Journal,* March 13, 1886: "There is under consideration the establishment in Breckenridge of a hospital under the supervision of the Benedictine Sisters of Chicago. Also a summer resort for invalids suffering from pulmonary or lung complaints. Father Chapuis is consulting and advising with our people generally about the matter."

The Chicago Benedictine Sisters provided material from their files regarding this Breckenridge effort. The material is mainly from "Where There Was Need".

A miner's hospital, supported partly by the county, was turned over immediately to the Sisters. An enclosed passage which was used as a laundry connected the main building with the Sisters' house. The hospital proper contained only one ward and one private room. Sisters Adelaide and Angela were assigned to duty at the hospital which became known as St. Joseph's. In Sister's little report she noted that there were two doctors who cared for the Breckenridge patients, one being Dr. Arbogast. Operations were performed on an ordinary table. Upkeep was guaranteed by an assessment of one dollar a month for each man plus voluntary contributions. This entitled the miners to the use of the hospital in case of need. Many men suffered from frozen limbs. For additional help the two nursing Sisters relied upon the teaching Sisters of St. Gertrude's Academy. This assistance was given at two a.m. on Mondays when they washed clothing and bed linen at the hospital. From 1886 until 1890 the Sisters performed this charitable work, then taught school. The Sisters moved to Canon City in June, 1890.

Residents clamored for a new Breckenridge hospital in 1888. Local papers voiced the issue:

Daily Journal   March 1, 1888

A NEW HOSPITAL

For many years our city and county have managed to get along with the most inadequate hospital accommodations. But the demand for hospital facilities has grown so great that the old rookery is no longer able to fill the bill, and it is absolutely necessary to the comfort of patients that the hospital be enlarged. As now constructed there is but one large room available for patients. But a single thought is required to convince any one that a half dozen patients, one perhaps crushed in a mine, another frozen, a third suffering with pneumonia, a fourth with disorders requiring private attention, and so on though the list, should not all occupy one room and furthermore there is absolutely no accommodation of a female inmate should one be sent there. Operations are sometimes necessary that ought not to be and cannot be successfully performed in the presence of other patients.

Imagine for a moment a patient requiring the profound quiet and freedom from excitement lying in the room where an amputation is being performed or other exciting operation taking place. To call such accommodations a hospital is a misnomer. We know this community well enough to know that they need but to be informed of the true situation of affairs to insure their wants being supplied.

The hospital, as conducted under the sisters' charge, is competent to receive any patient and assure them the very best treatment that can be received in any public institution in the state, but the building in connection therewith is totally inadequate to the requirements and we hope town trustees will see that it is remedied this season.

The condition was not remedied in 1888; it was not remedied before the Sisters left Breckenridge in 1890; there was not to be another hospital until August, 1906.

One of the outstanding Breckenridge residences at the turn of the century was known as the Charlie Sutton house on French Street, between Adams and Jefferson Avenues. County records show that Mary G. Sutton got title to the land by a tax deed, April-May, 1898, "for $248.92 as per order of County Commissioners." February, 1905, Mary G. Sutton transferred the property "and all improvements thereunto, consisting of one two-story frame dwelling and outbuildings"—plus two lots on the east side of the street with fence and barn—to Hattie L. Keables. A. E. Keables, husband, was business manager of The Summit County Mining Exchange. He owned considerable mine holdings, one of which was part ownership of the Masontown Mine, Mount Royal, near Frisco. (Masontown was completely destroyed by a gigantic snowslide sometime in the 1920's. The snake-like trail is clearly distinguishable on the mountain today.)

July 14, 1906, there appeared two articles in the Summit County *Journal* and the Breckenride *Bulletin*:

An appropriation of $2500 was made by the Commissioners to purchase the A. E. Keables residence for a county hospital, and the deal was consummated, the county to have possession of the property in thirty days.

COUNTY BUYS NEW HOSPITAL

The old ramshackle building posing as a county hospital will soon be abandoned. On last Saturday, the board of county commissioners purchased the Keables' property, consisting of several lots and a large steam-heated residence on French Street, which will be turned into a home for the ill and infirm on or about August 30. The County paid $2,500 cash for the place, including furniture, carpets, fixtures and kitchen equipment. The building is well-arranged for hospital purposes and the impression prevails that the County secured the property very cheap.

The Breckenridge *Bulletin,* August 8, 1908, wrote: "The old hospital building, (Washington Avenue and Harris Street) has been sold to William McManis for $25 and he is engaged moving it off the lots which are to form part of the new school ground."

The Sutton-Keables property was the County Hospital for many years. Today it is the beautiful residence of the Robert A. Theobalds.

Summit County Hospital. Formerly the Charlie (Mary) Sutton residence,
then the A. E. (Hattie) Keables residence. Became County Hospital
July-August, 1906. Courtesy—Denver Public Library Western Collection.

The Robert A. Theobald Residence. (Picture dated 1971)

Hospitals

A. E. Keables, Business Manager of Summit County Mining Exchange, held part ownership in Victoria Mine, Masontown Mining & Milling Co., Masontown, Mount Royal, near Frisco. Masontown (probably 10-12 buildings and cabins) was located on lower slope of Royal; Victoria Mountain is south of Royal. Courtesy—Denver Public Library Western Collection.

Snowslide coming down Victoria, crashed into Masontown on Royal demolishing mill and cabins, excepting two cabins to far north. Snowslide path clearly discernible fifty years later. Rubble still in existence. Picture —winter 1970-71. (Unverified date of snowslide—1920s.)

BRONCHO DAVE

A bouncing, lively, enterprising individual gave additional color to Breckenridge and environs in the 1880s and 1890s. He was familiarly known by the name of Broncho Dave—sometimes Dave Braddock, and occasionally by his given name, David Braddock. Apparently he was in his thirties or early forties when he appeared on the Breckenridge scene. Newspaper records give us less than twenty years of his life, leaving the earlier and later years unrecorded. Dave determined to make a business name for himself, and his activities were varied and interesting. He succeeded in getting a town named after himself.

We are introduced to Broncho Dave, December, 1880: "The largest couple we know of in town is Dave and his Broncho. Dave is a rustler and they both mean business, and when you want their services you will always find them ready either on the street or at the Domestic Bakery, Main Street." Dave's first business venture was the running of a stage line from Breckenridge to Swan City, Delaware Flats and Galena Gulch in Swan Valley. His advertisement appeared, 1881, in the Breckenridge newspaper:

DAVE'S BRONCHO STAGE LINE

On and after February 21st, Dave's Broncho Stage Line will leave the Grand Central Hotel and the Wilderness Postoffice at 8 a.m. for Swan City, Delaware Flats and Galena Gulch. For freight or passage apply to Domestic Bakery, 183 Main Street, or of Dave and his Broncho whenever you can catch them.

Broncho Dave's many business ventures knew misfortune. Running the stage line had hardly started when "some scoundrel shot one of Broncho Dave's horses, breaking his hind leg. The horse will have to be killed, and the miscreant who shot him ought to be served the same way." Other acts of malicious mischief followed. Dave's buggy whip was stolen; two months later the act was repeated. "As Dave knows the thief in the first case he will hold him responsible for both whips. If returned, no questions will be asked, but if not, trouble will follow. A young fellow whose name begins with "A" will take note of this and act accordingly." Horse and buggy pranks were common; sometimes they resulted in downright cruelty.

Summit County *Journal*   October 31, 1891

On Saturday of last week, C. L. Westerman made a trip to his placer claim up the Blue to look after some wood choppers, reported to be chopping down his timber for wood. He hitched his horse to a tree while he took a look through the timber to see the amount of wood cut. While he was away from his horse some one placed his buggy on the opposite side of the tree, the horse was hitched to, over a brush pile and set fire to it. When he returned the buggy was badly damaged, and the horse singed and blistered from his nose to his heels. A more brutal act could not be imagined. The horse is doing well and may recover. Mr. Westerman has offered a reward of $500 for the arrest and conviction of the guilty party.

Dave Braddock lived down Blue River, where Blue and Swan rivers converge, his house and barn a bit north of present-day High Tor Lodge. The railroad passed this point in the fall of 1882, and in 1884 Braddock ("Braddockville") was made a ticket station on the Denver

& South Park Railroad, primarily to accommodate the clientele of Swan River Valley. A few houses soon surrounded the station, but it always remained a small development. Dave's ventures constituted the business activity of Braddockville. In the summer Dave added ice delivery to his enterprises. Winter brought woes to running the stage. "The irrepressible Braddock, in order to keep open the road from Braddockville to Swan City, during the later weeks of winter, had to shovel nearly the whole distance." Ye Editor of Breckenridge newspaper frequently commented, "Dave is a rustler and bound to make his mark."

Wedding bells rang in Breckenridge; Father John L. Dyer united Eli Fletcher and Emma Nauman in marriage at the home of Mrs. Mary Fletcher. "After an ample wedding supper a graceful compliment was paid the newly married couple by a serenade from the Germania Band. Mr. and Mrs. Fletcher left for Braddockville, with the heartiest wishes of all who know them for success, happiness and prosperity. Eli will take charge of the Braddockville House. This hostelry is becoming an important point, and Eli will be likely to keep its reputation above par. A party is being arranged to make a trip to Braddockville next Sunday, to visit Eli and inspect the town." It was fashionable to take a buggy ride on Sundays, from Breckenridge to Braddockville, "where there was lots of excellent homemade ice cream for all callers." The year 1882 saw increase of activity at Braddockville:

Summit County *Journal*   January 30, 1882

Dave Braddock is erecting a fine hall for parties at Braddockville. It will be completed in the course of ten days.

Summit County *Journal*   February 3, 1882

Broncho Dave has completed his dancing hall and the painters are now finishing it up. A private party will be held there next week and some time in the following week a public ball will be given. The hall is one of the finest in the county and will no doubt become a popular resort.

Summit County *Journal*   February 25, 1882

The ball at Braddocks on the evening of the 28th will be one of the best of the season. The addition to his large stables will enable Dave to furnish shelter to all teams that may come on that occasion. Dave's facilities to properly entertain a large first class gathering are not equaled in the county.

But the Braddock Ball was postponed. Nearby Frisco had a gala celebration scheduled; Braddock's Grand Opening bowed in deference to Frisco. Frisco was ready for an historic occasion:

Summit County *Journal*   Monday, February 27, 1882

Journal Editor:

FRISCO

A Rattling Story Of This Ambitious Town

We "Friscocans" still live, and are full of ambition, life and energy. The latest novelty is an opera house, which is nearly completed, location at the Frisco Hotel. A large hall has been transformed into one of the nobbiest halls in the mountains; a large size stage has been put down, a drop curtain, several sets of scenes completed, and the hall papered in an artistic manner, a want long needed is now supplied. Several plays will be brought out in a short time by the Frisco Dramatic Asosciation; we have some artists, residents of Frisco, that are not unknown upon the stage. The Graff Opera House is the name of our pet.

Summit County *Journal*   February 28, 1882

Tomorrow night Frisco will be the friskiest town in the state: the opening of the opera house and the play to be followed by a ball is bound to make things lively. The initial performance at Graff's Opera House will be a Comedietta in one Act—"A Happy Pair" and a Farce—"Turn Him Out." A soiree will be given after the performance by Mr. and Mrs. J. J. Clinton of the Frisco Hotel. We understand that a number of Breckenridge society people contemplate attending the performance and ball.

Summit County *Journal*   March 1, 1882

Frisky Friscocans fling fluttering femininity fast and furious tonight at the dance at the Clintons.

Summit County *Journal*   March 2, 1882

The large number attending the ball at Frisco made it necessary to occupy both the spacious dining hall and the opera house. Kokomo, Ten Mile, Wheeler, Dillon, Braddock, Boreas attended; Breckenridge furnished upwards of forty couples.

Dave Braddock held his opening ball the following week. It, too, was a glittering social success:

Summit County *Journal*   March 8, 1882

Last evening Mr. David Braddock gave his opening ball at his new and elegant hall at Braddockville four miles down the Blue. The location is midway between the county seat and the towns on the Ten Mile, and at nearly the same distance from Swan City. It is an open plateau and here will be the depots of both the Denver & South Park and Denver & Rio Grande. Mr. Braddock has displayed excellent judgment in making these improvements and we sincerely trust that it will be a paying investment.

The buildings first erected here are, a dwelling house and saloon, connected; a stable to accommodate nearly fifty head of stock, and last but not least, a two story structure twenty-six feet by forty-five; the lower story furnished with Chicago lumber and the upper divided into several dressing rooms, altogether first class in design, finish and appointment.

The party was a pronounced social success, one of the most enjoyable of the season. The ladies pronounced the floor perfect for dancing, and the appointments elegant. The supper prepared under the personal supervision of Mrs. Braddock, received universal compliments, as well as the attention of those who enjoyed the contents of the groaning tables.

Broncho Dave's next commercial endeavor started in 1883, manufacturing and bottling a "temperance" drink. This was to be an adjunct to the drinking trade not desiring the stronger brands. Ye Editor reported it "a first quality article for bar purposes." The manufacturing establishment was at Braddockville. Business was good—"Broncho Dave is making oceans of temperance beer. This morning he was shipping forty-two dozen to Montezuma. Dave's beer is a very pleasant and healthful drink for this season of the year." It was time for another of Dave's misfortunes.

In late December, 1883, severe winds buffeted the Breckenridge area—"one of the most severe wind-storms in history. At Breckenridge the wind was fierce all day long, and at times it was feared the town would be picked up and dropped on the eastern slope of Mount Baldy."

During the night, about three o'clock in the morning, the building occupied by Broncho Dave as a bottling establishment (at Braddockville) was entirely destroyed. The front was blown out, which probably deranged the stovepipe and set fire to the building in the attic, as it was discovered to be on fire when the occupants of the dwelling first came out. The building, deprived of the support of the front, was shortly afterward blown down, together with its contents, entirely consumed. The dwellings close by, and stables, were threatened with destruction, but fortunately were saved. This is a sad blow to Dave, for although partially insured, his loss is quite heavy, and coming just at this time will make it worse. Dave will immediately resume his business with machinery and stock from Leadville, until he can get a new outfit from Boston.

It took more than wind and fire to stop Broncho Dave; he enlarged his manufacturing and bottling of "temperance" drink to establishments at Braddockville, Leadville and Breckenridge. At Breckenridge the business was located on the west side, next door to Hemingway's Smith Shop. Ye Editor again reported:

The place sounds as if it were all pop and fiz. When they are at work between sizzling and slopping they manage to fill a gross of bottles every three minutes. What the stuff is made of deponent saith not, but it tastes about as good as the best of the kind in the market, and being home manufacture it ought to be used at all the bars of the vicinity.

In early 1884 Braddockville got a post office. During the winter months the mail was carried on snow shoes to the nearby towns. "Miss Mattie Braddock made her first trip on horseback in late May, carrying the mail from Braddock to Preston."

Summit County *Journal*   February 2, 1884

It has been decided by the postal department to establish a new post office at Broncho Dave's, to be named Braddock, and will commence operations April 1, D. K. Braddock, Postmaster. Fossilized Breckenridgeians, ambitious Dillonites, dead and buried Frisconians and incipient Placervillians had better look to their laurels, for Dave is a rustler, and he may yet locate the metropolis of the Blue River Valley at his station. Stranger things have happened.

Evidently the enterprising Broncho Dave didn't have enough business undertakings to use up all his time and energy, so he added vegetable growing and marketing to the list. He experimented in raising rapid-growing crops, lettuce, radishes, and root crops, such as carrots and turnips. September, 1887, Broncho Dave "went through Breckenridge yelling like a Comanche Indian. Everybody went out to see what the matter was and found that it was Dave letting everybody know that he was selling radishes O! O!! and turnips O! O!! and such garden truck right from his ranch. Of course every woman bought an apron full. Dave Braddock is serving the finest vegetables ever sold in this market, raised at his ranch below town, pulled in the morning and sold in town here two hours afterwards as fresh and crisp as can be found anywhere—a treat that will certainly be appreciated by all who have been eating stale vegetables from two to five days out of the ground. Dave's son, Frank, will serve customers from his wagon on Sunday, Wednesday, and Friday mornings during the balance of the season."

Summit County *Journal*   June 25, 1888

Mr. and Mrs. Braddock have one of the cosiest homes in the county. This morning, through the kindness of Billy Hudson, we took a spin behind Colonel Ware's big team, a skip down to Braddock and showed us that the veteran Broncho Dave was putting in good work. We found him ploughing a new field beside his old one, which he has seeded to quick growing vegetables. Dave's labor for the last six years is making that piece of barren ground to blossom as the rose. He has lately added an enclosure of nearly one hundred acres, a good heavy rail fence makes it a first-class place to keep stock, and as it is all under an irrigating ditch, it will in a short time, be reduced to good grazing.

Dave's farming project received more than local attention. An article appeared in *Field and Farm* magazine, telling of his success:

Eight years ago Mr. D. K. Braddock commenced experimenting with crop growing in Summit County on the Blue, nine thousand, six hundred and forty feet above the level of the sea, where ice forms every night of the summer season. He has succeeded in growing a variety of crops such as peas, lettuce, turnips, rutabagas, and grows them in abundance. The gentleman expects to grow cucumbers next season, but will prepare to cover them with glass or canvas at night. He will also seed a hundred acres to timothy in the coming spring, which grows finely under the trickling waters of the Blue. Says Mr. Braddock: "Before I could succeed I had to learn what variety of vegetables would grow at our altitude. I found that the little dwarf peas, although of an early kind, would not do. They would grow but have no peas in the pods. Then I tried Lang's Early Variety, and found them a success. In the same way with turnips, I found the Milan and Munich and the Yellow Globe would do, while all others would fail."

In the summer-fall seasons "Dave Braddock's musical voice, heralding the wonderful productions of Braddock's Gardens, the highest in the world, is to be heard on the streets of Breckenridge." Some seasons, Dave said, "were most too wet for bananas, but all right for watermelons and pumpkins."

In 1891 another project was added to the list—running the stage line between Breckenridge and Lincoln City—fare for round-trip only fifty cents. But he had competition! "A freak of nature with a tin horn in his mouth tried to under-sell Dave. The competition wore a sign on his back announcing, "This goes for 25cts." Ye Editor again expressed himself: "The authorities of Breckenridge should look into this matter and rid the town of such a nuisance—Pueblo is suggested."

Mr. Braddock, Sr., father of the irrepressible Dave, paid his son a visit in 1887. "The old gentleman, who is far past his threescore and ten, is as lively and active and quite as hardheaded a Democrat as his son." At that time Broncho Dave announced himself as candidate for sheriff, subject to the decision of the Democratic convention. Whether Dave added politics and public service to his long list of endeavors is unknown to us. We hear little more of Broncho Dave, his farm, his railroad station. One of the last records is dated August, 1910, when the pathway was being cleared for the gold boat:

Braddock station will have new life infused into it next week. Four families will take up their residence there while the old junk-scrap machinery, etc., on the Colorado Gold Dredging Company's property is being loaded on cars for shipment; all the old placer pipe that has outlived its usefulness will also be cleaned up.

About the only remaining traces of Broncho Dave's "Braddockville" are the cinders where once the railroad and ticket-station had been. One dwelling-house and High Tor Lodge now occupy the town and farm of ambitious, genial, enterprising Broncho Dave. Colorado Highway 9 passes over what once was part of the town. Drive carefully when going through Braddockville.

Broncho Dave

Buffalo Flats area and Braddock buildings in center—far distance. Possibly Broncho Dave and one of his teams. Courtesy—Library State Historical Society of Colorado.

Braddock Railroad Station in distance. Date:—probably between 1892-1910—estimated by presence of electric lines (1892) and non-presence of gold boat diggings, 1910-1920. Courtesy—Library State Historical Society of Colorado.

Possibly Dave Braddock and his Breckenridge-Lincoln City stage line. Breckenridge-circa 1889. Note Fireman's Hall bell-belfry and hose-drying tower. Courtesy—Summit Historical Society.

INDIANA GULCH

CONGER'S CAMP—ARGENTINE—DYERSVILLE

WARRIOR'S MARK—ANGELS REST

At the south end of Breckenridge the waters of Indiana Gulch enter the Blue River. Like all other gulches of the area, it has been widely prospected for its precious minerals. The most famous, and probably most productive, of its mines was Warrior's Mark at the head of the gulch, some six miles from Breckenridge. The Denver and South Park Railroad coming down from Boreas Summit paralleled the east ridge of the gulch. The present-day road following the twisting roadbed of the old railroad adds extra miles of ascent to Boreas summit. Luxuriant growths of pine, spruce and aspen hide quite admirably many mining scars, and so it remains one of the area's most delightful spots. Real estate investors are rapidly changing its solitary seclusion.

Traversing Indiana Gulch, it is approximately six miles to Dyersville and Warrior's Mark mine. The circuitous Boreas Road is longer. Leaving Highway 9 at the south end of Breckenridge one travels five miles on the Boreas road and arrives at a horseshoe-shaped meadow, formerly the site of Conger's Camp-Argentine. At another mile and a half stands the old water tank of the D. & S. P. Railroad. Farther along— another two miles—one sees the ragged remains of Farnham. (Here an almost impassable jeep road descends into Indiana Gulch to Dyersville and Warrior's Mark.) Continuing another one-half miles on the Boreas Road one reaches the summit—11,482 feet above sea level. Descending the other side one comes to the old mining and railroad town of Como. Midway between Boreas summit and Como is Half-Way Gulch. Once a cabin waiting-station was there, and the miner-recluse, wanting to go to Como, could flag the train to a stop. Indiana Gulch and Boreas was, and still is, one of the most charming regions of Breckenridge area.

CONGER'S CAMP—ARGENTINE

About 1880 prospecting was promoted assiduously in Indiana Gulch. March, 1879, Colonel S. P. Conger discovered and opened the Diantha Lode, a short distance from Breckenridge, in Indiana Gulch. At the head of a beautiful mountain meadow Conger discovered his lode, and here Conger's Camp quickly sprang up. Its voting-power in November, 1880, was slightly ahead of the Ten Mile town of Frisco— Conger, 42; Frisco, 41. At the same time Wheeler, at the Vail junction of Highway 6, had 30 votes, Dillon, 15 votes. In one year's time Conger's Camp was about half the size of Lincoln City (French Gulch), Chihuahua and Decatur (in Peru Valley near Montezuma.) Chihuahua, Lincoln and Decatur had voting-power of 81, 75, 72 respectively. For a short time the settlement in Indiana Gulch was known as Conger's Camp, and the name is not unfamiliar today.

Across the gulch from Conger's Camp, south and west, Mount Argentine lifted its head into the skies. Just when the change took place is not known, but Conger's Camp, by 1881, was being called Argentine. And so it appeared on F. C. Cramer's maps at the turn of the century. An article in Summit County's *Journal,* March 26, 1921, entitled "Breckenridge Town Forty

Years Ago" indicated that Conger's Camp had become Argentine sometime in 1880-1881. The specific article was entitled "This is Argentine—Argentine A Swiss Chalet."

In crossing the range from Como to Breckenridge, the incoming passenger's attention is directed to the little village of Argentine, formerly and widely known as Conger's Camp. It resembles more than any other in Colorado (so European travelers say) a Swiss chalet. A beautiful location, surrounded by primeval forests and overlooked by towering mountains, near whose base it nestles like an infant at its parent's knee—this is Argentine. A score or more of buildings, from the cabin of the prospector to the well-built houses of prosperous mine owners, with several business buildings and the extensive sawmills of Seyball, Sutton & Co., comprise the town proper while at many a point on the mountain sides and in the sheltered gulches may be found bachelor parties and families industriously working out their fortunes on the lodes of the camp.

The foundation of the camp was laid by Colonel S. P. Conger in March, 1879, when he discovered and opened up the Diantha Lode. Following rapidly his remarkable discovery, a large amount of mining property was located, and has received considerable development. The coming season will undoubtedly witness more development than has been done in the past three seasons, and we trust to be able to chronicle its future prosperity. As one of the nearest mining camps to the county seat, its prospects and prosperity are directly connected with ours.

Breckenridge's *Daily Journal,* February 21, 1883, devoted a full page to write-ups of Breckenridge and nearby communities. Argentine had its write-up:

ARGENTINE

Known when first established as Conger's Camp from S. P. Conger the founder in 1879. It is located on the old stage road from Breckenridge to Como, across the Breckenridge pass of the main range, three and a half miles south of the former place and three-quarters of a mile west of the Denver and South Park railroad. Two daily mails are received and despatched, Mrs. Diantha Conger, postmistress. Several large corporations are mining in the vicinity, the Mining Co. of Hannibal, Mo., the Lake Shore Mining Co. of South Bend, Indiana, the Steadman Gulch Mining Co. of Wheeling, W. Va., the Stevens & Penfield Association of New York and Chicago, the Silver Glance Mining Co. of Denver and Argentine, the High Line Prospecting and Developing Company of Denver, Thompson, Moore & Co. of Harrodsburg, Ky., and several individual miners and operators. The mountains surrounding the place are rich in precious metals and are heavily timbered.

We get a few glimpses of the people and the life that was Conger Camp-Argentine's. Colonel Conger and his wife (Diantha) and a Mrs. Malaby got into the social news; a man by the name of Allen provided "spirituous" life for the community. Johnny Mitchael, the night watchman of railroad property, and a huge cinnamon bear provided excitement for Argentine an October night, 1886. The bear gave chase. "Johnny brought the bear to camp, or rather the bear brought Johnny. The entire force from Argentine turned out; his bearship made his way toward Breckenridge, and by the tracks he made he must have been a monster." Earlier in the year a mountain lion "run in the night trackwalker—east of Boreas—no one hurt, but badly scared." November, 1881,—"Conger's Camp is divided in its excitement; a mountain lion and a couple of big strikes bear the honors equally."

When Argentine gave its last gasp is not known. 1888 had a news item—"Yesterday's mail was seven hours late because of the derailment of two engines near Argentine." Ed Auge in his *History Of The Breckenridge Mining District* (reported January 25, 1938, in the Summit County *Journal*) wrote: "There are two freak veins in the Breckenridge Mining District, which are a puzzling proposition to all who have worked them. One is on the Diantha up Indiana Gulch. A blanket vein runs up the hill not over two feet from the surface. Several holes were dug through this vein and in some places there would be an ore streak a foot wide. Some of it looks like solid silver, but assays show it to be worthless. Near the top of the hill, a shaft was sunk in the 80's, and an old ore bin is still there filled with ore (?). Indications show that early day prospectors discovered this vein and thought they had a stake, but their dream must have been shattered by assay returns."

The camp rapidly disintegrated; only diehards remained to hunt elusive riches. A few scattered boards are now found in the open meadow. Among the trees, at the edge of the meadow, one finds stones outlining cabin sites. Hardly a remnant is to be found resembling a building or cabin. Conger's Camp—Argentine— passed away almost from remembrance.

("Argentine" was a popular mining-town name of Breckenridge area. Don and Jean Griswold, in *Colorado's Century of Cities,* write of "Argentine City" perched atop the continental divide near Gray's Peak and Argentine Pass. It was a booming silver camp of the 1860's.

Verna Sharp, *A History of Montezuma, Sts. John, and Argentine,* tells of the Argentine that came into being on the site of the former towns of Decatur and Rathbone in Peru Valley— four miles northeast of Montezuma.

The National Archives and Records Service, Washington, D. C., could not provide information of a post office at Argentine City. It did give information on the other two Argentines:

Argentine, Summit County, Colorado

Established as Conger on July 8, 1880
Name changed to Argentine on January 3, 1881
Discontinued on October 22, 1883
Postmasters: Date of Appointment:
George G. Gould   July 8, 1880
Diantha Conger   January 3, 1881

Argentine, Summit County, Colorado

Established on November 18, 1901
Discontinued on February 28, 1907
Postmasters: Date of Appointment:
Mrs. Julia Ritchey   November 18, 1901
Lizzie Smith (Declined)   March 16, 1905
Cora Williams   May 23, 1905
Hattie Southermark   December 3, 1906

DYERSVILLE—DYERVILLE—WARRIOR'S MARK

At the head-spring of Indiana Creek and Indiana Gulch, nature did its utmost before surrendering to timberline, nurturing a heavy stand of tall majestic evergreens. Aspen and pine became discouraged and stately, giant spruce claimed the last timbered heights for themselves. Water trickles forth from surrounding hills, the genesis of cold, refreshing stream. At this ancient primeval the little town of Dyersville (sometimes Dyerville) came into existence. Its name honored the beloved Methodist minister, the "Snow-Shoe Itinerant," John Lewis Dyer. Father Dyer was one of the first to prospect in that area and to

build a cabin at the location. In his book *Snow-Shoe Itinerant,* he writes:

Being well acquainted with the mountains and mining, I was paid good wages for locating claims. When the snow was deep, I went on snow-shoes (skis), always feeling that a preacher had a right to earn his living if he could not get it by preaching; but no right to leave his charge.

My practical knowledge made my services as a locater in demand. Sometimes I gave them to deserving young fellows, whom fortune had used roughly. Two such were Candell and Thompson. In the spring of 1880 they came to me for information. Snow was more than knee-deep. They were out of money, except enough to board them a few days, and put up a log pen, ten or twelve feet square, just large enough for them to stand up in and make a stopping-place. The next thing was a job of work. I was employed to sink holes on some claims, to hold them, and gave them employment. I bought tools for them, and we started up the mountains, I leading. Soon the trail gave out, and we broke a path in snow waist deep. We carried picks, shovels, tent, and blankets. It was hard climbing for the boys; but they said: "If that old man can get there, we must." And we did. I showed them where to dig. That day they had a shaft three feet deep, and slept in it at night.

They worked for some time, making fair wages—say three dollars per day—and then they and myself took up some ground in company. They also continued to work and prospect for themselves through the summer. Thompson found some float mineral, and followed it up to where it came up to the grass roots, and sunk a hole on it ten feet deep, and threw out several hundred pounds of rich mineral, gray copper, worth five hundred dollars to the ton. He staked his claim—one hundred and fifty by one thousand five hundred feet. He did not know how rich it was, and let one Parkinson have a fourth interest for one hundred dollars, and would have sold the balance for two hundred and fifty dollars, but his man failed to come to time. He kept the location a secret. I had not asked him where it was, but said: "You have got on my claim, I suspect." He replied: "You have no claim up there." I answered: "I prospected up there three years ago, and left my shovel to hold my claim." "Where is your claim?" he said. I inquired if he had been at the head of a certain ditch. "Yes," was his answer. "Well," I replied, "my claim crosses about

Indiana Gulch

thirty rods above that." "My claim," he said, "is not within three hundred feet of that."

I rode up, and found my shovel; and just up the hill-side I saw his corner stake, and followed to his works. I was pleased with his show for a lode, and was glad for his sake. Seeing the ground was vacant on each side of his claim, before I left I staked one claim south and four north of it. Unable to do the work myself, I took two or three pieces of his ore home with me, and told an assayer where it came from, and that I had staked the ground adjoining; and, as I had to attend to my church building, proposed to let him go in with me, if he liked the show; he to do my work for an interest. He went, and was pleased, and we made a contract. He looked at Mr. Thompson's prospect, and wanting some one to do the work, I suggested Thompson, as he would want to keep an eye on his own claim. He said nothing about buying the claim. When Thompson came in to our house, I told him they wanted to see him; and knowing that he had offered his claim for two hundred and fifty dollars, advised him, if they wanted to buy him out, not to sell for nothing. My wife named a thousand dollars, as it was easier to fall than to raise. He went and asked them twelve hundred; but they offered him a thousand, ten per cent down, and the rest in sixty days. He returned in a few minutes with his hundred dollars, and said it was the first time he had ever had that much at once. Then they wanted to see Mr. Parkinson, but told Thompson not to tell how he sold. Mrs. Dyer said: "You tell Mr. Parkinson to come here as he goes, and I will post him." He came, and then sold his fourth for five hundred dollars, ten per cent down. There were four of the company, and so they had the big thing, and—by doing the work agreed on—three-fourths of mine also.

The ore was very rich—from low grade to a thousand dollars a ton. But one of the parties assayed some of it, and showed me the certificate. It was so low that I never said a word to Mr. Thompson about it. I was disappointed in it. If anybody knew it was rich, it was those who bought it. In a day it was all over the camp that the boys had been swindled, the ore being fabulously rich. And, as a matter of course, the discoverers felt bad over the loss of a good thing. Everybody asked why they did not have it assayed. Because they had no money to pay on a risk, as but very few had received any benefit by the assays, and many considered it money out. Parties told them they were swind-

led, and that the sale could be set aside, and that on certain conditions they would have it done. What those conditions were I never knew. They were not to have anything except they could prove fraud, and so get the property back. So they went to law.

I had been asked by the assayer if I wished to have some of the Warrior's Mark ore assayed. I replied: "No, I have no interest in the lode." Afterwards he called me in and showed me his report on it, and it was lower than I had thought possible. I thought no more about it at the time, until after the sale. When they had me on the witness-stand, they questioned me as to the assay I had seen. I told them what I knew of it. "Did you tell either of the parties before the sale?" "No." "Why did you not tell them?" "Because I was taken back, and thought it would do them no good." This showed that they were not influenced by the assay. So the purchasers held the diggings, and the poor boys got no more. They were advised to compromise with the first party, but they would not.

Now the company goes to work, but soon winter is on, and snow anywhere from five to eight feet deep. Some good mineral was raised; but the water was strong, and they concluded to sell. The price was put at three hundred thousand dollars for the whole, including my interest. I was to have eight thousand, five hundred.

About the 1st of January, 1881, I began work on a log house. Had a good horse and sled, six miles away, at Breckenridge. Selected a place to build, and taking my horse, with chain and whiffle-tree, went eight rods, midsides in snow, and dragged in the first tree. And so, cutting and hauling logs, and going back home each day, returning to work in the morning with lumber, I finished my house. It was seventeen feet by seventeen, a story and a half in height, shingle roof, two floors, and doors. By the 19th of February I moved my wife and the last of our goods. By that time I had a hole against the bank in the snow to stable my horse. Laid poles on the snow, and put pine-brush for roof, and he was comfortable till his slab stable was built. We were within a half mile of the Warrior's Mark Lode, which was the center of attraction for mining experts and speculators. Men would come, and look, and send experts; then others would come. All wished to make money. Some would levy blackmail, under threats of spoiling the sale. After all the efforts, the property was not sold.

The weather becoming good, they hired a superintendent and about fifty men, and resumed work. In six months they took out, as well as I could learn, between seventy-five and eighty thousand dollars. During this time they stocked the property at three millions. After one dividend, it failed to pay any more for a time under the management. I took ten thousand dollars in stock for my part. At this time I began to look at the stock system, and concluded to let that be the last stock I would ever have anything to do with in mining. For these reasons: First, the amount is put at three times its worth; second, there are directors, clerks, and treasurer, president, superintendent, and bosses, all on pay, besides the hands. These, with mismanagement, wire-working, whisky, cards, and fancy women, beat the average lode. After several attempts to get pay out of the mine, a man took the property to work. He had secured more than half the stock, and had the control. He bought mine. I realized two thousand dollars.

I have given this sketch to show some of the difficulties of prospecting, selling, or running a mine. Yet mining is the business of the country.

Father Dyer's new-found wealth at Warrior's Mark did not measure up to expectations. Earlier the *Journal* had congratulated him:

> The venerable patriarch has at last struck it rich in his mining claim near the Warrior's Mark. The entire community rejoices over his success in this venture, and none more heartily than the *Journal*. He deserves it for his untiring zeal as the pioneer preacher of his church and the distinguished services he has rendered as a citizen.

The *Journal* of April, 1882, reported: "The source of wealth in this section just now, in the mind's eye of the hopeful prospector, is up Indiana Gulch, way above timberline or thereabouts. Within sight of the Warrior's Mark is the spot of all spots and a discolored piece of rock is the fortune seeker's glory. He will pick longer and harder on an empty stomach with a piece of copper-stained rock in his breeches than a pack of coyotes would follow a wounded deer. The smile may rise at their enthusiasm, but without their self-sacrificing efforts, where would our state be today?"

Not much of Dyersville and Warrior's Mark remains in 1971. Some decaying logs of three good-sized buildings are along the tumbling stream, marking the one-time community. Not one of them measures the 17 x 17 of Father Dyer's cabin. Remains of a few other buildings are on the east slope of the gulch. Warrior's Mark mine is a half-mile north and west of Dyersville; it is approached by a gently-graded road. Most of the mine buildings succumbed to hard winters of wind and snow; the sagging ruins that remain cannot last longer than a few more winters. Land investors encroach. The crystal ball reveals palatial homes and condominiums replacing the miner's lowly log cabin.

In 1886 and 1887 the voting-power of Dyersville (before woman suffrage) was seventeen—ten Republicans and seven Democrats. Political news, jury duty and news items reveal names of inhabitants—Thomas West, C. H. Pike, John Zwergle, John Stuber, Messrs. Wood and Abbett. There was no post office, and a nearby neighbor, Jerry Krigbaum, complained of this hardship. Dyersville did have a store—a branch of L. Adamson's Blue Front, corner of Ridge Street and Lincoln, Breckenridge. Adamson announced in the *Daily Journal*: "In transit from San Francisco for the Dyersville house, a choice line of California clothing and underwear. I have on exhibition at Dyersville a line of substantial well-made miners boots and gum goods that are selling on sight. Clothing at the Dyersville store at bed rock prices. Prospectors, miners and others intending to outfit are invited to call upon L. Adamson at the Blue Front, Dyersville or Breckenridge. Our motto to 'raise the standard and lower the price' will be strictly adhered to. Goods delivered free."

The *Daily Journal*, April 17, 1885, leaked the news that Warrior's Mark was in deep financial trouble—in debt to the tune of $19,000, of which $8,000 was due to workers. The mine representative lived in Breckenridge—"drove a carriage with a spanking team with gaudy plumes upon the horses—and could be seen at every game of stallion poker." There were threats of violence by the mine workers. Mr. James Fryer, superintendent, thought it best to slip out of Breckenridge in the early hours of morning before dawn. But a secret guard had been set to discourage just such a move. When he went to the barn to hitch his team, the alert guard persuaded him to return to the security of his household. When Mr. Fryer made a second attempt to go by train, he found some unwanted companions on the train with him. They persuaded him to get off the train with them at Farnham Station,

Indiana Gulch

atop Boreas Pass, and walk down to Dyersville and the Warrior's Mark Mine. Here he was compelled to restore funds he had borrowed from the mine's woman cook. Mr. Fryer's train companions rode back to Breckenridge on the next train, but he, stone broke, had to walk the six miles to town.

Warrior's Mark had its good and bad times. January, 1920, "they re-opened the old-time bonanza property which produced $96,000 worth of silver from shallow diggings." In February, 1920, "Warrior's Mark stock increased from $1,000,000 to $5,000,000. It was one of Colorado's wonder silver producers during former days of the high price of that metal. Several pockets that produced fabulous sums were encountered, and the mine was a steady producer for a long period." Such is the story of Dyersville and Warrior's Mark.

FARNHAM

Farnham was a near-neighbor of Dyersville, to the east, near the top of Boreas. The February 21, 1883, issue of *Daily Journal* had the following to say of it:

> This post office and station is located on the Denver & South Park railway, exactly one hundred miles west of Denver and half-way from Como to Breckenridge, and one and a quarter miles north of the continental divide, in the McBarnes mining district, celebrated for its high grade ores. A 500 foot switch has been put in by the company for the accommodation of miners and mill-men of the the vicinity. The mountain views from this point are unequaled in extent and variety, and preparations are under way for making it a first-class summer resort, with every variety of attractions. For information regarding the mining district, address W. H. Farnham, postmaster, who we guarantee will furnish necessary information to all making inquiries.

Breckenridge's Eli Fletcher was employed by Farnham & Company at Farnham Station on the Denver and South Park Railroad. In 1882 "our friend Fletcher came down from the eyrie of Angels Rest. He is not content with the quality of air furnished up there in rather insufficient quantity."

ANGELS REST

Not all was placid and serene at Dyersville. Nature did its best to make it so, but there was Angels Rest and Jerry Krigbaum! The pressure of years, traveling, and the demands of a heavy weekly preaching schedule had led Father Dyer to exclaim, "Where can rest be found?" Peace and rest were not to be found at Angels Rest and Dyersville!

On the east slope of Indiana Gulch, at Dyersville, was an establishment with the dubious title of Angels Rest. Both parts of the name are open to question. Rightly speaking, Angels Rest was a part of Dyersville. Angels Rest got its drinking water where Dyersville got theirs. The business clientele came primarily from Dyersville and Warrior's Mark. Both Jerry Krigbaum and Father Dyer were part-time prospectors; after that their aims in life were widely apart. Father Dyer's was spiritual; Jerry Krigbaum's was spirituous. Give the devil his dues— Jerry was good-natured, but more on the devilish side than the angelic.

In addition to his part-time prospecting, Jerry operated what he called Angels Rest—a place where food and spirituous drinks were dispensed. He was also dedicated to stir up some lively life at the far end of Indiana Gulch. One can, almost with certainty, pinpoint the exact location of Jerry's establishment. A large disintegrated log building on the east slope of Dyersville marks the spot. Its large tin can and bottle dump almost certainly locates Angels Rest. The dump has been thoroughly worked by the devotees of bottle-hunting—and what a rich treasure that dump must have provided! Large wooden boxes, once used for cupboards in the dilapidated structure, indicate that Wedding Breakfast Coffee was the favorite non-spirituous beverage of the establishment. Father Dyer built his cabin midwinter of 1881; Jerry Krigbaum waited until warmer summer weather. We learn to know Jerry by his activities reported in Breckenridge *Daily Journal*:

> June 13, 1881: The irrepressible Jerry Krigbaum, formerly of Conger's Camp (Argentine), now of Angels Rest or Dyersville, near the top of the range, was in town yesterday. Jerry vows he has struck it rich and will develop it if he has to borrow, beg or steal to do it. Just like him. June 20, 1881: Jerry Krigbaum of Angels Rest met with a serious accident yesterday in mounting a horse to go to South Park. The saddle being insecurely fastened and the horse feeling lively, Jerry was thrown and his leg broken above the ankle.

December 7, 1881: The denizens of Angels Rest are sadly out of place for mail facilities. With a railroad station in sight and a mail coach passing every day, yet they can't get the papers. Jerry the old angel is almost distracted over it. December 17, 1881: The ancient and wingless angel, Jerry, was down from the Rest this morning. He says nothing but the best will keep from freezing up his way. December 19, 1881: Father Dyer of Dyersville, adjoining Angels Rest, was in town this morning and favoured the *Journal* office with a call.

December 23, 1881: This being the first Christmas since the settlement of "Angels Rest," quite a flutter is apparent in the feathery group. The old he angel, Jerry, was down in town yesterday looking up supplies for the occasion. He took a two-horse sleigh load of truck out with him, the most noticeable article was the head of a ten-gallon keg filled up full of corn juice and well-surrounded with turkey, eggs, cranberries, oysters, butter, pickles, etc., etc., in too great a variety to mention. The old angel wants it generally known that they will have just the best lay-out to be found on that day and everybody will be welcome. The angelic old cuss was accompanied by a sort of sub-angel from the half-way station of Argentine. This unfeathered aspirant for angelic honors supplies the passers-by with spirituous comfort at the very unangelic place called Argentine, and in the language known to mortals he is called Allen, (no relative to Ethan.) He invites all passers-by to drop in at his place and he will give them something that will make quail look as large as turkeys and turkeys as large as condors. Shouldn't wonder.

December 29, 1881: The Angels of the Rest at the top of the range have not yet reported the kind of time they had at Christmas. We hope no ill has happened them for it's 1881 years since the last batch of feathered visitors of that kind visited the earth and it would be rough on them if they were in any way abused. Perhaps the oysters and things didn't agree with them.

December 30, 1881: The angels have been heard from. The old he angel, Jerry, was down this morning for fresh spirituous supply. Christmas passed gloriously, all the whisky was exhausted and the substantials soon followed, so the old one had to come down among dealers again. New Years at Angels Rest will be a grand free blow-out, everybody welcome, feathers or no feathers, angels of all denominations, character or color cordially invited.

WANTED: The man who found the line between the Angels Rest saloon and the watering place at Dyersville is hereby requested to return the same or call and get the mate. By order of J. T. Krigbaum.

February 20, 1882: Jerry Krigbaum came down from Angels Rest yesterday. It is stated on good authority that his mission was to attend church for the first time in ten years.

March 24, 1882: An angelic jamboree comes off tonight at the "Angels Rest" up among the clouds near Boreas, the occasion being the removal of the old he-angel's ten gallon keg from one log cabin to another. It is proposed by the unfeathered gang to make music in the air that will take the lead of that celestial concert of which all have read. Sorry that our reporter cannot take a balloon view of the affair as it would no doubt be worth reading.

March 29, 1882: Krigbaum reports having an assay of 650 oz. to the ton and claims to have a four foot streak of the truck which if O. K. will make Jerry one of the big guns of the section.

July 19, 1882: Jerry Krigbaum, better known as the he angel of Angels Rest, passed through town this morning for the Rest. The wife and little angels are down at Rock Creek.

Jerry's further doings elude us. Only once more we hear of him. May 18, 1886, *Journal* gives a list of Grand and Petit Jurors for the June term, 1886, of the District Court. Listed are: John Zwergle of Dyersville, J. Krigbaum of Braddock, and Barney L. Ford of Breckenridge.

After Jerry Krigbaum, Indiana Gulch needed a century's breathing spell.

Most substantial remains of Conger's Camp-Argentine (Indiana Gulch) 1971. Courtesy—Mr. Jack Caubin.

Jack and Lolly Caubin, and dog "Breck" (Breckenridge) at Argentine, Indiana Gulch. Courtesy—Mr. Jack Caubin.

Dyersville, 1964. (Robert L. Brown photo) Courtesy—Library State
Historical Society of Colorado.

Dyersville, 1971. Boreas Pass in the distance.

Indiana Gulch

Remains of Farnham near top of Boreas Pass-1971.

Remains of Jerry Krigbaum's "Angel Rest" establishment. Jerry Krigbaum reincarnated? No,—the Reverend Brian Duckworth, Methodist Chaplain of the University of London—summer, 1971.

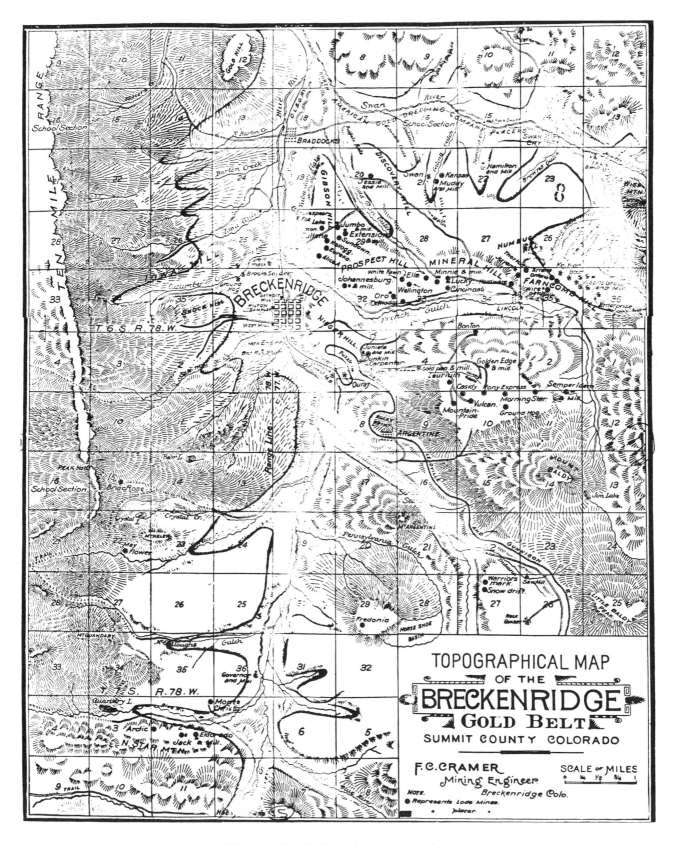

Map showing Indiana Gulch's Argentine.

Boreas Pass—Elevation 11,482 feet

FIREMAN'S HALL

Fireman's Hall, with quaint belfry and bell, was a Breckenridge Main Street landmark for many years. It stood on the east side of Main Street, north of Radigan's livery stables. A high tower was added to the south side. From a distance the shingle-siding of the tower looked like a massive brick chimney. The purpose of the tower was for draining and drying the fire hose. A window, on the east side, provided light; a smokestack, jutting forth mid-way up the tower, released smoke from the stove heating-unit. It was a picturesque sight, belonging uniquely to Breckenridge. The building was demolished in the spring and summer of 1941 by W P A (Work Projects Administration) and the lumber used to help erect another Town Hall—Fireman's Hall on the west side of Main Street. The new building never had the quaintness of the old.

Even to old-timers Fireman's Hall "was always there" on Main Street, but that was not true. Fireman's Hall had almost a decade of history before it came to the Main Street location. Like many other Breckenridge buildings—churches, blacksmith shop, newspaper office—it traveled from one place to another. Before the day of electric and telephone lines, moving buildings was a relatively easy thing to do. Fireman's Hall, with quaint belfry and bell, joined the building-moving brigade.

Thursday, June 10th, 1880, Breckenridge was threatened with destruction by fire. Two large forest fires broke out south of town and a third fire on the north side. A meeting was hurriedly called to formulate plans to combat the flames and organize a permanent fire department. (Previously, fire-fighting was a non-organized, volunteer activity on the part of the citizen-ry.) The meeting was brief—"it adjourned to fight the approaching flames which were threatening the city up the valley of the Blue from Gibson Hill. To meet the emergency Mr. Donald Fletcher was unanimously elected foreman and George Betz first assistant with power to appoint assistants to aid them in prosecuting the work of staying the threatening flames. During the emergency citizens of all classes turned out and worked side by side to avert the common peril, and to their exertions is owing the fact that the town still exists. Gathering clouds poured down an abundant shower of most welcome rain which dampened the fallen timber and dry leaves and it is hoped that the danger is measurably past." The hastily adjourned meeting was reconvened Sunday afternoon to establish a permanent and officially authorized fire-fighting organization. In the meantime, it was asked "that every citizen keep at all hours, day and night, in this emergency a fire bucket at hand ready for use on alarm being given from a triangle to be used until a proper fire alarm bell can be procured." They adopted resolution advising the Board of Trustees to purchase a suitable fire apparatus to protect the town. Establishing a fire department and building a fireman's hall moved rapidly. The *Daily Journal* reported:

On account of the fact that the trustees have no authority to issue bonds, the company is building a truck house on one of the county lots, donated for the purpose by the county commissioners. It is two stories high, 26 x 60; the first story to accommodate the apparatus, the second for a city hall for the use of company meetings and public entertainments. The funds for this purpose are loaned on long time by Judge Silverthorn ($2000 at 18% interest), a patriotic pioneer of the town. The location is a central one, on French Street, north of Lincoln Avenue. Surmounted by a tower, it is a conspicuous object among the fine buildings of the city; it will be completed about the 20th inst. The contractor is W. G. Taylor, one of the leading mechanics of the place. Contract for building, $1,617.63; grading lot, $50.00; laying foundation wall, $50.00; painting and papering contract, $147.00; Total, $1,864.63.

Fireman's Hall was erected on the French Street lot immediately south of Father Dyer Methodist Church. (This lot is the present-day space between Summit County Court House and Father Dyer Church.) It was town property.

Father Dyer Church and Fireman's Hall were in the process of construction at the same time. Father Dyer purchased his lot and got an early spring start on building, running into opposition with town commissioners on boundary lines. Voluntary help on church building wasn't as quickly performed as contracted labor on Fireman's Hall, so the latter was in operation before the Church. First church services were held in mid-August; Fireman's Hall didn't get started until June, but the July meeting (recorded in their minutes) took place in the "Hall of Hook and Ladder Company, Breckenridge—July 13, 1880."

The purpose of Breckenridge Fire Department wasn't only fire-fighting; the second-story of their building was designed for social purposes. A parade and a ball were planned for September 1st. It was a grand-opening ball—seventy-two tickets were sold at $3 apiece. When the expenses of supper, music, ticket and program printing were paid there was a net profit of $19.15. This was the beginning of social occasions for which Fireman's Hall was to be long remembered by "Breckenridgians."

Two of the first fires for the new department were at the Methodist Church and Silverthorn Hotel: "On Sunday, Nov. 12th, an alarm was given from the Methodist Church adjoining Hook & Ladder house, which was put out without difficulty." "On Nov. 16th an alarm of fire was given from the Silverthorn Hotel which was extinguished with little damage."

Breckenridge firemen had their welfare programs and rules of conduct. "In case of the sickness of a member it shall be the duty of the foreman to detail members to watch over the sick." In conduct matters: "Non-attendance at a day fire 50c fine; at a night fire $1.00. Non-attendance at annual meeting $5.50; non-attendance at other meetings 25c. Assisting in racing while returning from a fire or alarm 50c. Any attempt to introduce liquor into the house $5.00." (Evidently the rules changed by July, 1886: "There will be a full meeting to-night at Fireman's Hall as the boys are to get away with a keg of fresh lager—you bet." *Daily Journal*—July 13, 1886.) Next day's *Journal* reported that there had indeed been a "full meeting."

The firemen planned for another ball at the April 4, 1881, meeting "to christen and dedicate the bell purchased by the Town of Breckenridge when it arrives, or as soon thereafter as practicable." The ball was held April 28th.

The arrival of the fire bell brought problems to Hook & Ladder Company. The pastors of the Methodist and Congregational Churches, Dyer and Bickford, immediately petitioned the Town Trustees for permission to ring the bell for church purposes. The petition was granted. Hook & Ladder Company wasn't happy about it. A special meeting of the Company was called "to take action in regard to the course of the town trustees in giving permission to the churches to ring the fire bell." After much discussion a vote was taken on the question of bell ringing for church purposes and eight firemen were against it and seven were agreeable. It was voted then that a transcript of the vote be transmitted to the Board of Town Trustees "that the bell should only be rung for fire purposes." It was a close vote and it was a delicate matter to solve for fear of offending firemen and citizenry. Finally, five years later, November, 1886, "the meeting of town trustees on Thursday evening decided that the privilege of using the fire alarm bell for church purposes should be withdrawn, much to the disgust of some outsiders." Came the report the following Monday, "Yesterday the Fireman's Hall bell tolled as usual for church service; who is on top, the Town Trustees or Father Dyer?" Moving Fireman's Hall down to Main Street resolved the issue.

On a few occasions Episcopalians rented Fireman's Hall for services, but church usage was not encouraged. At the Company's July 12, 1881, meeting the matter was discussed: "An application having been made for the use of the hall for church purposes, it was moved that the matter be referred to the town council for adjustment as the majority of the company do not approve the movement." Bell-ringing may have been a determining factor. It must have been difficult, on Sunday, to know whether it was church service or a fire.

Daily Journal   February 6, 1882

Fireman's Hall

The board of trustees have nearly completed the improvements on the hall which will make it the finest room outside of Denver or Leadville. The floor was originally made of the best quality Chicago lumber and is still the admiration of all lovers of Terpsichore. A wainscoating three feet high has been placed on the wall all around the room and also on the sides of the stairway. The remaining portions of the walls are hung with the finest ornamental paper divided into panels by columns. The ceiling has been repainted in pure white giving a charming effect in contrast with the dark ground of walls. The work of the artisans will be completed some time during the week.

In the fall of 1882 the firemen decided to purchase hose and hose cart. "Mr. Bressler went to Denver and stated what our town needed to Mr. Bandhauer, chairman of the fire committee of the Denver council. Mr. Bandhauer said he thought he could serve the town and would ship a cart as soon as he could get the parts together. This morning the railroad company delivered a very neat and substantial truck, and it was received by the company, who housed it in the Fireman's Hall, ready for use."

In 1886 "Ye Editor" took up his pen against Fireman's Hall: "The Fireman's Hall is the shabbiest looking building in town. A little paint would improve its appearance amazingly." At a Trustee meeting, May 5th, it was "proposed that the town hall, otherwise known as the Fireman's Hall, be moved to a lot upon Main Street, where its spacious room might be a source of revenue."

At the July 6, 1887, Town Trustee meeting it was reported, "the removal of the Fireman's Hall was indefinitely postponed." Ye Editor resumed his sniping: July 19th—"The Fireman's Hall, if it is not sold or removed, should be cleaned up, repaired and painted. As it now stands, it is a disgrace to the city." July 22nd—"Repair the Fireman's Hall or sell it to someone who will take care of it." July 27th—"Some of the visitors today mistook the Fireman's Hall for a played-out livery stable. Cannot our city dads have it repaired and painted?"

December, 1887, saw action regarding Fireman's Hall. "On Saturday night the firemen held an enthusiastic meeting and by a close vote decided in favor of removal of the hall, but to what particular point was not decided upon." Whereupon Ye Editor commented: "The removal of this building to a proper position, its repairs and care, is just now the exciting question with our fire boys. A large number favor one location while quite as large a number favor another, and the two wings will fight it out on Saturday night next. That the hall should be removed and repaired is a non-disputed proposition. As it now stands the hall is a disgrace to the city and is enough to crush the pride of any department. Removed to an eligible site, repaired and remodeled, the hall instead of being an eyesore, a nuisance and an expense could be made useful, an ornament and a slight source of revenue to the department. By all means let the hall be removed and fixed up."

The Town Trustees, December 13th, acquiesced to the proposed plan—removal of the hall to Main Street. "Mr. Nashold stated the department could purchase the two adjoining lots just north of the Radigan livery stable for two hundred dollars. They proposed to grade them down to the street level, set the hall back four feet from the line of the buildings now on that side of the street, so as to give the apparatus a good start in going out, construct an outside stairway to the second story, divide the lower story into three rooms, the front for the apparatus of the three companies and the rear two rooms for meeting room purposes. They also asked that the trustees add fifty dollars to their former contribution and purchase the lots named. After discussing the project a motion was made making an additional appropriation to the department of fifty dollars for the purchase of the lots and that the foreman of each company together with the chief of the department be constituted trustees to hold the hall for the use and benefit of the respective companies for the term of ten years. The motion carried without a dissenting voice and the meeting adjourned." Now we are ready for the big move from French Street to Main Street. It had its thrills! It took a full month to complete the moving of Fireman's Hall. The distance was three blocks, two of which were down hill. Day by day progress reports appeared in the newspaper:

Dec. 14, 1887

This morning the volunteer force of the fire department set to work to grade the lots north of Radigan's stable for the reception of the hall.

Dec. 15th:

The gang of volunteer graders made very fair progress yesterday at the new foundation for the Fireman's Hall. Some portions of the ground being graded for the Hall is found frozen so hard that fires are built upon it to enable the brigade of pickers to get away with it. We learn that all the contributors to the fund for the removal of Fireman's Hall paid the amount subscribed with a single exception.

Dec. 16th:

Mr. John Dierks is working with might and main to get the hall ready for moving as soon as the foundation is ready for the building.

Dec. 19th:

Nobody working on the grading of the Fireman's Hall lots? Why?

Dec. 20th:

This morning at seven o'clock the thermometer stood ten degrees below zero. The firemen met last evening and determined to have their lots graded by contract which is to be let forthwith.

Dec. 21st:

Mr. John Baker and a partner has taken the contract of grading the Fireman's Hall lots to be completed by Monday night next. With such nights as last night it will keep them rustling to win at it.

This morning the fire alarm bell was taken down from its belfry on top of the Fireman's Hall. The contractors are raising the building so as to place the prepared skids under the frame preparatory to its removal. It has been well braced within so that moving it will not rack it to any great extent.

A COLD NIGHT

Last night and this morning was one of the coldest snaps on record in this locality. The evening was very cold, twenty degrees below zero was reached before midnight, at 2 o'clock it was 30° below, at 3 o'clock 38° at 4 o'clock 42°, at 5 o'clock 40°, at 6 o'clock 40°, at 7 o'clock 38°, at 9 o'clock this forenoon the thermometer showed 20° below zero, so that for twelve hours we enjoyed an arctic coldness that was suggestive if not refreshing.

Freezing was the order of the night, water pipes, flowers and everything subject to injury by frost received attention from the frost king. A suspicious feature this morning was our saloon men carefully examining their liquor bottles to see if the pure (?) liquors had frozen.

Dec. 22nd:

The old Fireman's Hall is up two feet from the ground and tomorrow it will be on runners and head for Main Street.

Four or five men are at work on the Fireman's Hall lots and it looks as if the contractors will come out winners. The hall may be expected to adorn Main Street by this time next week.

(They were too hopeful!)

Dec. 23rd:

The contractors who are removing Fireman's Hall say the Lord has gone back on them. Yesterday they flooded the space under the hall so it might freeze and the hall be slid out nicely on the ice. The two previous nights were cold enough to freeze a body of water four feet square into a solid block of ice, but last night only three quarters of an inch formed, scarcely enough for a skating rink, but 'twas ever thus.

Dec. 27th:

The Fireman's Hall is proving a heavy thing to start. This morning several hawsers parted and the hall never budged a peg.

Dec. 28th:

And still the Fireman's Hall is not sliding down Lincoln Avenue. The contractors are blasting a few large boulders that put in an appearance in the grading of the hall lots on Main Street.

Dec. 29th:

Contractor Deirks had to go to Leadville for heavier tackle with which to move the Fireman's Hall.

James McGee is engaged sinking post holes along the line of march of the Fireman's Hall from its old to its new location, for hitching posts that will be necessary to pull the structure from point to point. (This was the day that Fireman's Hall was to be in its place on Main Street; so far, it hasn't budged from its old location.)

Jan. 4th, 1888:

The Fireman's Hall will come a flying "when the clouds roll by" after Nashold's new capstan gets to work.

Jan. 5th:

The Fireman's Hall is coming and don't get in the way of it or something will happen.

Jan. 6th:

The Fireman's Hall is coming.

Jan. 7th:

Fireman's Hall has got straightened out on Lincoln Avenue and comes down hill like a barefooted boy on a coaster.

Jan. 10th:

The Fireman's Hall has reached Main Street.

Jan. 11th:

And now the Fireman's Hall will progress in a crablike direction, that is sidewise.

Jan. 12th:

The Fireman's Hall has not yet started on its southward journey up Main Street, but is taking quite a rest at the crossing.

Jan. 13th:

The Fireman's Hall took a lively start this morning but before noon an accident, the breaking of a large girder, delayed the moving for a couple of hours. But it has reached the front of its lots.

Jan. 14th:

At last the Fireman's Hall has reached its destination. This afternoon at half past two o'clock the last pull of the capstan was checked and the old hall stood over its future location. The letting down and alterations will be made next week.

Jan. 17th:

The Fireman's alarm bell was placed in the belfry of the hall yesterday.

Jan. 19th:

Mechanics are building the addition to the Fireman's Hall required for a side stairway.

Feb. 15th:

Mr. Nashold has relieved the belfry of Fireman's Hall of its unfinished appearance by placing a hand rail from pillar to pillar. It does not interfere with the sound of the bell in case of fire as the old lattice did.

May 19th:

The front of Fireman's Hall has been ornamented by having the names of the three companies painted on their respective doors. We presume should one of the Independents enter by the Hooks door that he would "about face," retire and enter by the proper door.

June 2nd:

Our Methodist friends ought to make an application to the town for the donation of ten or fifteen feet of the old lot of the Fireman's Hall. It would be a great protection against fire. They ought to take up a collection for the purpose of painting the outside of the church and clean up around it.

June 30th:

The corner of the M. E. Church that was injured by contact with the Fireman's Hall when the latter was removed last winter is still in its shattered condition. The contractors who removed the hall should have repaired the damage done long ago, but it is not too late yet.

Renovating and remodeling followed the move of Fireman's Hall to its new location. *Daily Journal*, January 25, 1888, reported: "The Fireman's Hall will be a perfectly remodeled hall. The removal of the platform at the front and closing of the stairway leaves the hall full size of the building for dancing purposes. The music stand will be in the annex and midway of the room so that calls can be heard equally distinct in all parts of the room. Hat room and ladies cloak room are off to one side of the dancing floor and all unnecessary interference is dispensed with."

Painting, papering and carpeting became part of the redecorating program. A series of balls and parties was announced to raise funds to pay renovating expenses. Ye Editor was moved to comment: "Fireman's Hall begins to look quite respectable. It is safe to say had the hall stood on its old site on French Street in its shabby condition there would have been but few attending."

Fireman's Hall was the scene of much social, cultural and community activity. While next to the M. E. Church it must have been a severe ordeal for Father Dyer, to whom the ball and the dance were anathema. Saturday night hilarity and Sunday morning solemnity weren't exactly counterparts. The ball, the dance, the social hop, the "old time sociables" were frequent, so much so that as early as 1881 Ye Editor wrote: "Fireman's Hall is becoming popular for all kinds of gatherings. Dates have to be secured weeks in advance." In addition there were dancing schools, lectures, militia drill, German Choir rehearsals. Occasionally, it was the place for a funeral service. Usually the 4th of July parades started and ended at Fireman's Hall, particularly when the hall was on French Street. The New Year's Eve ball was the big one. December, 1880: "The Fireman's Ball on New Year's Eve will be the event of the season. Parties from Robinson and Kokomo will be on hand, while from that little paradise among the rocks, Wheeler, where men never get old and boys are always men, will come a very pleasant party. Frisco, of course, will be on hand, and the Snake region will be duly represented by deputations from Dillon, Montezuma, Chihuahua and Decatur. Lincoln, Swan and Congers regions will come in force: so that one of the largest and best turn-outs may be expected from without, and of course, everybody in Breckenridge will be there."

Next to G. A. R. Hall, Fireman's Hall was the largest meeting hall in Breckenridge. G. A. R. Hall could accommodate 400 people; Fireman's Hall, an estimated 250-275. If the crowd was large, the affair was either at Fireman's Hall or the G. A. R. In later years roller skating was added to Fireman's Hall socials.

Breckenridge had need of good fire-fighting equipment. Frame buildings, shingle roofs, stove heating, over-heated flues and stovepipes—all contributed to the ever-present hazards and the many fires. Numerous calls came for fire-fighting. Pioneer Hook & Ladder Company, No. 1 (sometimes called "Hooks") was soon joined by two additional companies—Independent and Blue River Hose Companies. All were housed in the Main Street building. A system of taps for calling meetings was formulated. When a general meeting was called there were four taps of the bell, followed by a minute of silence, then repeated. A meeting of Hook & Ladder sounded two taps of the bell. Independents got three taps. Blue River was called by three taps, followed by one tap. The system worked for almost a half century. Breckenridge then replaced the fire bell with a new-fangled siren.

The Old Town Fire Bell

(An Editorial)

The early morning fire of Tuesday again demonstrated a fact that has been well known for a number of years. That is that the town fire bell atop the Fireman's Hall has long outlived its usefulness.

The old bell was installed more than fifty years ago and as far as we know has never been replaced. Time, weather and usage have worked their destruction on the old bell until it has lost its clear ringing tones. Many people will testify to the fact that the bell cannot be heard in a house more than a block away.

As our fire fighting forces must be recruited from our residents; it is imperative that the signal be of such a character that it can be easily heard at any part of town. Such is not the case with the old fire bell.

There is always danger from fire and especially so in a town where nearly all the buildings are of frame construction. Residents of Breckenridge must awaken to this danger and get some action before a real disaster overtakes us. We know of several places in the town where if a fire should start in the dead of night and the alarm immediately given, if the bell were not heard by a considerable number of people at once—most, if not all of the town, would be wiped out.

Let us then petition our town board to remove the old bell and put it in some prominent place as a historic relic and place atop the fire tower a modern electric siren which could be turned on at several different points and which would immediately warn everyone that the fire demon was to be combatted. Let not a matter of a few dollars stand in the way of this as anyone will agree that the matter is one of the greatest importance to the town.

October 19, 1934, Summit County *Journal* informs us that the Woman's Club Will Purchase Fire Siren:

A new fire siren for the Breckenridge Fire Department is to be purchased by the Woman's Club of Breckenridge and presented to the town. The cost of the siren and its installation will be approximately $200. When the siren is installed the warning of the fire will be given by the simple pressing of an electric button at the telephone exchange as soon as the fire is reported.

Money for the purchase of the siren will be raised by the Woman's Club in various ways. A food sale on the 17th of Nov., a New Year's dance and a card party. Mrs. Geo. Robinson is in charge.

A siren was presented in November. After six weeks trial it was found unsatisfactory. Another was ordered and received January 4th, 1935. It was to be tested 30 days before purchased. Evidently the second siren was satisfactory.

In 1941 the Works Projects Administration (WPA) came into the picture. January 14th work started on tearing down the old Town Hall and Fire House. Salvaged lumber would be used to help construct a 46 x 60 frame building on the west side of Main Street—"the site of the old Denver House just south of Eaton's Store." Plans called for a council room, town scales, hose rack and storage space for fire equipment and shop. The work was completed June 13th. "The new hall cost approximately $5,000, the WPA spend-

in about $3,600 for labor and the town spending $1,400 for building materials."

The fire bell is indeed one of the historic relics of Breckenridge. Research indicates that it is Breckenridge's oldest bell. It was cast in 1881 by the Buckeye Bell Foundry—VanDusen & Tift—Cincinnati. It came to Breckenridge in April, 1881, and has given almost a century of faithful service. It sounded the alarm of fire and called help for endangered homes and business places. When special help was needed it called friends and neighbors together. It called worshipers to divine service. It tolled the death of faithful members of the fire-fighting companies and stalwart citizens. Wherever its belfry moved it followed along to continue its service. When its time of usefulness was finished it was content to strike the hour of Firemen Meetings and toll the death of the membership. It now hangs in a little belfry above the fire engine house at Town Hall Center.

A new Firehouse is proposed for Breckenridge—a replica of the original—belfry included—a proud new home for the faithful old bell.

Fireman's Hall on French Street. Erected summer of 1880; Moved to Main Street location December, 1887-January, 1888. (Note proximity to Methodist Church at the right.) (Small buildings to left—present Court House site.) (Bell purchased April, 1881.) (Hose and hose cart purchased fall of 1882.) (Note beautiful louvered belfry.) Picture date:— probably fall of 1882. Courtesy—Library State Historical Society of Colorado.

Fireman's Hall on Main Street. (Bell restored to belfry, January 16, 1888.) (*Journal* reported the addition to the right, enclosing stairway and adding another second-story window. - January 25, 1888.) (Louver boards removed; Summit County *Journal*: February 15, 1888—"Mr. Nashold has relieved the belfry of its unfinished appearance by placing a hand rail from pillar to pillar. It does not interfere with the sound of the bell in case of fire as the old lattice did.") (May 19, 1888: "The front of Fireman's Hall has been ornamented by having the three companies painted on their respective doors.") Picture date:—probably summer of 1888. Courtesy—Denver Public Library Western Collection.

Faithful little fire bell followed Fireman's Hall to four different locations. (Probably Breckenridge's oldest bell.) Picture:—1971 at Town Hall-Civic Center.

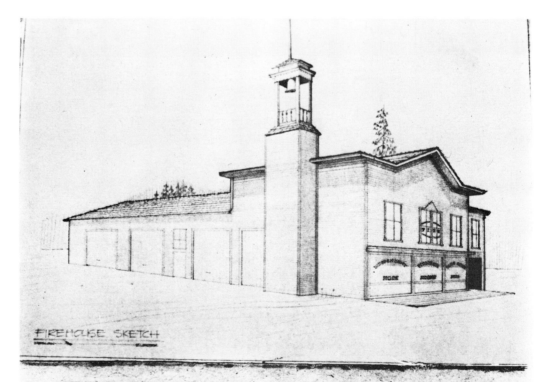

FIREHOUSE SKETCH

NEW BRECKENRIDGE FIREHOUSE PROPOSED
Plans for the new Breckenridge Firehouse are a copy of the old, original station.

(1971) Sketch of proposed new fire house and new resting-place for historic fire bell. Courtesy—Summit County *Journal*.

Main Street, looking north from Washington Avenue. Picture date:—shortly after moving Fireman's Hall from French Street to Main Street—January 14, 1888. Tall hose-drying tower is not built. (Date of drying-tower is not verified by any known record.) Courtesy—Library State Historical Society of Colorado.

(Looking east to west)—shows belfry, bell and drying-tower of Fireman's Hall. Electric light poles and wires indicate a picture date after March, 1892. Courtesy—Denver Public Library Western Collection.

Fireman's Hall

SISTER'S MUSTARD SEEDS

For thirty-five years an organization flourished in Breckenridge with the not-so-euphonius name of Sister's Mustard Seeds. Today, when the name is spoken or read, it provokes a quizzical look or a bit of head-scratching. It has, however, a logical and grammatical explanation and is the story of a noble endeavor. There is a sadness to the story because of the early death of the one who gave her name and spirit to the organization.

The Charles A. Findings were an early Breckenridge family. Charles Finding became a prominent and well-to-do merchant in the town. The "old Finding store" is an early Breckenridge building yet remaining on Main Street. In the spring of 1885 Finding gathered stone and lumber for the erection of a store building "as soon as mortar can be laid." A couple carloads of fine red sandstone were brought down from the range for the front of the building. Side walls were of mountain stone. All in all, it was one of Breckenridge's finest buildings. (In 1970 and 1971 the Summit County Investment Company and the Bank of Breckenridge took joint occupancy of the building, redecorating consistent with early Breckenridge decor.)

Mrs. Martha Finding was one of Judge Silverthorn's daughters. Marshall Silverthorn had the famous Silverthorn Hotel on the west side of Main Street, almost directly across from Finding's store. The Finding home, one of the show places in town, was on north Main Street. Later it was the Duane Miner home—Agnes (Finding) Miner. In recent years the Mine Restaurant was located there, but was totally destroyed by fire, January, 1971.

The Charles Findings had three daughters, born 1873, 1875, 1877—Agnes, Ada and "Tonnie." Agnes married Duane Miner and lived to the ripe age of almost eighty-two; Tonnie, unmarried, died at the age of twenty-eight, and Ada was a young girl of twelve years at her death. The baptismal names were Agnes Eleanor, Clara Ada and Charline Antoinette. The two younger girls went almost entirely by nicknames, however,—"Tonnie" and "Sister." Agnes was "Aggie" to many of her friends. In the family, among close friends, and in the community Clara Ada was lovingly called "Sister." "Sister" Ada Finding's Mustard Seeds organization is fondly remembered today by "old Breckenridge."

The official name was Sister's Mustard Seeds. It was an organization of young girls of Breckenridge, devoted to charitable deeds in Breckenridge and nearby area, but when hospitalization took place in Denver, ministrations of the young ladies reached the bedside there. A former member living in the city, or someone journeying to Denver, would minister in the name of Sister's Mustard Seeds. Into the second generation it continued as an active organization; at one time there were fifty-eight members in the group. Sister's Mustard Seeds is still remembered in Breckenridge, eighty years since organization.

Thursday, January 19, 1888, Breckenridge was shocked and grieved to read in the *Daily Journal*:

DIED

This afternoon, at about one and a half o'clock, Mr. Finding's daughter Ada, better known as Sister, died with membranous croup. The whole community sympathize with the bereaved family.

Another startling and strange announcement appeared in Saturday's *Journal*:

Thursday the *Journal* announced the death of little Ada Finding; it proved to be premature, it was a case of suspended animation, symptoms of life returning after a few minutes. The slight thread of hope was seized upon and every effort that science and attention and devotion could do was done to reclaim the almost lost life, but a night of effort was followed by death Friday morning. The agony experienced by the parents and sisters of the dying little one during those hours of suspense can only be imagined and not described. A large circle of friends were deeply interested and their sympathy went out to the parents in their distress.

DIED

FINDING,—On Friday morning, January 20, 1888, of membranous croup, Ada, second daughter of Mr. and Mrs. Charles A. Finding, aged twelve years. The remains were taken to Denver by this morning's train for internment. The body will be laid to rest beside a dear aunt, Mrs. Joseph C. Wilson, in Riverside Cemetery.

(Diptheria of the larynx is the disease called membranous croup.—*Summit County Journal,* December, 1880.)

In December, 1887, shortly before Ada's sudden and unexpected death, "Sister" attended the Sunday School held in the Methodist Church. The Findings were Episcopalians, but the Methodist Church was the only Protestant church in town holding regular services and conducting Sunday School. Children of other denominations participated in the Sunday School at the Methodist Church. Mrs. Samuel W. Jones was teacher of the young girls. Sunday School lessons during December were "Parables of Jesus." One Sunday was devoted to the "Parable of the Mustard Seed." A point to be emphasized by the teacher was, "A little word or deed may have in it the immortal life. It is for us to drop daily the little seed and leave the result with God." (Sunday School Lesson—*Christian Advocate,* December 18, 1887.) The story of Sister and her Mustard Seeds is unfolded in detail in a Service conducted in the Breckenridge Episcopal Church thirteen years later:

SPECIAL SERVICE FOR SISTER'S MUSTARD SEEDS

LIBRARY FUND

The special services held at St. John Baptist's Episcopal Church, on last Sunday evening, for the benefit of the Sister's Mustard Seeds' Library Fund, was largely attended, and greatly appreciated. Miss Agnes Finding presided at the organ. Rev. D. W. Galway, rector of the church, delivered the address of the evening, giving the history and work of the society carrying the peculiar name of "Sister's Mustard Seeds." The address was as follows:

The plant which yields mustard is pretty well-known; at least every one knows the bright yellow flower which in the months of May and June makes the cornfield golden. In a mild climate these plants grow to a height of four or five feet, and in the warmer climate and rich soil of Palestine they become much taller and more luxuriant.

In fact, it becomes a tree so arborescent that the finches and other little birds which are so fond of its seeds rest in its branches.

The design of our Lord's words is obvious, and the underlying thought in them is simple. It is that a little germ may have a large result, and a small commencement a conspicuous growth. And this truth has been beautifully illustrated in the history, growth and development of our little society called Sister's Mustard Seeds.

March 31, 1888—almost thirteen years ago—the society was organized and began its work in our midst. A brief history of its origin and work will be interesting to note. In the December (1887) number of the *Sunday School Advocate* there appeared an article entitled "Barrels of Joy," giving the story of a society of girls who called themselves "Mustard Seeds." Mrs. Samuel W. Jones, a devoted Sunday School teacher, called the attention of her class to the paper, pointing out the good each individual can do, however feeble the effort, in their own respective sphere. The seed thus sown fell on good ground, and took root, first in the heart of our beloved little friend, "Sister" Ada Finding, who was about twelve years of age. Ada asked Mrs. Jones to help her start a little society in Breckenridge and name it "Mustard Seeds;" but it was so near Christmas Mrs. Jones asked her to wait until after the holidays, as everyone was so busy. At this Ada felt disappointed, but Mrs. Jones promised to help her crochet some mittens for some poor little child. Ada worked with a loving will and finished two pair, which she gave to some poor children on Christmas morning.

Mrs. Jones, on account of illness, was not able to organize the society before Ada herself took ill and was called to join the "Mustard Seeds" in Heaven.

In the meantime the seeds of love had so grown in the hearts of members of the little class that they desired at once to begin to work for the Master, and on March 24, 1888, they met at the home of their teacher to organize themselves. In memory of "Sister" Ada Finding the little band was named "Sister's Mustard Seeds," for Ada was always known as "Sister." After asking God's blessing, help and guidance on their efforts, the little society embarked on the sea of existence.

Since then many new members have joined the society, a number of whom have grown to womanhood and have gone to live in other places; but, as they dropped out, their places were filled by others of the rising generation, till at present there are over fifty active members. These are working under the leadership and fostering care of the president, Miss Agnes Finding, assisted by her sister, Miss Tonnie Finding, and with Miss Josephine Wilson acting as secretary and Miss Clara Roby as treasurer.

The society meets once a week, save when prevented by sickness or disease among the members, and often I have personally found joy and inspiration in visiting them and seeing so many little hands at work making necessary articles of clothing, etc., for the poor and needy. They have cared for the sick and afflicted ones among us. Nowhere can their work in this respect be seen to better advantage than in the county hospital. Here a bed has been furnished and taken care of for years by them for the rest and comfort of the sick.

Among others I shall mention one case none the less interesting to us. Jennie Ruth, a little girl only seven years of age, had been a cripple for years. July last it seemed expedient that she should undergo surgical operation in order to recover the use of her limbs. Poor child! her mother was dead, and she had no relative who was willing and able to bear the necessary expense of sending her away for treatment. But then our little "Mustard Seeds" lent a helping hand. They sent Jenny, in charge of Mrs. Gaymon, to the Homeopathic hospital at Denver, and now we are happy to learn that she

has been greatly benefited there, and some of the little "Mustard Seeds" who are living in Denver visit her weekly and take her flowers and other little things to make her happy.

This is but one of the many cases that might be cited in which the society has done a great and lasting good.

In addition to their other work, for a few years past it has been their desire to have a public library, with reading-rooms adjoined, established in Breckenridge, where so many of the young men of the town and vicinity can profitably spend their leisure hours.

The first step in this direction was taken early last spring, when Miss Finding, president of the society, backed by a petition from the citizens of Breckenridge, wrote to Mr. W. S. Stratton, of Cripple Creek, Colo., bringing this matter under his notice; and in response to her request he kindly sent a check to the society to the amount of $500, and this sum has formed the nucleus for the library building.

Later, among others, a letter appeared in the *Journal* referring to the good work of the "Mustard Seeds" and emphasizing the need of a public library. This letter had the desired effect, and many of our citizens have liberally subscribed in aid of it. Who will not encourage this little society of workers? Who will not aid it in its noble work? We, this evening, ask for it your prayers, your influence and your contributions.

Gifts and subscriptions to the Library Fund totalled $1344.75. But the library, as a building and institution, never became a reality. For a time the library was in the home of Mrs. Minnie Roby, and then later became a part of the new school building, but the dreams of a place of its own, Breckenridge Public Library, did not materialize.

Sister's Mustard Seeds planned to provide a library where Breckenridge young men could spend time in profitable employment, instead of roaming the streets of town. Appeals, like the following, were made in behalf of the young men:

The library is not only for a place where our miners can go, but for anyone, and to get the young men who are growing up interested. They are not permitted to go to the saloons until they are of age, and they have but few places to go. If a place can be established and these young men become interested, who will attempt to estimate the good it may do? These Sister's Mustard Seeds want to secure a suitable building in a central location, furnish

Sister's Mustard Seeds

it, light and warm it suitably and comfortably, place therein a fine library, the leading news, scientific, pictorial, fashion and children's papers, the leading magazines and such reading matter as will attract all; and if sufficient funds can be procured, why could not a room for innocent dames be added?

Sister's Mustard Seeds struggled to get a library established in Breckenridge. Three years after raising their fund of $1344 the society was still without its library. Some were of the opinion that "if they continue to fail much longer they must as a mark of honor return the $500 to Mr. Stratton." We trace their plight:

Breckenridge *Bulletin*   February 6, 1904

Different locations have been discussed and at one time the library could have had the Edwin Carter lots and building for $500. This building would have been ample for the present with the large room for a reading room while the side rooms could be used for the office and the janitor, but the powers that were in charge, vetoed the purchase. This place seemed an ideal one with a large block of ground and natural trees, retired and quiet, close to town, and just such a place as would induce reading and study. It is hoped that the library will become a reality.

Summit County Journal   December 15, 1906

LIBRARY CLOSED

It is to be regretted that the small, but well-selected Sister's Mustard Seeds Library has had to be boxed up and stored for want of a reading room in which to the place the books.

The little society has struggled valiantly to have a library and free reading room in Breckenridge, but it seems that public sentiment is not in favor of it. At any rate the town officials and prominent business men do not seem disposed to do the part in the good work that has been asked of them.

The society had agreed to furnish the books and librarian, provided a reading room is furnished in which to keep them.

We know the Mustard Seeds would gladly do it all, but their funds are not sufficient, and it seems this worthy enterprise is to be abandoned for want of public spirit—at least for the present.

The Library revived with the opening of the new school building in 1910. This, too, proved temporary respite.

Summit County Journal   December 4, 1915

SISTER'S MUSTARD SEEDS TO CLOSE THEIR LIBRARY

Sister's Mustard Seeds regret to announce that they will be obliged to close their library in the school building and store their books, as the school finds it necessary to use the room occupied by us for their own library. We trust that we will be able at some later date to open and maintain a free reading room and library, and the earnest cooperation of the public is solicited to help us attain this end.

Apart from special contributions made to the library project, funds for the far-reaching charitable work of Sister's Mustard Seeds came from the sale of handwork, chocolate sales, baked goods, lawn socials, and similar fund-raising activities. The vast amount of charity performed by this group of young girls is truly remarkable.

Summit County Journal   September 15, 1894

Sister's Mustard Seeds have kept steadily and quietly at work during the past two years accomplishing much, but preferring to follow the command of the "Master"—"Take heed that ye do not your alms before men." In order to increase their funds for the winter's work and for the benefit of society, will, on Saturday of this week, have a Chocolate Booth in the Arcade Restaurant on Main Street, where chocolate, tea and coffee will be served at noon and from 5 to 7 o'clock p. m. at 5 cts per cup, also homemade bread, cake and pop-corn, and if popular will serve chocolate each Saturday during the time of regular meetings through the winter.

During the last two years they have met together each week and sewed for two hours, making and repairing over 500 pieces which they have given away besides piecing three quilts, two of which are completed. A large number of persons have been assisted by money. Fancy work is a special feature of their work and the result of their labor finds ready sale. Go and take a cup of chocolate or coffee with the little folks.

Summit County Journal   September 22, 1894

The Chocolate Booth of the Sister's Mustard Seeds opened last Saturday, and was tastefully arranged. The viands served were palatable and were served on fine china. This society of young girls has done much good in an unostentatious manner and should receive the financial support of all. The *Journal* acknowledges the receipt of a tray well filled with delicious cake and chocolate.

Sister's Mustard Seeds desire to thank most heartily the *Journal* and all friends who so kindly remembered them last Saturday with donations and kind words. The receipts were $19.80.

Fifteen years later Sister's Mustard Seeds were working in the same manner and with the same success:

Summit County Journal   February 20, 1909

The Sister's Mustard Seeds met with Miss Florence Tresler last Saturday afternoon. This little society, under the leadership of Miss Ella Foote, is gaining in favor and numbers to exceed all winters. Forever hallowed in our memories and enshrined in our affections will be this little band of workers. This is surely a child-garden, where a few hours Saturday afternoon are intelligently spent listening to some good book, plying the needle; where they are also taught to seek light and power to promote usefulness and charity toward our own citizens as well as sending sunshine abroad, and where the child's social nature is to be considered and provided for—all of which is sufficient to assure these children that confidential companionship, sympathy and devotion of mind and heart to such work will cleanse them from all selfish interferences. Their motto is:

> "Do all the good you can,
> in all the ways you can,
> to all the people you can."

When the demise of the organization, Sister's Mustard Seeds, occurred is not clear; it seems to have been sometime between 1920-1925. What was written about them in 1900 could have been repeated years later:

> To replenish the losses, other strong and willing young girls have come upon the scene of life and valiantly identified themselves with the society and its purposes, and today the membership numbers over fifty as bright, cheerful, active and self-sacrificing sisters as can be found anywhere in the state. Their mission on earth is a Christian one: to care for the sick, clothe the needy and relieve the distressed. During its life this little band has carried cheer and necessaries into the homes of many families, and their noble deeds could be ennumerated by the score.

The deeds and charity of Sister's Mustard Seeds are recorded in the Book of Remembrance. Some are living today—children and grandchildren—who know the stories of the good deeds of Sister's Mustard Seeds. The solid silver communion set, chalice and paten, was presented to St. John's Episcopal Church, Breckenridge, by the "Little Mustard Seeds" in memory of "Sister" Finding. The pulpit chair in Father Dyer Methodist Church was presented by Sister's Mustard Seeds in memory of Helen and Theo Jones, members who died during a diptheria epidemic. Mrs. Samuel Jones was Sister's Sunday School teacher. Truly the teacher spoke to the heart of a little twelve-year-old girl:

> "A little word or deed may have in it the immortal life. It is for us to drop daily the little seed and leave the result with God."

The result was—Sister's Mustard Seeds—forever enshrined in the heart of Breckenridge.

SISTER ADA FINDING MONUMENT
Riverside Cemetry, Denver
(Scroll)
"Little Sister"
"How We Loved Her"

Finding Sisters (Left to Right)

"Sister"—Clara Ada; Born 1875; Died January 20, 1888.
"Aggie"—Agnes Eleanor; Born November 23, 1873; Died October 20, 1955.
"Tonnie"—Charline Antoinette; Born 1877; Died October 24, 1905.
(Agnes Eleanor and Charline Antoinette-Baptized All Saints Day, November 1, 1891-St. John The Baptist Episcopal Church, Breckenridge.)

Silverthorn-Finding Burial Plot—Riverside Cemetry, Denver.

Charles A. Finding Building. Built 1885. Picture:—1971.

Interior Charles A. Finding store. Two wall calendars are dated November-December, 1891; two others dated January, 1892—indicating picture date, January, 1892. Courtesy—Mr. Melvin Gaymon.

Agnes (Finding) Miner with "Sister's Mustard Seeds" meeting in her home.

"Sister's Mustard Seeds" in the Agnes (Finding) Miner home.

DYNAMITING THE CHURCH BELL

Moving Fireman's Hall had its sequence; no longer did the minister of the Methodist Church have a bell to ring, calling his flock to Sunday worship. Ringing the fire alarm bell for church services had been an annoyance to fire department, town trustees and many of the citizenry. For two and a half years thereafter the Methodist Church was without benefit of a bell. Then in 1890, during the pastorate of Florida F. Passmore, a bell was purchased. The Summit County *Journal*, June 1890, tells the important happening:

> The new bell for the M. E. Church has arrived and is mounted on a pair of tressles at the rear of the church, whence its muffled peals are at times sent forth to call the faithful to service. It is hoped it will soon be hoisted to a proper position. Our Methodist Church friends purpose raising their fine bell on four high posts for the present. It will be a desirable addition to our Sunday morning out-of-door music.

The original church building, erected by Father Dyer in 1880, was of simple design, 24 x 48 feet in dimension. Windows and doorframe were square-topped; there was no belfry. The building very much resembled a plain country schoolhouse. Acquisition of a bell meant that a belfry had to be built; this was done in the summer of 1890.

Florida F. Passmore became one of Breckenridge's most colorful individuals. He was Georgia-born, raised in Tennessee. His first appearance in the general area was at Alma, South Park. There he engaged in mining, living in a tent. He was not a minister of the gospel at the time. Rev. J. R. Shannon, Methodist presiding elder, met Passmore at Alma. Rev. Shannon later said, "His prayer was of such a spiritual kind that I recognized he was a man of strong brain force. I encouraged him to enter the ministry. He was a man of spotless character and spotless life. Everybody around Alma and Fairplay had the highest respect and esteem for him as a man of godly character. He believed that God was calling him to the ministry, and that the Lord's hand was upon him."

In those days many came into the Methodist ministry by way of a probationary period that included serving in a church while completing prescribed courses of study, under the supervision of the Conference. College and theological seminary training were not required; in fact, they were the exception. Father Dyer said, "I hadn't been to college —hadn't even rubbed my back against one—but I felt bound to preach." Upon completion of the probationary period, candidates were ordained, if their trial work and study were satisfactory.

Passmore was about forty years of age when he began his ministerial training. Sometime during the Conference Year 1882-1883, Florida Passmore began as a "supply minister" in the Fairplay-Alma churches, and continued there for a number of years. In 1884, he was elected to deacon orders, and in 1888 ordained an elder. In August, 1889, Florida Passmore was appointed to the Breckenridge Methodist Church, (at the age of forty-five years.) He became one of the most remembered ministers to serve that church. He lacked the "polish" and formal education of his neighboring Episcopalian brother, Rev. Hodder, who was highly esteemed in the community for his scholarly ability. Hodder gained publicity in his way; Passmore equaled in another.

Father John Dyer, builder of the church, was also renowned—but in a far different way from Florida Passmore. The point of emphasis in the Passmore and Father Dyer ministries was similar, the difference being in personality and method of promoting the ministry. Both were genuinely concerned about their flocks and the community. Father Dyer had a deep compassion for the frailties of mankind; Florida Passmore moved in the realm of the "crusader," seeking to change mankind's shortcomings willy-nilly. Father Dyer commanded respect and cooperation from the community; Passmore provoked scorn and opposition from many. It must be brought to mind, however, that Florida Passmore's five-year pastorate in Breckenridge was the longest pastorate until the present one. It must also be recognized that his difficulties were not within his church, but with the town citizenry. Records attest that membership, Sunday School and Church attendance, were at the highest during his pastorate. A number of commendable improvements and additions were made to the M. E. Church during Passmore's pastorate. At no time is there evidence that his congregation opposed him or his ministry.

The story—Dynamiting the Methodist Church Bell—has found its way into a number of publications. Stories, vague in details, make the rounds of Breckenridge. But for the real story, we must turn back the pages of time eighty years. It was not the man's fiery preaching alone, as many think, that caused the violent upheaval. Passmore's activity extended beyond the pulpit. Other factors were present that made the time, the place, and the preacher opportune.

A Saloon Law went into effect in Colorado, April 7, 1891. (See SALOONS—AN ACT, printed at end of chapter.) The law was popular with some; it was bitterly opposed by others. Breckenridge, for the most part, detested the saloon law. Two aspects of the law were particularly obnoxious—Sunday closing of the saloon and the 12:00 midnight closing on week nights. Brother Passmore mounted the white charger of the crusader to have the law enforced in Breckenridge. He visited all the saloons, demanding that saloonkeepers obey the law. Threats of law enforcement reinforced his demands. If law officers were inclined to be lax in their duty, Passmore had another card up his sleeve—forfeiture of bond on law officials. He got results. The Summit

County *Journal*, August 1st, 1891, came out in protest:

Last Sunday was the Sunday of Sundays; all the saloons in town were closed and their usual habituates were compelled to loaf around the streets. Miners, in from the hills, stood upon the sidewalks looking wistfully to the right or left for some retreat from a condition of misery. To make matters worse, the day was damp and dull. The workings of law here was such as to show the sheer nonsense of such legislation for a camp in the midst of the mountains. The law was conceived in the brain of a fanatic, enacted by a body of imbeciles, signed by a doughface, and in a camp like Breckenridge would be enforced only by an impracticable enthusiast. Monday last, a mournful cuss brought in twenty-four stanzas of alleged poetry, of which the following six lines are a fair sample:

On the twenty-sixth day of July, year ninety-one,
The drinking community of this town was undone,
On complaint of the parson, by order of the Judge,
All thirsty old topers were deprived of their budge,
An eye-opener, a cocktail, a plain morning dram
Was denied the bum, the boss, and the hard-working man.

An editorial, "Sunday Closing," appeared in the same issue of the *Journal*:

Last Sunday Breckenridge enjoyed the result of silly laws placed at the disposal of any crank who may from any cause see fit to demand their enforcement. The state law directing all saloons to be closed on Sunday and at 12 o'clock every night and not opened before 6 o'clock in the morning was, on the complaint of the Methodist pastor, enforced. If the complainant was representing any large portion of the community there would have been an excuse for it, but he stated, we are informed, before the court, that this act was his alone and that he alone was responsible.

The closing worked a great inconvenience to the mass of citizens who came from the hills Saturday night, and to make it worse the day was dull and damp, with no place to sit down. Those whose homes were on the hills soon left so inhospitable a place and went to their lonely cabins.

This class of legislation raises the question whether an individual has rights that majorities must respect. If it is wrong to enter a saloon on Sunday it cannot be right to enter on Monday. If the majority have a right to interfere with what a man drinks, it likewise has a right to say what he shall eat and wherewithal he shall be clothed. So long as a citizen in his drinking, eating, and clothing wrongs not any other citizen, or infringes on no rights of others, then the majority in restraining him becomes a tyrant in fact, and no right is safe from its encroachment.

It is unfortunate that the moral backbone found in members of the Colorado legislature is so flexible as to allow the enactment of laws that cranks can utilize to the public's discomfort. This Sunday closing law was not asked for by any respectable number of citizens in any mountain town or county in the state. The city of Denver, weighed down with cathedrals, churches, chapels and colleges, and crowded with night prowlers, policemen, preachers, priests and professors may have faintly asked for some such law, but why afflict the whole state with such an abomination?

We will place the town of Breckenridge against any similar town in the country for peace and good order. Its worst element is well-behaved and liberal. The bell that on Sabbath calls saint, sinner and hypocrite to services was in great part paid for by saloon men and gamblers. The church in which the saloon business and card-playing is denounced, was mainly built by sporting men's money, and every impecunious corpse that is given a decent burial by contribution carries a fair share of the contributions from the tabooed classes. We speak advisedly when we assert that the seven saloon owners of this city will compare favorably for business honesty, public spirit and individual rectitude with any class in the community.

The customs of the country, ever since settlement by white men, has sanctioned the Sunday open house and until public sentiment demands it the enactment of such laws as the Sunday law is a mistake, and their enforcement the act of an impractical enthusiast or malicious persecution for personal motives.

The *Journal* has ever favored good order and all progressive movements, always favored church congregations, with all thereunto belonging, for the general advancement of the interests of the public. What men believe cuts no figure so long as their practices and general conduct are conducive to general good. The *Journal* will be pleased to support them.

Meanwhile Breckenridge was seething. "Ye Editor" wrote, "Would it not be more in keeping with their calling for non-taxpaying transient professional gentlemen to let the taxpaying permanent residents see that statutes of the state are enforced?" The trouble had only started; more was to come. Retaliation would be forthcoming.

CHURCH BELL DESTROYED

On Monday night last (August 17, 1891) some miscreant, not having the good name of the town nor the safety of sleeping residents in the neighborhood before his eyes, ascended the Methodist Church to the belfry and there so arranged an explosive that a few minutes afterwards destroyed the bell, hurling the fragments in all directions, the shock awakening nearly all the sleepers in the town.

Tuesday morning an investigation showed that the bell and iron frame was utterly destroyed, the belfry so shattered as to be dangerous in its present condition, it must be effectively repaired or taken down.

The vandal act has been the town talk and no one has been found to sanction it, no clue to the perpetration has been discovered. It, no doubt, was the work of some hair-brained crank who has the misfortune to be on the other side. The mayor should offer a reward to secure the arrest and conviction of the perpetrator of the outrage. Every good citizen will sanction all efforts to enforce order and protect property.

No doubt some will attribute the act to the friends of the saloon element, but there isn't evidence to sustain the charge nor is there anything yet developed to establish the fact that the explosion was not the work of some friend of the church to regain the sympathy that the fanatical course of the parson has forfeited. The probabilities in the case are a fair stand off.

The unreasonable and unchristlike course of the pastor in the part he took in the Sunday closing business was calculated to develop just such retaliation in the mind of a cracked-brained opponent, but we did not believe there was one in town. It is an old saying, "For every Jack there is a Jill," so the parson has found his natural opponent as he ought to have anticipated.

Nearby communities added fuel to the fire when they printed their comments on the bell dynamiting incident. The Leadville *Democrat* said, "The M. E. Church bell was destroyed by a crowd of toughs." The Dillon *Enterprise* jumped onto the wicked fellow who destroyed the church bell and said, "The fellow ought to be hung." The Como *Record*, commenting on the Dillon *Enterprise* recommendation, said, "We hardly think, however, that the good level-headed citizens of our neighboring county will act upon this advice in case the offender is caught. We would recommend as a substitute for hanging that the fellow be washed in the cool exhilarating waters of the Blue River, and be sentenced to go to church for three Sundays thereafter in succession, and hear brother Passmore preach the Gospel." There had been previous reactions to Brother Passmore's stand on saloon closing:

> The *Journal* neither defends nor assails any class from a personal motive. But it seems there is a large portion of the citizens of our town, as well as other places, that think every line in a paper is controlled or directed from a personal motive. One class, whose whole object is to look after the almighty dollar, wonder, and so express themselves, how much the *Journal* was paid for "that article." Another class think and express their thoughts that because the *Journal's* elder takes a drink, when so inclined, that it was a personal restraint that irritated him and inspired it. Another class insinuate that it was to secure and hold the goodwill of the saloon element, etc. to the end.
>
> Now brethren, disabuse your minds of all such nonsense. The *Journal* does not change its editorial tone or sentiments for any consideration, either money, appetite or favor. Of the former, it has enough for present use without selling itself; the second is within control; and for the third, while desiring the good will of all, the *Journal* would not stultify itself to win the good will or avoid the ill will of every man in Colorado. What it believes to be right, it will maintain; and wrong, it will denounce, with a perfect indifference as to whom it may please or displease. All are equally at liberty to cuss or discuss the course of the *Journal* and can, while doing so, have the pleasure of knowing the *Journal* cares not a cuss what they do.
>
> J. C. Fincher, Editor

The barbs of criticism were needling and goading the preacher. The Crusader dug up an old law of twenty years' vintage from the Colorado statute books—the Gambling Law of 1866. (See copy printed at end of chapter.) Salt was poured on open wounds. The Gambling Law had been only haphazardly enforced periodically.

When its strict enforcement was demanded, Ye Editor bellowed:

MORE INTERFERENCE!

On Saturday last considerable commotion was caused by the announcement that all gambling was to be stopped in town on complaint of a parson of one of the churches, and Monday found the saloons duly quiet and no games running. The proprietors, employees and frequenters of such places could be seen in little knots discussing the situation. Of course the sudden check of these popular resorts caused a derangement of business, but is that all? Admitting that saloon men and gamblers are non-producers, they receive money at their bars and games and pass it out the same as a merchant, a lawyer or a preacher, and there is no great portion of the community would ask that either of the last three callings should be driven from the community. The saloon man and the gamblers of this city are among our best citizens so far as pushing any public enterprises is concerned. Their taxable property foots up to quite a sum, their investments in mining are heavy and often to the full extent of their ability, and their contributions to the funds of the town in licenses, water rents, taxes and monthly fines foots up to quite a respectable figure, and it is a sum that the town would not get but for their business. It amounts to the neighborhood of five thousand dollars per year. Their places of business are orderly and quiet, they never interfere with others, no neighboring business man has ever complained of their presence, and the tax payers have been relieved of a great burden by their tolerated existence. Cut off the revenue derived from these sources and town property will be so taxed that the more a man owns of it the poorer he will be. It will not pay the taxes to say that these men derive their income with which to pay these taxes from those who earn it, for if it remained in the original hands it would return no revenue to the town. If spent, as it probably would be, in the same way, the original producers would go to Denver or Leadville and blow in all their pile in one continued round of pleasure and return to work when exhausted. The difference being that some other town would reap the benefit, while all the responsibilities and expenses would have to be borne by the tax payers here.

It is true the complaint and its result are in keeping with the law of the state, so far the

Rev. complainant has the best of it so far as the law goes. But the law is not in accord with the desires or wishes of a large majority of the tax paying people, we venture to say not one tax payer in Summit County asked for its passage, further we will venture the assertion that not a tax payer in this representative or senatorial district asked for the passage of any such law. It was contrary to general custom of the districts and no complaints were heard thereon.

After showing that the burdens of the honest working tax payer will be more than doubled it is well to ask at whose instigation. The church building in which a tolerated Sunday worker by Sunday work earns his salary is exempt from taxation. The transient resident who in an untaxed pulpit earns his salary by Sunday work pays no taxes and owns no property by which the assessor can reach his pocket. The preacher who is here today and away tomorrow is not so much of a benefit to the town as a resident, saloon man or gambler, who invests all his earnings in living and property. The one is, if you please, a resident non-producer, the one invests what he gets over and above the cost of his living, while the other puts it down in his jeans and skips to pastures new. The respect that should be shown the interests of others should have called a check upon a non-tax payer before he deliberately doubled or trebled the burdens of others. The law has put it in the power of any one citizen, be he worthy or worthless, either for what he knows to be a dishonorable, or what he deems a worthy, object to thus interfere with the customs and habits and derange business of a whole community.

So far as the *Journal* is concerned, it is not ten dollars in or out of its coffers whether a card is turned or a glass of liquor is sold or bought in the town. But if town taxes are doubled, water license increased, it will be a matter of some consequence. Saloons and gambling rooms are on a par with churches, those who do not wish to visit them are not compelled to, so long as our fellow citizens do not annoy or interfere with us their going to either of the places is none of our business.

Even the law-enforcement agencies joined in the hue and cry:

A CARD FROM THE SHERIFF TO THE PARSON

To the Rev. F. F. Passmore:
Dear Sir: While the officers of Summit County are enforcing the laws with your assistance and insistence, why do you overlook the person and shortcomings of yourself—the Rev. F. F. Passmore—why has he not been arrested long ere this for disturbing the peace? There will be no lack of evidence in the case, it cannot be successfully denied but that he has caused more disturbance in this county than all the saloon men and gamblers put together. It is safe to say that any judge or jury, upon evidence that could be presented, would bring in a verdict of guilty. Why should you not help defray the expenses of the city? Come, old pal, F. F., get down to the truth, in your card to the public you avoid the facts as satan does holy water. Did you not write to my bondsmen that if I did not enforce the laws against gambling in this county you, the Rev. F. F. Passmore, would bring suit against said bond? Did not I come to the parsonage and talk with you on the subject of gambling, and can, or will, you deny that we talked over the matter of shaking dice and playing cards for drinks, and that I told you it was foolish to make arrests for such actions, that cases of that kind could not be made to stick. Can you, or dare you, through the columns of the papers deny that you told me that if I failed to stop gambling in the county that you would immediately proceed against my bondsmen, and that I must get down to the shaking of dice and playing cards for drinks or you would bring suit?

Come now, pard, if you expect to retain my society you must act square, quit crawfishing, because I despise a backslider and recollect that a liar is worse than a thief, but neither can enter the kingdom of heaven. In the name of the Godly and the ungodly,

I remain respectfully yours, F. F. Brown,

Sheriff of Summit County

The sequel appeared in another short notice in the *Journal*: "A burlesque of a trial for shaking dice came off before Judge Davis on Thursday last, at which a non-taxpaying gentleman arrayed in sacerdotal robes played the role of prosecuting attorney. The taxpayers footed the bill."

All these happenings must be considered in the light of the last decade of the 19th century. It was a decade in which Sabbath observance was a warring issue. It plagued the Columbian Exposition held in Chicago, 1892. "Sabbatharian cranks are flooding Congress with petitions praying Congress to deny any further aid to the Columbian World's Fair unless the managers promise to keep the big show shut up on Sunday." Attempts were made to open the Exposition for business on the Sabbath (Sunday). It met with strong opposition. The strongest opposition was that people would not attend on Sundays. Attempts to operate the Fair on two or three Sundays were sufficient to close the gates. Another attempt was made near the close of the Exposition; the results were the same. The open Sunday was a big issue in those years. Most States had enacted laws regarding Sunday observance, Colorado included.

Furthermore, most church denominations expressed themselves strongly on the issue. What was happening in Breckenridge was happening in Denver, and elsewhere, in enforcement of the laws regarding the Sabbath. Churches in Denver were having their battles on the issues. Rev. Passmore's denomination, the Methodist Church, was in the vanguard. The Methodist Church was just as emphatic on the temperance issue.

Lest we are tempted to judge Florida Passmore too harshly, let us keep in mind the tenor of the times, the laws of the States, the position of his Denomination and his particular Conference. Ridicule, persecution and annihilation were his rewards for taking his ordination literally and seriously.

Finally the matter of Sabbath observance went to law. Brother Passmore made formal charges against one of the saloonkeepers. As reported by the local newspaper, it was a farce—a Gilbert and Sullivan operetta:

The *Journal*   February 6, 1892

On Tuesday last the county court saw a set-to between the law and the gospel on the Sunday closing question. The Rev. Passmore had lodged a sworn information against M. J. B. Dewers charging him with a violation of a state statute against saloons being open on the first day of the week called Sunday. Precisely at four o'clock Judge Eastland in all his dignity and a biled shirt directed under-Sheriff Dunn with his varnished countenance and new clothes, to call the court to order. The long rigmarole and double-barreled charge was read, informant, defendant and counsel for both sides together with a large crowd were present and the fun began. Judge Shock, counsel for the prosecution, asked that the Rev. Mr. Passmore be allowed to address the court in the

opening. Judge Clark, counsel for the defense, had no objection provided the Rev. gentleman would confine himself to the law and evidence and not spread all over the country with a gather-them-in sermon. The parson checked himself when he was about to go into a protracted-meeting exhortation, and finally sat down to catch his breath. Back and forth went the charges and counter-charges. The parson got to his feet again and charged, "These saloon men had violated their word of honor which they had given him not to open on Sunday; they all were men not to be relied upon," and finally he shook the American flag until the eagle screamed.

The court decided the case in favor of the defendant and thereupon declared him discharged to the satisfiaction of all except the complaining witness and his two friends. The taxpayers of the county have the bill to foot.

During the bickering and sniping church activity proceeded in its usual way. The Ladies Aid Society met regularly and promoted its socials and fund-raising activities. Projects of the church were promoted and accomplished. Attendance was good. Reports and jibes came from the newspaper. October 10, 1891: "The *Journal* is pleased to learn that a new church bell has been ordered to replace the one maliciously destroyed a few weeks ago. The new one is to be two hundred pounds heavier than the one destroyed." October 24, 1891: "Brother Passmore is happy once again, the new church bell has arrived. It is hoped the tone will be at least as good as its predecessor." June 18, 1892: "The M. E. Church is being remodeled and given quite a churchy appearance. The square-topped windows and door have given way to very neat pointed arched ones. The interior has been neatly papered and the outside of the church painted. Brother Passmore will hardly feel at home amid all this finery."

Breckenridge newspapers are not available for a few years in the mid-nineties, so we do not know the week-by-week squabbling regarding Florida Passmore and his adversaries. The Methodist Conference returned Passmore year after year to Breckenridge where he was unwanted by many of the town citizenry. In March, 1894, he was hung in effigy and a note delivered to leave town promptly. Florida Passmore did not scare. He remained until the Methodist Conference appointed a new pastor to Breckenridge.

Passmore's closing of Breckenridge saloons was not of extended duration. It was reported March, 1892, that Breckenridge saloons were open on Sunday and running full blast. And that was only eight months after the dynamiting of his bell. Had the Crusader eased up on reforming? Or had he moved to larger fields of endeavor? The latter was true; he graduated from little Breckenridge to big Denver.

Passmore remained as pastor in the Breckenridge church, but the objects of his crusading were now the resident bishop of his denomination, prominent leaders of the Church, both clergy and laymen, and Governor Evans of the State of Colorado. Crusading was now on a larger scale, but as devastating as in Breckenridge.

Adverse winds began to blow for Passmore within the Methodist Conference. Within two years a full-fledged storm had arisen. In 1895, upon personal request, Passmore was given "location"—released from the Conference with permission to go where he wished *outside* the Conference. Immediately he changed his mind and asked "supernumerary relationship"—released from an appointment, but at liberty to preach within the bounds of the Conference. Supernumerary relationship was given on the basis of "personal infirmity." (Passmore's only known infirmity was difficulty in hearing.) He now became front-page news in Denver newspapers and his crusading movements gained momentum.

Rocky Mountain *News*   June 12, 1895

MUST GO TO TRIAL

Rev. F. F. Passmore Is Too Much Of An Anarchist
His Sermon On Personal Righteousness Is Offensive
Plain Words From An Unvarnished Tongue Lead
To Arraignment
Offender Maintains His Right To Free Speech
And Will Not Be Silenced

The closing sessions of the Methodist conference of Colorado at Trinity Church yesterday were convulsed over the consideration of the case of Rev. F. F. Passmore. Mr. Passmore, it will be remembered, is the preacher who in a sermon at the People's Tabernacle last winter arraigned some of the most prominent leaders of the Methodist Church in Colorado, both laymen and clergy, for complicity with the li-

quor traffic and other public evils. He accused them of preaching prohibition and then voting the Republican ticket straight and helping to put the most corrupt ring in the state in office. Chancellor McDowell, Governor Evans, Dr. McIntyre and several other prominent Methodists came in for a severe drubbing on this account, Passmore saying that they had joined hands with the lowest slum element to elect the Republican ticket, and were to just that degree responsible for the liquor traffic. He scored Governor Evans for running street cars to make money on Sunday, and said the reason Evans was not denounced from the pulpits of the denomination was because he was rich and able to contribute large sums to the church. Long before this, Passmore had preached so furiously against saloons and saloon people, while pastor of a charge in Breckenridge, that dynamite was placed in the church and the belfry blown off, presumably by those whom he had angered by his boldness. Therefore it was plainly seen that something must be done with the fearless preacher at the conference this summer. His uncompromising way of casting the truth around promiscuously in large, unadulterated fragments was disconcerting to his more conventional and mildly spoken brethren, to say the least.

Therefore, on Monday, Mr. Passmore was "located," which is a technical term to signify that he was removed from the conference and cast forth to go where he would. Yesterday morning, however, this action was reconsidered and Mr. Passmore was reinstated in the conference as a "supernumerary." This means that he is still a member of the conference and at liberty to preach sermons within its boundaries whenever called upon, but that he will have no regular charge for a year. Ministers often are relieved from duty for a year in this way for illness and various reasons.

After his reinstatement in the conference a committee, composed of some of the most eminent members of the conference, was appointed to confer with Mr. Passmore and see if they could not bring him to a realizing sense of the errors of his ways. They labored long and earnestly with the fiery reformer and finished by asking him, once for all, if he would cease in the pulpit the use of personalities which had caused so much trouble and scandal in the church in the past year and was contrary to the discipline of the Methodist Church.

Mr. Passmore replied distinctly and unmistakably that he would not stop; that he

Dynamiting

would continue in the way that he had begun, and that no power should hinder him from speaking what he believed to be the truth. It was the last straw. The committee went back to the conference and made its report and Mr. Passmore was straightway cited for trial. The charge is upon "unministerial conduct," and the trial will occur in the near future.

The Denver *Republican*   June 12, 1895

It was decided to refer the case of Rev. F. F. Passmore to Presiding Elder Madison of the Greeley District, endeavoring to show the fiery reformer "the error of his way and repent for the peace of the conference and the honor of the church." Bishop Foss, Dr. Earl Cranston, Dr. J. R. Shanon, Dr. W. C. Madison and Dean A. C. Peck were appointed the committee to confer with the erring brother. Dean Peck reported that the gentleman had declined to change his "plan of reform." He concluded with "This will make history some day, brethren." His remarks were met with coldness.

Editorship of the Summit County *Journal* passed from J. C. Fincher to J. W. Swisher, but the tone was the same toward Passmore. (Swisher wrote a series of articles lambasting the preacher, entitled, "Brother Passmore and Madeline.") June 15, 1895, Swisher wrote:

The M. E. annual conference was held in Denver last week and among other things it was decided to try Bro. Passmore for anarchism and insubordination. The speeches and harangues of Mr. Passmore, on which the charges were preferred, contained too much truth to suit the modern political Christian and for that reason he must be silenced. Had they charged him with being a pestiferous nuisance, mischief breeder and liar, we could have furnished a witness to the charges. According to the Rocky Mountain *News,* F. F. Passmore has been "located." We presume the word "locoed" was intended.

Methodist Conference, 1896, was held in Leadville. The consideration of formal charges against F. F. Passmore was taken up. Everything possible was done to keep the matter quietly "within the conference family." File "A" was read, containing the charges. The accused replied, "Not guilty." A formal trial went into operation. The Conference found the specifications and charge sustained. The penalty was determined—"expulsion from the ministry, but

not from the Church"—File "B." Files "A" and "B" were courteously and effectively withdrawn from public inspection, but the story "leaked" to the newspapers:

Rocky Mountain *News*   August 29, 1896

PASSMORE EXPELLED

The Methodist Conference At Leadville
Expells Rev. F. F. Passmore From the Ministry

The only question before the Methodist conference today was the matter of Rev. F. F. Passmore, who appears to have given the church throughout the state a great deal of trouble, and no little annoyance. Mr. Passmore was on trial during the day on the charge of immorality and defamation of character. His immorality consists in his uttering what are claimed as untruths, and the defamation of character arises over the violent attacks he has made on the character of Bishop Warren of Denver. These attacks were embodied in a series of articles which have appeared in various reform papers throughout the country. The charges against Mr. Passmore were sustained and his punishment fixed at expulsion from the ministry, but he still retains his membership in the church.

The trial was held behind closed doors, but after its conclusion the ministers talked freely in regard to the case. There seems to be no personal feeling against the man, but his utterances are considered highly objectionable. He has been engaged in an earnest crusade against intemperance, and appears to think that the pillars of the Methodist Church have not taken the interest in the subject which they should as servants of God.

A political phase is given to the subject owing to the charges made against Bishop Warren. Mr. Passmore takes the ground that in voting or working for the Republican or Democratic tickets both of which parties are in favor of licensing the saloons, a minister of the gospel practically leagues himself with the saloon element and his position is against that canon of the Methodist discipline which asserts that the licensing of the liquor traffic is a sin. Taking this position, he has bitterly attacked Bishop Warren and accused him of being in league with the saloon-keepers and drunkards, and equally if not more guilty than they are. This sort of utterance, even his friends consider highly injudicious, tending as they do to weaken their influence and bring the church into disrepute.

Rocky Mountain *News*   September 2, 1896

Refuses to Be Read Out Of The Methodist Church

Will Imitate Myron W. Reed

In The Meantime The Heterodox Preacher Will Carry His Case To The Judicial Conference And Thence To The Highest Authority

Rev. F. F. Passmore may yet fill the pulpit of an independent church, organized and conducted on the plan pursued in the Broadway Temple, and located in Leadville. After his expulsion from the ministry of the Colorado Methodist Conference last Friday, he was interviewed by various citizens of the Cloud City, who desired to formulate plans for such an organization. Mr. Passmore preached to great crowds on the street every night during the conference. The erratic ex-minister has money of his own, however, and is not dependent upon a salary from a congregation for his support. Mr. Passmore's plan is now to carry his case to the judicial conference, which is composed of ministers belonging to conferences contiguous to the Colorado conference. Should he suffer a repetition of his defeat there he will carry his case to the general conference which is the highest tribunal of Methodism.

Passmore carried his appeal to the Judicial Conference, meeting in Omaha, December, 1896. The action of the seventeen-member judicial conference was: "The case of F. F. Passmore, appealed from the action of the Colorado Conference, expelling him from the ministry, was refused a hearing on the ground of forfeiture of all rights to appeal on the part of the appellant, and the action of the Colorado Conference confirmed by a unanimous vote." The step to General Conference was not taken by Bro. Passmore.

Walter J. Boigegrain, in a doctorate thesis, The Methodist Church in Eagle-Colorado River Valley—1880-1906 tells of Florida Passmore coming to the Rifle Circuit during the year 1895, when Passmore held his supernumerary relationship. There were no serious consequences to the first-year's revival meetings, but when a second series of meetings was held the following year, the results were far different. Passmore tried to take the congregation and church building of Grand Valley away from the Methodist Church. Passmore had to be forcibly ejected from a Quar-

terly Conference meeting. Court litigation took place, but Passmore and his followers lost the case. Boigegrain wrote: "Any explanation of why the Passmore incident took place seems impossible. If this minister caused dissension, it is probably also true that he possessed some highly admirable qualities."

Isaac H. Beardsley, for many years secretary of the Colorado Conference, wrote in his book, *Echoes from Peak and Plain*:

Florida F. Passmore was born in Union County, Georgia, August 12, 1844; moved with his father, when six years of age, to Polk County, East Tennessee; came to Colorado in April, 1879; joined the Methodist Episcopal Church in 1880; licensed to preach in November, 1880, at Alma, Park County, Colorado, by the Rev. Earl Cranston, presiding elder; admitted to Conferences in 1888, and ordained to local orders as an elder at the same time, having been ordained deacon previously. He was pastor at Alma and Breckenridge, each five years. At the latter place he made a valiant fight against rum and sin in high places, and brought out the opposition of the baser elements. August 17, 1891, an attempt was made to blow up the steeple of his church with dynamite, and those "of the baser sort" hung him in effigy, March, 1894, ordering him to leave town, threatening his life in case of non-compliance. True to God, his own conscience, and the law of the Church he remained at his post until relieved by the expiration of his term. He became a supernumerary in 1894-95. He is a man of good natural abilities, firm in his convictions, and possesses an uncompromising spirit. In his recent history, he has denounced unsparingly some of the prominent members of the Conference and the resident bishop, without cause, as most of the brethren think, dealing in bitter personalities. His brethren bore with him long and patiently, but to no effect. In 1896, charges having been brought against him, he was expelled from the ministry. In all that he has done, he claims to have the Divine approval.

So little is known about Florida Passmore apart from his fiery preaching and valiant crusading. Apparently he was unmarried; there is no mention of wife and family. No pictures are available, except the newspaper sketches. Reportedly, he was a large-sized man and physically strong. Breckenridge lads found him a capable boxing instructor. He was fearless; threat of physical force or power of pen and printed-page failed to cower him. The story is told of a young man, who thought himself a pug, asking a business man if he would pay the fine if he would go out in the street and lick that preacher. The business man replied, "Yes, I will pay your fine, but I will not pay your doctor bill."

Passmore's preliminary trial by his ministerial brethren was held December 6, 1895, in the pastor's study at Trinity Methodist Church, Denver. Crowds of curiosity-seekers sought admission, but the trial was closed to the public. A former Breckenridgian was, at the time, living in Denver; he was admitted as a witness *for* the defendant. It was none other than our friend, "Ye Editor," of Summit County *Journal*—Jonathan C. Fincher. This "witness for the defendant" had lashed the preacher unmercifully with the editorial pen in the columns of his Breckenridge newspaper.

What finally happened to Florida Passmore? Again, as in so many Breckenridge stories, the trail is lost. The independent tabernacle in Leadville did not materialize; perhaps Passmore found another "Cloud City" for his crusading.

Muddled stories of the dynamiting of the bell still make the rounds of Breckenridge, from saloon to church. The only-known remnant of the dynamited bell rests on the northwest window-sill in Father Dyer Church. It is a twenty-two pound iron hammer. It was not the clapper to sound the joyous call to worship on Sabbath mornings, but the hammer to strike the outside of the bell in funereal tolling. It is the memorial of Florida F. Passmore—"for whom the bell tolls." The way of the crusader and reformer is not easy.

Present day bell purchased after dynamiting incident in 1891.

SALOONS.

(H. B. 203.)
AN ACT

To regulate the keeping of saloons and other drinking places or resorts, and imposing penalties for a violation of such regulations.

Be it enacted by the General Assembly of the State of Colorado:

SECTION 1. That no saloon, tippling house or dram shop shall have or keep in connection with or as a part of such saloon, tippling house, or dram shop any wine room or other place either with or without door or doors, curtain or curtains or screen of any kind into which any female person shall be permitted to enter from the outside or from such saloon, tippling house or dram shop and there be supplied with any kind of liquor whatsoever. If any person shall be convicted of a violation of any of the provisions of this section, such person shall be fined in a sum not less than fifty dollars, nor more than two hundred and fifty dollars, or by imprisonment in the county jail not less than two months nor more than twelve months or by both such fine and imprisonment at the discretion of the court.

Wine rooms.

Penalty.

SECTION 2. Every saloon, bar or other place where spirituous, vinous, malt or other liquors are kept, sold, bartered, exchanged and given away or are kept, sold, bartered, exchanged or given away, shall be closed and kept closed from twelve o'clock at midnight until six o'clock in the morning of every day in the week, except Sunday or the first day of the week, and on Sunday or the first day of the week as aforesaid the said places hereinbefore in this section mentioned shall be closed at twelve o'clock at midnight on Saturday of each and every week and kept closed until six o'clock in the morning of the following Monday of each and every week; that during the time and times herein specified in which the said saloons, bars and other places are to be kept closed, no liquor of any kind whatsoever shall be sold, bartered, exchanged or given away, and no person or persons whomsoever, other than those connected with the business of carrying on or keeping the said saloon, bar or other place or places as aforesaid shall be permitted to be or remain in or around the same, but all and every such person or persons shall be expelled and put out of the same. Any and every person convicted of violating any of the provisions of this section shall be punished by a fine of not less than one hundred nor more than five hundred dollars or imprisoned not less than six months nor more than eighteen months or by both such fine and imprisonment at the discretion of the court; and if it shall appear that a person or persons not employed in and about the business as aforesaid, shall be permitted to remain in the said saloon or other place or places as aforesaid, such fact shall be *prima facie* evidence in favor of the guilt of the accused party or parties.

Saloons shall be closed at midnight.

Closed on Sunday.

When closed no person permitted to remain in or around premises.

Penalty.

SECTION 3. The courts are to construe this act liberally so as to effectuate and carry out the intent of the legislature in its enactment.

Act liberally construed.

Approved April 7th, 1891.

AN ACT

TO SUPPRESS GAMBLING AND GAMBLING HOUSES

Be it enacted by the Council and House of Representatives of Colorado Territory:

SECTION 1: That if any person shall keep any room, building, arbor, booth, shed or tenement of any description, to be used or occupied for gambling, or shall knowingly permit the same to be used or occupied for gambling; or if any person, being the owner of any room, building, arbor, booth, shed or tenement of any description, shall rent the same to be used or occupied for gambling, the person so offending shall, on conviction thereof, be fined in any sum not less than thirty dollars, nor more than five hundred dollars, or be imprisoned in the county jail not less than ten days, nor more than thirty days, or both, at the discretion of the court; and if the owner of any room, building, arbor, booth, shed or tenement of any description, shall know that any gaming tables, apparatus or establishment is kept or used in such room, building, arbor, booth, shed or tenement, for gambling and winning, betting or gaining money or other property, and shall not forthwith cause complaint to be made against the person so keeping or using such room, building, arbor, booth, shed or tenement, he shall be taken, held, and considered to have knowingly permitted the same to be used and occupied for gambling.

SECTION 2. That if any person shall keep or exhibit any gaming table, establishment, device or apparatus to win or gain money or other property, or shall aid, assist, or permit others to do the same, or if any person shall engage in gambling for a livelihood, or shall be without any fixed residence and in the habit and practice of gambling, he shall be deemed and taken to be a common gambler, and upon conviction thereof, shall be imprisoned in the county jail not less than three months nor more than one year, and be fined in sum not less than two hundred dollars nor more than five hundred dollars.

SECTION 12. This act shall take effect and be in force from and after its passage.

Approved January 20th, A.D. 1866.

Keeper of room used for gambling or person permitting same to be used for gambling, or landlord renting room &c. to be used for gambling—how punished.

May be fined or imprisoned, or both. Duty of owner of any room, building, &c., knowing the same to be used for gambling— to complain forthwith of the person so using.

Such owner failing to complain, liable to penalties.

Common gamblers— what persons so considered.

Penalties.

REV. MR. PASSMORE: "I appeal to the committeemen.

Passmore On Church Trial — The Rocky Mountain *News,* December 7, 1895, Page 1. Courtesy—Library State Historical Society of Colorado.

Passmore On Church Trial — The Rocky Mountain *News,* December 7, 1895, Page 1. Courtesy—Library State Historical Society of Colorado.

PASSMORE LISTENS.

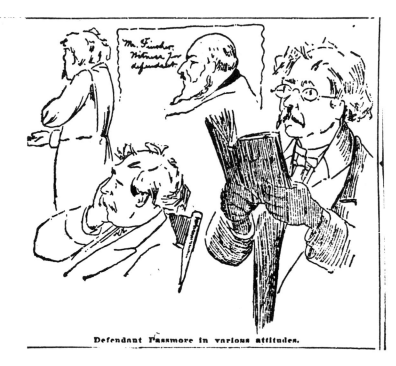

Defendant Passmore in various attitudes.

Passmore On Church Trial — The Denver *Republican,* December 7, 1895, Page 1. Courtesy—Library State Historical Society of Colorado.

THE BULL IN THE CHINA SHOP.

Cartoonist's portrayal of Rev. Passmore attacking the Methodist Discipline, the Methodist Church, Governor Evans, Bishop Warren, Elder Madison, Chancellor McDowell, Sheriff Wilson, Rev. McIntyre. Rocky Mountain *News,* December 8, 1895, Page 1. Courtesy—Library State Historical Society of Colorado.

Dynamiting

PUG RYAN

Ed Auge was a long-time resident of Breckenridge. He was also a chronicler of Breckenridge historical events, sharing his stories through the columns of the local newspaper. In a series in the Summit County *Journal*, 1938, appeared Auge's stories of two hold-ups that took place in Breckenridge in the summer of 1898. Of the two, the story of "Pug Ryan" is more bizarre. Auge was almost an on-the-scene reporter for the event; he missed being one of the main characters by only ten minutes.

Summit County *Journal*   January 28, 1938

In the summer of 1898 two hold-ups took place in Breckenridge which old-timers have not forgotten. The first one was in June in the game room of W. P. Knorr's saloon. Two brothers, Bob and John Etzler were running the games when two masked men entered through the back door and at the point of six-shooters, took the tin money racks from the tables. Bartender Theodore Stanaker opened fire as they were leaving, which was returned by the hold-ups. No one was hurt but one of the bullets went through the window of the fireman's hall where the dancing club had dances every Saturday night. As the Kempton Show Company was at the G. A. R. Hall for a week the dance had been fortunately given up for that night. Another bullet just missed Dave Cowell's head. Although nearly forty years have passed since this hold-up, Dave still shudders when he hears it recalled. The kids trailed the robbers for a long ways picking up nickels, dimes, quarters and half dollars that they dropped in their flight. These hold-ups were never caught.

On the night of August 11, 1898, everything seemed to be stepping along nicely in the game room of the Denver Hotel. The rattle of chips could be heard as the faro bank, roulette wheel, crap table and stud poker games were busy. Bartender Ed Brewer was busy answering the bells and serving the stimulating refreshments to the game buckers. Shortly before midnight the writer, (Ed Auge), accompanied by Charles Gilbert, left for the Oro Mine where the Minnie employees were boarding and bunking, never thinking of what they missed by not staying ten minutes longer. Just about midnight four masked men entered through the back door carrying six-shooters. The accidental discharge of one of the guns as they entered the barroom upset their plans. The contents of this discharged gun went through the ceiling. Robert Foote had several thousand dollars in his safe which had been left by others for safe keeping. No doubt this was what the hold-ups were after, but now they had to do things quick and make their get-away. They immediately lined up the bunch and after taking the money from the barroom till and from the game tables proceeded to rob individuals. While three men held the guns leveled, another took the watches from Ed Brewer, George Ralston and Robert Foote, and also a diamond valued at $250 worn by Foote. They then departed with their loot. Some, who were in the lineup, had several hundred dollars in cash upon their person, which the stickups didn't exactly overlook, but the discharge of their gun made them uneasy. Louis A. Scott, alias Pug Ryan, the leader of the gang, had done some spotting before the hold-up. Charles Levy, the old time Hebrew clothing man who roomed at the Denver Hotel at the time, would sit by the stove and doze away until about 2 a.m. before retiring and always had from $600-$800 in his pocket. Pug had him spotted and intended to get him, but to his disappointment, this was one of the few nights during the summer that Levy retired before midnight. Others who had the pleasure (?) of looking down the barrels of the six-shooters were Chas. Messner, George Tyler, Lou Weir, Al Brewer, George Forman, Frank Roby, Wm. Passmore, Harry Whitehead, John Kelly, Ed Radigan, Dick McKellup and Sam Blair.

Those were the days when a freight train, which carried passengers from Denver to Leadville, went through Breckenridge at 4 a.m. The morning of August 12, 1898, found this train pulling out with a large crew of passengers bound for Kokomo, where a bunch of toughs living in a cabin close to town, were the suspected holdups. Jerry Detweiler, who was serving his first year as sheriff, appointed Ernest Conrad of Breckenridge and Sumner Whitney of Kokomo as deputies. A reward of $100 was offered by Robert Foote for the capture of the bandits. Conrad and Whitney slipped away from the crowd and entered the cabin of the suspects. They searched them and finding nothing on them made an apology and departed thinking they were not the men. After talking the matter over for a few minutes they changed their minds and came to the conclusion they were the men after all. Then followed a blunder that cost four lives. They went back into the cabin and this time the suspects were prepared for them. Conrad demanded that they let him look under the blankets and as he lifted them up Pug Ryan fired twice killing Conrad and wounding Whitney. Pug made his get-away but Whitney shot Dick Bryant and wounded Manley, who lived but two hours after he was shot. He confessed all before he died. After being buried, his friends came for his body, and after he was taken from the ground Ed Brewer's watch chain was found on his person. The fourth member of the gang was never accounted for. Whitney died about two months later.

Breckenridge was a very excited town on the afternoon of August 12, 1898. The streets were filled with maddened people who were anxious to catch Pug Ryan. The most conspicuous man was Bob Etzler, who rode up and down Main Street on horseback with a rifle on his shoulder and acted as though he meant business. Pug eluded the maddened people and remained at large for four years, being captured in Portland, Oregon in May, 1902. Sheriff Detweiler and deputy sheriff William Lindsay of Kokomo, father of Mrs. Ed. Farnham, made the trip to get him. Fearing he might escape from the Breckenridge jail, he was placed in the Leadville jail. He didn't do a thing but escape through the sewer pipe. He then made a big blunder by going right to his home in Cripple Creek where he was well known and was standing on a street corner talking to old acquaintances when arrested by the Cripple Creek marshal. His trial took place in Breckenridge in August, 1902. He was defended by J. Maurice Finn of Cripple Creek, who was assisted by Attorney James T. Hogan. The District Attorney was Frank E. Purple, who was assisted by Sam Jones who made a talk to the jury that sent Pug Ryan to prison for life.

The first juryman to be examined and chosen was Carl Fulton, who was postmaster at Swandyke. When asked by the District Judge Frank Owers why he wished to be excused, Carl said, "I live in Swandyke and not in Breckenridge, therefore I know nothing about the case." The Judge smiled and said they needed twelve men just like him, so Carl had to serve. Other jurymen were W. H. Lawyer, Montezuma; E. M. Cox of Dillon; R. H. Lee, Lakeside; Wm. Robinson, Breckenridge, father of County Treasurer George Robinson; Geo. Truax, Ed Dwyer, Robinson; Harry Smith and Geo. Louage of Breckenridge; John Lasky and L. S. Shane of Slate Creek and J. H. McDougal of Swandyke. The following is an extract from Sam Jones' talk to the jury:

"I see a beautiful happy home up Main Street, three young children, a loving mother, and a loving husband and father. Suddenly a mist came over this home." Pointing to the defendant he said, "Gentlemen of the jury, there is the mist! Oh! Pug Ryan we got you. Four long years, but at last. We cannot give you the gallows, but we will give you the nearest to it."

During the trial Mrs. Whitney, widow of one of the victims, recognized Pug Ryan as the man who ate at her table the day before the holdup. Capital punishment was not in vogue when the crime was committed, so life imprisonment was the limit which he received.

During the summer of 1908 Allie Carlson, with her two cousins Bertha and Bryan Murrell, were playing by a big log in Kokomo. They found a watch which proved to be the very one that Pug Ryan took from Robert Foote.

Ed Auge included in his story the finding of the robbery loot as it was printed in the Summit County *Journal*, 1908:

On Monday afternoon, a bunch of Kokomo children held a luncheon on the summit of Jacque Mountain. Returning home the children of Gus Carlson happened to come down the path which Pug Ryan took going up in making his get-away from the incensed Kokomo people. There on the mountainside the Carlson children picked up an old watch and chain. Directly another gold watch was found. Of course the children were excited and naturally ran home with their treasure.

When papa Gus arrived home in the evening and heard the story of the find, he at once recalled the 1898 tragedy and commenced to investigate. He found the first clue to ownership of one of the watches in the monogram, R. W. F., which it bore.

He called up the *Journal* by phone and said he had R. W. Foote's and another gold watch and a pearl-handled revolver and narrated how he came into possession of them.

A morning later Mr. Foote was appraised of the recovery of the forgotten time piece. He took in the situation at once and said, "My diamond is on that hill too; it will be found where the watches were picked up, and I shall take the morning train to Kokomo."

Sunrise next morning found Mr. Foote and Chet Acton knocking at the door of the Carlson home in Kokomo. The children were aroused and they led the way to the lone treasure spot. Acton scratched in the dirt at the spot pointed out by the children and in an instant uncovered the big diamond, to the great joy of him who was ruthlessly deprived of it ten long years before. The second watch proved to be the property of Ed Brewer then residing in Glenwood Springs.

After the shooting which took place toward evening on August 12, 1898, Pug with the plunder ran up the hill. It is now evident that as he ran he wrapped up the watches, diamond and revolver (and possibly Ralston's watch which was never recovered) in a handkerchief and hid them behind the old log. Year by year the log decayed and piece by particle blew away. Also the handkerchief rotted, exposing the timepieces to weather and the shining gold to the eyes of passersby. Sliding dirt had covered the diamond, but it was there just the same.

Auge's accounting of the "Pug" Ryan thriller seems to be the authentic record of this Breckenridge story, told and retold. Other accounts have been written, but they vary little and differ only on a few minor points. The Denver *Times*, August 13, 1898, recorded the hold-up story and the happenings at Kokomo—"Hounds Are Out—Pug Ryan Cannot Long Escape the Law—Excitement Is Running High." The *Times* also recorded Manley's deathbed confession:

I, Dick Manley, being on my death bed, make the following statement, believing my end near and wishing to confess before going before my Maker. I am a married man, 24 years old, was born in Henrietta, Clay County, Texas. That I, Dick Bryan, and Hugh Ryan, started out from Victor about a week ago to do such work as we've been doing. We came to Breckenridge and got in with a tall, light-complexioned, slim fellow about five feet nine inches, who steered us to the place we held up last night. This fellow had been working for Knorr, whose place was held up a few weeks ago. This man, Lewis, went ahead of us and came out and said, all was well, and Bryan and Ryan went in; Bryan had a short shotgun and so did Ryan. One was quick on the trigger and it was fired accidentally. We got three gold watches and $50. We walked all night and came up to the cabin where the shooting of today took place. There we calculated to sleep. This man Lewis had a long, light mustache. The officers came down to the cabin and talked awhile and went out and come back and said: "Boys, we must see what you have got under those blankets," and Dick Bryan and Ryan jumped up and pulled their guns and the officer was shot. In the excitement I could not see who shot the other man. I went to run out and got my finger shot off as I was going out the door. This is the truth, gentlemen. We were all going to Leadville tomorrow night and hold up the Pioneer saloon and games. I know nothing about the hold-up you had here on the 3rd of July, and I've only been with these people a little while. Ryan, the fellow that got away, is called "Pug" Ryan, and is a short man, sorter heavy-set, weight about 160 pounds and was bloody when he left and run away, after the shooting.

(Signed)   Dick Manley

Another series of articles appeared in the Summit County *Journal*, from December 24, 1954, to April 15, 1955, entitled "Thar's Gold in Them Thar' Hills." The Pug Ryan story received considerable attention in these stories. George Ralston's watch was reportedly the most valuable watch in town, an heirloom valued at five hundred dollars. Two men at the Denver Hotel that night who escaped being robbed were Frank Roby who hid under a billiard table and William Passmore who crawled under a bench.

(William Passmore, mentioned in the story, seems not to have been related to the preacher, Florida Passmore. William E. Passmore was manager of the local Sampler of the Denver Smelting and Mining Company.)

The articles, "Thar's Gold in Them Thar' Hills," recounted the excitement of Pug Ryan's trial: "Spectators vied for seats and some brought lunches in order not to lose their places. Some of the romantically inclined, but misled, young ladies of the town displayed an undue interest, ogling Pug Ryan, much to the consternation of their elders."

The Breckenridge *Bulletin*, June 27, 1908, gave an interesting write-up of the finding of Pug Ryan's loot at Kokomo:

One in the habit of reading dime novels would not in a thousand of them find a more romantic incident than happened this week at Kokomo, which calls up a tragedy of ten years ago. We will review the tragedy, then give the incident. (We omit the tragedy part since that has been recounted.)

The children did not find the diamond or the Ralston watch, but Foote and Acton, when piloted to the spot, commenced to search for them, with the result that the diamond was dug out of a pile of worm dust, from a rotten tree, in a few moments. It is the property of Mr. Charles Moessner, now of Hastings, Nebraska, and will be returned to him. Mr. Foote was just wearing it the night it was plucked from his bosom. One of the watches started to run when it was wound. The revolver is quite rusty and of little value save as a relic. (Breckenridge *Bulletin,* July 4, 1908, mentioned: "Charles Moessner, of Hastings, Nebraska, arrived Thursday for his regular summer's visit in Breckenridge. He will take the diamond home with him which was found near Kokomo last week, and which had laid in the dirt for ten years since the Pug Ryan robbery.")

Auge wrote that Ed Brewer's watch was in perfect running condition, when found, ticked off the seconds accurately as before. After cleaning and oiling, Robert Foote's Elgin ran as before and is still in perfect running condition. The pearl handled 38 calibre six-shooter, with three bullets missing, was doubtless the weapon that killed Conrad and Whitney. "For many years," Auge wrote, "these articles of value, priceless as relics, were to be seen in the Denver House curio cabinet." Other stories are to the effect that personal effects, taken from the dead robbers, Dick Manley and Dick Bryant, were on display in one of the stores of Kokomo. For days following the killing a resident of Kokomo paraded the streets displaying the boots of one of the dead bandits. The precise location of these relics is presently unknown, with one exception. The gold Elgin watch of Robert W. Foote is now a prized possession of his great grandson, Robin G. Theobald of Breckenridge.

"During his imprisonment in Canon City, Pug Ryan became unruly and vicious and was subjected to solitary confinement. He was mentally deranged when in 1931, after twenty-nine years imprisonment, he died at the penitentiary."

The last commentary on Pug Ryan was in the July 10th, 1931, Summit County *Journal*— Death of "Pug Ryan" Recalls Early Day Event. "Arthur L. Scott, alias Pug Ryan, 61 years old, a life termer at the Colorado State Penitentiary, was buried on Woodpecker Hill, near the prison Saturday afternoon. Scott completed his life sentence for the murder of three officers at Breckenridge, Colorado, in 1898. Four convicts took the rough pine casket to the burial grounds and Chaplain L. A. Crittenton conducted a brief service."

BOREAS

In Greek mythology the four winds—Boreas, Zephyrus, Notus and Eurus—were worshiped as deities. Boreas was god of the north wind, Zephyrus of the west, Notus of the south and Eurus of the east. Boreas and Zephyrus have been most celebrated by the poets, Boreas for his rudeness, Zephyrus for his gentleness.

Boreas was enigmatic, perplexing, baffling. At times he cut a dashing figure, again he was extremely crude. Sometimes he was calm, and then he was boisterous. He was gentle, he was vicious; he was tender, he was brusque. He was unpredictable—peaceable and raging, loving and sadistic, placid and murderous. At play he was mischievous, a rascal, a scoundrel, a rogue, a scamp. At times he played for the sheer joy of playing; in another moment he was playing for keeps. Sometimes he appeared stupid, at other times there was ingenuity and cunning to outwit the wisest. Inexplicable, incorrigible, the mood of the moment was Boreas.

Boreas was pathetic. He was burly, strong and sturdy. With wings outstretched, curly beard and hair snow flecked and speckled, garments gracefully flowing in the wind he was the epitome of rugged strength and manliness. But he loved the nymph, Orithyia, and she desired gentleness. Boreas tried desperately to play the lover's part, but met with poor success. He could not breathe gently like Zephyrus, nor softly sigh as his brother. Orithyia did not like the lack of gentle-loving on the part of her suitor.

To complicate matters Orithyia's parents did not look with favor on Boreas courting the maiden. They had conceived a hatred for all who lived in North country, and they refused to give the maiden to Boreas. They were foolish, however, to think they could keep what the North Wind wanted. One day, when Orithyia played with her sisters on the bank of a river, Boreas swept down in a great gust and carried her away to a distant land, married her, begat two sons, Zetes and Calais. To our regret, the mighty Boreas had a streak of meanness, jealousy and viciousness that came forth on occasions with little provocation.

Hyacinthus was a young lad of extraordinary beauty. Apollo, son of Zeus, god of poetry and music, greatly admired the young Hyacinthus. One day Apollo was teaching Hyacinthus to throw the discus. Boreas was a by-stander, and he was jealous of the handsome young lad and also of Apollo's favoritism. When the young lad threw the discus into the air, Boreas blew a blast from his nostrils that caused the discus to halt in mid-air, boomerang, and return to strike the head of the young man with a vicious blow. Hyacinthus, a deep gash in his head, fell to the ground dead. A flower, thereafter called the hyacinth, blossomed from the blood-soaked ground where his wounded head rested.

Boreas—North Wind—took up dwelling in the high mountainous caverns. There he remains as inexplicable as ever, fairly gentle at times, vicious and murderous when on rampage. It is believed he has a cavern in the lofty heights overlooking Breckenridge, the heights that bear his name, Boreas.

Boreas was in a surly, disagreeable mood in the late fall of 1898. It had been ten years since he had been on a real bender. At that time, March of "88," he had struck New York City with a vengeance. What caused his peevishness at that time is not known. Pleased with his success, he broadened his activity to include most of the eastern States and the northern mid-west.

The blizzard of "88" is reluctant to give up its reputation as grand-daddy of all storms.

What ruffled the querulous North Wind in 1898-1899, we know not, but his fault-finding didn't abate from fall of "98" to spring of "99." If anything, it progressively worsened. Boreas struck with a vengeance and moved into fiendish viciousness, insatiable of nothing short of murder. Forever debatable is the issue of which was the greater storm—"88" or "98." What Boreas missed in "88" he included in "98" with equal severity. Some say "88" had more severe blizzard winds to add to the heavy snowfall; others says blizzard conditions of "98" equalled "88," and furthermore, the storm covered a far wider area. The East had deeper snowfall in "88" than the West; Boreas reversed it in "98" and gave greater depths to the West. High winds and fierce cold were a standoff. Boreas blasted the winter of 1898-1899 without favoritism toward East or West. Some hold the opinion that the Big Storm of 1898-1899 was localized—that it centered in the Rocky Mountains—mostly Breckenridge. Not so. Boreas ranged and rampaged far and wide.

Fall Season, 1898, in Breckenridge area, followed somewhat the usual pattern, except for a heavy snow-storm in mid-September. Beautiful weather followed this early snowstorm, leaving the high peaks whitened and the lower slopes opportunity to bedeck themselves in glorious aspen gold. Old-timers knew that sometimes it could remain pleasant, and almost snow-less, until Thanksgiving and Christmas. Fall and Winter do not follow set patterns in the Rocky Mountains; sometimes it is an early winter, sometimes late. Breckenridge has learned to take the seasons as they come.

Carl Fulton, owner of a mine at Swandyke, up Swan Valley, decided to stay and work the winter at his mine. In addition to the mine, he had a small stamp-mill that could handle about five tons of ore every twenty-four hours. Between the mine and the mill he could keep busy during the winter months. Also, he had invested $5,000 in his project, and he was eager to get returns. During the summer and early fall his pack of thirty-two "jacks" had carried (each jack) two to three hundred pounds of ore from mine to mill, thrice daily. But the snow came about the 15th of September and his jacks had to be taken down to the valley for the winter.

Fine weather followed that first September snow. Then, the afternoon of the twenty-seventh of November, snow started to fall, and by nine o'clock the next morning it was five feet deep on the level. It snowed every day until the twentieth of February. By the middle of December snow-slides were coming down the slopes and the mine and stamp-mill had to be abandoned for the winter. June 1st, Fulton returned on snowshoes and found that his mill had been knocked down, broken in pieces, and the rubble carried across a deep gulch and deposited on the opposite slope—the $5,000 investment was lost.

(The first stage got over the mountain from South Park to Swandyke, July 4th, and Carl Fulton's father from Ohio was one of the passengers. H. J. Fulton remained at the mine, helping his son during the summer and fall months of 1899. October 22, 1899, began a beautiful Sunday with sun shining brightly. H. J. Fulton and George Sunderling hiked across the mountain to Montezuma, on a seven-mile trail. After visiting in Montezuma they started home. A raging blizzard came up, the two men perished. The body of H. J. Fulton was not found until June, 1900, and now rests in the family plot in Valley Brook Cemetery. We recount this, for there are some who believe that Fulton's life was lost in the "Big Storm" of 1898-1899, but it was the winter of 1899-1900.)

Stories of the "Big Snow" of 1898-1899 are almost unbelievable. Much of our information of the Breckenridge area comes from old-timers who told their stories in later years. There is little variance in the accounts and the dates. Ed Auge wrote his remembrance of the Big Snow and the Blockade in 1935. E. C. Peabody chronicled his account of "The Big Snow" in the early 1950s. (Peabody's story appeared in installments in the Summit County *Journal*, March 26, 1954 to April 30, 1954. Auge's appeared on March 29, 1935.) We regret that Breckenridge papers for the time of the Blockade are missing. Auge wrote:

The Fall of 1898 was very beautiful until the first week in November when the first heavy snow fell. It kept up its pace very steadily and by Christmas huge snow-banks had accumulated on Main Street. Trains began to stall, and two days without a train seemed to take place quite often. On February 4, 1899, a train ar-arrived, being the first one in about a week, but could get no farther than Breckenridge. This train departed February 5, and no train was seen again in Summit County for a period of eighty days.

This was the famous "Blockade" of 79 days, February 4th to April 24th. The "blockade" refers to the period when Breckenridge was without train service. The "Big Snow" extended from November to June. Supposedly, the intensity of the storms decreased and became intermittent in mid-February, but enough snow, plus occasional snows, was on hand to keep the blockade in effect until April 24th, as far as train service was concerned.

Mail service, to and from the outside world, was only occasional. Eli Fletcher and Will Fletcher made a trip to Como on skis for first-class mail. "About March 1st, all able-bodied men, both young and old, volunteered to shovel out the wagon road over Boreas to Como. The men, and all the horses in town, completed the job in about ten days, and then mail and necessities were freighted by team and sled over Boreas until the train could run again."

Boreas had managed a "dilly" this time. Snow fell day after day, all day long, and with no sunshine. If it were not snowing at daybreak, the mountains were shrouded in gray, so dense that only a few trees at the base showed their frozen silhouettes. But soon the fine flakes started sifting downward and then a heavy white curtain descended again. Willows and low shrubbery were completely covered; railroad cars, unused cabins—anything that did not fight back became white mounds or a part of the level surface. Great stretches were white meadows. The wind drifted the snow to fantastic heights. Main Street of Breckenridge was tunneled in three places so people could cross from one side to the other. Others snow-shoed overhead.

What was happening in Breckenridge was being duplicated in all nearby towns and villages —Alma, Fairplay, Dillon, Frisco, Wheeler Flats, Kokomo, Leadville, Montezuma. Kokomo, it was reported, became a "city of whiteness." There "the heads of people, when walking on the street, were brought to a level with the tops of two-story houses. One night a trampling in the snow overhead was heard, and the occupants of the house, on looking, found a burro had unconsciously made his way to the very top of the house, and there stood, looking calmly about him." "A

freight train that was left standing at Wheeler (now the junction of the highways going to Vail and Leadville) was buried completely out of sight, and in fact, there was nothing left to show where it stood. Snow had levelled it so completely that there was not a sign of track or coaches."

S. T. Richards tells of snow-shoeing from Breckenridge to Como—an eleven hour trip to cover eighteen miles—"shoeing over the tops of trees, plunging head first into a forty-foot drift. I was loaded with four pounds of gold in one pocket and a sackful of mail and packages strung across my shoulder. I'll shoot the next man who asks me to carry fifty pounds of mail when I contemplate making a snow-shoe trip."

Thomas Painsett made a trip over Boreas along the same route and in the same manner:

Boreas is the most elevated station on the South Park Railroad and is the rendevous of the scattered forces of the north wind. There they recuperate and radiate. There they gather and scatter, pack and pile the waters they have congealed into flakes. There they mock and hide the works of man. At the top of Boreas a telegraph station and a section station are maintained. True the operator of the electric key can safely communicate with the world below when the storm king is angry and erects his barriers, but the mountaineer who braves the elements warring on the pass risks a shroud in the drifts.

I had started from Breckenridge at 8 o'clock in the morning, in order to get away from bacon rinds and frozen potatoes into a community where butter and eggs were on the bill of fare. As I neared the top of Boreas a smoke signal cheered me, coming from a piece of stovepipe that seemed to be planted in a drift. Buried beneath was the stone building used for train shelter and turntable. That pipe denoted present safety, and perchance a meal, and hope for the flesh pots of Denver.

I had provided myself with a couple of pint bottles of liquid ballast for an emergency, and here the emergency appeared. Food was scarce for an unexpected pilgrim on his way to the haunts of men. While I nestled close to the sources of that smoke and thawed into the resemblance of a human being, they sampled the ballast and decided that I was an angel sent to inform them that with firewater the storm king could be defied, if only for a minute.

I glided down the mountain like lightning, came to a halt at Como by running one of my shoes on either side of a telegraph pole and hanging onto the lower cross-tree. I continued the next day to Grant to catch the train. I had two companions to guide on the last day, who were anxious to reach home. They are now my sworn friends and will never swear at a stove-pipe in good running order. At Grant I sold my snow-shoes to a man who wanted to see that stovepipe and his family over the range.

South Park started digging out in mid-February and the blockade was broken to Como. Some of the first arrivals from Como had been stranded for nearly a month. The first train to hack its way through the snow and ice was made up of a rotary plow, five engines, a flanger, and then the passenger coaches. Fifty men with picks and shovels were aboard. It took three days' fighting against the tremendous masses of snow to accomplish the break-through. A rotary following lifted the snow over the sides of the cuts and clear of the tracks. Drifts forty and fifty feet deep covered South Park.

A reporter for Rocky Mountain *News* wrote, "The people of Denver can't realize the amount of snow there is in the mountains. It is beyond all imagination and I am afraid the destruction by snow-slides and washouts within the next few weeks will be enormous. The oldest inhabitants never saw such great "combs" of snow on the mountain tops as exist now, and as soon as these are softened up a little by the sun they will cause slides that will sweep everything before them. One slide has come down Mosquito Creek already. Luckily there was nothing in the way but a few telegraph poles, and if the company wants these back again they had better take a basket along to gather them." Denver, strangely, did not receive snow in devastating amounts. There were a few weeks that stores weren't crowded, but "sunshine and pleasant breezes came to Denver February 13th, and brought out crowds. It was the first time in two weeks that stores were crowded and streets filled with a joyous throng."

Boreas eased up a bit on the mountains and Denver, but he was far from being sated. There were other parts of the country that needed attention, and they were not to be denied. Boreas needed a vacation—new scenery—the snow was becoming "old stuff" to Denver and the moun-

tains. That was an insult to Boreas, and Boreas didn't like insults.

Boreas, with renewed strength, lashed out viciously in every direction, east, west, north and south. The whole United States would remember the winter of 1898-1899. Denver's Rocky Mountain *News*, February 14th, had large first-page headlines:

EAST AND WEST IN THE GRASP OF
THE STORM KING

Blizzard of Almost Unprecedented Severity
Sweeps All The States Lying East of the
Mississippi River
Business Paralyzed and Railroads Unable to
Run Trains
Intense Suffering of the Poor of the Large Cities
Washington, D. C. Buried in Snow Drifts and
Uncle Sam Shuts Up Shop for a Day
Thermometers Throughout the South Hovering
Around Zero
Many Fatalities Reported

Another front-page headline emblazoned:

BOREAS GONE TO MARDI GRAS

Storm King Forsakes Colorado to Pay His
Compliments to New Orleans

The New York *Times*, not given to sensationalism, gave pages one and two to storm news —it was the big news!

THE STORM KING HOLDS FULL SWAY

New York and Its Environs Fast in Winter's
Clutches
Traffic at a Standstill Rivers Choked with Ice
and The Port Practically Closed
Much Distress Caused
Governor Roosevelt and Mayor Van Wyck
Take Measures For Relief
Coal and Provision Famine Threatened

STORM PREVAILS IN ALL QUARTERS

Heavy Snow and Extreme Cold Afflict the
Entire Country
Gulf States Suffer Badly
Washington is Snowbound and Business There
is Practically Suspended
Low Temperature in Kentucky

The prevailing storm extends from New England to the Gulf and as far West as Oregon at the north and Texas at the South. The South has not been spared, and Washington in particular has suffered severely, the fall of snow now having reached more than twenty inches. Some thermometers in Kentucky registered as low as 39 degrees below zero. Pennsylvania is suffering much; Harrisburg is stormbound—20 inches of snow in 24 hours with drifts ten feet high in the city. The most important feature of the weather is the extreme cold prevailing throughout the Gulf States and Tennessee. The region of heavy snow extends from Virginia to New England, while the general storm has moved rapidly since Sunday night from Florida to the New England States.

And so went the news—Baltimore is at a standstill—Lebanon, Kentucky had 39 degrees below zero. At Paducah, Kentucky, a negro mother and child were frozen to death. Coal jumped from $2.25 a ton to $4.00—and some places to $6.00 a ton. Atlanta, Georgia, experienced the lowest temperature ever known —8½ degrees below zero. Anniston, Alabama, had 15 below—cold almost unbearable—many with frostbitten hands, faces and ears. Two negroes were found frozen to death at Montgomery, Alabama. In Savannah, Georgia, a negro was found frozen to death. Macon, Georgia, had six inches of snow and zero weather. The wharf at Memphis, Tennessee, is icebound. Birmingham, Alabama, had 10 degrees below zero. "The Birmingham Carnival Society has called off the Mardi Gras celebration which was to have been held the 13th and 14th. The town is full of visitors suffering in the cold." Columbia, South Carolina, had eleven inches of snow. New Orleans registered six above zero, but the dampness of the atmosphere made it equivalent to 10 degrees below zero in other places. It almost put an end to the Mardi Gras reveling. Cumberland, Maryland, reported two hunters dead. Watertown, New York, had a death from exposure. New York boroughs had drifts of snow six and eight feet high. Long Creek, Oregon, reported that thousands of range horses are said to be starving to death in eastern Oregon because of the snow. And LEADVILLE, KOKOMO, WHEELER AND DILLON, COLORADO, were in the New York *Times* report:

Leadville, Colorado, February 13: Two prospectors on snow-shoes arrived in Leadville today from Wheeler. It took them four days to make the trip of fourteen miles. They report that the wagon roads are covered in some places for two miles at a stretch, with snow slides and drifts twenty to thirty feet deep. There is enough food at Wheeler and other towns around Kokomo and Dillon to last ten days with care, but stock is suffering. There has been no suffering so far in any of the mining camps, but fuel and provisions are running short.

Boreas, indeed, had ranged far and wide— and furiously!

Life in Breckenridge did not come to a standstill during the Big Snow and the Blockade, although supplies were dwindling, store shelves were emptying. Meat, eggs, milk and supplies of this kind were the most difficult to obtain; fresh fruit and vegetables were soon non-existent. When Mrs. Christ Kaiser went out to the barn to milk her cow she found it butchered and strung up. The butchers at the Christ Kaiser Market explained, "It was done in the name of necessity." Mrs. Peabody's cow, in a barn in the alley near the Catholic Church, was spared. Mrs. Peabody daily expected her cow to be demanded as a sacrifice for the same reason. Perhaps the nine-foot snow drifts around the barn made it too difficult an operation. E. C. Peabody wrote:

It has been said Breckenridge never had such a sociable time as that winter. Certainly never since has any time equaled that winter. Four dances were held every week. Professor Clisbee had a dance for juniors and beginners at the G. A. R. Hall every Saturday afternoon— 50c, boys and girls paying alike. Professor Clisbee's Saturday night dance was for the general public. At the same time Saturday night, the "Club" held a dance in Fireman's Hall. On Wednesday nights Professor Clisbee had a dancing class in the dining-room of the Occidental Hotel. Ladies who did not want to dance could attend free of charge. In addition to the dances, young people had their own age-group parties at various homes—dancing and having a good time. Refreshments were not often served because of dwindling supplies. The "elite," and the non-dancing society, had their "Five Hundred" card games in their homes. Fuel was not a serious problem. The few who used coal had coal-bins filled before winter set in; wood could be cut and hauled in from the nearby woods, during hours when the snow had a hard crust. Thus the social life was "endured" in the weeks of snow and blockade.

Another writer, telling of life in Kokomo during the hardships of that winter, said, "But

God was kind to us. We had neither sickness nor death in our little camp that winter." It is an amazing fact that fatalities in the high country were almost non-existent during this severe and unusual winter. But Breckenridge did have one sad happening:

LOREN WALDO

Loren Waldo was a young man of twenty-seven years. He was not exactly a newcomer to Summit County, having spent six or seven years in the area. When he first arrived he was a single man, employed at Dillon as a telegraph operator for South Park Railroad. Then came the panic of "93" and the Railroad followed its policy of giving preference to married men for work. Waldo turned to another occupation, bookkeeper and salesman, finding work at Dillon, Como and then Breckenridge. For a year he was in the employment of J. H. Hartman & Bros. whose store was on Main Street, near Lincoln Avenue. The store's specialties were groceries, miner's supplies, hardware and tinware. Early in 1898 Waldo married Minnie Volkart of Denver. The young bride remained at her mother's home, 1855 Lafayette Street, until additional funds could be earned to set up housekeeping.

"Big, kind-hearted Waldo" was industrious and well-liked in the community. Later, it was to be written, "the business circles of Breckenridge lose a sturdy and popular member, his young wife and relatives keenly miss a loving husband, dutiful brother and obedient son."

Business was dull at Hartman's Store in early February. The Big Snow and Blockade had curtailed work for many people, and so the people were carefully spending their "coppers," buying only the necessities. But even necessities were being emptied from shelves and new supplies were not forthcoming. The extra services of a bookkeeper and salesman were not actually needed, and Loren knew it. Perhaps, too, loneliness of a young husband for his wife could have been a factor. Maybe the appearance of last-year's left-over supply of valentines on the shelves was the determining factor. Whatever the motive, Loren decided he was going to Denver.

Waldo was acquainted with the use of snow-shoes; he owned a fine pair of ash "shoes." He gave notice to Mr. Hartman. Saturday noon, February 11th, Waldo, Eli Ruff, and a railroad employee left Breckenridge on snow-shoes to go to Como and thence to Denver. The three arrived safely at Boreas Station on top of the mountain, but Waldo was very tired. The other two men continued their trip to Como without him. About 5:20 o'clock, with darkness descending, Waldo resumed his way, although Agent Soper pressed him to stay over night until he was completely rested. There would not be another resting place until he reached Half-Way Gulch (half-way between Boreas and Como) where the Railroad had a cabin shelter for those wanting to flag the train. But the young husband wished to continue his journey, so he started out into the night.

In his last letter to his wife, Waldo spoke of returning to Denver, but did not hint at making the attempt on snow-shoes. His wife did not approve of this mode of traveling and had strongly objected whenever the subject was mentioned. In her reply letter she urged her husband not to take any chances or expose himself to an unnecessary danger. But Waldo had lived in the mountains for six or seven years and considered himself an expert snow-shoer, even though his wife seemed to have strange presentiments of evil in connection with these trips and was greatly worried until she knew he was safe. When the Blockade started, letters could not be sent or received. Waldo did send a few telegraphic messages, but in none of them was a word said about the proposed snow-shoe trip until the day of the departure.

Atop the Rocky Mountains, during a blowing snowstorm, can be a harrowing experience. The descriptive words *dangerous, fierce, wild, savage,* are much too mild. One soon learns that stronger phrasing is needed—*ferocious, violently cruel, vicious, ravenous, villainous, fiendish, diabolical, infernal.* The traveler loses all sense of direction, whereabouts are obliterated, no spot is familiar. Human strength ebbs until nothing remains to combat the elements. Then comes the desire to rest and sleep. Waldo recognized the inevitable, and took a notebook and pencil from a pocket and tried to write,—Dearest Minnie . . .

For the first few days Mrs. Waldo bore up bravely. While fears for her husband's safety naturally oppressed her, she continued in a hopeful frame of mind, expecting each day to bring some word that her husband had reached his destination in safety. But the dreary days passed on, and "hope long deferred maketh the heart sick." Hoping against hope, she began to believe that her worst fears were to be realized. No word forthcoming for ten days, a telegraphic message was sent to Mr. Hartman, bringing his reply, "Loren left Breckenridge February 11th and there has been no word of him since." A dispatch came from Como, in which the belief was expressed that the unfortunate man had perished. "The young wife burst into a wild paroxysm of tears and then swooned away."

Searching parties from Breckenridge hunted for the body of Waldo, but without success. The young man's father joined the searching parties. All attempts met with failure. The father berated the two men for deserting his son at the top of Boreas. The question arose, "Could it have been murder?" The white mantle over Boreas kept its secret for a long time.

Meanwhile Boreas, tiring of his far-flung rampage, swished homeward for rest in his mountain cavern. On the homeward flight he came by way of Georgetown and Silver Plume to view his devastation in those mountain towns. It was beautiful to him; snow was deep, threatening combs were overreaching the high peaks. His snow-flaked eyes wandered over hills and gulches. Here and there cabins and mine buildings showed defiant occupancy.

Snow had been piling on the mountains for many weeks. It drifted into every nook and crevice. Even while the East was getting its lashing, a fierce gale raged around Georgetown and Silver Plume, heaping more snow on the whitened hills. Saturday and Sunday were blizzard days. But Silver Plume did not worry about snowslides; snowslides in the area were not much in its history. Cabins on the hillside housed families and the mines were being worked.

Monday morning dawned fair and sunshiny. After breakfast some of the miners basked in the sunshine outside their cabin doors. Dominic Destefano started down the hillside to Silver Plume. He whistled and sang snatches of old Italian songs. He was a fortunate man—he had work, a wife, two small daughters, a cozy cabin with straggling geraniums in blossom at the windows, a flock of chickens in a coop to produce fresh eggs and some good Italian dishes; he had relatives living nearby and working at the mines, sharing reminiscences of the homeland to which, someday, they would return with a fair measure

of wealth. Why shouldn't Dominic be a happy man? He owned the world. Boreas appraised Destefano and his strutting, quickened steps—"Another of those self-satisfied, cocksure men!" Boreas gave a snort! The heavy-laden combs on the high peaks above Willehan and Cherokee gulches trembled, then moved—and snow, rocks and trees rushed down the mountainside.

A few were dug out of the slide, more dead than alive—Antonio Migretto, Antonio Laleano and Guiseppe Corcunio; they survived. Mrs. Destefano's body was found, clasping in her arms her younger child; the other child was found nearby as though the mother had been rushing to her. The bodies of Peter, Joe and John Tondini were uncovered, as well as Gerondo Guenzi, G. Bietto and Enrico Novaria. Some of these were married, but their wives had remained in Italy. Dominic Destefano was buried too deeply to be found before spring thaw. Seven black caskets and two white caskets were in the Silver Plume opera house for the funeral services, and then were taken to the cemetery to be buried in one large grave.

Boreas returned to the high country and oozed into his cavern for a much-needed rest. Let the winter recuperate now as best it could. In late May, Boreas emerged, sufficiently rested for a leisurely blow over the hills. A number of good-sized mounds were on the high peaks, sure to be there for a head start on next winter's snows. Only little mounds remained here and there on slopes secluded from spring sun. Boreas lazily swished down the mountain side to where a body now lay exposed in the sun—not quite to Half-Way Gulch. Near the one hand was a notebook, a page fluttered alongside. A removed glove was by the other hand—and a pencil. Boreas gave a good sniff and the piece of paper soared in the air and gently floated to a resting-place in the crevices of a rockslide.

It was evident to Boreas that Zephyrus, his brother, had been roaming the hills, sighing his soft, balmy, life-giving breath. Tiny yellow blooms hugged the warm earth, and the delicate, cup-like, lavender anemone garlanded the body of Loren Waldo. Boreas snorted his disgust, "Humph! Another Hyacinthus!"

They found Loren Waldo's body Saturday, June 3rd. The searching party included James Craig, J. Painsett, and the father, Nathan Waldo. James Craig, Breckenridge, saw the body first, at a lonely spot among fallen timber, one-quarter mile from the South Park Railroad track, and one mile on the Boreas side of Half-Way. The body was in a fair state of preservation. They removed it to Como for an inquest, thence to Denver for burial. All Waldo's possessions— watch, letters, money, clothing and other valuables were found intact. The suspense and mystery of Loren Waldo's disappearance was over. "Big, kind-hearted Waldo" lost his life trying to break the blockade and return to his beloved wife.

BOREAS

— STORM KING —

GOD OF THE NORTH WIND

Picture: "The Classic Myths; The Gods Of Heaven"

Library State Historical Society of Colorado

Seven-engine train struggling against the 1898-1899 Big Snow.
Courtesy—Mrs. Ted Fletcher

Fighting the Big Snow. Courtesy—Mrs. Ray McGinnis.

Banker and Mrs. George Engle crossing Main Street, Breckenridge, via a snow tunnel, Big Snow 1898-1899. Courtesy—Denver Public Library Western Collection.

Main Street, Breckenridge—Winter of Big Snow—1898-1899.
Courtesy—Denver Public Library Western Collection

Main Street, Breckenridge—Winter of Big Snow—1898-1899.
Courtesy—Library State Historical Society of Colorado

Boreas Pass — Beautiful in summer and fall seasons; ferocious in winter wind and snow. (Picture-1971) (Altitude-11,482 feet).

2. Post Office Entrance at Summit House, Top of Boreas Pass. Summit County, Colorado. Summit Historical Society.

Boreas Pass in winter's grip. Note: man standing at telegraph pole — brick chimney and stovepipe protruding above snow right of pole. Courtesy—Summit Historical Society.

20-foot monument in Silver Plume, Colorado, cemetery. Inscription: "Sacred to the Memory of the Ten Italians—Victims of an Avalanche— February 12, 1899. Erected by the Public." (Background mountain, scene of the avalanche.)

WHITE GLOVES AND WALLPAPER

Summer and fall of 1942 marked the end of gold-boat dredging in the town of Breckenridge. It also marked the end of another era in Breckenridge history.

When the gold boat took its last chomping, gritty bite from the river bed at the south end of Breckenridge, there lay behind it five miles of barren, spewed-out rock piles to mystify future, first-time visitors to the area. The once-happy, rapid-flowing, fairly-deep, picturesque Blue River now seeped a tortuous course through gold-boat tailings. Lure of gold decreed that the river be dredged to bed-rock—thirty, forty, fifty feet deep.

In these "mountains" of rocks lie almost a half-century of gold mining history in the Breckenridge area. In the early 1890s almost all the known methods of taking the precious metal from the earth had been employed—all except dredging stream beds to rock bottom. The idea of dredging was in the minds of a few, among whom was Benjamin Stanley Revett. In 1896 Revett's dream materialized, when he saw his gold-boat take a first bite at Colorado mineral-bearing ground. Other companies joined the act. When the last mouthful was taken in 1942, Swan Valley, French Gulch and Blue River Valley were ravished for miles and miles.

Gold-boat dredging in Summit County had its dying gasps before final surrender. In the 1930s there were spasmodic spurts and stops. In August, 1939, operations suddenly ceased. A statement came from Blue River Company that sufficient funds were not available for operating expenses. In September, 1941, Erland F. Fish, Boston-New York, bought the Blue River Dredging Company and the Tonapah Shops from Bankruptcy Court. The Bankruptcy Court sold all scrap iron to the Kenyon Iron Works of Denver, who immediately had a crew clearing the scrap iron from the placer and lode claims and around the shops.

Gold-boat dredging had been at a standstill for two years—and then came Pearl Harbor, December 7, 1941. April 28, 1942, the Blue River Dredging Company started operating again. Three and a half months later came the blow to Breckenridge economy:

GOLD MINING IN SUMMIT COUNTY COMES TO A HALT THURSDAY

Gold mining in Summit County came to an abrupt halt Thursday, October 15th, at midnight. The Blue River dredge was the only major operation at work at the time. The dredge is now in the process of being dismantled. Due to uncertainty as to the length of the war, it was believed the proper thing to do. The issuance of WPB order L-203, closing all gold operations, affected twenty men working on the dredge. Men from the dredge will no doubt find plenty work in zinc and lead mines under development near here.

This marked the demise of almost fifty years of gold-boat dredging in and around Breckenridge. It was a blow to Breckenridge economy and social life.

The writer made his first visit to Breckenridge in the summer of 1939. The gold-boat was in clanging operation. A visit in 1940 found Breckenridge with the look, the feel, the silence of a ghost town. Visitors, and they were "mighty sparse," peered through cracks of boarded-up buildings, snooping into the past. No one seemed to care; in fact, there were few people around to care. Beyond the huge rock piles were doorless, window-less buildings, wide open to snoopers and weather. Some were shacks; others, two-story in height, spoke of spaciousness and a certain measure of affluence. A few elaborate "mansions" had toilet facilities adjoined by an enclosed walk-way, protection against wind and weather. Faded remnants of shredded wallpaper clung to walls, dangled in festooned strips, or added bits of color to floor debris. Beautiful patterns of wallpaper spoke of the elegance that once belonged to Breckenridge.

An old-timer reminisced, "Yes, Breckenridge had its day. There was a white-glove social life—concerts, lectures, chautauqua; they were white-glove affairs! It is hard now to imagine what the town was like in those days." Breckenridge, indeed, had its white-glove and wallpaper days.

The 1860 descent on Blue River was for gold. Dwelling-places were not of major consideration. Canvas-covered wagons sufficed as a lodging place, or a tent, or a "bower-house" of tree boughs, or a hastily-constructed log cabin. Finding of gold brought establishment of stores and business places, thereby giving a measure of permanency to the camp. Families arrived; dwelling places received more attention. The 1860 boom dissipated, but a fair living was made by those who stayed and "tied to it."

Social life, though not worthy of the terminology "high society," stirred with the influx of additional miners and families into Breckenridge and nearby gulches. The *Miners' Record*, William Byers' Tarryall newspaper, told of Breckenridge's social occasion, 4th of July Celebration, 1861:

> Our national independence was celebrated here with great interest and enthusiasm. A large concourse of people, consisting of men, women and children, assembled about noon and repaired to the beautiful grove a short distance east of town, conducted by Col. E. P. Elmore, Marshal of the day. The exercises were opened by prayer from the Rev. M. Hubbard. The Declaration of Independence was read by Judge G. G. Bissell, after which orations were delivered by Dr. E. D. Leavitt, J. V. Carpenter, Esq., and Gov. R. W. Steele. The intervals between the orations were occupied by songs from Capt. Preston of Miners' District, and also by the German Glee Club of Breckenridge, both of which were exceedingly entertaining.
>
> The audience then retired to the Breckenridge Hotel (Marshall Silverthorn, Proprietor) where they partook of one of the finest and most complete dinners ever served on the Western Slope of the Rocky Mountains. Here we found the table spread with all the luxuries, from the oyster beds of the Atlantic to the silvery rivulets of the Western Slope, in which the speckled trout so greatly abound.
>
> The day having passed, no small share of the time being spent in drinking of numerous toasts, and the best of music having been secured for the occasion, consisting in part of William P. Pollack and Jack Spirry of French Gulch, the assembly crossed over to the Colorado House (J. Crissman, Proprietor) where they engaged in dancing, which was vigorously prosecuted until 12 o'clock, when a supper was served by the gracious landlady, which in variety and excellence cannot be surpassed, even in countries affording much greater facilities. The dance was then renewed and kept up until nearly the break of day, when all started to their homes, apparently much pleased with the proceedings of the day and night, and all convinced that Breckenridge has two hotels that cannot be beaten in Colorado.

Lincoln City, in French Gulch, had its own Fourth of July Celebration "from dawn of dewy morning until shades of evening and the large bonfire." Mr. Bunday and Dr. Paige conducted the celebration. The opening ball in French Gulch was announced for Lincoln City, July 25th, and "no pains will be spared that it be one of the most recherche affairs of the season." For many years July Fourths were gala social gatherings and patriotic demonstrations of great significance in the mining community.

The most important social occasion of the early mining camp was the ball. It was held frequently. Not much provocation or preparation seemed necessary to stir up a ball; it was a welcomed institution in a life otherwise humdrum and tiresome. The town hostelry, or one of the larger-sized cabins, sufficed as a ballroom. About all that was required were dancing partners, a fiddler, a supper; that constituted a ball. "Cutting the pigeon wing" and dancing "the light fantastic" "until the wee sma hours anant the dawn" was one of the chief diversions of the time. Preachers castigated the ball as the devil's favorite device for destroying religious effort in the camp. So it often proved. Whenever there was confrontation between the ball and religious service, as to time and place, it was easier to make the decision in favor of the ball. Some chers, like Father Dyer, considered the ball the most demoralizing influence in the mining camp. For others it was the bright spot in a life of loneliness and gloominess.

Few of the balls of the early camp reached the society pages of Denver's Rocky Mountain *News*, for most of the reporters were men and not too adept at writing a "woman's column." Then, too, the ordinary mining camp wasn't the place of the latest Parisian styles; frippery more often characterized the "elegance" of the small mining camp. As time, prosperity and permanency came to the camp a refined elegance unfolded.

The second gold boom came to Breckenridge in 1880. The rush was on again. Population was reported at 8,000. All the sordid attractions of a booming mining camp rushed to Breckenridge. "There was general hubbub from dark to daylight." Twenty-five dollar town lots soared to fifteen hundred. The boom spent itself in eighteen months. Property values descended as rapidly. In 1881 a fine two-story, ten-room house, well-furnished, was offered for $250 cash. It was advertised a number of weeks before it sold.

After the boom of 1880 passed Breckenridge assumed a fairly fixed pattern of life. Those who survived two booms were considered "permanent." Social life advanced. Homes became more elaborate. Some were generously alluded to as "mansions." They were not the mansions of Denver and the mining towns of Leadville, Central City or Georgetown. But they were Breckenridge's mansions.

Civic matters received attention in the 1880s. Lincoln Avenue organized "a stump pulling squad to rid the street of stumps and obstructions that infested it." There was a creditable change in the appearance of the thoroughfare. "Old sheds and tent skeletons which have marred the elegant thoroughfare, Ridge Street, are being removed. Ridge is destined to be the showy street of the town." Main Street was cleared of boulders and mud holes. Ye Editor prodded civic projects—"The hole in the street left by the removal of Miller's scales would make a good cellar. Won't someone buy it and move it away?"

As early as 1882 Turks' general store advertised wallpaper. In the 80s and 90s merchants competed for the business. Morgan advertised: "Morgan has all the late styles in wallpaper. 4000 rolls of wallpaper for sale at Morgan's. If you want good wallpaper cheap, go to Morgan's. He only charges you freight for wallpaper. The most magnificent patterns of wallpaper ever seen are at Morgan's." Breckenridge wallpapered.

Corduroy came into style. "Go one eye on Brown's corduroy pants, they will make you wink. Brown's corduroy pants and suits will stand the wear and tear. They are iron clad." Corduroy was the style in men, women and children garments—"Buy it by the yard, if you wish."

Tight lacing was in vogue for ladies. "At a ball at Silver Plume a young lady, while dancing, suddenly fell to the floor. She died on the following Sunday. The cause of death is announced to have been tight lacing." An editor commenting on the fact said: "Those corsets should be done away with, and if the girls can't live without being squeezed, we suppose men could be found who would sacrifice themselves. As old as we are we'd rather devote three hours a day, without a farthing of pay, to prevent corsets, than seeing these girls dying in that manner. Office hours almost any time."

A new, fashionable edible graced the dining table in 1888. "Hamburg steak is a new venture in beef, it is after the fashion of prepared ham, only better. If a right good dinner of beef steak, tender and juicy, is desired, try a Hamburg steak. All the virtues of a good tender steak, minus the bone, can be obtained. Enterline and Keyser are doing a wholesale business in that line just now."

Music and drama came into the civic picture. A minstrel company was organized "and would soon be before the public as exponents of modern art." It was composed of gentlemen of experience and ability and proposed, after a season in the mountains, to make an extensive tour in the states. The Breckenridge Mannerchor was organized in 1881; "This musical organization bids fair to become a permanent and prominent institution. Although established when a large proportion of the population was absent, yet at the third meeting, twenty-three had joined or signified their intentions of doing so. The practice meeting yesterday at Fireman's Hall developed the fact that most of the members were the possessors of voices much above the average, many of them being well-cultivated. Mr. Henry Yust, who has recently come to the county, is the conductor and acquits himself with credit. Peter Engle, principal tenor, has a fine voice and has

White Gloves and Wallpaper

paid considerable attention to its cultivation. Gus Jander is too well known as an accomplished basso to need notice. The music books were received a few days since, but are a terror to a yankee reporter. Fireman's Hall proves to be a fine room for vocal efforts." The Teutonia Leiderkranz, in 1886, "is making creditable headway and soon will be able to rank as one of the best singing societies in the state."

Social affairs kept pace with the new elegance. Thursday night, November 4, 1886, there was

A WEDDING IN STYLE

Last night, at the Arlington House, there was an event which was known to be on the tapic for several days. Mr. Christ Kaiser, of the popular meat and vegetable market firm on Lincoln Avenue, and Miss Ida Sandell of Lindsburg, Kansas, were married by the Rev. J. L. Dyer of this city. The ceremony was performed at 8 o'clock in the presence of about thirty couples, friends of the young groom, and comprising creme de la creme of the town and vicinity. After the ceremony the guests were invited to partake of a wedding supper that was already spread. The dining room was decorated in a most tasty manner for the occasion, and the meal, it is unnecessary to add, was everything that could be desired, and every luxury possible to obtain in this section was at the disposal of the guests. For the occasion the landlord brought out his Arlington House table set, every article of plate, cutlery or silverware bearing the name of "Arlington" thereon. After supper, music and dancing was continued until 2 o'clock in the morning when the assembly separated. The bride was the recipient of a very fine collection of needed house-keeping articles such as tableware of the choicest character, lamps, chamber toilet sets, etc., all of the finest and in ample abundance. A more pleasant party never met in the town upon a more happy occasion, nor was ever a party more royally entertained. The young couple start off on their united journey for life, amid the good wishes of all friends who were present, as well as the hosts of friends who were not present.

Calithumpians made their appearance for the wedding celebration. "Calithumping" was the "charivari" or the "shivaree" or the "belling" of other parts of the country. It was a mock serenade to newlyweds, usually on the wedding night or after return from the honeymoon. The crowd gathered stealthily around the residence, then came a sudden blast of deafening noise—horns sounded, buckets and pans were beaten, bells rung, etc. The newlyweds were expected to make an appearance and respond with an appropriate treat.

Last night the calithumpians were out on the occasion of the Kaiser and Sandell wedding, but were properly quieted by the groom coming down handsomely with fruits and candies, and he forestalled the boys of larger growth by directing one of the saloons in town to throw open its bar at a certain time to his friends. Christ knows how things ought to be done.

Social life accelerated considerably in the 1890s. It was fashionable to send calling cards. The ladies of Breckenridge were "at home" on stated afternoons. The etiquette of the social call was adhered to strictly. Cards were sent in advance telling when guests would be received. These afternoon calls were made with great formality and were "dress-up" occasions.

Lectures, lyceum, chautauqua and concerts were white-glove affairs. Lodges, of which there were many and dating from very early Breckenridge history, increased social gatherings. The Mason's "annual" was formal—elaborate gowns, fresh flowers for the ladies; dark suits worn by the men. Dancing was usually the feature of the evening, and often the band was imported from Leadville. The annual Fireman's Ball was a gala event. The Redman's annual masked ball had almost a fifty-year existence. Be assured it was properly conducted. All participants were required to enter a small room to remove masks so that the guard could be sure no rowdy, undesirable hoodlum gained entrance. The G. A. R. Hall was used when an exceptionally large crowd was anticipated. Home-talent productions, touring stage companies, children's recitals, prominent lecturers—all graced the G. A. R. stage. Social life was lively and varied.

Card parties were popular—progressive whist, euchre, and five-hundred; poker had its devotees. Like the ball, card-playing was anathema to many of the religious exponents. Winter had its sledding and snow-shoe parties; summer had its picnics and garden parties. Men folks had their saloon social gatherings; they didn't have far to walk from one to another. Nor can one omit the socializing around Geo. B. Watson's

Warm Stove Mine. "This mine was located in the back part of George B. Watson's store. It received its name on account of the big bodies of ore that were taken out beside a comfortable warm stove. Solid gold was taken out in slabs by the ton. This ore was shipped to Fairyland where it was treated in the Hot Air Smelter and brought large fictitious returns.

"All the miners belonging to this crew were also great hunters and had many daring exploits in pursuit of lions, tigers, and grizzly bears. Edwin Carter, the great museum man, whose museum is now in City Park in Denver, could not begin to compare with these hunters." O. K. Gaymon, who was editor of the Summit County *Journal* at the time, published several of their experiences.

"The superintendent of the Warm Stove Mine was George B. Watson and Judge William Guysleman had charge of the hunting gang. Others who belonged to this gang of miners and hunters were Ed Collingwood, Judge D. W. Fall, Dr. J. F. Condon, Col. C. L. Westerman, Jake Conrad and A. W. Phillips."

There were also strawberry socials and the oyster suppers sponsored by the churches. The community Christmas Tree-Program-Social was always held at the Methodist Church. Presents could be left under the tree for anyone and Santa would deliver them at the program.

Nearby communities had their socials. Carriages and sleighs transported the partying crowd to Lincoln City, Braddockville, Frisco and ripsnorting Wheeler Junction. Life was never dull for Breckenridge.

Homes became more elaborate and stylish in architecture and furnishings. The Charles Finding residence was one of the finest in the town. Barney Ford's house, corner of Main Street and Washington Avenue, was a show-place. Ben Stanley Revett's "Swans Nest" along Swan River was modeled on the lines of an elaborate English estate. Construction had just begun on this house when it was learned that visitors were coming from England. They had just six weeks before their arrival. The builders said it couldn't be done. Revett said that it must be done. By working night and day the house was completed in time for the honored guests.

Breckenridge advanced socially to where a class-system developed. It caused Ye Editor of the *Journal* considerable distress:

Summit County *Journal*   January 16, 1892

The city of Breckenridge is following in the steps of its seaboard rival, New York. The latter has its McAllister's Four Hundred, while the former has its Fourteen. Members of the four hundred are all descendants of the old Vans of the days of Peter Stuyvesant, but the fourteen of Breckenridge's select are composed of men whose residence here ranges from twenty days to twenty years, and the line that divides the utterly-too-too class of society from the outer world is drawn at saloonists and gamblers, with a very heavy strain in favor of topers and poker. To exclude poker players would deprive the select organization of too many shining lights, while to close the sacred gates to all who take a nip would be to have no dancing masculinity at all in the circle, and there must be a line somewhere. Now these cruel excluders little thought of the results of their action on the night of the first fandango. The excluded met in solemn convocation upon their situation. One of the solicited declared he would not go where his good friends were debarred, and to drown grief he proposed a bottle of Mumms Dry. An acrobatic friend, a terpsichorean friend and a dudish friend agreed to join him and lament their ouster from good society, so while the ins danced the outs drank, and both ends of society made a night of it. In view of the history of the utterly-utts, the chautauqua, the social reunions and the free whisky and gambling club leaves a lingering and longing hope to the excluded that "ere the robins nest again" the present cloud on the horizon of their happiness may be cleared and dances will not be opened with prayer and closed with benediction, and all who properly deport themselves may once again be allowed to join the mazy dance.

But, exclusiveness persisted. "There was another select gathering one evening this week. Cards, etc., were issued; as usual, *The Journal* was left out." In the summer came further announcement: "J. B. Dewers, the popular proprietor of the Corner, has gone to the extravagance of buying a saddle horse, next will be a carriage with his coat of arms on it. But still the charmed circle of the elite fourteen is not open to him,—hence he is not happy." Another exclusive party followed: "On Wednesday evening there was a select dancing party in a private hall on Main Street, we cannot give particulars, but we are assured it was a fine affair. Men of blood, even if not members of the 400, were there. Brecken-ridge is becoming all together too excruciatingly exclusive, in other words it is becoming alto-gether too-too-too."

There were various nationalities represented in the mining industry and they were assimilated into the life of the community. All mention of Barney Ford, and his popular "Chop House," was highly respectful. A few other Negroes were successful in prospecting and freely mingled with the saloon society. Whether a place was made for the Barney Fords, and others of his race, in what was considered Breckenridge "high society" is not revealed through the newspapers. Chinese were acceptable to operate laundry establish-ments, but emphatically "No!" as mine laborers. Ye Editor wrote, April, 1884:

By our local columns it will be seen there is likely to be trouble in our quiet camp on ac-count of the incoming of celestials. While de-siring to see no man imposed upon or abused on account of his nativity, nationality or reli-gion, we are not favorably impressed with the idea of flooding our town with a class of labor which is calculated to drive out white labor, empty our school houses and supplant our churches with joss houses, reduce our store-keepers' stock to the smallest variety and cheap-est and commonest articles. Once introduce that class of labor and Breckenridge will soon find a lower level than it has held for the last three years. Right on the eve of what bids fair to be a season of permanent prosperity, we regret to see this element of disturbance brought in. It is all in vain to moralize over the matter, saying it is wrong to abuse these poor people, etc. Abused they will be, either in public or private, by men who realize that these men will render worthless the labor of those who have struggled through a long winter to be here to take advantage of summer work. These Chinamen are brought here nominally to work placers, but once here and their introduction into all kinds of labor will soon follow. The parties importing them should be made to feel the weight of public sentiment in the matter. If there is any property around here so poor that it will not pay to be worked by white men, it had better lie idle rather than introduce a kind of labor which will eventually drive out that which has made America what it is. While sym-pathizing with the downtrodden of all the world, America, and Americans, cannot afford to de-grade its own laboring class to give them asy-lum, even if the desire to make money out of their degradation does lead some few to prove treacherous to their race. Let the compromise of '80 be adhered to.

Summit County *Journal*   June 16, 1888

Thursday quite an excitement was created at Lincoln by the arrival of a flock of Chinese who were to be put to work on a placer mine in that neighborhood. Their arrival was the signal for demonstration, all the workingmen about town followed the wagon to where the celestials were to alight. At that point the driver was directed to return with his load of humanity to where he started from, which he proceeded to do. The gentleman who had engaged them pro-tested, but in vain. The whole affair was very quietly conducted, but with sufficient decision to carry conviction that the men were in earnest and Chinese were not required and would not be tolerated in that neighborhood.

At the turn of the century Breckenridge society was definitely delineated. Columns were beginning to appear in the newspaper, contribu-tions from a pen in the hand of a woman. Sis Orinda, in her column "Social and Personal Pot-Pourri," gave the woman's touch:

We heard of a dainty little luncheon that was given on the Q.T. to a precious few one day this week—where the table was beautifully laid for six, with white damask, cut glass, hand-painted china, and, oh, such a profusion of roses and hyacinths, and the lunch served with the skill of an artist. We are not jealous that we were not there, not at all, but wish to let our friends know that society "do move" and will continue to move.

As Breckenridge moved into the twentieth century increasing signs of social elegance ap-peared. Exquisite cut glass and hand-painted dishes graced the china closets of all the finest homes. Painting china became a favorite activity among the elite and a few produced results of artistic merit. Later wood-burning was added and the new craft became the "in" thing among the members of the social set.

Mrs. Hilliard, wife of L. F. Hilliard, assayer, set the town back on its heels by arriving from Ohio with a table service for eighteen. This in-cluded two covered tureens, seven platters, num-erous vegetable dishes, as well as eighteen break-fast, lunch, and dinner plates; bone dishes and butter chips.

Mrs. O. K. Gaymon, whose husband pub-lished the Dillon *Enterprise*, and later the Summit County *Journal*, used imagination to place herself "out front" on the social scene. When she entertained she put a drop of peppermint in the cut glass tooth-pick holders. Mrs. Gaymon is remembered for many such delicate effects. (The writer saw some of her collection of beautiful cut glass and painted china in the home of her son, Melvin Gaymon of Breckenridge.)

Early in the 1900s George H. Evans, a British engineer, arrived to take charge of the Goldpan Shops. The company was there to do hydraulic mining, but they got little gold so they were gone from the Breckenridge scene by 1906. The Company had holdings in South Africa and Alaska and so the Evans did much entertaining for dignitaries who came to Breckenridge on business. The B. Stanley Revetts also entertained lavishly at Swan's Nest for world travelers and business associates. The railroad switch, for the private cars that brought these guests into town, was located directly in front of the present Breckenridge Inn. While the Evans and Revetts lived in Breckenridge private cars arriving and departing were common. Not so common, however, was the German Prince who came in on one of them.

Breckenridge *Bulletin*   May 28, 1904

PRINCE VISITS BRECKENRIDGE

Prince Hohenlohe and Party Arrive on Special Train, En Route to Frisco, and are Amazed at Large Placer Plant. Were Presented with Gold Nuggets.

Tuesday afternoon will be remembered for a long time on account of the visit paid our town by Prince Phillip Ernest Furst zu Hohenlohe Schillingsfurst, his sister, Princess Elizabeth Pass Hohenlohe, Frau Borgins, the guests of Mr. Frank B. Wiborg of Cincinnatti.

The Royal party was accompanied by Ben Stanley Revett, C. L. Westerman, W. F. Robinson, and others. The prince, princess and count were well pleased with the hearty welcome extended to them.

After the visit in Breckenridge the royal party boarded the train for Frisco, taking with them a pleasant remembrance of their short but interesting visit to Breckenridge.

At Frisco the royal party remained all night. Mr. and Mrs. A. B. Colcord of that place doing the honors as host and hostess. A visit to the Excelsior mine and mill was made by all. The Excelsior property belongs to Mr. Wiborg and Mr. Colcord is superintendent.

The royal members were greatly pleased with all they saw in Summit County and will ever think of the vastness of the resources of the mineral deposits in the mountains surrounding Breckenridge and Frisco.

Because of the entertaining required Mr. Evans had a ballroom built onto his house. When the electric car came into vogue in the cities, Mr. Evans secured one for his wife, Birdie. But she could not use it in Breckenridge because of the rocks in the streets.

Children were also part of the social scene in Breckenridge. The following item was taken from the Breckenridge *Bulletin* and concerns Mrs. H. G. Culbreath whose father, George Engle, was the Banker of Breckenridge.

Little Miss Elizabeth Engle celebrated her fifth birthday Thursday by her parents taking a number of her playmates to "Goose Pasture," south of town, and giving them a picnic dinner and general good time. Elizabeth is a general favorite among Breckenridge little folks, and they all like to be entertained by her, because there is nothing so good going that it is not furnished for their amusement and happiness, as was the case Thursday. The little ones were chaperoned by Mrs. Engle, and Mr. and Mrs. W. H. Briggle, and taken in a three-seated carryall. Just a word with any of the little ones present tells that they had a most excellent time. One little boy, excitedly relating the events of the day said: "And we eated bushels of ice cream. Mrs. Engle is the bestest cook, for she fried some of the ice cream as hard as burned potatoes."

The settlers who inhabited Fort Mary B that first winter on the Blue, when only the barest essentials were at hand, would have been greatly surprised to have looked in on Breckenridge at the turn of the century. Life, even in the remote mountains, had assumed a refinement and a polish that would have astounded those early pioneers. Life—and death, too.

Summit County *Journal*   August 29, 1891

Our enterprising undertaker, Mr. M. H. Huntress, has added to his large stock of necessary articles for his business, a fine hearse, one containing all the essentials necessary to impress the beholder with the solemnity of its mission. This is the first and only hearse that has ever been in Summit county. The deacon must have felt a worthy and justifiable pride in his business to invest a thousand dollars of his savings in this new addition to his stock in trade.

White Gloves and Wallpaper

Breckenridge elegance displayed by wife of Judge William Thomas.
Courtesy—Summit Historical Society.

Breckenridge Gold Boat, 1939

Deserted Breckenridge, 1940.
(Writer's car in foreground-parked
on wrong side of street.)

Mining was primary objective in Breckenridge early days; social life secondary. Joe Sharron and his oxen team. Courtesy—Library State Historical Society of Colorado.

Arrival of supplies by wagon train. Courtesy—Denver Public Library Western Collection.

Lincoln Avenue, between Ridge and Main Street. Dated 1880 or 1881. Courtesy—Library State Historical Society of Colorado.

Main Street, Breckenridge. Dated 1880 or 1881. Buildings—J. A. Turk & Co.,—Drug Store—Arlington House—Levi Clothing Store. Courtesy —Denver Public Library Western Collection.

White Gloves and Wallpaper

LODGES

Breckenridge Chapter No. 79. Eastern Star,

Meets in the Masonic Hall every second and fourth Tuesdays in each month.

MINNIE ROBY
Worthy Matron

GOLDIE C. ACTON, Secretary.

Breckenridge Lodge No. 47, A. F. and A. M.

Meets in Masonic Hall, Washington Ave. and Main St., on the First and Third Saturdays of each month. Visiting brothers in good standing always welcome.

GEO. ROBINSON,
Worshipful Master.

WM. McADOO
Secretary.

Breckenridge Camp No. 305.

Meets on Second and 4th Tuesdays of each month in G. A. R. hall. Visiting choppers cordially invited to attend.

JOHN VALAER,
Consul Commander.

HARRY YORK,
Clerk.

Mt. Baldy Tent No. 6 K. O. T. M.

Meets second and fourth Thursday of each month, in Bradley hall

J. D. GALLOWAY
Commander.

W. T. KEOGH, Record Keeper.

Summit Circle No. 140, Women of Woodcraft.

Meets in Bradley Hall the Second and Fourth Wednesdays in each month. Visiting neighbors invited to attend.

JENNIE CARTER
Guardian Neighbor.

BELLE MARZ
Clerk.

Joseph A. Mower Post, No. 31, G. A. R.

Meets every Second Friday evening in each month at their hall. All visiting comrades in good standing cordially invited to attend.

WM. McMANIS,
Commander,

C. L. WESTERMAN Adjutant.

Mt. Helen Homestead Lodge No. 2066. Yoemen

Meets in Bradley hall on the first and third Tuesday in each month.

MAUDE BREWER
Foreman

EDWARD CARTER,
Correspondent

Mt. Helen Rebekah Lodge, No. 102, I. O. O. F.

Meets in Odd Fellow's Hall on Second and Fourth Fridays of month. Visiting members welcome.

MRS. VALAER,
Noble Grand.

MARY HALLEN
Secretary.

Sacajawea Council, No. 51, D. of P.

Meets in Bradley hall on Second and Fourth Mondays in each month. Visiting members in good standing invited.

MRS. R. E. FOREMAN,
Pocahontas.

BESSIE WHITEHEAD,
Keeper of Records.

Blue River Lodge No. 49, I. O. O. F.

Meets at Odd fellow Hall every Monday night. Visiting brothers in good standing cordially invited to attend

Horace Spradling
Noble Grand.

Ed. Carter
Secretary.

Kiowa Tribe No. 6, I. O. R. M.

Meets at Bradley Hall on the First and Third Thursdays of each month. Visiting members in good standing always welcome.

W. H. FOREMAN
Sachem

ELI FLETCHER,
Chief of Records.

Park Encampment No. 4, I. O. O. F.

Meets in Odd Fellows Hall, first and third Fridays of each month. Visiting patriarchs cordially invited to attend.

C. W. BURNHEIMER
Chief Patriarch.

GUS. HALLEN, Scribe.

Gold Nugget Lodge, No. 89, K. of P.

Meets in Grand Army Hall on the First and Third Mondays of each month. Visiting Knights in good standing cordially invited to attend.

W. E. STOUFFER,
Chancellor.

W. B. BRIGGLE,
K. of R. and S.

"Stag" Social Life. Johnnie Dewers' Saloon. One of the numerous places of liquid refreshment in Breckenridge. Dewers (#2) shot and killed by Dr. J. F. Condon, August 4, 1898. #6—Bob Lot—successful Negro miner. Courtesy—Denver Public Library Western Collection.

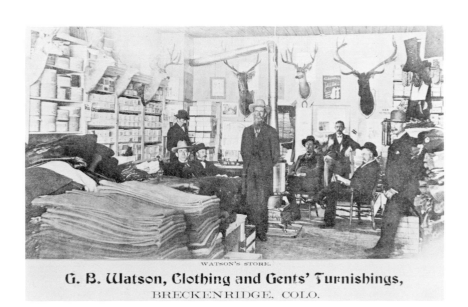

George B. Watson's famous "Warm Stove Mine" where more gold was "mined" than the entire Breckenridge area produced. Courtesy—Mr. Melvin Gaymon.

White Gloves and Wallpaper

Ben Stanley Revett's "Swans Nest"—Swan Valley. (Structurally un-
changed-1972.) Many treasures disappeared when looted, January, 1919.
Courtesy—Library State Historical Society of Colorado.

RESIDENCE OF B.L. FORD, BRECKENRIDGE.

One of Breckenridge's early day show places, as pictured in *Hall's History
of Colorado,* Vol. 3, page 160. (Barney Ford's "Chop House" was a
popular Breckenridge dining place.) ("Chop House"-destroyed in the big
fire of May, 1896.) Courtesy—Denver Public Library Western Collection.

Charles A. Finding home—one of Breckenridge's "mansions." First floor—library, parlor, music room, dining room, kitchen; second floor —bedrooms. Later was the home of Duane and Agnes Miner (nee Finding). In the 1960s was "The Mine" Restaurant. Totally destroyed by fire, January 11, 1971. Courtesy—Mr. Melvin Gaymon.

Parlor of Finding home. Courtesy—Mr. Melvin Gaymon.

White Gloves and Wallpaper

Parlor of Finding home, looking toward Music Room. Courtesy—Mr.
Melvin Gaymon.

Music Room of Finding home; Grand piano partially showing, right
foreground. Piano now possession of Robert S. Foote, Frisco, Colorado.
Courtesy—Mr. Melvin Gaymon.

The Tom Brown's Parlor. Recent years—"Ore Bucket" Restaurant. Courtesy—Mrs. Ray McGinnis.

Breckenridge parades were "dress-up" occasions. Courtesy—Denver Public Library Western Collection.

White Gloves and Wallpaper

ROUGH AND SHADY

Bayard Taylor, noted writer and lecturer, who made a short visit to Breckenridge, 1866, said: "Thin air and alkali water invigorates every function of the system." He added, "Alkali water is anaphrodisiac," which he thought was rather an advantage than otherwise in a new country, where the population was largely of the male sex. His pronouncement is open to question; the alkali content of the water seems not to have been a major deterrent in high country.

One of the "Letters to the Editor" that came forth from the series of articles, "Thar's Gold in Them Thar' Hills," Summit County *Journal*, 1955, was concerned that Breckenridge was being pictured in an unfavorable light:

Your recital of Breckenridge history is well-done and interesting. However, I feel compelled to register a protest to a subheading in your latest installment.

Over the story of the murder of a saloon-keeper by a doctor on the town's main street in the late '90's appears this heading: "Where There's Gold There's Gunsmoke," creating the impression that gunplay was as natural a feature of a gold-boom town as hilarity, dancing drinking, gambling, prostitution, etc.

In your next issue you may be recalling the murder, a few years later and in the same block of main street, of a bartender-gambler by one of the town's grocers.

Both killings were the result of suspected improper attention of one man to the wife of the other. Both involved respected business men and both resulted in acquital by juries on pleas of self-defense.

In my recollection these killings were the only ones to mar the eighty-year history of this fine community. Quite a record, I think.

The gold-boom days should be praised for other things, too. Then no padlocks were needed on the doors of stores, dwellings, etc., in the town or even of isolated well-stocked miners' cabins on the surrounding hills, where the latch-strings were always out for any hungry prospector or hunter. Burglaries were as rare as murders. No virtuous woman was unsafe on the town's streets or on lonely trails through the hills, day or night.

The good old gold-boom days! They were in many ways the happier days!

'Twasn't always thusly. Breckenridge has not been greatly different from the customary run of mining towns and communities, in respect to the "rough and shady." You name it, and Breckenridge knows about it. In proportion to size, Breckenridge compares favorably (or unfavorably) with other communities.

Inasmuch as this chapter deals with individuals of prominence we will be discreet and not use the real names. Exact dates will not be given to help further researching. Like Nathaniel Hawthorne, in *The Great Stone Face*, we give our most prominent characters descriptive names according to their occupation—more explicitly, their wayward preoccupation. Instead of the rich Mr. Gathergold, the illustrious soldier, Old Blood-and-Thunder, the orator-statesman, Old Stony Phiz, we give our main characters the names of "Marshal" Incognito, Libertine Gayblade, Aggrieved Husband and August Silvermane.

The Leadville *Herald Democrat* carried a story that was reprinted in the Breckenridge newspaper. The individual involved was a prominent man of Breckenridge, who falsely posed as town marshal of Breckenridge. "Marshal" Incognito's wife had gone back east to Iowa to visit relatives, leaving Mr. Incognito at loose ends. Came the news:

PROMINENT MAN DEAD

Mr. Incognito, well-known in this camp, a few days since went to Leadville. This morning's *Democrat* announces his death as follows:

At about half-past 8 o'clock last evening, as Officer Maney was standing in the Central Theatre, he was approached by Ellen Smith, a colored woman of much notoriety, who told him to "hurry up and come down the street, there is a man dead."

Following the woman the officer soon brought up before the door of 149 State Street. He found the door locked and was compelled to break it in. Getting inside, he was confronted by an individual, known as Mrs. "Hoodoo" Brown, who was wringing her hands, crying, moaning and conducting herself in a manner highly exciting. She pointed to the figure of a man lying on the floor beside the bed. The officer went to the side of the man and lifting one of his arms, felt the pulse, finding he was dead. Officer Maney recognized the man as one Mr. Incognito, to whom he had that day been introduced. Coroner Nelsen, Marshal White and Officer Roberts were summoned, and arrived in a few minutes after the discovery had been made.

Mr. Incognito had been in the city for the past four days, and represented himself to the officers here as marshal of Breckenridge. He was known to have had a sum of money, amounting to over $400 on his person on Tuesday night. The clothes of the dead man were searched, but nothing, with the exception of a few minor articles, discovered. A little later a pocketbook, identified as belonging to the dead man, was found on the floor beneath the bed. The body was then removed to the coroner's. Mrs. Brown, Ellen Smith and "Banjo Bob," a man who delivered several bottles of beer at the house during the afternoon, were placed under arrest and taken to the city jail, and a thorough search made throughout the building. Several parties residing on the premises were placed under arrest. A post-mortem examination will be held for the purpose of ascertaining if any poison had been administered to him.

Other details were forthcoming, that led to the belief that Mr. Incognito was murdered by one or more blows upon the head with an instrument of the nature of a lead pipe or a tightly filled sand bag. Indications are that the murderer will soon be in the clutches of the law.

Mrs. Incognito had been visiting in the midwest, and telegraphed that she would return and "the funeral will take place as soon as practicable after her arrival." She did not, however, state the exact time of her return. Mrs. Incognito returned on the morning train. Losing no time, funeral arrangements were hastily made for two o'clock that same day, under the auspices of Miners and Prospectors Association. Before the sun sank behind the hills Mr. Incognito was resting in Valley Brook Cemetery.

Another prominent man "kicked over the traces" and provided Breckenridge with its most news-worthy scandal:

On Friday of last week the social and business circles of Breckenridge were suddenly brought face to face with a real scandal, and considering the prominence of all parties concerned, the luscious tale of duplicity and dishonor has not lost any of its flavor, even up to this time—and we might add, that it is still hot on the firing line.

The appearance of Aggrieved Husband, a cool Kentucky gentleman, with determination in his mind, and a gun in his pocket, seeking to avenge a wrong that is usually righted in the South with guns that kill, on Main Street, pacing to and fro, waiting in vain for the wrecker of his home to emerge from his business place, that the life of one or the other might be ended then and there, was the first notice the public gained "that there were about to be something doing."

Instead of meeting Aggrieved Husband's challenge, Libertine Gayblade flew out the back door and took a rapid transit route to the railway station, where he was lucky enough to catch a train that was going in the direction of safety—Denverward—as time was the essence of the situation.

The next day Aggrieved Husband instituted divorce proceedings in the county court. Wife of Aggrieved Husband asquiesced, admitted the charges, and assented to an immediate determination of the case. After hearing testimony, the jury speedily rendered verdict for the plaintiff, and court ordered bill of divorce granted instanter.

Aggrieved Husband had been South for a few weeks, and when he returned he found affairs somewhat different than he ever expected. A little detective work, on his own, provided the answer.

In his testimony to the court, plaintiff expressed that he was heartbroken, but believed that divorce would be the only way to protect his two children financially. He expressed deep regret for his wife's family, "one of the best in an Eastern State." Mrs. Aggrieved Husband left immediately for her parents' home. Mr. Aggrieved Husband sold his home and office and departed for the South, "carrying with him the sympathy of 98% of the people of this town."

EVER BEEN SHOCKED?

You have all heard of shocks and many of you, no doubt, have experienced them to a more or less degree. Some are pleasant, some the reverse, some physical, some mental; and again some can only be designated as peculiar. It is with the latter that this account deals.

This is the same Libertine Gayblade who is as completely ostracized from society in his home town as a small-pox patient would be. This is the same Libertine Gayblade who made a lucky get-away from Aggrieved Husband's gun a year ago. This is the same Libertine Gayblade who made a fortune here, but now, when safely away from home, says that morally, socially, commercially and otherwise the County is N.G. and that he proposes to knock it on any and every occasion. This is the same Libertine Gayblade who says he is writing the history of ten men in Breckenridge and it will be enlightening. This is the new scandal:

On Flag Day (June 14th), a lady of this town, with her husband and children, was enjoying a dish of ice cream at the pavillion in City Park, Denver, when her little girl becoming sick, she sought the ladies' toilet. Trying a door she found it locked. After a reasonable time, she tried the door again; it was still locked. She sought a nearby policeman, who volunteered assistance.

On the policeman's demanding that the door be opened at once, it was opened and out came a blonde woman with a partially filled glass of booze in her hand. Immediately following her was one of our townsmen, Mr. Libertine Gayblade, carrying a half-filled bottle of whiskey. It is enough to say the Breckenridge lady was somewhat shocked. Ever been shocked?

One of Breckenridge's newspapers picked up the story anew, in a page one, column one item:

Mr. Libertine Gayblade seems to be getting into the mire deeper and deeper as the days go by. It is the old, old story of a man's sins finding him out. There seems to be an inevitable something in the fate of every man which evens up scores with him pretty well before he passes in his checks at the jumping off place.

Mr. Gayblade came to town last Sunday, smoked out of Denver by articles published concerning his Flag Day celebration with a dizzy blonde at City Park. His main object seemed to be to scare the newspapers with threats of libel suits, etc., but before he left town he was presented with another bunch of trouble which will keep him guessing for some time to come.

Monday the sheriff served papers on him, for $25,000 damages for alienating the affections of Aggrieved Husband's wife. It is all old history to Breckenridge—the record of this degenerate and libertine. We have his record with other women, and his Denver record is a peach.

Libertine Gayblade did attempt a libel suit against Breckenridge newspapers, but it proved a dud. In answering the libel suit threat, the publishers replied:

In the first place, his character can't be libeled. Furthermore, he is a blowhard, a barnacle on our citizenship. All we would need to do is get Madam De Webster, Madam Alice Perry, and other "beauties" of former days to speak "on the woman question." He made a record with these two notorious characters, named Alice Perry and Madam De Webster, which is too rotten to mention.

He simply degraded himself in this community, until he became a menace to common decency, a detriment to the business interests of the town, a stench in the nostrils of society, and an all-around undesirable citizen. No man or woman, no judge or jury, would censure our stand on this commercial and social vulture who parades in human form. This is the human ghoul who says he is libeled.

Later, Mr. Libertine Gayblade made another of his quick, sneak-in visits to Breckenridge, and this time he was encountered by another business man who was outraged by the former's business practices. Mr. Gayblade "got thoroughly licked and left town with a badly battered up phiz."

The trouble happened near Butcheck's blacksmith shop about 9 o'clock. Libertine Gayblade was on his way up town when Second

Prominent Business Man met him at this point. Without a word, Second Prominent Business Man planted a right uppercut square into Gayblade's mouth, knocking him down as though he had been kicked by a mule. Mr. Gayblade picked up a rock for defense, when Second Prominent Business Man went at him again.

Mr. Libertine Gayblade's face and nose were quite badly swollen, and we understand that some of his front false teeth were put out of commission, his injuries requiring the immediate attention of Dentist —————. Gayblade left for Denver on the 11:30 train; Second Prominent Business Man pleaded guilty to assault and battery and was fined $3, this being the minimum penalty.

The newspapers carried more of the gory details, the alienation of affections suit, etc. Libertine Gayblade wanted the case tried in Denver, claiming that Summit County would not give a fair trial. Finally, the suit went to court in Leadville. Aggrieved Husband evidently won the suit, for another suit was instituted a few years later for $1,750 "due on account."

Another affair, in the general category, sent a man to Canon City penitentiary for the remainder of his life:

With great reluctance, we publish the fact that Breckenridge has a sensation—a scandal—the gravity of which, as the facts come out, threaten to place an old man, gray with age, past the age of 60, before the public as a licentious debaucher of the chastity of females of tender years, and to stifle the life of one of our brightest and most promising high-school girls.

The young girl had been hired as kitchen-help in Mrs. August Silvermane's boarding house. She had successfully averted the attentions of Mr. Silvermane for a time, but then was "forcibly robbed of her virtue, by a married man, who heretofore stood high in this community." The young girl had much "corroborating evidence to strengthen her strong case, in addition to the presence in the court of her off-spring." The sentence of the court was 10-12 years in the penitentiary. Mr. Silvermane ended his days behind prison bars.

Breckenridge, like most all mining towns, had its "fancy houses." Breckenridge *Bulletin*, August, 1900, registered a complaint about the "Illegitimate houses across the Blue." This seemed to be the center for these establishments, particularly in the neighborhood of the railroad station. The "Blue Goose" was a bit farther south and west. Another establishment, "Minnie's House," was on the east side of town, conveniently located along the pathway to Wellington Mine and other mines of French Gulch. It was said, "Breckenridge distinguished itself in yet another way. Its pest house was located within the town limits and its sporting houses were on the outskirts." According to an old timer, this was absolutely unique in a mining camp. Most mining camps kept their pleasures close at hand and their pains as far away as possible.

Breckenridge *Bulletin*, May 27, 1905, reported: "Every feminine resident of the red-light district has accepted terms of the court to seek new fields and pastures greener, not later than May 20. Some went to Alma, some to Denver, and one or two to Goldfield (near Cripple Creek)." Similar edicts had been given before, but there was always a returning. Summit County *Journal*, October 17, 1908, had a sordid tragic story:

HALVERSON TIRED OF BUTTERFLY LIFE

Monday evening Breckenridge was treated to a real sensation—a tragedy in a sporting-house on Evergreen Heights. There, by his own hands, Carl Halverson "went the route" as a result of making too close alliance with booze and fallen women. Others have chased these tempters before; many are on their trail now; none ever permanently conquer both, and a majority shuffle off at Station S (suicide) on the broad and gilded road that leads straight to perdition.

Halverson and wife were newcomers in Summit County. He worked for the Central Power Company at, or near Dillon. She, with his consent, was an inmate of "Minnie's House." There she led a life that was anything but lady-like. According to her story she went on the sporting stage before she married Halverson.

Last week he came up from Dillon armed with a gun which he had purchased from C. A. Miller. He went to Minnie's to make trouble, which he did. His wife was afraid of him, so much so that the landlady had him locked up. Monday evening he sought entrance at the house, with the avowed purpose of shooting his wife. After the latter had been secreted in a closet, the landlady allowed him to enter the house.

On making inquiries for "Pearl," his wife, and receiving the information that the "jewel" had flown, he deliberately walked to the center of the parlor floor, and, placing the muzzle of the gun to his right temple, pulled the trigger. The bullet crushed the skull on the right side and came out near the left ear, passing straight through the head. A jury was impaneled, and the findings of the jury being as above given.

Reading of old newspapers shows that Breckenridge had its full share of the "rough and shady." And, Bayard Taylor, you were wrong about the alkali water—dead wrong.

MADDENING MYSTERY

"TOM'S BABY"

PART I

Breckenridge had, and still has, a maddening mystery—what in the world happened to "Tom's Baby"? From the time the infant came to light of day and had his birth-cleansing, the child has been a mystery. Few babyhood details are known. While yet a youth his whereabouts were fairly well obliterated. Now that he has passed fourscore years he has left no definite trace of a lifetime.

Is he alive? Did he die an early death? Has he slipped away, awaiting future reincarnation? Is he tucked away—an unknown identity, an unrecognized celebrity? Was he kidnaped, as some suppose? Is he far away? Is he close at hand? Does he exist, or doesn't he? Could the story of his birth be no more than "a legend that has hung over from colorful pioneer days?" (as one closely connected with his destiny conjectured). These are some of the haunting questions about "Tom's Baby."

Tom's Baby was Breckenridge's prize gold nugget. In fact, it has almost undisputed claim of being Colorado's largest gold nugget. Some say it was United States' largest nugget. And there are some who foolishly believe it was the world's largest nugget. The mystery of its disappearance, its whereabouts, lack of definite information fired the imagination of many. It remains a present-day topic of speculation.

Story upon story is related of Tom's Baby. Supposedly, it was seen here—or there; "so-and-so saw it at such-and-such a place." All stories to the contrary, it remains as elusive as the English Scarlet Pimpernell of the French Revolution:

"We seek him here, we seek him there—

That demmed elusive pimpernell."

Fascinating, elusive Tom's Baby remains a baffling mystery. Is Breckenridge's infant, like Philadelphia's Charley Ross, forever destined to be a mysterious, unsolved child-disappearance—an haunting enigma? Many have joined the search, but the unanswered question remains—"what happened to Tom's Baby?"

One question, at least, can be answered with finality. Tom's Baby was not an unfounded legend. Verified information refutes that. Phyllis Campion Bullock-Webster, daughter of the wealthy mining-banking John F. Campion, (who supposedly had the nugget in his gold collection) raised the question of it being only a "legend of colorful pioneer days." She proposed to search her deceased father's papers, but at the time of her own death, (February, 1965), no information had come to shed light on the mystery.

CLAIMS OF ITS WHEREABOUTS

Claims galore have been made of the whereabouts of the celebrated nugget. Old-timers are almost willing to take an oath they saw it on display somewhere during their early years. Or parents, relatives, acquaintances saw it, so they say. On and on it goes, endlessly. If it were everywhere claimed, it was a well-traveled baby. The only thing lacking is proof that it was "here or there."

One of the most persistent stories is that Tom's Baby journeyed to Chicago's World Columbian Exposition, 1893. J. C. Smiley's *History of Colorado* (1902) states, "Tom's Baby, with several other, but smaller nuggets, was sold to the Chicago World's Fair Commissioners for $15,000." Supposedly, afterward, it went to

Chicago's Field Museum. Chicago newspapers, of the time, shed no light on Tom's Baby; Field Museum knows nothing of it.

Colorado had an outstanding exhibit at the Chicago Fair with Breckenridge gold as the main attraction. The Denver *Republican*, May 30, 1893, announced:

GOLD FROM SUMMIT

THE BRECKENRIDGE EXHIBIT IN PLACE AT THE WORLD'S FAIR PROVES A CENTER OF INTEREST

A Big Crowd Surrounded It All Day Yesterday

Chicago, Illinois, May 29, (Special)

> Colorado's big pavilion in the Mines and Mining Building was closed this morning until 11 o'clock. At that time the ropes were cast aside from the entrance to three ordinary-looking showcases in the center of the pavilion. It was not the showcases that attracted the people, but their shining golden contents, and everybody went into raptures over the beauties of the ore. It was the first display of the Breckenridge gold exhibit from Summit County, and the costly metal was sent out in three showcases, which enclosed altogether about $15,000 worth of specimens.

> E. J. Collingwood, in charge of the exhibit, began the work of unpacking the ores from the Wells-Fargo strong box at 9 o'clock, and assisted by Assistant Chief Heikes of the Colorado exhibit, and the young man who had taken most of the ores from the Summit County's earth, had them neatly displayed in the showcases by 11 o'clock, at which time the public was admitted. An addition to this display is expected in a few days. The value of the exhibit when complete will be $100,000.

(The reference to the young man who had taken most of the ores from Summit County's earth, quite likely was the young man who found Tom's Baby. World's Columbian Exposition followed six years after the discovery of Tom's Baby.)

The *World's Columbian Exposition, Chicago, 1893*, (by T. White and W. Igleheard, describes Colorado's exhibit as follows:

> A circle of marble columns of native material adorns the Colorado space, and the low parapet is faced with new light-colored varieties of Colorado onyx. The Breckenridge collection of gold nuggets and free gold is valued at a quarter of a million dollars.

Again, there is no specific mention of Tom's Baby.

Another story, equally persistent as World's Columbian Exposition story, is that of the State Museum (The State Historical Society of Colorado) and the Denver City Park Museum of Natural History.

State Museum came into existence in 1879, but its collections were housed several places in Denver. Rooms in the Capitol building were used until erection of the present structure, 1915, at 200 E. Fourteenth Avenue. Some claim Tom's Baby was seen at the Capitol building, and later at the State Historical building.

The first unit of City Park Museum of Natural History, (originating from Breckenridge's Edwin Carter collection of mounted animals and birds), officially opened in 1908. (Previous to this, a small eastern section had been completed in 1903 and housed the Carter collection.) John F. Campion's gold collection was one of the outstanding attractions of the Museum of Natural History. The *United States Geological Survey— Geology and Ore Deposits of the Breckenridge District, Colorado*, 1911, pictures five of the largest gold specimens of the Campion Collection at City Park Museum. (All five of these specimens are on display today.) Tom's Baby wasn't pictured in the 1911 *Geological Survey*, nor is it in the present-day exhibit at the Museum. But stories persist—Tom's Baby was seen in both places—State Historical Museum and City Park Museum of Natural History.

John F. Campion had mining interests at Leadville, Colorado, and in the Breckenridge Wapiti Group at the top of Swan and French Gulches. Campion possessed a valuable collection of gold, and supposedly, Tom's Baby was included. However, we must use the term *supposedly*, for there is no valid evidence that Colorado's large nugget was in the collection.

John Campion died July 17, 1916. There is no mention in his will of the gold collection. But, as in the case of many of his benefactions, the City Park Museum gift could have been made years before his death. The Denver *Post*, October 17, 1920, wrote of "Campion's Last Labor for Colorado," saying, "The Museum of Natural History at City Park may be said to have been built up around the Carter Collection of wild animals of Colorado, which collection Mr. Campion, Joseph A. Thatcher and others obtained as the nucleus of the museum. An exhibit of native gold, given by him to the museum, is so rare and valuable that it is specially guarded against burglars."

Pasquale Marranzino, writing in the Rocky Mountain *News*, January 13, 1955, revived the old question, "What Became of Tom's Baby?" His premise was, "The cloak of Colorado history, and the dim light of time, keep hiding the fact that somebody kidnaped Tom's Baby."

It was purchased by the rich and powerful John Campion, who, as founder and angel of the State Historical Society, said that his famed mineral collection would be willed to the society. That valuable and irreplacable collection is an important exhibit of the Denver Museum of Natural History, but Tom's Baby isn't a part of it. Some time in history—nobody could tell me exactly when, the Campion collection was switched from the State Historical Society to the Museum at City Park—but Tom's Baby did not arrive at the Museum with the collection.

The piece, at today's gold prices, would be valued at approximately $6,000 melted down. But its size and perfection made it a museum piece, as Campion intended.

But somewhere, somehow, Tom's Baby was kidnaped or lost, and there's another story that says the howling of the wind on Breckenridge Farncomb Hill is the ghost of Tom Groves calling for his lost baby.

Marranzino published another story the following week—"Disappearing Gold Nuggets."

The other day I wrote wistfully of my desire to get my hands on Tom's Baby. Tom's Baby was one of the largest gold nuggets ever delved out of Colorado quartz. It was part of the John Campion mineral collection, but got pilfered or lost in the last century.

My efforts to locate Tom's Baby are of no avail. But since then I have found that if, indeed, Tom's Baby has been kidnaped, that dastardly act can't compare to the wholesale liberation of a $100,000 display of nuggets that used to be owned by the State Historical Society.

Walter Scott, state director of mines, remembers that a fabulous collection of nuggets was encased in some glory at the society's exhibit hall around 1915. The collection was a great tourist attraction and school kids paraded by to oooh and aah at the dull gleaming metal which meant the world to them.

One day an inventory of the properties of the museum caused officials to open up the nugget case and weigh its contents.

The weighing and examination disclosed that a clever highgrader had lifted the whole collection, nugget by nugget, and had left instead gilt-painted rocks.

Stories persist that Tom's Baby was seen at the State Museum or the Museum of Natural History. There is a valuable collection of crystallized, wire, and gold nuggets at the Museum of Natural History, displayed through heavy-plated glass, encased in a strong metal vault. Special attractions are the large pieces of Farncomb Hill crystallized gold. These were on display, 1911, as the largest gold specimens.

For a number of years, a replica of the famous Australian "Welcome Stranger" nugget was displayed at the Museum of Natural History. Perhaps this confused some as Tom's Baby.

Mrs. Louisa Arps, formerly a cataloguer at Colorado State Historical Society Museum, informs us that, "In the mineral exhibit at the Colorado State Historical Society Muscum—2nd floor—is a small piece of gold, labeled:

#11256
Gold nugget from Tom's Baby,
14 pound gold nugget,
Farncomb Hill, Lincoln, Colorado.
Donor: Mrs. Mary Hilliard Williams,
January 21, 1960

Mrs. Mary Hilliard Williams was godmother of Mrs. Oral K. Wilson (neè "Frankie" Gore of Breckenridge.) (Hilliard was the "ponderous assayer" who cleaned and weighed Tom's Baby.) Mrs. Williams states that the small gold piece was not a gift to the Museum, but a *loan*. It is to stay there, unless the town of Breckenridge builds a museum, at which time it is to be taken to that place. Mrs. Wilson thinks the small piece of gold, loaned to the Colorado Historical Museum, probably fell off the large Tom's Baby when it was being assayed in the Williams' (Hilliard) living room.

Mrs. Arps is of the opinion that Tom's Baby is languishing in Denver Museum of Natural History's vault in United Bank of Denver.

April, 1970, the writer saw the small piece of gold at Colorado State Historical Society Museum. It was labeled, as described by Mrs. Arps,

Maddening Mystery

but had been moved to the attic storage room of the Historical Society building. It is a small piece of gold, no larger or thicker than a dime, and rests in a jeweler's silk-lined ring box. The ring box is in a small, locked showcase with other items.

Tom's Baby has been seen other places—so the stories go. One thought it was at Smithsonian Institute. (Smithsonian has no record of the nugget.) Another thought it was seen at Peabody Museum, Harvard University. (Peabody replied: "The Minerology Museum of this University does indeed have many specimens of Breckenridge gold, chiefly of the wire type, but unhappily we do not possess the large nugget, Tom's Baby.")

Before Chicago's World Columbian Exposition, Tom's Baby was to have been exhibited at the November, 1891, Mining Congress, meeting in Denver. The Congress was a gala event to celebrate the opening of the new Colorado Mining Exchange Building. Colorado's fabulously rich mining tycoon, the Honorable H. A. W. Tabor, was temporary chairman of the Congress. The Rocky Mountain *News* gave description of the dazzling gold display at the opening of the Mining and Exchange Building:

> One of the finest and largest exhibits of pure gold, just as it comes from the mine, ever made is now open for public inspection at the Mining Exchange headquarters. The exhibit is from Summit County, and it all comes from the vicinity of Breckenridge, on Farncomb Hill. The aggregate value of the collection is about $100,000, and as proof of the honesty of the big crowds that daily inspect the nuggets not a cent's worth has yet been missed, though some of the pieces could easily be concealed in the palm of the hand. The exhibit is but a nucleus, large as it is, of what is proposed to make it

for the world's fair at Chicago in 1893. Many of the nuggets weigh a pound and a half and more, and under a magnifying glass reveal some wonderfully fine markings. The collection, all in all, is one of the most rare, costly and beautiful ever exhibited, and will prove a card at the world's fair.

But again, there is no specific word about Tom's Baby.

World Conclave of Knights Templar met in Denver, August, 1892, and it was announced beforehand: "The people of Breckenridge will dazzle the vision of the conclave visitors with a display of gold worth over $10,000. The display will be placed in the exhibit room of the Mining Exchange Building. One of the nuggets which will be shown weighs thirteen pounds." (No write-up at the time of the conclave mentioned a thirteen pound nugget on display.)

Tom's Baby was supposed to have been at the St. Louis Fair, 1904. It is also claimed the baby was "in a display at a bank in Leadville around the turn of the century." And there are others who say they saw it on display "in the window of a cigar store at Denver's Albany Hotel."

There are a number of present-day Breckenridge people who claim they saw Tom's Baby thirty-five and forty years ago at City Park Museum. They say it was in a "glass safe" in the basement and was labeled, " Tom's Baby." One said he was warned by a guard "to keep his hands off, because if he touched the safe all the bells in the world would ring."

That elusive Tom's Baby was "here-there-and-everywhere"—but what really happened to him? One would think there would have been more detailed publicity about him and many photographs taken of the bewitching youngster.

Colorado Exhibit—World's Columbian Exposition, Chicago, Illinois, 1893.
Courtesy—Chicago Historical Society.

Colorado Exhibit—World's Columbian Exposition, Chicago, Illinois, 1893.
(Young man at center-rear display cases-possibly "Tom's Baby" discoverer.) Courtesy—Chicago Historical Society.

Maddening Mystery

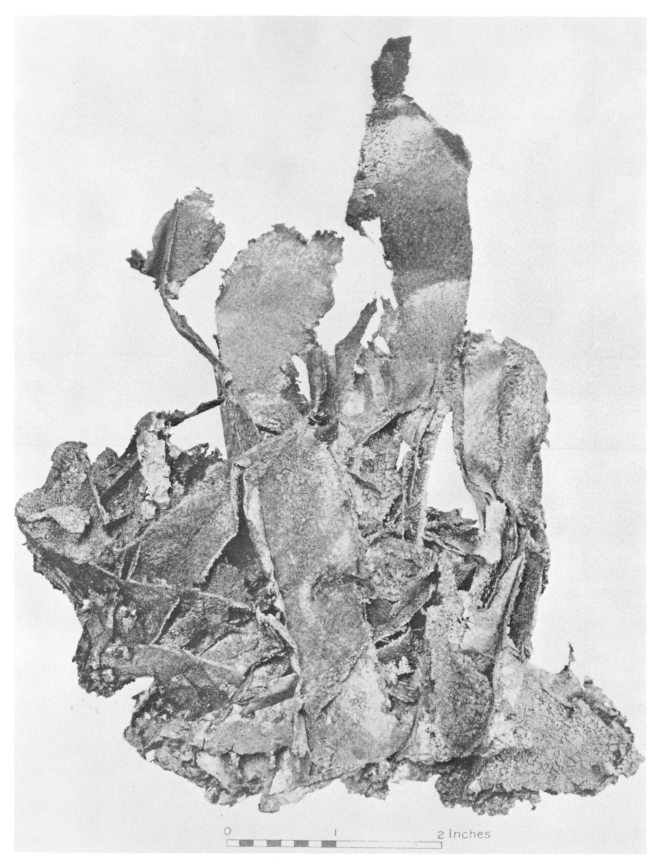

Picture:—*United States Geological Survey—Geology and Ore Deposits of the Breckenridge District, Colorado*—1911 (page 80). John F. Campion Gold. Denver City Park Museum of Natural History. (Largest piece of crystallized gold on display.)

A.

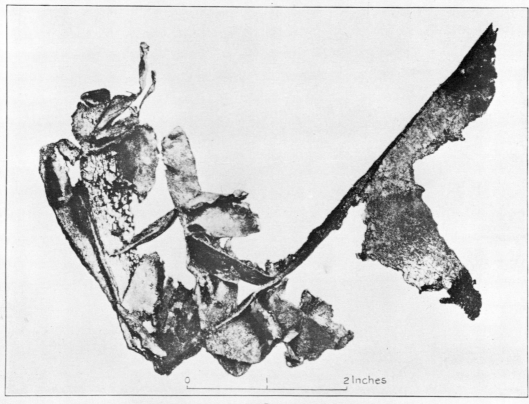

B.

NATIVE GOLD FROM FARNCOMB HILL.

Both illustrations are natural size. The upper shows the usual intersecting plates. The lower illustrates particularly well the grouping of implanted octahedral crystals, partly in parallel orientation. Photograph by Schwartz from a specimen in the Campion collection, Colorado Museum of Natural History, Denver. See page 81.

Picture:—*United States Geological Survey—Geology and Ore Deposits of the Breckenridge District, Colorado*—1911 (Page 82). John F. Campion Gold. Denver City Park Museum of Natural History. (Largest piece of crystallized gold on display.)

A.

B.

NATIVE GOLD FROM FARNCOMB HILL.

Both illustrate on natural scale the size and delicacy attained by some of the crystal-coated plates. The lower figure shows octahedral crystals in parallel orientation. Photograph by Schwartz from a specimen in the Campion collection, Colorado Museum of Natural History, Denver. See page 81.

Picture:—*United States Geological Survey—Geology and Ore Deposits of the Breckenridge District, Colorado*—1911 (Page 84). John F. Campion Gold. Denver City Park Museum of Natural History. (Largest piece of crystallized gold on display.)

TOM'S BABY

PART II

(Birth of Tom's Baby)

The birth of Tom's Baby, and the immediate events following are, like all other events of his life, surrounded with many different stories and interpretations. We set forth the different stories, but favor the story as it came from the Breckenridge newspaper, local Summit County records, and mining periodicals of the time.

Breckenridge was wildly excited Saturday afternoon, July 23, 1887. Two young men, Tom Groves and Harry Lytton, rushed into town bearing a gold nugget of unusual size and beauty. That's the beginning of Breckenridge's maddening mystery. Breckenridge's *Daily Journal*, Monday, July 25th, told the story in news items and editorial:

AN IMMENSE NUGGET OF GOLD

On Saturday last, Tom Groves and Harry Lytton, who are working on the Fuller Placer patent on Farncomb Hill, struck a pocket of gold nuggets from which they, in four hours, removed two hundred and forty-three ounces and nine pennyweights of gold. The largest nugget, when taken out, weighed fully one hundred and sixty ounces, two pieces were broken off, leaving the nugget as now shown weighing 136 oz. 5 dwt., which is, we believe the largest nugget ever found in the State. Yesterday hundreds of visitors called on Colonel Ware at his office at the concentrator on the west side, to feast their eyes on the find.

The largest nugget previously found in this county was in McNulty's Gulch placer mine on the upper Ten Mile many years ago, that was valued at $475, but that was not more than one-fifth the size of the present find. Although this vicinity, during the last two years, has sent out thousands of fine specimens of nugget gold, this one dwarfs them all. It will be sent to Colonel Carpenter in Denver, that Denverites may learn that there are other inducements in Colorado besides Denver town lots.

"TOM'S BABY"

When the big nugget of gold was found on Saturday afternoon by Tom Groves and Harry Lytton, Tom was so elated and fondled the find so affectionately that the boys declared that it was "Tom's Baby" and so it goes. It will probably be a long time before "Tom's Baby" will be retired as Colorado's big nugget.

136 oz. 5 dwts.

That is Summit County's latest champion nugget. Where is the district that can knock that chip off our shoulder in 1887?

SUMMIT'S GOLD

The exhibition of the "Tom's Baby" nugget must not be allowed to divert the attention of the friends of mining from the fact that this nugget is but an incident to Summit's production of gold. This section has been pouring a steady stream of gold into the metallic currents of the country for the last three years. Hundreds of nuggets have preceded this "baby" nugget, and even in its native bed it was surrounded by a greater amount of gold than was contained in itself. It is no longer subject to question that the ridge between French and Swan, especially near the foot of Guyot, is filled with a closely woven net work of gold-lined seams, the value of whose content no man can form any conception. The "Tom's Baby" nugget came from a point ninety feet below the surface, and certainly shows no decrease in the richness of the deposits as depth is gained.

Denver newspapers, Monday, July 25th, made recognition of the discovery. The Rocky Mountain *News*, page 1, column 1, and the first article at the top of the page gave the heading:

NABBING A NUGGET

A Thirteen Pound Gold Nugget Found In One Of Summit County Gulches
A Big Gold Nugget Found
Special to the *News*
Breckenridge, Colo., July 24

Yesterday two leasers in the Colonel Ware property in American Gulch struck a pocket from which they took a nugget weighing thirteen pounds, five pennyweights, and considerable gold in smaller pieces, the entire lot weighing 243 ounces. The big nugget is now on exhibition at Colonel Ware' office.

The Denver *Republican* reported:

The discovery of a nugget of gold near Breckenridge, weighing over thirteen pounds, is an event of no little interest. The nugget is the largest ever found in Colorado, and it deserves a place among the large nuggets found anywhere. It shows that the gold mines of Colorado are not all exhausted. There may still be many such nuggets as this in the mountains, waiting for someone to find them. One thing is sure, that only those who hunt for them will find them.

Breckenridge's *Daily Journal* gave further enlightenment of the first week of life for Tom's Baby:

Monday, July 25th:

Tom's Baby is the general subject of conversation all over town today. Colonel Carpenter was in town yesterday, he came over from Alma to see Tom's Baby. He saw the infant and insisted on taking it to Denver, but its foster parent would not allow it to go until its face was washed and the infant made presentable. It will be sent to the Colonel tomorrow.

Tuesday, July 26th:

Yesterday a party of officers and others, on a special train on the D. & S. P. Railroad, stopped over long enough to visit Hilliard's Assay Office, to take a good look at Tom's Baby that was in the process of cleansing. Some of them are old Coloradoans and they all declared that it was the largest nugget they had ever beheld.

Thursday, July 28th:

Tom's Baby was sent to Denver this morning in charge of Conductor Jones, with directions to let the infant be shown to any enquiring people along the line. Mr. Jones was quite proud of his charge.

Friday, July 29th:

Tom's Baby weighed 160 oz. when first taken out, and 136 oz. after its face was cleaned. Last Saturday, in four hours, Tom Groves and Harry Lytton took out 246 oz. of nugget gold on the Gold Flake vein, part of which was Tom's Baby.

Saturday, July 30th:

Colonel Carpenter came up from Denver by last night's train, and will return by tonight's train. He received Tom's Baby all right.

The *Daily Journal*, in its last issue for 1887, December 31st, had one more item:

TOM'S BABY

Don't forget Farncomb Hill contributed the boss nugget of 1887, known as Tom's Baby, weight thirteen pounds, found in a crevice on the Ware-Carpenter placer patents.

There are other stories of the finding of Tom's Baby. One is that "Tom Groves was going hammer and jack against the side of Farncomb Hill when he splintered off a hunk of quartz that hit his foot. He picked it up to throw it out of his way and noted that it was heavier than ordinary quartz. So he smashed with his hammer and laid open the quartz jaws on one of the finest whole pieces of gold ever mined in the State." Another story is that it was in the ore pile and was going to be tossed aside, when Tom noticed its unusual weight. Closer investigation revealed the nugget.

A delightful story is told of Tom sending to Denver and having a seamstress fashion a black pillow and blanket for the baby. Just like any proud parent, he folded back the blanket to display the baby upon request of admirers. It appears, however, that Tom did not have the baby in his possession long enough to send for such a blanket, or do much displaying of the infant.

There is a document in the Summit Clerk's Office, Breckenridge, dated March 1, 1887, and recorded March 16, 1887, Book 61, page 3. The instrument is entitled "Agreement of Lease."

The Lessors are M. B. Carpenter and A. J. Ware; the Lessees are Charles Kern, John Hartman, Martin Hartman. The property involved was: Carpenter Mining District, Gold Flake Lode or Vein, near head of American Gulch, United States Mineral Survey No. 85 on Farncomb Hill, being the vein just discovered by said Hartmans and Kern. Specific stipulations were listed:

The Lessees are granted to have and to hold for two years, except in case of sale of property;

Not to be sublet without written consent of Lessors;

To keep accurate accounts and to render monthly statements—first of each month—showing the amount of all ore and gold and the yield of the same;

To deliver as Royalty 25% of mill returns, or mill retorts, or free gold, delivered to the office of A. J. Ware (Breckenridge) as soon as free gold is mined or milled, without offset, deduction, or any change whatsoever.

It is expressly agreed that the Royalty in kind of all free gold mined shall be delivered to said Ware, or Agent, the day after the same is taken from the Mine.

And the said Lessors expressly reserved to them the property and right of property in all minerals to be extracted from said premises during the term of this Lease.

While there is not a similar agreement officially recorded, it is assumed that Thomas W. Groves and Harry Lytton, leasing from the Ware-Carpenter properties on Farncomb Hill, were bound with similar agreement. The stipulations of the Hartman-Kern-Carpenter-Ware (Lessee-Lessor) seems to have been followed, step by step, in the case of Tom's Baby.

The following items appear in the *Mining Industry*, published in Denver:

July 29, 1887:

The thirteen pound gold nugget, found at Breckenridge the other day, is the largest ever discovered in the State. Col. M. B. Carpenter made a flying trip to Breckenridge to inspect the big thirteen pound nugget, found in one of the mines of which he is an owner. He will have it on exhibition here in a few days.

August 5, 1887:

Hiram Johnson, of Breckenridge, was at the Brunswick this week, and it is safe to say he deposited a big lot of Summit Gold at the Denver Mint.

August 12, 1887:

Col. A. J. Ware, of Breckenridge, is in the city and ready to wager a thousand dollars that his thirteen-pound nugget, lately found on one of his lode claims, will be eclipsed by another three times as large and valuable within the next ten days.

August 26, 1887 (from Breckenridge):

The leasers on the Ware-Carpenter property are getting rich, and those beautiful and valuable nuggets which have astonished and delighted the people of Denver and other localities in which they have been exhibited, scarcely excite comment here; they are so common. On Saturday last, John Hartman, of J. H. Hartman & Bros., who has a lease on the Ware-Carpenter property, presented his bookkeeper, Ed Hanash, with a gold nugget of rare beauty. Its intrinsic value is about $150, and when Col. A. J. Ware learned that Mr. Hartman intended it as a gift to Mr. Hanash, he generously declined to accept the royalty due him and his associates. Such acts of generosity, in appreciation of faithful services, renew the ties of friendship, and are sources of pride and satisfaction to all concerned in them. The Gold Flake is only one of a dozen veins embraced in the Ware-Carpenter property, to say nothing of over 2,000 acres of placer ground of demonstrated richness.

September 16, 1887:

A request has come from the 16th Triennial Exhibition of the Massachusetts Mechanic Association. The request came from a Mrs. Olive Wright for one carload of mineral, which should consist of the finest cabinet specimens, including the wonderful Ware-Carpenter nugget, also a miner's suit of clothes, lamp, etc., and implements of his trade. The answer to the request was, "No, Mrs. Wright. Mining is a masculine employment, not feminine. The Boston people, and crowds of visitors, will scarcely get a view of the Ware-Carpenter nugget, unless they come to Denver, but some enthusiastic miner may donate some cast-off canvas suit and brogans."

August 31, 1888:

A sale of the Ware-Carpenter property on Farncomb Hill has taken place. Senator Hearst of California, Senator John P. Jones of Nevada, and Senator Gorman of Maryland were among the purchasers.

The Summit County *Journal* spoke out on this sale:

The organization of the Victoria Company and the purchase of the property in Georgia and American Gulches, heretofore owned and controlled by Col. A. J. Ware and M. B. Carpenter, threatens to lead to some slight difficulties. The lessees, of whom there are quite a number, do not think it a square deal, and the creation of the new company was merely to terminate their leases, as their leases stipulate that in case of sale the lease is to end.

Tom's Baby is now being known as the "Ware-Carpenter Nugget." How, and when, and where did Colonel Carpenter and Colonel Ware dispose of Tom's Baby? Whose baby was it—Tom Groves'?—Alfred Ware's?—Mason Carpenter's? At least we know that "Tom's Baby" *did* exist.

"TOM'S BABY"

PART III

(Godparents of Tom's Baby)

From the beginning, Breckenridge had a preference for the east side of Blue River. West of the Blue was a sagebrush flat with occasional willow clumps. Pine and spruce shunned the flat, preferring the nearby slopes. Lincoln Avenue bridge conveyed traffic across the river, connecting with the road going west and north to Valley Brook Cemetery and Two-Mile Bridge. Before 1880 few people selected building sites in what could be called "West Breckenridge." But "West Breckenridge" was not always to be a nonentity. The picture changed with the "1880 Boom." Father Dyer tells of the 1880 boom in his book, *Snow-Shoe Itinerant*:

Breckenridge experienced a characteristic boom. A report was spread that about Breckenridge were immense bodies of gold quartz and carbonates, three feet deep. People of all classes came across the range, and, of course, the inevitable dance-house, with degraded women, fiddles, bugles, and many sorts of music, came too. There was a general hubbub from dark to daylight. The weary could hardly rest. Claims were staked out everywhere, and the prospector thought nothing of shoveling five feet of snow to start a shaft. Saloons, grocery-stores, carpenter-shops, and every kind of business sprang up, including stamp-mills and smelters. All classes were excited beyond all good sense. Town-lots, that could have been bought before at twenty-five to fifty dollars, brought fifteen hundred dollars. Corrals, log-heaps, and brush thickets were all turned into town-lots. Those owning ground thought it worth ten times more than it was. The excitement was almost as great as when they thought the Indians were coming.

In about a year most of the excitement in town-lots had passed over; and in eighteen months building had quit, and the camp went down. Town lots went down as fast as they went up.

The Summit County *Journal,* June 14, 1881, concurred:

Real estate is not quite so flourishing as it was a year ago in this town. Then a few greedy ones thought they had the world by the heels and all they had to do was to ask their price and get it. Today lots with houses on can be bought for less than was demanded for the naked lot one year ago, and yet the future of Breckenridge is today far more promising than it was then, but the excitement of the hour based upon nothing, carried men's judgment away as if by a whirlwind.

"West Breckenridge" got additional shots-in-the-arm in the 1880s. The Wilson Smelter was built along the cemetery road, north of Breckenridge and near the mouth of Cucumber Gulch. Later the Smelter was changed to a concentrator and it had a change of names—Breckenridge Concentrator—Jones' Mill. The Mill was demolished near the turn of the century, but its towering smokestack remained a landmark for years, until it toppled ahead of the gold boat.

Central Park, on the west side of the Blue, was a favorite place for outings. It boasted a grandstand for speakers, dancing, parlor skating and other appropriate enjoyments. Building of the Denver and South Park Railroad depot on the west side of the Blue, north of Lincoln Avenue, spurred other building activity—homes—the redlight district. August 7, 1882, the first train arrived in Breckenridge, and thereafter "West Breckenridge" gained importance. In the summer of 1887 Alfred J. Ware's large concentrating mill (sometimes called Ware-Carpenter Concentrator), south of Lincoln Avenue, was being rushed to completion.

The first half of the 20th century saw the goldboat inching through Breckenridge, gouging the riverbed and "West Breckenridge"—not stopping until it came to Ware-Carpenter Concentrator. There—midnight, October 15, 1942—the clanging, clattering goldboat took its final bite. The shrill whistle sounded for the last time, engines stopped, the boat quivered—the valley became deathly quiet. Behind, "West Breckenridge" lay in a grave, overlaid with mounds of jumbled rocks.

Into the 1880-setting came four men whom we call the godparents of Tom's Baby. Another, Harry Lytton, dropped into immediate obscurity.

THOMAS W. GROVES

The 1880 United States Census listed a Groves family living on High Street, Breckenridge. According to the census record, the household consisted of Cathrin (sic) Groves, mother, age 59; J. T. Groves, son, age 33, born in Pennsylvania; and one boarder, unnamed. Why John D. Groves, husband-father, and Thomas W. Groves, son, are not listed, is left unexplained.

A Quit Claim Deed, dated July 12, 1880, and recorded December 26, 1881, was made between James MGlee and Catharine (Catherine) D. Groves, for a piece of real estate, to the value of $20. It was described: "50 foot front by 125 foot depth, west side of the Blue River, fronting 50 feet on the south side of Lincoln Avenue, and adjoining David Eledery's residence on the West, and adjoining Father Dyer's lot on the East." Presumably, this became the home of the Groves family.

The number of documents recorded in Summit County's Clerk and Recorder office would indicate that the Groves family was not destitute. In 1881 Thomas W. Groves, Jeremiah T. Groves, and John Groves got title to the Dushore Lode and Mining Claim for $500. John Avery and Alfred J. Ware, in 1885, transferred the undivided one-half, Survey No. 83, California Mining District to Thomas Groves, Jerry Groves, John Groves and Lizzie Groves. In 1885, E. C. Moody and H. H. Irwin deeded to Thomas W. Groves "the undivided one-half interest in the Key West Lode, and to the Bond Holder Mine or Lode, for the price of $16,000." In 1886 it was the Amazette Lode for $300. January, 1887, Colonel Alfred J. Ware transferred to his daughter, Bessie E. Ware, "the undivided (⅛) interest in the Groves-Ware Mining Claim at the head of Humbug Gulch on Farncomb Hill. No, Tom Groves was not exactly destitute.

July 23, 1887, brought the startling news of the discovery of Tom's Baby. About the same time Tom Groves secured one-twelfth interest in the Gold Dust Mine. If Tom Groves had been considered an ordinary miner-prospector up to this time, his status now was greatly changed. News items about him began to appear in the Summit County *Journal* and in mining magazines. The *Daily Journal*, September 26, 1887, noted: "Tom Groves visited Denver last week for the first time since 1879. He expressed himself duly surprised at the vast changes in the city; he had to employ a guide for the first few days, lest he should get lost or mixed up with the people who crowded around him." Another item, April, 1888, reported: "Tom W. Groves, who has been away for several months, came in on last night's train, looking and feeling well and happy after his sojourn." Th *Mining Industry* magazine noted a number of Tom's visits to Denver.

July 7, 1888, *Daily Journal* had an interesting news item: "Mr. Thomas Groves, and sister, and Miss Bessie Ware came up from Denver by last night's train. They propose spending a few days fishing." July 12th report was: "Mr. Thomas Groves, and sister, and Miss Bessie Ware returned to Denver by this morning's train. The party was down the Blue fishing yesterday." Could a romance be blossoming between Tom Groves and Bessie Ware?

Perhaps a more lasting fame than his "baby" was coming to Tom Groves and his brother, Jerry. The Breckenridge *Daily Journal*, December 1, 1887, announced:

TOM AND JERRY

This delicious drink will be served to all comers at the Denver Hotel bar (Breckenridge) on Sunday morning, next, by that expert mixologist, Bob McCollum. Don't fail to sample McCollum's Tom and Jerry on Sunday morning.

"Tom and Jerry" is a concoction (according to the *American Heritage Cookbook and Illustrated History of American Eating and Drinking*) of eggs, sugar, Jamaica rum, ground all-spice, cinnamon, cloves. "To a ladleful of the mixture in a mug, add some bourbon, boiling water or hot milk; dust with nutmeg and float some cognac on top." That, according to the book, is a "Tom and Jerry."

"Many a bartender, up to the present century, laid claim of inventing or naming it—but solid historical documentation has somewhat befogged." Perhaps Breckenridge has a claim to "Tom and Jerry"—at least it had Tom and Jerry Groves, and it was serving "Tom and Jerrys" in 1887.

In December, 1887, there was an agreement between Thomas Groves, Jerry Groves, Lizzie Groves and Bessie Ware with the Victoria Gold Mining Company "for an undivided one-half of the Ware and Groves Mining Claim for a consideration of $8,000."

Colonel Ware died April 19, 1891. In settling the estate the Ware Mill, west of the Blue River, and at the south end of Breckenridge was transferred to Charles H. Beattie by "the sole heirs at law of Alfred J. Ware, deceased—Mason B. Carpenter, Bessie E. Ware, and Harry C. Ware—for the sum of $25,000."

In 1893 Jerry Groves died, intestate, "leaving as his only heirs Thomas W. Groves, Elizabeth Ware, his sister, and Catharine Groves, his mother." (The father, John Groves, died February, 1888, at Leadville and was buried at Leadville.) Who was Elizabeth Ware?—none other than Lizzie Groves!

Tom Groves faded from the Breckenridge scene. His name is mentioned at Leadville and Twin Lakes. Later, April 4, 1904, there was a document recorded between Thomas W. Groves (of Teller County, Colorado) and Ellis J. Hoyle, Matthew W. Hoyle and Josefilimi Kirk (of Summit County) transferring his one-twelfth interest to the Gold Dust Mining Claim. Thomas Grove's signature was notarized by Chas. A. Vanatta, Teller County. Vanatta was a well-known attorney at Cripple Creek, Colorado, around the turn of the century.

The names of John Campion, Alfred J. Ware, Mason B. Carpenter, Bessie E. Ware, Thomas W. Groves were involved in litigations, settling the vast Campion estate, particularly in the Wapiti holdings. Tom Groves was named in a 1921 case where he, and others, were listed "in default and judgment by default." Another proceeding in 1941 ended in like manner. Tom's whereabouts appeared to be unknown shortly after the turn of the century. He is not listed in Colorado's Bureau of Vital Statistics that records almost all deaths in Colorado since 1900. We know considerable about Tom Groves—but not enough about him and his "baby."

ALFRED J. WARE

Colonel Alfred J. Ware comes into the Tom's Baby mystery as part-owner of the Ware-Carpenter Concentrating Mill and as part-owner of the gold mine from which the famous 13 pound nugget was taken. Also he claimed the 13 pound nugget as his nugget, and was willing to wager $1,000 that a larger one would be found on his mining claims.

Alfred J. Ware was born in Ohio, 1838. He studied law, and at an early age was admitted to the bar. Caught with the enthusiasm to come West, he came to Leadville in 1872, thence to San Juan mining country, and from there to Breckenridge. His concentrating mill at Breckenridge was completed in the summer of 1887. Ware maintained a home in Denver, 3260 Lawrence Street, and a cottage in Breckenridge. His mother, Mrs. M. F. Ware, and a brother, William Ware, lived in Breckenridge. Alfred Ware died of pneumonia at his Denver home, following a week's illness, April 19, 1891.

After Alfred Ware's death, the Ware Concentrating Mill, (or the Ware-Carpenter Mill) was sold to Charles H. Beattie. The following year it was spoken of as the "Price Mill, formerly the Ware Mill." Two years later, the mill was purchased by Pankhurst and Whipple. Colonel Ware's mining interests, around Breckenridge, were mostly on what is known as Farncomb Hill, at the head of Swan and French Gulches.

The *Mining Industry* and *Tradesman*, June 18, 1891, had an article entitled "Summit County—Golden Nuggets." It wrote:

Since the beginning of 1885 there has been a pretty good supply of pure gold nuggets taken from Farncomb Hill; at some seasons the output has been remarkably prolific and of exceeding great value, the nuggets ranging from a half-ounce to fourteen pounds in weight. These specimens of Farncomb Hill gold are scattered all over the world. At one time the late Col. A. J. Ware had a cabinet containing several thousand specimens, ranging from the largest and tiniest leaf of almost no weight, to the solid chunk of pure native gold weighing fourteen pounds. Dealers in specimen of nuggets in this town have sold hundreds of pounds of these nuggets, and at no time has the supply entirely ceased, although it has varied considerably.

Alfred J. Ware's modest will is on file at Denver Probate Court. Inventory of the estate does not mention a gold collection. Valuable items in the inventory were: a $2,000 solitaire diamond, one gold watch $250, one saddle and bridle. Son Harry decamped with these items and daughter Bessie had a warrant issued for his pickup and arrest.

While the estate was in process of settlement, Miss Bessie had two changes of name— Bessie E. VanNostrand (former name before marriage viz. Bessie E. Ware) and Bessie E. Heaton, nee Ware. If there was a romance with Tom Groves, evidently it did not come to marriage.

The Groves family was not entirely out of the Ware family picture, however. Mrs. Lizzie M. (Groves) Ware claimed an interest in the estate as wife of the deceased. Bessie Ware disclaimed ever knowing of such a person. A summons was served, December 26, 1901, "in the matter of the Estate of A. J. Ware, deceased, to Lizzie M. Ware (Cripple Creek, Colorado), Bessie E. Heaton, and Harry C. Ware, heirs at law of the deceased, and M. B. Carpenter, defendants. The lawyer presented a bill to the estate for legal services:

$15 To answer the petition of Lizzie M. (Groves) Ware who claims to be widow of the deceased;

$25 To prepare answer to suit of Lizzie M. Groves, claiming to be widow of A. J. Ware, deceased;

$60 To three days trial Lizzie Groves case in District Court, that plaintiff was the widow of A. J. Ware, deceased.

Later we read, "then Lizzie M. Ware, who had been and was the wife of Alfred J. Ware, comes to withdraw and dismiss petition." The last we hear of Lizzie (Groves) Ware was that she was present at a public auction of Ware interests, and there was "received from Lizzie M. Ware, for sale of 5/16 interest in the Double Decker Lode Mining Claim, Lake County, Colorado, $500, August 25, 1902." The Wares and Groves were very much in the mix-up of the Tom's Baby mystery.

MASON B. CARPENTER

For being one of the most important figures in the Tom's Baby mystery, Colonel Mason B. Carpenter succeeded in keeping farthest in the background. For such a prominent person, he is little known. For disappearing from sight, he almost equals Tom's Baby.

Mason B. Carpenter was born in Vermont, October 7, 1845. He was Sergeant-Major in the Thirteenth Regiment Vermont Volunteers. At twenty-two years of age, he was Official Reporter of the Vermont House of Representatives, and then Assistant Secretary of the Senate from 1869 to 1872, and Secretary of the Senate the following year. He moved to Chicago in 1873 where the legal firm of Hutchinson and Carpenter was formed. He also organized the First Regiment of Illinois Guards and was Captain of the Regiment. Carpenter married Fanny Brainard in 1875, and shortly thereafter moved to Denver, Colorado, where he pursued the legal profession. Carpenter was elected Colorado Senator and served two terms as president of the Senate. When candidates were proposed for election of mayor in Denver, 1891, a correspondent suggested Senator Carpenter "as a most fitting candidate for the mayor's chair. He is the man who made the first move toward purifying the office by removing from it the control of the police force. More than to any other one man, the fact that Denver has the system now is due to him."

This praiseworthy gentleman has his signature affixed to many documents relating to mining interests in Summit County, particularly Farncomb Hill. He was associated with Alfred Ware in the Ware-Carpenter Concentrating Mill. He was allied with Ware, Campion and Groves in mining ventures. Carpenter wrote a handbook on mining laws which was considerd an authority into the early part of the 20th century.

According to Breckenridge's *Daily Journal*, Tom's Baby was taken to Denver and delivered into Mason B. Carpenter's care. A few days later the newspaper reported that Carpenter said he "received it all right." Numerous periodicals spoke of Tom's Baby as the Ware-Carpenter nugget. Many other names have been associated with the nugget, but it seems the last specifically-named person to have Tom's Baby in his possession was Colonel Mason B. Carpenter. The *Mining Industry*, July 8, 1887, wrote:

Considerable work is being done on the Ware-Carpenter mines, and nuggets and retorts of great richness are being secured. They are also sluicing from some of the lode dumps and getting big pay. Outlook for Summit County is good this year.

July 15, 1887:

During the week there have been some fine specimens of native gold on exhibition at the office of M. B. Carpenter in the Tabor Block, in this city. They are from the Gold Flake lode, on Farncomb Hill, at Breckenridge.

Mason B. Carpenter had offices, for a number of years, in the Tabor Block, 16th and Larimer, listed as Mason Carpenter and William McBird. In 1900 the listing was Carpenter and McBird in the Ernest and Crammer Building, 17th and Curtis. From 1905-1911 Carpenter was listed alone at this last address.

Mason Carpenter died at the Chicago home of a daughter, Mrs. W. P. J. Dinsmoor, March 9, 1913. Another daughter, Mrs. Margaret Upley, Leadville, Colorado, was the only other survivor. Probate Courts at Chicago, Denver, Leadville and Breckenridge show no will recorded in his name. Mason B. Carpenter had Tom's Baby in Denver; what did he do with it?

JOHN F. CAMPION

To associate John F. Campion, the copiously wealthy banker and mining tycoon, with Tom's Baby would be a "natural." Tom Groves had some working capital; Colonel Ware and Colonel Carpenter had a measure of financial means—but John Campion had wealth. The names of Groves, Ware, Carpenter and Campion were yoked together in business interests, but they were not equally yoked together financially. It would be reasonable to conclude that Tom's Baby went into John Campion's gold collection, if anyone purchased it for a private collection. So it has been assumed by many people. But, to date, no one has come forth with definite proof of such a transaction by Tom Groves, Colonel Ware or Colonel Carpenter. Although Campion had a vital interest in the Colorado Historical Society and the Denver Museum of Natural History, there is no record that either institution received Tom's Baby. Campion's voluminous will, Denver County Probate Court, is a family document; provisions for institutions and benefactions had been made during his lifetime; the estate went to family members.

It is difficult to believe that the beauty and exhibition-value of Tom's Baby would not equal, if not far exceed, its intrinsic value. In that period of fabulous mining wealth, surely there were many who coveted it in a mining collection. Surely it would not be permitted to go the way of the melting-pot! Haunting questions arise, "Why didn't more publicity attend its supposed public appearances?" "Why were not more photographs taken of it in the many places it was supposed to have been?" "Why were the people so closely connected with it so silent on the subject?" "Why?—Why?—Why?"

"West Breckenridge" (foreground)—1870s. Note turbulent Blue River. (River was turned by Spalding party, fall of 1859.) Note road (foreground) going north to cemetery and Two-Mile Bridge. Courtesy—Denver Public Library Western Collection.

"West Breckenridge" (foreground)—1880s—before arrival of railroad. Courtesy—Denver Public Library Western Collection.

"West Breckenridge"—(foreground)—1890s—after coming of railroad. View taken from Shock Hill. Courtesy—Denver Public Library Western Collection.

Ware-Carpenter Concentrator—original building in foreground. Later additions were made and numerous changes of ownership and name. Courtesy—Mrs. Ted Fletcher.

Maddening Mystery

"August 7, 1882, the first train on the South Park ran into Breckenridge. During fall months of that year the road was extended to Dillon and Keystone, and the following year the line was constructed from Dickey to Leadville. But not till September, 1884, did the then Denver, South Park & Pacific operate regular trains between Dickey and Leadville. The tracks of the Denver & Rio Grande were completed to Dillon in the fall of 1882." (Summit County *Journal*, August 11, 1906—"24 Years Ago."') (Dickey sank in the depths of Dillon Reservoir.) Courtesy—Denver Public Library Western Collection.

Courtesy—Denver Public Library Western Collection.

Mason R. Carpenter.

Denver *Times,* March 11, 1891, page 2.
Courtesy—Denver Public Library Western Collection.

A large smelter was erected in the 70's nearly a half-mile north of town, alongside the old road to the cemetery. The high stack, made by expert stonemasons, stood for many years after the building was dismantled. To the old timers this high stack, or tower, as it was often called, was a relic of one-time prosperous days in Breckenridge. It was blown down in 1923 by the Tonopah Company, in charge of Joseph Hopkins, to allow No. 1 dredge to work the ground. The smelter was near the spot where Fort Mary B once stood.

The U. S. Geological Survey, 1908-1911, page 109, wrote: "Various attempts at smelting in the district were made prior to 1890, but of course were unsuccessful. The brick stack of the Wilson Smelter, built in 1880 and afterwards converted into the Breckenridge 20-stamp mill, marks the site of one of these enterprises just north of town. The mill has long since disappeared." (The mill was also known as Jones Mill.) (Note similarity to large chimney at Hall's South Park Salt Works, pictured in "Softly Beautiful" chapter.) Courtesy—Mrs. Minnie Thomas.

After turning the Blue River (1859) a road was constructed west of Blue River, continuing two miles and then crossing to east side of the river on "Two Mile Bridge." Pictured is the high smokestack of Wilson Smelter-Breckenridge Concentrator-Jones Mill . . . a landmark for many years as one travelled north from Breckenridge. Courtesy—Mrs. Ray McGinnis.

Breckenridge in the 1890's, showing Wilson Smelter-Breckenridge Concentrator-Jones Mill at far right. Courtesy—Mrs. Minnie Thomas.

Maddening Mystery

PART IV

(*Extravagant Claims*)

Extravagant claims have been made regarding Tom's Baby. Even as late as 1937 a Breckenridge author wrote, "Tom's Baby was the largest nugget in the world at its time of discovery." Two publications in 1970, with stories originating in Colorado, had similar statements. Poppycock!

Tom's Baby was not the world's largest nugget in 1887. It was far from being the world's largest nugget. Moreover, it was not the United States' first large nugget nor the United States' largest nugget. On this point, the most we can say is that it was Colorado's largest gold nugget. Even this point might be disputed.

Tom's Baby, when discovered, was reported as "fully one hundred and sixty ounces." Gold being weighed at troy weight, 12 oz. per pound, determined the weight of the nugget as 13-plus pounds. But we are told, "two pieces were broken off, leaving the nugget weighing 136 oz., 5dwt." (The dwt, or pennyweight, is 1/20 of a troy ounce.) Thus, Tom's Baby, minus the broken off pieces, weighed 11-plus pounds, troy weight. One pound troy is 0.822857 lb. avoirdupois. Thus 13-plus lb. troy would be about 11 lb. avoirdupois; 11 lb. troy would be about 9 lbs. avoirdupois.

There is no way of determining that large gold nuggets are .999 fine, except by the melting process; therefore, one has to distinguish between gross or net weight and value—before and after melting. For almost a century the price of gold was $20.67 per troy ounce; in 1934 it was raised to $35.

Tom's Baby has the reputation of being Colorado's largest gold nugget. We must, however, list other claims that have appeared in print. The Breckenridge *Daily Journal*, June 5,

1888, wrote: "The latest fifteen pound nugget from Farncomb Hill is the topic of the hour."

The Breckenridge *Democrat* amplified the item: "A NUGGET. One of the miners employed in the Bondholder tunnel yesterday took out a solid nugget of crystalized gold weighing within a few pennyweights of 15 pounds, which, when dressed and cleaned of all other substances, will tip the scales at about 13 pounds, and is worth about $3,000. The nugget was found in the face of the tunnel, at a point where the crevice widened somewhat, and very near to the point of contact between the slate and quartzite dyke that extends across the claim in a north-easterly and south-westerly direction."

An item in the *Mining Industry*, July 28, 1892, speaks of "two nuggets taken from Victoria property a couple years ago, weighing 13 and 15 pounds respectively."

The *United States Geological Survey*, 1911, *Geology and Ore of the Breckenridge District, Colorado,* by Frederick Leslie Ransome, says:

> The heaviest single mass ever obtained from Farncomb Hill came from a tunnel on the Gold Flake vein and was found by H. J. Litten (sic) and others about 1887. It was jocularly named "Tom's Baby" by the miners and is reported to have weighed 13 pounds.

The Summit County *Journal*, January 23, 1915, told of "another strike of free gold in the carbonate vein in the Dunkin Group, yielding $30,000 in three days. One piece, said to weigh eighteen pounds, and an eight pound chunk of gold, were exhibited at Engle's Bank for an hour or more and were admired by many of our town's people."

Reports of this kind have come from time to time, so we must say, *supposedly*, Tom's Baby was Colorado's largest nugget.

UNITED STATES NUGGETS

It comes as a surprise to many people to learn that North Carolina was one of the earliest and greatest producers of gold nuggets in the United States. While no authentic references can be obtained as to the actual discovery of gold in North Carolina, it is reported that gold mining was done in the State previous to the Revolutionary War. The State of North Carolina, Department of Conservation and Development, provided a bulletin, "Gold Deposits in North Carolina," published in 1936, which states: the first authentic record of gold being discovered in North Carolina is the finding of a 17-pound nugget on the Reed plantation in Cabarrus County, in 1799. The statement is taken from John H. Wheeler's "Historical Sketches of North Carolina, 1584 to 1851." The report continues:

The first piece of gold found at the Reed Mine, was in the year 1799, by Conrad Reed, a boy of about twelve years, a son of John Reed, the proprietor. The discovery was made in an accidental manner. The boy, above named, in company with a sister and younger brother, went to a small stream called Meadow Creek, on a Sabbath day, while their parents were at church, for the purpose of shooting fish with bow and arrow, and while engaged along the bank of the creek, Conrad saw a yellow substance shining in the water. He went in and picked it up, and found it to be some kind of metal, and carried it home. Mr. Reed examined it, but as gold was unknown in this part of the country at the time, he did not know what kind of metal it was: the piece was about the size of a small smoothing iron.

Mr. Reed carried the piece of metal to Concord, and showed it to a William Atkinson, a silversmith, but he not thinking of gold, was unable to say what kind of metal it was.

Mr. Reed kept the piece for several years on his house floor, to lay against the door to keep it from shutting. In the year 1802, he went to market at Fayetteville, and carried the piece of metal with him, and on showing it to a jeweller, the jeweller immediately told him it was gold, and requested Mr. Reed to leave the metal with him and said he would flux it. Mr. Reed left it, and returned in a short time, and on his return the jeweller showed him a large bar of gold, six or eight inches long. The jeweller then asked Mr. Reed what he would take for the bar. Mr. Reed, not knowing the value of gold, thought he would ask a "big price" and so he asked three dollars and fifty cents ($3.50)! The jeweller paid him his price.

After returning home, Mr. Reed examined and found gold in the surface along the creek. He then associated Frederick Kisor, James Love, and Martin Phifer with himself, and in the year 1803, they found a piece of gold in the branch that weighed twenty-eight pounds. Numerous pieces were found at this mine weighing from sixteen pounds down to the smallest particles. The whole surface along the creek for nearly a mile was very rich in gold.

The veins of this mine were discovered in the year 1831. They yielded a large quantity of gold. The veins are flint or quartz.

I do certify that the foregoing is a true statement of the discovery and history of this mine, as given by John Reed and his son Conrad, now both dead.

> January, 1848
> George Barnhardt

(Later reports add to the above statement that Mr. John Reed, after learning the real value of gold, went back to the jeweller and recovered about $3,000.)

Thomas Jefferson Hurley, in his booklet *Famous Gold Nuggets of the World*, 1900, listed nuggets from the North Carolina Reed Mine as follows: 28 pounds, 17 pounds, 16 pounds, 13¼ pounds, two 9 pounds, two 8 pounds, 5 pounds, 3½ pounds, two 2 pounds, and 1¾ pounds, and an even peck of gold the size of beans and peas. Hurley says, "The Reed Mining Claim holds the world's record for the greatest production of gold nuggets, both as to size and quantity."

The second greatest find in North Carolina, according to Hurley, was on the property of the United Goldfields Corporation, Albemarle, Stanley County. "This mine produced a 10½ pound nugget, one 8½ pounds, another 5¾ pounds, and one weighing 3 pounds, besides a dozen of about 1 pound, and a couple quarts of smaller pieces."

North Carolina is not to be overlooked when one studies gold-production and nugget-production in the United States.

Famous Gold Nuggets of the World (1900) was compiled by Thomas Jefferson Hurley, Member of American Institute of Mining Engineers and American Geographical Society. His book has disappeared from the shelves of Denver Public Library and Colorado School of Mines Library, Golden. One copy is in the basement vault of State Historical Society. The Historical Society provided the writer with a zeroxed copy of the sixty-four page booklet. Page twenty-six of the booklet has a blurred picture labeled:

"TOM'S BABY"

The Largest Gold Nugget Ever Found in Colorado
(156 Ounces or 13 Lbs. Troy.)
Taken From Gold Flake Mine on Farmcomb (sic) Hill,
Summit Co., Colorado
July 23, 1887.

Hurley gives only a short paragraph to Colorado's contribution of nuggets:

> Outside of California few nuggets of note have been found in any of the Pacific Coast States and territories. Colorado's biggest nugget, known as "Tom's Baby," weighing 156 ounces, or 13 pounds troy was taken from the Gold Flake mine on Farmcomb (sic) Hill, Summit County, Colorado, July 23d, 1887. We have been unable to get reliable information with reference to other great nuggets found in Colorado, but we learn that last January a man in Denver found a nugget worth about a dollar in the craw of a turkey gobbler. An effort to locate the ranch where the gobbler spent his happy boyhood days failed, and that placer ground, so far as known, is still to be discovered.

California is on the top of the list for the largest nugget in the United States. There were many good-sized nuggets produced by California. The "Second Report of the State Minerologist, California," 1882, tells of the first specimen of gold, remarkable for its size:

> Late in the summer of 1848, a young soldier of Stevenson's regiment, while riding along the Mokelumne River, stopped to get a drink from a stream, and discovered a gold nugget, weighing between twenty and twenty-five pounds. He hastened to San Francisco and placed his prize in the hands of Colonel Mason for safety, who sent it by General Beale to the Eastern States, the exhibition of which in New York fanned the smouldering flame, and the na-

tion began to realize the importance of newly acquired California.

The Report continues:

> In California, November, 1854, a mass of gold was found on Carson Hill, Calaveras County, which weighed 195 pounds troy weight, or 2,340 troy ounces, the value of which, assuming the gold to be .900 fine, was $43,534. This is the largest piece of gold ever found in the State. Several other nuggets, weighing from six to seven pounds, were found at the same locality.

The Carson Hill nugget has been described as resembling the branch of a tree, four to five feet long and five inches in diameter. Not only was it California's largest nugget, but it holds the record of United States' largest gold nugget. The listing of California's nuggets of size would include more than a dozen larger than Tom's Baby, ranging from 1,596 troy oz. to 186 troy oz., thus surpassing Tom's Baby of 160 troy ounces.

Prize nuggets have been found in a few other states. Nevada produced the Osceola nugget of 24 pounds. Montana's nugget, found at Snow Shoe Gulch, Little Blackfoot River, valued at $3,356, was a trifle larger than Tom's Baby. Alaska is reported to have had an 182 oz. nugget, valued at $3,367.

WORLD'S LARGEST NUGGET

Australia lists the "Welcome Stranger" nugget as its largest and the world's largest, having a gross weight of 2,520 oz., or 210 troy pounds. It had a net weight of 2,284 oz., 190 troy pounds. (Some have claimed Carson Hill nugget the world's largest, but the comparison was made between 2,284 oz. net weight against 2,340 oz. gross weight.)

There is another sometimes spoken of as Australia's largest nugget and the largest nugget the world has ever known. It was found, October 19, 1872, at Hill End, New South Wales, Australia, by Messrs. H. L. Byer and B. O. Holtermann, and goes by the name of Holtermann nugget. Gross weight of the "nugget" was 7,560 ounces, or 630 troy pounds. Measurements were 4 foot-9 inches in height, 2 foot-2 inches in width, and an average 4 inches in thickness. The Holtermann nugget is omitted from Australia's listing of larger gold nuggets, "because technically speaking it was not a nugget, but a mass of gold *in situ* in reef." When reduced, the gold content was about 3,000 ounces, or 250 troy pounds. The gold content exceeded Carson Hill nugget and Welcome Stranger, but "technically" it is not considered a nugget—it is spoken of as a "mass of gold," "conglomerate," "a slab of gold." Its gold content was the greatest.

Welcome Stranger nugget is almost universally known as the World's Largest Nugget. Found in Victoria, Australia, February 15, 1869, it measured "about 21 inches in length and 10 inches in thickness, and was about 98.66% pure gold—gross weight 2,520 oz., net weight 2,284 oz.

Poor Tom's Baby is far outclassed as the world's largest nugget—now, or at the time of its discovery. And, furthermore, it is eliminated as United States' largest nugget. About the best we can give is a 99 44/100% rating of being Colorado's largest nugget.

SIZE OF TOM'S BABY

What was the size of Tom's Baby? Here, again, we are stymied; there seems to be no known description as to height, width, thickness. Trying to estimate its size by comparison with other nuggets is difficult. Nuggets, tossed and shuffled for ages in stream beds, tend to have all loose particles removed, and often are described as beans, peas, pigeon eggs, goose eggs, boulders. Such nuggets cannot be equated with nuggets of loose composition. The famous nuggets of Farncomb Hill were of crystallized gold, wire and leaf, gathered together in beautiful design and various sizes. (Some have described Tom's Baby as looking like a "head of lettuce.") "It is estimated that nuggets of the crystallized gold type would have dimensions greater than a solid, well-rounded nugget—possibly as much as 50% greater size." Tom's Baby came from Farncomb Hill and supposedly belonged to that intricate and beautiful family of crystallized gold. When found, its gross weight was 160 ounces; after its "face-washing" and pieces broken off, it was 135 ounces.

Gold is heavy. Many finders of nuggets sensed gold immediately by the weight of the object. An extraordinary weight in the ore pile was suspicious and hopeful. A seven-pound (84 troy oz.) solid, boulder-shaped nugget is pictured in Hurley's *Famous Gold Nuggets* as resting easily in the palm of a hand. Tom's Baby was about twice this weight.

Hurley's *Famous Gold Nuggets of the World* tells the story of Harry Ellis and wife in Alpine County, California. They had come to California for the husband's serious lung trouble, eking out a living on a small ranch. Grizzled miners stopped by the ranch for food and lodging. One miner, ill for several weeks, was nursed back to health. For recompense, the miner told of a certain canyon in the foothills where his benefactors could profit in the gold-bearing gravel.

For days the young husband and wife trudged through the gulches, seeking gold—but to no avail. They abandoned the search and returned to their ranch. One afternoon, as Mrs. Ellis was driving home the family cow, she was seeking stones to throw for the amusement of the dog. She saw, in the coarse gravel, a dark, dull yellow stone and picked it up.

"I knew from the moment I picked it up," says she, "that I had found gold, because it was so heavy, but as I had never seen a real nugget, I was afraid my husband would laugh at me."

Mrs. Ellis got $2,250 for the find. Based on the gold rate of the time, it probably weighed about 108 oz., or 9 pounds troy. It is still kept for exhibition purposes. It is phenomenally clear and the size of a croquet ball, but very rough and battered by rolling and tumbling in water for ages.

The 17-pound nugget, found on the North Carolina Reed plantation, was described as "about the size of a small smoothing iron." The "smoothing iron" was the old-fashioned, heavy iron used for ironing clothes. A smoothing-iron can easily rest on the palm of a hand. Descriptions of nuggets, comparable to Tom's Baby in weight, put us in the realm of "a croquet ball" or "a small smoothing-iron." One, however, has to keep in mind the nugget formations of Farncomb Hill, increasing the size beyond the solid nugget.

One might say Tom's Baby was a good handful of baby.

"Welcome Stranger"'—Found in Moliagul, Victoria, Australia, February 15, 1869. Gross Weight: 2520 Ounces; 210 Troy Pounds. Net Weight: 2284 Ounces; 190 Troy Pounds. Courtesy—La Trobe Collection, State Library of Victoria. (Not to be reproduced without permission. Permission granted May 18, 1971 for publication in *Blasted Beloved Breckenridge* by T. A. Kealy, Principal Librarian.

THE WELCOME STRANGER NUGGET.
Valued at £9,534.

Courtesy—State Library of Victoria, Australia. Permission granted *Blasted Beloved Breckenridge* to reproduce.

"HOLTERMANN'S CONGLOMERATE—Found at Mill End, New South Wales, Australia, by Messrs. H. L. Byer and B. O. Holtermann, October 19, 1872. 4-foot, 9-inches high; 2-foot, 2-inches wide; 4-inches average thickness. Gross Weight: 7,560 Ounces, 630 Troy Pounds; Net Weight: 3,000 ounces, 250 Troy Pounds. Picture: From the original in the Mitchell Library, Sydney, Australia. (Not to be reproduced without permission and payment of $10 fee. Payment made and permission granted.)

WORLD'S LARGEST MASS OF GOLD
54 inches in height; 5½ inches thick.

Carson Hill Nugget
2340 ounces,
value $77,220

The author owns the only model that was ever
made of this nugget, and the above picture was
taken from this model.

This picture appears, page 5, in John Gaarden's *Gold Nuggets of the World*, Gaarden Publishing Company, Hollywood, California, 1940. Its claim of "World's Largest Mass of Gold" is disputed—also its $77,220 value. The "'Second Report of the State Mineralogist"—'1882—(California) put the value $43,534, "assuming the gold to be .900 fine." Quintin Aune, Geologist, California Division of Mines and Geology, gave the information: "Inasmuch as the 2,340 ounce figure for the Carson Hill 'nugget' rounds off to 195 pounds (troy), it is probably the rough weight of the raw nugget, including some naturally alloyed silver and minor impurities. Very few nuggets weighing over about 200 ounces troy were ever preserved. (We have one of that size on display in our San Francisco mineral museum.) The Carson Hill mass of gold is no exception."

"TOM'S BABY."

The Largest Gold Nugget Ever Found in Colorado—(156 Ounces or 13 Lbs. Troy.) Taken From Gold Flake Mine on Farmcomb Hill, Summit Co., Colorado, July 23, 1887.

Thomas Jefferson Hurley—*Famous Gold Nuggets of the World*—1900 page 26.

Gold Nugget from Atlin Lake District, British Columbia.

The Atlin Lake District, British Columbia, gold nugget (Hurley's *Famous Gold Nuggets of the World,* page 14) weighed 84 ounces (7 Troy pounds). The 17-pound (204 ounces) nugget from North Carolina Reed Plantation, was described as the size of a "smoothing iron." The Ellis, Alpine County, California, nugget—probably 108 ounces (9 pounds Troy) was likened to a "croquet ball" in size and shape. All fit easily into the palm of a hand.

Maddening Mystery

TOM'S BABY

PART V

(Romanticizing Tom's Baby)

Tom's Baby has been romanticized to the extent of obscuring reality. We cannot give him all that has been claimed for him. But we do know he was an extraordinarily handsome tyke. We know that he has warmed the hearts of many proud Coloradans. He has been the inspiration of many a lonely prospector grubbing the hills and gulches of the Rocky Mountains. Many have envied Tom Groves, and would be mighty pleased to have a baby like that one. Hearts have been saddened for the "lost baby." Hope lives on that Colorado will yet see his sunny face and snuggle him to heart again. You see—"Tom's Baby" is Colorado's Baby—and we love him.

Two other stories have attached themselves to Tom's Baby and we must include them. One is strange; the other is pathetic.

The Denver *Post*, July 5, 1965, ran a story entitled "Fabulous Archie Still Has the Golden Touch," written by John Kobish:

An inmate of the Colorado Penitentiary with a genius for making phony crystallized gold has created what is believed to be an almost perfect replica of the largest specimen every found in Colorado.

Archie Virgil Willson, 43, serving 2 to 6 years for confidence game, has duplicated "Tom's Baby," a 167 ounce nugget found in 1887 near Breckenridge.

Willson, whose fake gold has fooled even some jewelry experts, made the replica in his spare time at the prison.

Safety Manager Al Capra, the convict's defense attorney, says Willson has turned down an offer of $10,000 for the specimen.

The story goes on to say that Willson is willing to rent the nugget for display, and that three Denver banks have asked to display it. The "nugget" was created out of rock, lead, and 18-karat gold leaf—but the process kept secret. In order to keep his secret from other inmates, he often mixed his compounds in bed, under blankets. Archie secured his supplies from a Denver Art Supply firm, via prison officials. "He used photographs of the original to work from, read all the material about Tom's Baby he could find, even contacting the heirs of Lytton for descriptions of the nugget." "Willson has built a glass-enclosed box and leather carrying case for the imitation." "Willson began selling the phony gold in 1962, and in a year had netted $5,000 from 36 sales all over the West. His gold-making and selling activity landed him in prison. He is eligible for parole and should be released from prison shortly, Capra said. Archie has determined to put his art to use in practical and legitimate ventures."

The estimated value of Tom's Baby, 160 ounces, 1887, at .999 fine, $20.67 per ounce, would have been $3,211.20. At the 1934 rate, $35.00, it would have been $5,600. Usually, untested nuggets were reckoned at .900 fine. Archie's $10,000 offer far exceeded the real value of Tom's Baby.

The second story in the Tom's Baby saga has pathetic overtones—the story of Tom Wintermute.

The Summit County *Journal*, April 29, 1955, had an article entitled, "Did Tom Wintermute Take Fabulous Tom's Baby East?" The *Journal* goes on to say, "The story was inspired by E. C. Peabody, when he unearthed some interesting clues as to the probable whereabouts of the fabulous nugget, known as Tom's Baby, the present whereabouts of which is shrouded in mystery. An advertisement from the Denver *Post* in 1931 announced the 43rd Anniversary

Sale at A. T. Lewis & Son, at 16th and Stout, Denver." Part of the advertisement is as follows:

1888-1931
Tom Wintermute's "Baby"
A Magnificent Gold Nugget—
A 14-Pound Gold Nugget
12 Pounds Of It Pure Gold!

This amazing piece of news was stirring the little town of Breckenridge when A. T. Lewis moved from Breckenridge to open his first store in Denver. It was news that spread to Eastern cities and interested moneyed men of New York, Philadelphia and Boston in the mining industry of Colorado. This gold nugget was sold for $3,500 and was exhibited in Wall Street. Tom's Baby played its important part in bringing capital and people to the State.

"It is Mr. Peabody's recollection," the *Journal* states, "that Tom Wintermute had a bank in Breckenridge."

Yes, Tom Wintermute did have a bank in Breckenridge, on Main Street, next to the Grand Army of the Republic Hall.

Tom Wintermute was a promising and highly-respected young man in Breckenridge in the mid-eighties. Summit County *Journal*, March 28, 1885, tells us:

> One of the most notable weddings of the camp was celebrated Tuesday evening, **Mr.** Thomas Wintermute and Miss Clara Remine entered life's journey together. A large attendance of our townspeople were at the Remine mansion to witness the ceremony. The newly-wedded pair were the recipients of many, various and costly presents from their many friends.

The Remine family came to Breckenridge from Central City. Clara was born in Central City, and the move to Breckenridge came in the 1860s when she was a small girl. She was one of the most popular young ladies of Breckenridge. The Frisco Graff's Opera House opened February 29, 1882, with the presentation of a one-act Comedietta—"A Happy Pair" and a Farce—"Turn Him Out." A Frisco Dramatic Society was organized, and Miss Clara Remine, of Breckenridge, played prominent parts in the performances.

Fifteen months after the marriage the *Journal* noted, "Thomas Wintermute purchased the old Miller safe from Whyte's Restaurant. Mr. Wintermute can make good use of it in his new business." At the same time the Wintermutes

were about to welcome their first-born, but Mrs. Wintermute's health was in precarious condition. June 24th, 1886, the *Journal* stated: "Mrs. Wintermute's condition was reported as much improved today." A short time later complications set in, and Dr. Lathrop was called from Denver and gave ten days complete attention to Mrs. Wintermute. Health seemed to be returning and Dr. Lathrop went back to Denver. July 31st, the *Journal* reported, "As we go to press, Mrs. Thomas Wintermute is lying in a very critical condition; the chances are against her recovery." August 2nd *Journal* told the sad news:

> DIED: Wintermute, on Sunday morning, August 1st, at 5 o'clock, Mrs. Clara Wintermute, aged 24 years. Yesterday morning at the old family residence on Main Street, Mrs. Thomas Wintermute, after a lingering illness, breathed her last. A year ago last March her marriage with Mr. Thomas Wintermute was looked upon as the beginning of a promising, and all hoped for, long married life. But man proposes, God disposes. About seven weeks ago she gave birth to her first-born, a promising little girl, but she was never to rise again and take her place among her friends. A large concourse of friends gathered at the desolate home to pay respects to the departed.

It was a year later, July 23, 1887, that Tom's Baby was discovered. In the July 25th newspaper, that told Tom's Baby news, was also an item stating that the "new bank building is to have an elegantly tiled floor laid in a few days." April 4, 1888, the Breckenridge *Daily Journal* announced:

AN ELEGANT WORK OF ART

> Mr. Thomas S. Wintermute has suspended in his fine bank parlor an elegant picture, a likeness of his deceased wife. The picture was enlarged from an excellent photographic likeness, and the artist certainly caught the inspiration of the sun's rays in the transfer, for the reproduced picture is quite as good a likeness as the photo. The old acquaintances of the late Mrs. Wintermute should call and see the picture.

April 21st, another newspaper item appeared, regarding Thomas Wintermute:

> Mr. Thomas Wintermute returned from Denver by Tuesday morning's train. During his visit to the State Capitol, Mr. Wintermute in-

dulged in a drive behind a two thirty nag, which ended in himself and companion being unceremoniously landed in the street, the injurious effects of which are plainly visible in T. W.'s disfigured countenance. He will not sit for a portrait for some days to come.

A month later there was shocking news:

A BANKER DERANGED

Yesterday our community was somewhat startled by the actions of Thomas Wintermute, the local banker. In the morning he seemed to be drinking more than usual, and in the afternoon he entered the procession to the cemetery with the Kiowas Tribe of Redmen. On the way to the grounds he retired to the willows beside th road and took several drinks from a bottle of liquor, and at the point of a cocked pistol of large size ordered Mr. Crawford of the firm of Baker and Crawford to stop and take a drink. He stopped, but did not drink. At the cemetery he visited the grave of his late wife, and kneeling down inserted the muzzle of the pistol in his mouth as if with the intention of suiciding. Mr. John Roby and family being there, Mr. Roby spoke to him, saying, "Tom, don't do that." He withdrew the weapon and fired three shots in the air. Marshal Reeder, hearing the shots, went to the spot to see what was the trouble. On his approach Wintermute covered him with his gun and declared he would shoot him if he came nearer. As the marshal was unarmed, and noticing a wild look in the man's eyes, he used only kind words and Wintermute left for town. It afterwards transpired that he had punched Judge Richardson in the abdomen with the same gun before starting in the procession. After returning to town, during the evening, he swallowed a dose of morphine, and when noticed was fast yielding to its fatal influence. Friendly hands were called to the rescue and from ten o'clock until daylight the insensible form was kept in action. After daylight he was brought to the Denver Hotel and has been receiving the constant attention of friends. Consciousness returned about six o'clock, but fears for the result are still entertained.

It will be remembered that a few weeks ago he met with a severe accident while in Denver, and some of his most intimate friends have noticed that in many things he has been a little off ever since. His mother has been telegraphed and is expected here as soon as cars can bring her.

Came the news:

Tuesday afternoon, June 5th, at about six o'clock, Thomas S. Wintermute, who had been failing all day, breathed his last, in the 26th year of his age. His remains were at once transferred to the Fireman's Hall and were taken in charge by the Kiowas Tribe of I. O. O. R. M. The funeral took place Thursday afternoon at two o'clock from the G. A. R. Hall. Funeral obsequies were conducted under the direction of the State Officers of the I.O.O.R.M. who were present for that purpose.

Summit County *Journal,* June 13, 1888:

The friends of the late Thomas Wintermute are pleased to learn that the examination of the deceased banker's accounts at the bank have proven everything straight as a string, with more funds in the bank by a trifle than the accounts called for—whatever faults he may have had, Mr. Wintermute was a strict businessman.

If Tom Wintermute played a part in the Tom's Baby story, it would have been during the last ten hectic months of the young banker's life. There is no valid information to that effect. Tom Wintermute's concern seems to have been centered on his own baby and his departed wife. In Breckenridge's Valley Brook Cemetery, southeast corner, is a small monument with a cross mounted on a pedestal. On it is inscribed, "WINTERMUTE, Clara Remine 1863-1886, Thomas Stinson 1863-1888." In springtime anemones garland the graves. Nearby Cucumber Creek gurgles, splashes, and keeps up an age-long requiem.

In those peaceful surroundings, we ask ourselves—"Are all lips now quieted that could tell the answer to the mystery, What happened to Tom's Baby?"

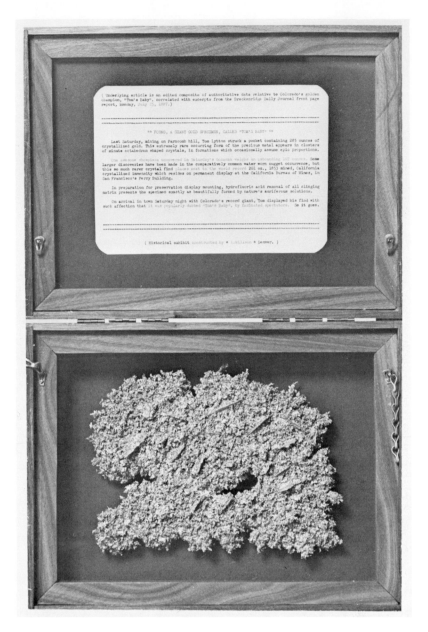

Archie Willson's Imitation Gold
Courtesy—Photo-Graphics Internationale, Arvada, Colorado

Thomas-Clara Wintermute grave—Breckenridge Valley Brook Cemetery.

Maddening Mystery

TOM'S BABY

PART VI

The writer intended to conclude the narrative of Tom's Baby with the story of Tom Wintermute. Leave it there—an unsolved mystery—the baby gone forever. But Tom's Baby is an insistent kid. He's lost. And he keeps crying to be found. You can't stop hunting for a crying child that wants to found.

What about City Park Museum safety deposit vault in United Bank of Denver? Could it be that Tom's Baby *is* languishing there? What about Archie Willson's phony gold? Where did he get his information for making a phony Tom's Baby? How reliable was his information? What about an 1898 item in the Summit County *Journal* that spoke of a "good half-tone engraving of Tom's Baby?" Tom Wintermute's sad story didn't quiet Tom's Baby.

Came a sudden, unexpected thought. Perhaps the different specimens at City Park Museum are dissected parts of Tom's Baby. The largest specimen seemed to bear resemblance in height and shape to the most common picture of Tom's Baby. Could this be the answer? Were they the skeletal remains of Tom's Baby after gangue had been removed?

More trips were made to City Park Museum to study the nuggets. If only one could see the reverse side of the largest specimen, perhaps it would have some identifying features that would link it with the most common picture of Tom's Baby. But you don't ask the Museum to unlock that valuable display so you can study it more closely.

From the beginning of the research, Jack Murphy, Curator of Geology at City Park Museum of Natural History, took an active interest in Tom's Baby. In the summer of 1970 he made the surprise announcement: "We're planning to remove the gold collection, weigh it, photograph it and properly catalogue it; would you like to be present when we do it?" The writer was there at the appointed moment. And had his hand photographed, holding the largest nugget of the Campion Collection!

The measurements of the largest nugget are approximately six inches wide and seven inches high. Its weight is 17.03 ounces, as converted from 529.6 grams. Both sides were photographed and appear in these pages. It was a sight to be long remembered—this outstanding specimen of Farncomb Hill gold, glistening and sparkling under bright photographic lights.

A plaque, describing the John Campion crystallized gold at City Park Museum, reads: "This unique collection of gold was obtained from Farncomb Hill, near Breckenridge, Colorado. The gold was found imbedded in a matrix of iron oxide, which has been removed by hydrochloric acid, leaving the gold in the form in which it was originally deposited from the auriferous solutions."

Tom's Baby received a "face-washing" at the time of its discovery. Even in the gentle cleansing a few pieces separated from the nugget, reducing it from 160 to 136 troy ounces. Conceivably, the baby got a thorough bath at a later date in hydrochloric acid. If so, pieces like the Campion collection could have been the result.

Gold is malleable—adaptable, yielding, ductile. It can be hammered, pounded, or pressed into various shapes without breaking, or returned to its original shape. Gold, silver, copper and tin are malleable; they can be beaten into thin sheets. It is possible for a number of pieces to come together into a cluster, forming a large "nugget." It is just as possible for the "nugget" to be separated and divided into a number of "nuggets." This could have been the fate of Tom's Baby.

Geologists have their definition of a true nugget—"a small mass of metal in place such as gold or silver, found free in nature. The term is restricted to pieces of some size, not mere 'colors' or minute particles. Fragments and lumps of vein-gold are not called 'nuggets' for the idea of alluvial origin is implicit." (*A Dictionary of Mining, Mineral and Related Terms—Department of the Interior Bureau of Mines.*)

There are geologists who claim that Tom's Baby was not a true nugget, according to definition. It was a cluster of crystallized gold pieces. Popularly, is it known as a "nugget." Ralph H. King, Chief of Information Service of Montana Bureau of Mines and Geology, after seeing a picture of Tom's Baby, wrote: "Most gold nuggets, as recovered from placer deposits, have been rolled and tumbled and battered by other rocks to the extent that the soft gold is rounded. Your photographs show a "nugget" that seems remarkably angular and delicate. It certainly had not been transported far nor been long subjected to stream action. Might it have been taken directly from a vein? Gold in a calcite vein can be readily cleansed with hydrochloric acid to remove the gangue."

And what about Archie Willson's phony "Tom's Baby?" Denver's former Safety Manager, Al Capra, was Archie Willson's defense attorney. Jack Brockman, attorney, was Capra's assistant at the time. Brockman did much of the "leg work"—investigating for the trial that put Archie behind Canon City prison bars. A letter to Attorney Capra received this answer:

Archie sold his reproduction because of financial distress. It has been valued at various prices, ranging from $10,000 to $20,000. It is being stored at Security Title Company, 1597 Wadsworth Boulevard in Denver. The owner has posted a $25,000 bond and the Security people are also heavily bonded. The reproduced nugget may be viewed upon making arrangements with Vice-President Jack W. Brockman of Security Title Company.

The owner of reproduced "Tom's Baby" is willing to negotiate for its sale in case any of your acquaintances are interested.

Arrangements were made with Jack Brockman of Security Title Company to view Archie Willson's phony "Tom's Baby." Another unexpected happening occurred. The writer was photographed holding Archie Willson's creation.

Archie Willson's gold-making was the subject of a story that appeared in *Inside Detective Magazine*. The story is entitled "I'm the Man Who Makes Gold." Archie related in the story:

I arrived in Colorado in the spring of 1963 as a tourist. The first thing I did was to head for Colorado's famous museum at Denver. I wanted to study Colorado's supply of gold products, to familiarize myself with the local product.

In the museum display was the John Campion gold collection—all crystallized gold. A nugget is common compared to crystallized gold. And I have the process to make this!

Archie's downfall came when he created two nuggets exactly alike and by coincidence they came into the hands of two dealers in neighboring towns. The dealers compared the specimens and had doubts that two nuggets could be marked identically. When the nuggets were drilled and tested, Archie landed in jail.

Now comes more mystery to the "Tom's Baby" story. Two pictures appeared, both claiming to be "Tom's Baby." One could easily be likened to the "head of lettuce" Tom's Baby; the other looks like a rough-sided slab of coal. One has the delicate features of the famous Farncomb Hill crystallized gold; the other (not clearly photographed) has the gaunt grace of a chunk of broken cement. The two pictures are widely different. One appears a masterpiece; the other, a clod. Which one *is* "Tom's Baby?"

Summit County *Journal*, January 15, 1898, printed the following: "In the January 6th issue of the *Mining Industry and Review* there appeared a good half-tone engraving of the "Tom's Baby" gold nugget, which was taken out of the Gold Flake Mine (one of the present Wapiti company's properties): it weighed 136 ounces after being cleaned and after considerable loose gold was taken from it. It is the largest nugget of gold ever mined in Colorado. A copy of the paper should be secured and sent to your friends who have the Klondike fever, it might effect a cure. Editor Wynkoop has always shown a kindly interest in Summit County and his generosity in having the engraving made should be appreciated."

Copies of the January 6, 1898, *Mining Industry and Review* were not available at Denver Public Library, State Historical Society, Colorado University Library, nor the Colorado School of Mines Library. The *Union List of Serials* reported that copies were in New York Public Library and Chicago Public Library. The New York Public Library provided the picture and copy.

Mining Industry and Review provides us with our earliest dated picture of Tom's Baby. Evidently it was the source material of *Mining Reporter* and Hurley's *Famous Gold Nuggets of the World*. *Mining Reporter* misspelled Farncomb (Farmcomb), and Hurley followed suit. Hurley was probably the source material for Archie Willson and his phony gold "Tom's Baby" nugget.

Archie Willson was not the only one to take a hungering look at the Campion Collection of crystallized gold at City Park Museum. The Summit County *Journal*, March 3, 1923, ran a story, "Museum Gold Again Target of Burglars." (Most of the story was reprinted from the Denver *Post*.):

A plot to attempt to steal the gold at the museum in Denver was nipped in the bud last Saturday. Most of the gold came from Farncomb Hill, near Breckenridge. This is considered the greatest collection of crystallized gold in the world, most of it being donated to the Museum by the late John F. Campion.

In reviewing the attempted robbery, the following is the account in the Denver *Post*:

A carefully-formulated plot to break into the Colorado Museum of Natural History at City Park, knock out the night watchman, and blow open a safe containing a gold ore exhibit valued at more than $100,000 was frustrated Friday night by the arrest of three men, the police announced Saturday.

C. E. McClaine, 25 years old, of 3306 Lawrence Street, was in an automobile containing drills, ropes, heavy comforters and other paraphernalia for a big safe-blowing job when he was picked up by detectives near his home, according to Chief of Police Williams and Captain of Detectives Rinker.

"McClaine is an ex-convict," Rinker said. "Bullock is widely known as 'Diamond Blackie.' Buxton is called 'Slim' among a large circle of acquaintances. They had all plans made to break into the museum, knock out the night watchman and then drill into the safe containing gold leaf, gold ore and other valuable exhibits. They also had an eye on some radium ore."

According to the police, the robbery was to be attempted Saturday night. The men planned to make another inspection of the museum and surroundings Friday night, it is alleged. They already had made several visits there and mapped out the ground.

The plot is declared to have been the most complete and ambitious since the holdup of the federal reserve bank car in front of the mint and the theft of $200,000 in $5 bills.

A tip to Chief Williams revealed the scheme. Some persons, whose identity the police are concealing, heard the plotters making their plans and notified the chief. The arrest of McClaine kept him from keeping an appointment with the other two men at Sixteenth and Larimer Streets, Rinker said.

Bullock, Diamond Blackie, is declared by Rinker to have conceived the idea of stealing the gold exhibit, which is one of the largest in the United States and was donated to the museum by John F. Campion.

According to the captain of detectives, Diamond Blackie came through Denver last summer with a small circus and on a visit to the museum noticed the gold ore. He and Buxton are alleged to have come to Denver recently from Salt Lake City to carry out the robbery plot, which has been germinating in Bullock's mind for months.

"If they had tried to pull off any such robbery they would have run into a lot of trouble they apparently did not anticipate," said J. D. Figgins, museum superintendent, Saturday. "There is a system of burglar alarms which would have instantly communicated a signal of the danger to the city hall and the police station. Moreover, the safe is a guaranteed twenty-four hour one, that yeggs would find quite a problem. There isn't just one night watchman, either. There are two guards on duty all night and an electric light floods the exterior of the vault at all times."

Several years ago some nuggets were stolen from a case at the museum, but this is said to be the first time a plot to steal the entire exhibit ever was uncovered. Several scintelloscopes of radium were stolen nine years ago.

Maddening Mystery

Police are endeavoring to get more details of the plot which they alleged the trio under arrest admit in general outline.

Attempts to get the Museum's safety deposit vault opened at Denver United Bank meets with no more success than Diamond Blackie's efforts at the gold collection. Mrs. Louisa Arps was asking for its opening in 1954-1955, but was unsuccessful in her endeavors. The writer's requests, 1970-1971, met with the same result. If Tom's Baby is "languishing" in City Park Museum's safety deposit vault, it has had a long, undisturbed sleep.

What happened to "Tom's Baby?" Is he alive; does he exist? Is he far away; is he near at hand? Which of the two pictures shows the real "Tom's Baby?" Jack Brockman says, "Never underestimate a con man; he always researches his subject thoroughly." There's a good imitation "Tom's Baby" around. Better drill and test before buying.

"Tom's Baby" remains Breckenridge's baffling mystery.

Front view of the largest crystallized gold nugget of the John F. Campion gold collection at Denver City Park Museum of Natural History. Courtesy—Denver Museum of Natural History; photography by Robert R. Wright, Curator of Photography. (Writer present when photographs were taken—summer of 1970.)

Reverse side of largest John F. Campion gold nugget on display—Denver Museum of Natural History.

Maddening Mystery

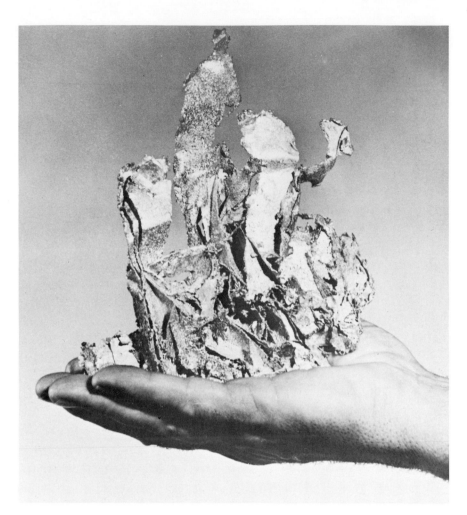

Writer's hand holding the largest crystallized gold nugget of the famous John F. Campion gold collection at Denver's City Park Museum of Natural History. Courtesy—Denver Museum of Natural History; photography by Robert R. Wright, Curator of Photography.

Writer holding Archie Willson's phony "Tom's Baby." Permission granted by Jack Brockman, Vice-President of Security Title Company, Wadsworth Avenue, Denver. Courtesy—Photo-Graphics Internationale, Arvada, Colorado.

The picture most commonly portrayed as "Tom's Baby" (before face-washing, while appendages were attached). Courtesy—Denver Public Library Western Collection.

"TOM'S BABY"
—136 OZ. 5DWTS.

Picture of "Tom's Baby" as it frequently appears in newspapers, magazines and pamphlets. (Some pictures of "Tom's Baby" are shown, minus the two base appendages.) Courtesy—Summit County *Journal*.

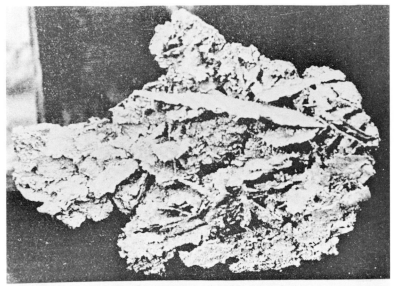

A SUMMIT COUNTY GOLD NUGGET, WEIGHT, 26 OUNCES.

Mining Reporter Magazine, Vol. 40, #25, Dec. 21, 1889, p. 370: This 26 ounce nugget ranks with McNaulty Nugget, found a number of years earlier than "Tom's Baby." McNaulty nugget found at McNaulty's Gulch, Upper Ten Mile, and valued at $475. At current rate, $20.67 per ounce, this nugget had $537.42 value, depending on .999 purity. Nugget much smaller than "Tom's Baby." Courtesy—Denver Public Library Western Collection.

A SUMMIT COUNTY (COLORADO) NUGGET.

This picture appears in *"Secrets of the Rocks"*—S. M. Frazier-Denver-1907. It is a perpendicular reproduction of "A Summit County Gold Nugget, Weight, 26 Ounces." Its similarity to the generally believed "Tom's Baby"—minus appendages—is evident. Sometimes it is labeled "Tom's Baby." Courtesy—Denver Public Library Western Collection.

"TOM'S BABY."

The Largest Gold Nugget Ever Found in Colorado (156 Ounces or 13 Lbs. Troy. Taken From Gold Flake Mine on Farmcomb Hill. Summit Co. Colorado July 23, 1887.

A second "Tom's Baby" (different in appearance and delicacy) makes appearance in publications. First discovered by writer in Thomas J. Hurley's *Famous Gold Nuggets of the World*—1900—page 26. Writer concluded it an imposter—far different from the well-known, generally accepted "Tom's Baby." Further research brought disturbing discoveries. (Note the spelling of "Farmcomb"-sic-for "Farncomb." Courtesy—Library State Historical Society of Colorado.

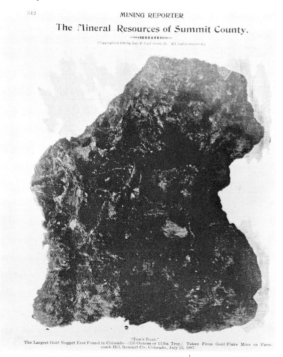

Picture appeared in a publication earlier than Hurley's *Famous Gold Nuggets of the World*"—*Mining Reporter* Magazine, Vol. 40, #23, Dec. 7, 1899, page 342. "Farncomb" is misspelled "Farmcomb." Appears to be Hurley's information and picture source. Courtesy—Denver Public Library Western Collection.

ADDENDUM

Quest for "Tom's Baby" has been related, step by step, as it unfolded over a period of five years; all leads were painstakingly researched. The writer hoped the nugget most commonly believed to be Tom's Baby was the real one. It appeared far more delicate of feature. Final research, however, pointed to the one that had lesser appeal. The earliest-dated picture didn't favor the writer's choice.

Bessie (Ware) Van Nostrand provided the photograph for Editor Wynkoop's engraving in the January 6, 1898, *Mining Industry and Review*. We could not dismiss Bessie (Ware) Van Nostrand lightly. Surely her information was firsthand. She was a friend of Tom Groves. Her father built the Ware-Carpenter Concentrator. Ware and Carpenter owned and leased the mine where "Tom's Baby" was found by Groves and Lytton. Ware and Carpenter had royalty rights on all gold discoveries from their leases. At least for a brief time the nugget was in possession of both Ware and Carpenter. Shortly after it was found the nugget was called the Ware-Carpenter nugget. Bessie's photograph, linked to the earliest-discovered picture of Tom's Baby, added authority. No other authenticated photograph, from 1887 to 1898, came to light. Evidence tightened; here the story seemed destined to end.

Then came startling news—the Museum of Natural History opened its box in United Bank of Denver, December 21, 1971. Gold nuggets *were* in the box stored in the safety-deposit vaults. It was not a metal safety-deposit box, but a wooden, cube-shaped box, 24 x 24 x 24 inches. Jack Murphy, Curator of Geology, Denver Museum of Natural History, wrote to the author: "The specimen boxes are all there, neatly packed in paper and individual specimen boxes, and they include quite a range in size. Most of the pieces are small. However, there are two large specimens that are of interest. One is quite similar to the largest crystallized leaf we presently have on exhibit at the Museum; the other is more massive and not as finely crystallized. Nothing can be determined about these large speciments until they can be weighed and studied further. Mr. Allan Phipps, President of the Board of Trustees, has given his permission for you to inspect the specimens at that time."

Tuesday morning, February 8, 1972, was the date set for photographing, weighing and cataloguing the Campion gold in United Bank of Denver. Seven officials of Denver Museum of Natural History (including the Curator of Photography) and the author were present. It was a never-to-be-forgotten sight and experience.

Clearance was made at an outer office before armed guards unlocked a massive steel gate for admittance into the chambers of safety-deposit vaults. A guard escorted the writer down corridors of vaults to a locked room. Announcing name and getting favorable response from within, the guard unlocked the door—and there displayed on a long table was the glittering gold of the Campion Collection—crystallized gold of all sizes and shapes—almost 200 glorious, carefully selected specimens of Farncomb Hill gold. One sweeping glance quickly scanned the display. At the end of the table was the large specimen.

"That's it! That's it! That's Tom's Baby!"

The largest piece of gold had a marked resemblance to Editor Wynkoop's engraving. A smaller piece was quickly spotted that bore similar color and composition; the two fit together perfectly. Sometime—somehow—the two had parted.

The writer's allotted time (before weighing and cataloguing work) was about twenty minutes —time enough to have three cameras flash a number of pictures—the writer holding "Tom's Baby." Museum officials stood on both sides, "guarding" the writer and ready to support him if he capsized under the excitement. (All pictures of the writer holding "Tom's Baby" show the two pieces of gold—the smaller piece in the palm of the left hand.)

A complete description cannot be made of the sight. The writer was so enthralled, entranced, captivated by "Tom's Baby" that the many other glittering treasures received only hasty glances. Undoubtedly, even the smallest cluster was of great beauty and value, worthy of minute inspection. But "Tom's Baby" was the end of a long quest—a hoped-for-desire—an attainment never fully expected. Other glorious gold was glimpsed, but the writer was *seeing* the long-lost "baby," and *holding* it in his hands! No wonder it was named "Tom's Baby"—it was thrilling to cuddle.

"Tom's Baby" does not have all the delicate and intricate features of many Farncomb Hill specimens. In shape, it does resemble a small slab of concrete. It seems basically solid gold with delicate Farncomb Hill leaf and wire gold here and there on its surface. Average thickness is ¾ inch, tapering down to thinner edging. The background of solid gold is of a deeper, bronze-like color, sprinkled and touched with spots of glistening, wisp-like gold unique to Farncomb Hill. In size, it is approximately 10¼ x 6¾. It is amazingly heavy; one feels need to use both hands to support it. Blindfolded, one would believe he were lifting a chunk of iron or steel. Other pieces have broken from the nugget; some may be in the collection. Twenty breath-taking minutes were much too short to photograph all its features on the mind.

Later weighing showed the larger piece weighing 78.3 troy ounces, the smaller 24.6— almost 103 troy ounces. What happened to the other pieces—whether they will ever be found— why and how they were broken off—whether they exist or have been lost or melted—all remain unknown at the present.

The second-largest specimen appeared, without doubt, to be the nugget described in *Mining Reporter Magazine* (December 21, 1899) "A Summit County Gold Nugget, Weight 26 Ounces."

Has "Tom's Baby" really been found? One feels reasonably sure it has. The general outline compares favorably with Editor Wynkoop's engraving. An engraving, however, does not duplicate all the fine details of a massive piece of crystallized gold. Thirty-three ounces are still missing from the 136 oz. 5 dwt. reported in Summit County *Journal,* July 25, 1887; fifty-seven ounces would be needed to restore it to its size when taken from the earth:

> The largest nugget, when taken out, weighed fully one hundred and sixty ounces, two pieces were broken off, leaving the nugget as now shown weighing 136 oz. 5 dwt., which is, we believe, the largest nugget ever found in the State. Yesterday hundreds of visitors called on Colonel Ware at his office at the concentrator on the west side, to feast their eyes on the find.

(Listing the nugget as 13 pounds is on the basis of the original 160 ounces—12 ounces per troy pound.)

Some of the missing pieces may be among the many clusters of the Campion Collection. Perhaps some went into other hands and collections. These are some of the unknowns. It would have been of great assistance to future researchers if the Campion Collection had come with detailed cataloguing—or that "Ye Editor" had chronicled more about "Tom's Baby."

John F. Campion gave Colorado the finest, most valuable collection of Farncomb Hill crystallized gold in existence. Museums, over the world, boast pieces of this extraordinary gold, but none can equal the collection brought together by John Campion. Archie Willson wasn't faking when he said, "A nugget is common compared to crystallized gold." Most nuggets are dull in color; Farncomb Hill gold sparkles and dazzles.

A crate of John F. Campion papers, left in custody of Colorado University Norlin Library, Western History, was opened January, 1972. Letters in it verified that Ben Stanley Revett and Mason B. Carpenter associated with John F. Campion in business dealings. The papers also revealed that Tom Groves and Van Nostrand were in Campion's mining ventures at Victoria (top of Farncomb Hill—name later changed from Victoria to Wapiti, March, 1894.) Revett wrote to Campion—June 11, 1893:—"Saw Lizzie Groves. She says Tom will go up to Victoria to work if we want him." July 11, 1893, Revett wrote: "Kindly send cheque to the German National Bank, Denver, and I can give personal checks against my account to settle with Groves, etc." December 18, 1893, a letter from Revett to Campion stated: "World's Fair Breckenridge Gold Exhibit—Can get the bulk of this for you at any time, per verbal conversation with you." Revett spoke of Gold Flake Mine (where "Tom's Baby" was found) as "Bonanza of the Hill." Ben Stanley Revett assisted Campion in acquiring his valuable collection. A collector, possessed of John Campion's zeal for the best, could never remain content without acquiring Colorado's largest nugget.

Jack Murphy, Curator of Geology at Denver Museum of Natural History, said that public display of "Tom's Baby" will not be made by the Museum until a special, secure display vault is constructed. Furthermore, he added, it is doubtful that the total Campion Collection will ever be on display at any one time. It is too valuable to take such a risk.

United Bank of Denver guards glimpsed the table of glittering gold when they unlocked the door to admit the eight persons permitted in the room. One guard said to the writer as he was leaving, "And to think that wooden box has been around here for years—marked 'Colorado Museum of Natural History'—and we supposed it was filled with dinosaur bones."

"Tom's Baby," did you travel far and wide? Were you in all those places they said you were? Or were you safely resting in the Campion Collection all this time?

Colorado, take good care of our "baby."

Engraving-Picture of "Tom's Baby" that appeared in January 6, 1898, *Mining Industry and Review*. Summit County *Journal*, January 15, 1898, wrote: "In the January 6th issue of *Mining Industry and Review* there appeared a good half-tone engraving of "Tom's Baby" gold nugget. Editor Wynkoop has always shown a kindly interest in Summit County and his generosity in having the engraving made should be appreciated." A sketched engraving of a large gold nugget cannot compare with an actual photograph in exactness of shape and minute details. The above is a picture of an engraving. Courtesy—New York Public Library.

Denver Museum of Natural History officials and author at the opening of safety-deposit box at United Bank of Denver, February 8, 1972, revealing "Tom's Baby" and the fabulous John Campion Gold Collection.

Left to Right: Jack Murphy (Curator of Geology), Mark Fiester (Author-*Blasted Beloved Breckenridge*), Allan R. Phipps (President of the Board of Trustees), Dr. F. A. Cajori (Honorary Curator of Minerology), Charles T. Crockett (Assistant Director). Courtesy—Denver Museum of Natural History, Robert R. Wright, (Curator of Photography.)

Denver Museum of Natural History officials and author at the opening of safety-deposit box at United Bank of Denver, February 8, 1972, revealing "Tom's Baby" and the fabulous John Campion Gold Collection.

Left to Right: Bruce E. Dines (Trustee), Allan R. Phipps (President of the Board of Trustees), Mark Fiester (Author-*Blasted Beloved Breckenridge*), John A. Ferguson, Jr. (Treasurer-Board of Trustees.)

Bruce Dines, Mark Fiester, Allan Phipps studying large nuggets of the
John F. Campion Gold Collection-United Bank of Denver-February 8,
1972.

Robert R. Wright (Curator of Photography-Denver Museum of Natural History) and Jack Murphy (Curator of Geology) photographing and cataloguing John F. Campion gold.

Author of *Blasted Beloved Breckenridge* holding "Tom's Baby" and almost two hundred glittering crystallized gold nuggets of the John F. Campion collection are spread on the table before him. United Bank of Denver—February 8, 1972.

Courtesy—Denver Public Library Western Collection (Frank Hall's *History of Colorado*, Vol. II, page 17).

The fact that Colorado has the largest and most valuable collection of Farncomb Hill gold in the world—under guarded care of Denver Museum of Natural History—is entirely due to the foresight, dedication and philanthropy of John F. Campion. He has given to Colorado a priceless treasure.

Unanswered questions still remain. Did the golden hoard see light of day since ending of the 19th century? Why has its whereabouts remained so secretive? Where are the missing pieces of "Tom's Baby?" The "Maddening Mystery" is not completely solved.

EDWIN CARTER

Miniature to Magnificent

A miniature, modest cottage, 111 North Ridge Street, Breckenridge, and the magnificent, spreading Museum of Natural History, Denver City Park, share a common claim—the life and work of "Professor" Edwin Carter. The humble gave birth to the magnificent.

Many were the tributes paid to the life and work of Edwin Carter, but the finest, most-comprehensive, came from the report sent by the Denver correspondent of the Chicago *Record* to his newspaper at the time of Carter's death:

> Hunters and scientists in every part of the world will deplore the death of Professor Edwin Carter, "the log cabin naturalist," whose collection of Rocky Mountain fauna, at Breckenridge, in this state, is the only one extant.

> In a humble log cabin at the foot of a snow-capped mountain and commanding a superb view of the entire valley of the Blue River is stored the Carter collection, which has been visited by scientists from all parts of the world, and by many curious tourists, and which has been pronounced the finest private collection of fauna in existence. Thousands of dollars have been offered for the rarest specimens which were secured by the indefatigable naturalist but Professor Carter refused to part with anything that he could not duplicate, his object being to found a Rocky Mountain museum to be located at Denver. Now his dream is to be realized after his death, as John F. Campion, one of the wealthiest mine-owners of Colorado, has taken up the matter and has interested other capital, so the Carter collection will soon be removed from Breckenridge to a suitable building in Denver.

> Professor Carter gave up wealth and fame for the sake of science. He came to Colorado in the Pike's Peak gold rush, being one of the first-comers in Russell gulch, the Klondike of the West, in 1859. In 1860 he joined a party bound for California gulch, where Leadville now stands. He took up a placer claim, which he finally sold, and then prospected over the state of Colorado with varying success, finally locating at Black Hawk, where he engaged as assistant to a furrier, in order to learn the rudiments of taxidermy. His curiosity and interest were aroused by the pelts which he handled and he determined to devote his life to the gathering of all the specimens of birds and animals of the Rocky Mountain regions. He went to Breckenridge in 1868 and then settled down to the accomplishment of the one object which he had in view. He sold out his mining interests, which were considerable, and, in spite of the fact that he was deemed one of the finest judges of placer ground in the state of Colorado, he refused to locate and work valuable claims, preferring to wander over the mountain ranges, rifle in hand, studying the habits of animals and birds and bringing to his log cabin such specimens as he lacked. When his cabin was filled with mounted specimens and hundreds of carefully preserved pelts he built a larger structure and kept on with his work. Owing to the fact that Colorado is the sportsmen's paradise and thousands of hunters come to the state annually in quest of big game, many animals have become entirely extinct in the last few years. The birds of the state, too, have been ruthlessly slaughtered and the wisdom of Professor Carter's early start in his work is now apparent, as there are hundreds of specimens in the log cabin that cannot be duplicated.

> In order to secure enough money to enable him to pursue his life work, Professor Carter sold many duplicate specimens to naturalists in all parts of the world and most of the Rocky Mountain fauna in the great museums of this and other countries came from his cabin and

were mounted by his hand. He also purchased of other taxidermists and collectors specimens that his collection lacked, and in this way he made his exhibit well nigh perfect. He had a marvelous knowledge of the habits of the birds and animals of the Rockies, and, as an instance of the thoroughness which characterized his work, his collection of ptarmigans includes one for most every day of the year, thus enabling students of natural history to note the many changes which occur in the bird's plumage. His skill as a taxidermist and his art in imparting lifelike poses to stuffed animals equalled his gifts of observation, and the mounting of his specimens is said to be unexcelled. Professors of learned societies in all parts of the world traveled to visit the Carter museum, in order to gain knowledge in the fast-disappearing fauna of western America. They were always treated with distinguished courtesy by the modest, re-tiring naturalist, who seemed almost a part of the grand, inspiring wildnerness which he made his haunt. No information was withheld, and a conversation with Professor Carter on his fav-orite theme was regarded as equal to a course in textbooks of natural history.

The museum at Breckenridge presents be-wildering sights as the visitor enters. Stuffed buffaloes and grizzlies, brought down with Car-ter's own rifle, occupy the center of the room, while around them on every side are life-like mountain lions, strange-colored birds, nests full of rare and beautiful eggs, and piles of valuable and skillfully tanned pelts. The loft is full of skins and plumage, and there is hardly a foot of vacant space in the building, so closely are the valuable specimens packed. Professor Car-ter was unable to make an estimate of the num-ber of specimens he had gathered, but the total will mount into the tens of thousands. He was engaged in the work of classification when he died, and this work alone will require years of effort on the part of the experts who will take it up.

The plans for the removal of the Carter museum to Denver will be carried out.

Edwin Carter was born June 1, 1830, at Oneida, New York; he died February 3, 1900. The local newspaper, February 10th, erroneously listed his age as 63. The mistake was rectified the following week: "In last week's *Journal* we gave Professor Carter's age as 63, which was an error. Had he lived till next June, he would have been 70 years of age." His tombstone, in Valley Brook Cemetery, reads: June 1828-Feb. 1900— again, a conflicting birthdate.

Although Carter was one of the early ar-rivals at California Gulch (Leadville), he did not remain there long. Selling his property, he returned over Fremont Pass, down Ten-Mile Creek and camped at Salt Lick below the site of (old) Dillon. He held claims at Salt Lick and prospected down Blue River into Middle Park. Mining endeavors also took him to the head of Swan Valley to Humbug and American Gulches. He was present there during the placer gold ex-citement of those camps during the early 1860s.

Professor Carter was intensely interested in Masonic Lodge work. His library of Masonic books was undoubtedly the most complete in the area. He was a charter member of the Parkville, Georgia Gulch, Summit County Lodge, No. 2, A. F. & A. M., organized in 1860, and also one of the organizers of the Breckenridge Lodge No. 47, A. F. & A. M.

Edwin Carter's introduction to taxidermy is somewhat befogged by narrators. Some say it was at Black Hawk; others say at Georgetown. Some say he learned it as assistant to a furrier; others say he hired a German furrier, who was also a good taxidermist, and was taught by the German. By the time he settled at Breckenridge, 1868, he was well established in the art.

Carter's first dwelling place and workshop in Breckenridge was believed to have been the small cabin at the rear of the present building. The larger building, known as the museum was built in 1875. Mr. Carter was always fearful of fire destroying his valuable collection, so the mu-seum was separated from all other buildings on his property. As further fire protection, he pur-chased the plot of ground on the east side of Ridge Street—between Ridge and French Streets, extending from the Methodist Church to Carter Avenue.

Summit County *Journal*   February 10, 1900

Professor Carter's museum was better known by scientists of distant parts of the world than by the people of Colorado. Among his visitors were professors of learned societies, collectors of natural specimens, tourists and men who traveled long distances to study the most remarkable collection ever made in the field of natural history by an unassisted indi-vidual. Professor Carter was one of the most modest and retiring of men and he never boasted of anything he had accomplished. He was proud, however, of the fact that his collection was the greatest of the kind ever made by any one man acting entirely independent of outside agencies. A number of his stuffed animals are pronounced by experts to be the finest specimens extant, and his collection of birds' eggs is a wonder even to those most familiar with the subject.

Professor Carter was a child of nature. He never married, and his entire time for the last quarter of a centuy was devoted to enlarging his collection.

Many overtures for his valuable collection were made at different times, but the professor allowed no tempting offers of wealth to divert him from the one object—the establishment of the nucleus of a museum in the capital of the state.

If Professor Carter had kept a guestbook at his museum, on his birthday anniversary, June 1, 1892, there would have appeared a long list of Denver's and Colorado's must influential leaders. The Summit County *Journal*, June 4th, gave complete coverage:

On Wednesday last our little mountain city was visited by a party from Denver consisting of state, county and city officials and influential citizens among whom were: Governor J. L. Routt, Ex-Governor J. B. Grant, Ex-Governor J. A. Cooper, Ex-Attorney General S. W. Jones, Mayor Platt Rogers, D. H. K. Steele, Col. G. E. Randolph, Colonel Longstreet, General B. Brooks, Oscar Reuter, City Engineer Hunter, Thomas S. Clayton, County Treasurer Hart, County Assessor Aggers, W. J. Curtis, F. A. Kenner, Albert Nelson, H. C. Lowrie, T. G. Anderson, H. C. Twombly, Egbert Johnson, R. W. Speer, Corporation Counsel Ellis and son, A. A. Blow, William N. Byers, John H. Poole, City Attorney Williams, County Clerk McGaffey, Sheriff Burchinell, E. M. Ashley, Colonel John Arkins and son, Joseph E. Bates, Thomas E. Poole, Peter Magnes, R. P. McDonald, Robert S. Roe, Auditor James T. Smith, Judge W. E. Beck, Hon. John D. McGilvray and the members of the board of supervisors, Hon. M. D. Currigan, and the members of the board of aldermen, President S. H. Elbert of the chamber of commerce, President E. M. Ashley of the manufacturers' exchange, members of the Denver school boards, representatives of the daily press.

The party came by special train and they were met at Boreas by a committee from this city, headed by Mr. Ed. Collingwood. The train arrived at our depot at 1:30 p.m. and the excursionists were met and welcomed by a goodly turnout of citizens and the mutual greetings of friends soon made the visitors realize that although for some of them it was their first visit to Breckenridge yet they were among friends and acquaintances. The party proceeded to the Denver Hotel where minehost Foote had prepared a dinner of mountain trout fit to serve all the crowned heads of Europe. As the guests were seated at the table Mayor Westerman was introduced and formally welcomed the visitors as follows:

"Gentlemen, it is an honor and a pleasure for me to welcome you here today. You who represent a city that all Coloradians feel proud of, as the growth of the city of Denver shows to the world the energy and push her citizens are possessed of.

"The people of Colorado feel proud of our young state and desire to excel in all they undertake, for within her borders there are to be found the resources that at no distant day will place her as one of the strongest and most powerful states of our glorious union.

"Our little town of Breckenridge that you have done us the honor of visiting today, is but a speck compared to the world, but it is within our power at the world's fair at Chicago to make the grandest display of native gold that has ever been collected together for man to see. If we assist in capturing a prize there, we shall feel that we have helped to add one more laurel to our state.

"It is our wish and desire to show you gentlemen a small sample of this gold while you are here with us so that you may judge of its value and beauty. I again in the name of the people of Breckenridge bid you welcome."

After which the guests fell to with a will and a relish that was a pleasure to witness. It was particularly observable that Martin D. Currigan, the democratic delegate-elect to Chicago was very fond of trout, he declared he could see a half dozen boys catching them while he was eating and that if the stock in the Blue didn't give out for once he would have his fill of fine fish; alas an alarm of fire called the bulky alderman from his feast.

(The visitors were treated to an exhibition of how our fire boys get out at fires. A false alarm was struck and the machines rattled out, grabbed a plug, turned on water—all before Alderman Currigan could get that last fish tail from between his teeth.)

The party then visited Professor Carter's museum, their mission being to capture both the owner and his museum and transport them to Denver. After looking over the wonderful work of Mr. Carter's they were unanimous in the verdict that it must and shall go to Denver. Proposals were exchanged and in a few days will decide whether they will be accepted or declined.

The visitors were shown various quantities of gold specimens by those having them, John Klinefelter, Mayor Westerman, Charles Finding, William Briggle, the Denver Hotel Hiram Johnson and others showed up their golden stores to the great gratification of the visitors. A few were driven about town and out to some of the neighboring mines, others strolled about town for an hour or so until nearly six o'clock when all assembled at the depot, before starting Mayor Rogers made a congratulatory speech and Gov. Routt delivered the farewell address after which amid the cheers of the assembled Breckenridgians and the screeching of Price Mill's whistle the train started homeward.

The town had been duly and patriotically decorated. American flags were everywhere displayed. At all flagpoles the star-spangled banner was hoisted. The clerk of the weather for once was kindly considerate; the day was bright and could not have been better. All parties enjoyed themselves, many until "the wee sma hours annent the twal" gave notice that it was time to retire.

A letter from Mr. Carter followed that important visit of dignitaries:

Breckenridge, Colo.
June 10, 1892

To His Excellency Governor Routt
Mayor Rogers and Members of the
Committee
Gentlemen,

I respectfully submit, for your consideration, the terms and conditions upon which I shall be pleased to co-operate in an effort to found a Natural History Museum in your City.

I will sell my collection of birds and mammals for the sum of twenty thousand dollars ($20,000.00) upon the following terms to wit: Five thousand dollars ($5,000.00) in cash to be paid when the collection is boxed and ready for transporting and fifteen thousand dollars

($15,000.00) to be paid at the expiration of six (6) years or at the close of contract.

The title to be vested in the City of Denver in perpetuity.

To be located and housed in suitable buildings for Museum purposes in the City Park.

There shall be provided for maintenance an annual appropriation of not less than ten thousand dollars ($10,000.00) said sum to be applied to the care of exhibits, salaries, collections, transportation, preparation of specimens and all expenses connected therewith.

The Museum shall be open and free to the public at all reasonable hours.

That I shall have general charge (under advisory control) and direct the collecting and preparation of subjects in the department of zoology, and be paid a yearly salary of three thousand dollars ($3,000.00) for the term of six (6) years.

Should you consider my proposition with favor I can have the collection boxed and ready for shipment on or before the first of April, 1893.

Respectfully,
Ed. Carter

A long, dry spell seems to have set in following Carter's June, 1892, letter. Little correspondence is available to indicate progress of the proposed sale. In the meantime, Colorado Springs gave consideration to purchasing the exhibit. Two very important documents were formulated during this time which could have played a significant part in the future of the exhibit. One document concerned Banker George Engle and the other, William H. Wilkinson. Banker Engle was one of Carter's closest friends and later was administrator of Carter's estate. Wilkinson had been a one-time partner with Carter in securing the museum specimens. Wilkinson held a $1,500 unpaid share in the exhibit. The Wilkinson agreement was properly signed, notarized and recorded in Summit County records. The Engle document was signed by Judge W. M. Clark and Edwin Carter, but not notarized and recorded. The Engle-Carter document appears in the Administrator's papers of the Carter estate. The only given explanation for Carter's Bill of Sale to Engle was that he hoped by so doing to side-step the complications and involvements of the Probate Court in the event of his death. Mr. Engle did not bring the document to public attention in settling the estate. In the hands of a less-trustworthy individual, it might have caused disturbing complications. Of Wilkinson, we shall hear more later.

In the five years, 1892-1897, there was more dickering about the museum sale. Carter asked for an expensive building program at City Park. The Committee asked a reduction of the sale price from $20,000 to $10,000. In this period John F. Campion, the mining magnate and millionaire, assumes a leading role in the negotiations.

THE IBEX MINING COMPANY
John F. Campion, Manager

Leadville, Colo.,
Sept. 15th, 97

Professor Edwin Carter.
    Breckenridge, Colo.
Dear Sir:—

Referring to our conversation the other day in regard to the proposed museum at Denver I think it is only fair to you and myself that I should give you an idea of what the Denver people who have expressed a desire to assist the enterprise are willing to do. To begin with, I do not believe for an instant that they will agree to raise One Hundred Thousand dollars. I know they will agree to pay for your collection at the price you gave me, they will also raise money to pay you, and one other, a fair salary, and in addition to this they will raise enough money to pay the running expenses of the institution. Their idea is to start in a moderate way, and gradually interest the citizens of the State in the institution. That many of the proposed Trustees will contribute quite liberally, I have no doubt, but I am quite certain that they will not agree to raise the sum of money you mention to me. In fact, the conversation I had with you last spring left the impression in my mind that you realized the necessity of starting the institution in a modest way and let it gradually grow. Personally, I am quite certain that no other plan will succeed in Denver. It may be that Professor Slocum of Colorado Springs thinks he can make it succeed on different lines in Colorado Springs. In the latter town such an institution would be purely a local enterprise, and could not be made anything else. Individually, I should not take the slightest interest in it, as I feel an institution of the kind under discussion should be built for the State and the West, or not at all. I make it a practice in life to be perfectly frank with my fellowmen in all my business relations with them, and I do not wish to undertake what I feel is an impossibility, or,

commit you to agreeing to a certain line of policy, if your judgment leads you in another direction. I expect to go to Denver in about 10 days, and would be glad to hear from you, before calling the meeting of the proposed trustees, which I had intended doing, shortly after I get home. With kind regards,

Faithfully yours.
John F. Campion

John F. Campion
Equitable Building
Denver, Colorado

Denver, Colo.,
Oct. 5, 1897

Professor Carter
    Breckenridge, Colo.
My Dear Sir,

Your letter of 2nd is at hand. Your idea of the way to do the thing is quite right and I feel very certain that once we get the institution under way it will meet your expectations. My first object is not to scare contributors away before they get interested. Once we get them interested it will be very much easier to increase our requirements and I have no doubt about the money to carry out all practical plans will be forthcoming. I fully understand and have so explained to the parties with whom I have talked, that the money you are to receive, viz Ten Thousand dollars, is only a partial payment on your collection and that you are to be publicly given the credit of being one of the donors of the collection. I feel quite certain that the institution will not confine its operations to any one department of Natural History. I expect to be back here by the 12th and hope I have the incorporation papers of the institution filed by that time and I really think it would be wise for you to be present if you can spare the time to make the trip. Kindly let me know if it would be convenient for you to come down if we secured your transportation and advise you of the date of the meeting by letter or telegraph.

Faithfully yours,
John F. Campion

The Denver Museum of Natural History provided an excerpt from the minutes of a meeting held December 13, 1897, "to consider ways and means for the establishment of a Museum:"

The call for the meeting was explained by Mr. Campion, Mr. Merritt and Prof. Carter, which last named gentleman made a proposition that he would turn over to an organization of twenty-five gentlemen, who should incorporate as "The Colorado Museum and Library Association," his collection of stuffed animals and birds, now located at Breckenridge, Colorado, and valued by experts at from thirty to fifty thousand dollars, provided that a suitable fire-proof building shall be erected with ample floor space for the proper exhibition of said collection, and the payment of ten thousand dollars be made to him, and further provided that he should be guaranteed a salary as curator in charge during his lifetime. After due consideration it was determined to appoint a committee on ways and means, to prepare plans and arrange for organization, report to be submitted at a future meeting.

Our next correspondence is dated a year later:

John F. Campion
Equitable Building
Denver, Colorado

December 31, 1898

Prof. Edwin Carter,
     Breckenridge, Colo.
My Dear Sir:

I beg to inform you that recently a very considerable interest has been manifested in this community looking to the establishment of the proposed Colorado Museum of Natural History. During the first week in January a committee will be appointed that will canvass the city, and I presume during the month of January we shall definitely determine whether or not the funds can be acquired to carry out the work in which we are both so much interested.

On the whole, the outlook is quite favorable for a speedy and satisfactory conclusion towards acquiring the money that will be required to start our work. I fully realize how important it is to you that this matter should be determined as quickly as possible. That Denver is clearly the ideal locality of all others in the State, in which to place the Museum, I fully agree. You can rest assured that, when this matter is taken up in the near future, it will be pressed forward as speedily as possible, and, unless we can arrive at a satisfactory solution of the financial problem connected with the enterprise during the month of January, it will, in that event, be extremely doubtful if it can be done for some time to come. However, as I have already stated, I feel at present very hopeful that our endeavors to secure the necessary

financial aid to start the enterprise will meet with success. I shall promptly advise you as quickly as we can determine what can be done. Wishing you the compliments of the season, I am,

Faithfully yours,
John F. Campion

Another year passed and now we hear from the man largely responsible for miles and miles of Summit County stone piles—Ben Stanley Revett, General Manager of The NORTH AMERICAN GOLD DREDGING COMPANY. Seven and a half years passed since that IMPORTANT VISIT in 1892 when Denver dignitaries "were unanimous in their decision that Carter's Museum must and shall go to Denver." In December of 1899 it didn't seem much more of a reality than it did in June of 1892. And Edwin Carter's health was no longer at its best.

THE NORTH AMERICAN GOLD DREDGING
COMPANY

B. Stanley Revett
General Manager
Denver, Colo.,
December 7th, 1899

Prof. Edwin Carter,
     Breckenridge, Colo.
My dear Mr. Carter:—

Last evening in coming through Leadville, I had the pleasure of meeting Mr. John Campion and spent an hour or two with him, in which we discussed the possibility of some immediate action in regard to taking hold of your museum on the lines which you have outlined and its immediate removal to Denver.

I must confess that I have wronged Mr. Campion in saying that he was unnecessarily dilatory and slow in getting some action taken on the removal of your museum and putting it on a satisfactory basis to yourself and all concerned in Denver.

In conversation with Mr. Campion, he states that he was very much surprised to find that $16,000 which was supposed to have been appropriated by some special taxation, and which Mr. Gallup had said to several parties, had been set aside for the furtherance of your museum had been politically disposed of and no such fund was at present in existence.

Mr. Campion has recently been doing some very faithful work on behalf of yourself and your museum and is prepared to make the following proposition:—That within thirty days he will pay you $10,000.00 for your own particular benefit to do with as you may see fit. The understanding being that you will turn over your collection to a committee composed of Mr. David Moffat, J. B. Grant, Joe Thatcher, Frank Trumbull, Governor Thomas, Harry Bryant, J. T. Jeffries, and my humble self, who will obligate ourselves in writing to remove yourself and your museum down to Denver, place it in a suitable fire-proof building, and it for the tenure of your life to be placed in your jurisdiction and direction so soon as the committee may be able to decide that they are enabled to furnish ample funds to carry out your wishes and to place the museum on a strong and lasting financial basis such as you have always desired.

I have spent the greater part of today in going fully into the matter with the Gentlemen above named and I am more than gratified to find such kindly interest taken in the enterprise.

Mr. D. H. Moffat has expressed himself in the warmest and most sympathetic terms and I am satisfied that not only he, but many of the old residents in the state who have heretofore been apathetic will fall into line and do everything in their power to further and enhance the museum, not only with such funds as they may have at their disposal but with their strongest and kindest efforts.

I had purposed leaving to-morrow evening for the East but I find every one, so kindly disposed toward taking some immediate action toward the removal of your museum to Denver that I have decided to stay over until Monday evening and have arranged with the representative men, not only of this town, but of the state to hold a meeting Monday afternoon for the immediate consideration of subscribing the necessary money to carry out the plan as above arranged.

If I am to be successful in this matter, it is necessary that you should come down here on Sunday Morning's train. I will meet you at the train, take you to the hotel, where no one, except those interested in the furtherance of our undertaking, will know that you are in the city.

Mr. Campion and myself wish to talk matters over with you, so that when we go before a committee of representative men of this city that we shall be able to know just what you will accede to and what immediate money will be necessary for us to raise.

I know, of course, that you are not feeling yourself and have recently been very much un-

der the weather, but I do not think you are too unwell to come down here and talk with all of your friends what can and is best to be done.

Your statement that you wish to send East and get a suit of new clothes is of minor importance to yourself and all those interested in the matter. I will pledge myself that if you will come down here on Sunday morning that by the time you are required to be visible on Monday, to have you clothed in your right mind from broadcloth to sack cloth and ashes, or if necessary, a suit of armor.

In addition to the necessity of your coming down on the above, there are one or two matters that have occurred to me relating to the Salt Lick ground, that make it necessary for you to come down to have a few minutes talk before I leave for the East.

Mr. Campion showed me your letter in which you state that you do not wish to leave for a lower altitude until compelled to do so, and I wish to reiterate what I have said before that a trip for only a few days will do you good.

If you will come down here as I have suggested, in fact as I demand, having postponed my trip East in order to meet you, I am satisfied it will do you not only a world of good physically but be a very pleasurable experience for you to find that you and your life work have so many friends prepared to stand by you in every way they are possibly able for the furtherance of your worthy undertaking.

Immediately on receipt of this, I wish you to get Charlie Walker (a neighbor-friend) and tell him that you are going to Denver and that you wish him to accompany you, sending me a wire that you are coming down and I will meet you both and then we will arrange matters for you.

I will see to it that you are comfortably housed, clothed in the most appropriate style and that your friends are on hand to greet and meet you in most satisfactory way to accomplish that which is nearest and dearest to your heart and those who know yourself and your undertaking.

So far as water works are concerned, do not let this distress yourself as Martin Currigan is trying to finance the water works of this city, so we can devise some plan to furnish the city with a more important plan, and you will have our permission, if it be necessary, to make water every five minutes, but in this I am only joking.

I really and sincerely want you to screw up your courage to make a special effort to come

Edwin Carter

down here on Sunday morning and as to the remaining matters, leave them to me and I am satisfied that you will be satisfied with your visit. If I was not, I would not have written you as above.

I am just as sincerely interested in seeing your museum moved to Denver as you are in having it substantially installed, and unless you come down as I have suggested Mr. Campion and myself will be very bitterly disappointed as we have made a special effort for your coming down in order that no further time may be lost and that we may get some immediate action in moving your museum to Denver.

I trust that you will pardon my writing so fully but you know that I have had this matter at heart for some time and such being the case, I shall hope to have a telegram from you, that yourself and Charlie Walker will arrange to arrive Sunday night and that I may have the pleasure of seeing and meeting you both at the depot.

Please do not say you cannot, for all things are possible to those who will try.

Fraternally yours,
Ben Stanley Revett

Professor Carter made the trip to Denver with the purpose of making a final proposition to its citizens. Upon his return to Breckenridge he seemed in a more hopeful mood over the prospect of the ultimate consummation of his museum dream than ever before. Nevertheless, nothing more than a verbal agreement was made.

Time was running out. Seven and a half years had passed since the Colorado dignitaries visited the Breckenridge museum at 111 North Ridge Street. The 19th century ended; the 20th began. No museum building was being erected at Denver City Park. Nothing of the Carter collection had been transferred to Denver. Not a dollar had been paid to seal the agreement. Breckenridge was still the home of the famed "log-cabin naturalist." The dream was still a dream.

The new century had hardly begun when it became apparent that Edwin Carter's health was a serious matter. Carter lived alone; his brother, sister, two nephews and a niece were "back East" in New York State. Neighbor-friend, Charlie Walker, sent word to the brother, Theodore Carter, Oneida, New York. Theodore interpreted the message differently than Charlie Walker intended:

Breckenridge, Colo.
January 8, 1900

Dear Sir:

Mr. Edwin Carter is not well and is started on the road to Galveston, Texas. We do not know how far he will get. He left here yesterday and should be in Denver today, and is to be examined by Dr. Stedman before he leaves Denver.

Mr. George Engle—Banker at this place—wished to write to you and asked your address. Mr. Carter refused the address and positively forbade his writing.

I have got to be so old that I do not care whether I am forbid or not. And it is not at all likely that he will be pleased with what I am doing now.

My wife and I were gone from here for four years until last June. When we returned we realized that Mr. Carter had failed greatly. He seemed to be starving. His food did not assimilate, and all we could feed him and all we could do for him did no good.

My wife—Mrs. Walker—has the key to his house. Everybody has the care of it. There is no one stopping there when he is gone.

We wish to hear from you if you receive this letter.

Yours truly,
Chas. A. Walker

Evidently the reply to his message was annoying to Walker, assuming that Mr. Carter was as good as dead. Walker's reply of January 12th reads:

Dear Sir:

Your telegram received. I wish to state that I have nothing to do with Ed Carter's property in any way, shape or manner, and moreover that he is alive yet. And that we hope he will live many years after this and in good health. Our latest advice is that he is feeling better and we think he is on his way now to Galveston.

Yours truly,
Charles A. Walker

Came the shattering news:

CARTER DIES OF ARSENIC POISON!

Summit's Naturalist Succumbs
To Arsenic Poisoning At
Galveston, Texas

For the past eighteen months, owing to the arsenic poison absorbed by his system in preparing specimens for mounting, the professor's health has been gradually declining, and it was only about a month ago that the persuasions of his friends were successful in getting his consent to try a lower altitude, and he decided to go to the gulf coast in Texas.

On the 7th of January the late professor and Mr. T. M. Hudgins departed from Breckenridge—not on a mission of pleasure, but on a journey that Mr. Carter's friends hoped would restore him to his usual robust health; but alas, the trip was postponed too long. From here they went to Denver, and, after a few days' rest, the journey to Galveston was accomplished without serious results.

It was hoped that the soft Gulf breeze of the salt ocean would impart new life to his tottering frame, and for the first few days following his arrival his friends were encouraged. However, despair soon followed and, after three weeks of careful nursing, he, on February 3rd, peacefully passed from the active scenes of earth to that happy home beyond that the Scriptures tell us awaits the reception of the just and truly good.

Denver was severely jolted with the news of Carter's death. What about Carter's Museum? Will Denver get the museum? Had payment been made for the museum? Was there a will? Governor Thomas' reaction was, "Carter's death may prove a public calamity. His passing before the fruition of his hopes is to be deplored. It simply shows that action should always be prompt in such affairs. I wish it might have been accomplished during Professor Carter's life."

Consternation prevailed among all the dignitaries involved in the Museum transaction. Senator Merritt, Secretary of the Carter Museum and Library Association, believed "Carter Museum Safe In Possession Of Denver." "He thought that it was thoroughly understood at the December 18th meeting that the museum was to be transferred to Denver—but the senator was by no means certain that a bill of sale or a contract had been signed. If such a paper existed it was probably in the possession of Mr. Campion. He must have left a will. The professor was a man of sterling integrity, and if he had any warning of his death he must have insisted upon leaving some paper before he passed away. I think it is likely that we will learn that he prepared a will."

John Campion telegraphed from California —"the contract was verbal."

Governor Thomas was asked in regard to the legal phase of the matter, if the heirs entered suit for possession of the collection. "It would have been much better had some part of the money been paid to Mr. Carter. The matter should have been attended to ten years ago, and if it had not been for Mr. Campion's initiative move, we probably would never have had the collection, that is, if we get it."

While Denver was in turmoil as to the future of the museum, at Galveston Carter's body was placed in a handsome casket and entrained for the home journey. The body was met at the train by Senator E. W. Merritt, representing the Carter Museum and Library Association; Chris Kaiser, representing Breckenridge Lodge No. 47, and Charles A. Walker, representing the citizens of Breckenridge. On Thursday the body was taken to the state capitol building where the public viewing was from 10 a.m. to 3 p.m. The *Rocky Mountain News* showed a picture of Carter's casket in the Capitol with the caption of the article "First Private Citizen Accorded Public Honors."

The casket lay at the archway in front of the main stairway to the second floor, and was surmounted and surrounded by floral tributes that would do honor to a king. Large and beautiful floral tributes came from Denver's leading citizens and organizations. A large American banner hung in graceful folds from the archway, forming a fitting background for the scene in which one so loyal to his commonwealth was the principal. Masons stood about in groups and conducted the visitors past the casket, showing every honor to the living in the name of the dead. On Friday the funeral party goes to Breckenridge, the former home of Professor Carter, to confer the last rites of the Masonic Order, and where a waiting populace awaits with tears the last view of a beloved citizen.

Funeral Services at Breckenridge were conducted by Lodge No. 47, A. F. & A. M. in the Mason Lodge Hall, Sunday afternoon, February 11.

SLEEPS IN VALLEY BROOK

A Large Concourse Of Citizens Follow
The Remains Of Prof. Carter To
Their Last Resting Place.

After lying in state at Masonic Hall for two days, the remains of Professor Edwin Carter were interred in Valley Brook Cemetery Sunday afternoon. Notwithstanding a fierce storm was raging and the bitter cold temperature, everyone who could secured a rig and joined the funeral cortege, while many followed along behind on foot.

The procession left Masonic Hall about 1:30, headed by the members of Breckenridge Lodge No. 47, A. F. & A. M., who conducted the entire ceremonies. At the grave the impressive ceremony of the Masonic fraternity was read, which was interspersed with appropriate songs by a choir of male and female voices accompanied by an organ.

Considering the weather conditions, the mark of respect shown the remains of Professor Carter on this occasion, was certainly a high tribute to his irreproachable character as a man and excellent reputation as a citizen. His place among us is one that can never be refilled, and the memory of his life and its noble work will live long after the present generation is no more.

After the funeral came the settling of the estate and all the unhappy involvements that too frequently attend such matters.

Breckenridge *Bulletin*
Saturday, February 17, 1900

While the people of Breckenridge and Summit County at large will greatly regret losing the Carter museum there are not any who will approve of the methods attempted by the secretary of the Colorado Museum and Library Association last Monday relative to this collection.

Hardly had the last sad rites of the funeral ceremony been performed before the gentleman referred to above and his associates were in the museum going through Professor Carter's private papers and making preparations to remove the museum to Denver. Teams were standing at the door ready to haul things to the depot. Had the authority for this act been ever so good, which we fail to find was the case, it would have looked a little more decent to have deferred the action for at least 48 hours after the burial of the man, who had spent his life in the work of making the collection, or until the proper steps could be taken or permission secured from those in authority for the removal of the same.

In justification of his conduct, Secretary Merritt claimed ownership of the collection by reason of a resolution passed by the Museum Association on the 18th of December last, in which Professor Carter concurred, and the supplementary authority given him by Mr. George Engle, who was temporary custodian of the property.

Mr. Engle, however, denies that he gave any such authority, but says that, being in charge of the collection, he was anxious that an inventory be taken so that there could never arise any controversy relative to just what was in the collection at the time of the professor's demise. This subject, Mr. Engle says, was broached to Mr. Merritt on Sunday evening, and it appears that the latter gentleman took "inventory" to mean "move," and at 7 o'clock Monday morning he was on hand at the museum, pulling and dragging specimens around, for which Professor Carter had refused hundreds of dollars, as if they were bales of cotton or sticks of cord wood. Not only this, but started out to collect all the specimens in the possession of private individuals on the presumption, we suppose, that they also belonged to the museum.

As soon as these proceedings came to the ears of the county judge, who was ill at his home, he immediately issued administration papers to Mr. Engle and placed him in charge of the collection, upon which the moving was stopped at once.

Mr. Merritt also claimed that himself and associates came to Breckenridge for no other purpose than out of respect for the late professor and to show same by attending the funeral. To a certain extent this may be true, but their subsequent actions do not prove that "respect" was all that brought them to Breckenridge. He also states that it was not the intention to move the collection for at least a year, still he comes here with a document of some kind from the president of the Colorado & Southern railroad which acts like magic on Agent McDade in furnishing cars for loading the specimens into, notwithstanding the fact that the cars were previously promised to other parties, not to mention the remark overheard by one of our citizens, that "possession is nine points of the law."

But aside from any opinion our people may have of the right and wrong in the case, if, as Mr. Merritt claims, he had any right to the collection, why did he need Mr. Engle's or anyone else's authority to take possession of the same? If he was satisfied that the copy of the resolution he had was sufficient authority for him to take possession, why didn't he and his attorney go to the county judge and ask that an administrator be appointed and this collection set aside as the property of the association?

As near as we can get at the facts in the case, the situation is that the collection was to go to the Museum association upon the payment of a certain consideration. As yet not a dollar of this consideration has been paid, nor is there a scratch of a pen with Professor Carter's signature attached which shows that the association has ever been placed in possession of the property, and it is folly for the heirs or the administrator to give up the collection on hearsay. If they did, doubtless they would not have enough specimens to go around.

However, it is the universal desire that the museum be located in Denver, and it is hoped that the association and the professor's heirs may get together on some ground that will facilitate this end.

Carter had no will. Banker Engle kept silent about the Bill of Sale made out in his favor. The natural heirs were in the driver's seat. A cat-and-mouse game was played. It was not easy to get a committal from the heirs. They prepared "A Statment Concerning the Carter Collection" and presented it to the Carter Museum and Library Association. The demands were practically the same as Mr. Carter's original offer in 1892. The price had returned to $20,000, instead of the $10,000 finally agreed upon. J. A. Thatcher, President of First National Bank, dealt with that in a letter to Administrator Engle:

March 28, 1900

George Engle, Esq.,
    Breckenridge, Colo.
My Dear Sir:—

Messrs. Moffatt, Campion, Frank Trumbull and myself were appointed a Committee to settle with the Carter heirs for the payment of the Carter Collection.

As you probably know, we have not found it very easy to arrange with them. They wanted to add considerable to the price; but we have about agreed, and they are to be paid the full sum of $10,000, which is the amount settled and agreed upon by Mr. Edwin Carter and ourselves before his death, but they still want us to pay all costs of administration, attorney's fees, etc.

Now, my object in writing you is to ask you in the name of the Committee, and for the Colorado Museum & Library Association, if you will give or donate your administrator's fees on this payment of $10,000.

I assure you the donation would be greatly appreciated by our Committee, and duly acknowledged by the Association, which after all, is really organized for the benefit of the entire state, and which some day, we believe, every citizen of the state will take pleasure in and be proud of.

    Very truly yours,
    J. A. Thatcher
    Committee Chairman

Banker George Engle acquiesced to Thatcher's appeal. His final records on the estate show that no commission was taken on the $10,000 from the Museum Committe. The administrator's fee on the $10,000 would have amounted to $600.

Dickering on the museum deal seemed endless; the clincher came from one who had remained, more or less, in the background. April 14th, 1900, Administrator Engle wrote one of the heirs:

Mr. Wm. H. Wilkinson, old partner of Mr. Edwin Carter, was here for several days looking after his interests. Before going to his home, he told me that he had put a Bill of Sale in escrow in a Denver Bank, running to the so-called unorganized society of Natural History for the sum of $1500. The Bill of Sale in escrow was to be taken up on or before June 13th, 1900. He further said that should the above society not make haste and put things in shape according to Mr. Carter's wishes, and the heirs not able to make satisfactory arrangements with them so far as their interest is concerned, that he (Wilkinson) would be compelled to ask for a division of the collection after the time of above Bill of Sale in escrow had expired."

A division of Edwin Carter's collection was the last thing in the world that the heirs, the Museum Association, or anyone else wanted. To parcel out the collection would decrease its value and lower its worthwhileness. The administrator got in touch with the estate lawyer; the lawyer advised as to procedure; May 31, 1900, an answer came from Denver National Bank:

Geo. Engle, Esq.,
    Breckenridge, Colo.
Dear Sir:—

As telephoned you this morning, I today deposited with the Denver National Bank to the credit of your bank, for your use as administrator for the Carter Estate, $10,000. Also had the bank confirm the same by cipher message, as per your request.

I also received from the bank your draft of $1500, payable to my order, and with the same took up the Wilkinson bill of sale for like amount, made to John F. Campion, Campion having assigned the bill of sale to you, and I now enclose it herein, as it properly belongs to you.

I am very glad to have this Carter business finally settled up. It has been a long and rather annoying matter; but it was very important that we had a legal right to the property before paying for it, for I was acting for an institution that may last for a century, or more, and I wish to express my sincere thanks to you for the assistance you have given us in this matter, which I assure you is duly appreciated by the trustees of the institution.

Very truly yours,
J. A. Thatcher
Denver National Bank President

The big hurdle had been accomplished; the $10,000 was in the estate. Edwin Carter's museum was shipped to Denver and temporarily stored in the Capitol building until the museum could be constructed. (Work started on the Denver Museum building November 18, 1901, and a small portion was completed June, 1903).

There were other aspects of the estate to be settled. Some claims were readily approved, others appeared not genuine but couldn't be disproved, and one claim had to have litigation to determine its outcome. Settling the estate dragged along two years, driving some of the heirs almost to distraction. Previous to Carter's death the museum had been admission-free and thereby tax exempt as a public institution. After his death the County viewed it differently and imposed a tax of $242.40 for 1900; $306.80 for 1901. The heirs yowled. Mounting fees and costs made them despair that anything would remain in the estate.

Administrator Engle had one consuming desire to be fulfilled—that his friend Carter have a tombstone erected on his grave. The heirs didn't want additional expenses. "The Masons spoke of honoring their most-distinguished member; couldn't they sponsor it?" "What about Breckenridge paying honor this way to their illustrious citizen?" Neither the Masons or Breckenridge made any overtures. Administrator Engle con-

sulted the lawyer: "Yes, it possibly could be considered one of the funeral expenses; there had been a precedent of that kind in Illinois." Finally the heirs agreed—"it would be only decent to set apart a fair sum for the same"—"but we implore you, don't make it costly; it would not have been the wish of Edwin to have an elaborate stone erected—something of fair size and quality." "We beg to urge you not to set aside any large amount for the same. Would not fifty dollars be sufficient to erect a suitable monument? Please do not set apart a large amount—we beg you! Suggest that Breckenridge add to the amount. He honored Breckenridge in his life: Let Breckenridge honor him in his death." An item, "$250 for monument," appears in the estate expenses. Had it not been for perseverance on the part of George Engle, Carter's grave might have been another of the unmarked graves in Valley Brook Cemetery.

Two other Carter memorial projects died aborning—a memorial park and a memorial library. At the turn of the century Breckenridge real estate property wasn't marketable. Carter's heirs couldn't understand why that "valuable property doesn't sell quickly—the most desirable building lots in town." But it didn't. The editor of the local paper came forth with a praiseworthy suggestion—why not a Breckenridge Edwin Carter Memorial Park? The two pieces of property on the east and west sides of Ridge Street could be incorporated into a lovely park.

HERE IS AN OPPORTUNITY FOR BRECKENRIDGE
TO ACQUIRE A SMALL PARK

Now that the baseball grounds and picnic grove have been taken up as placers, Breckenridge is destitute of any and all public grounds suitable for park purposes. Now, while the opportunity presents itself, the town authorities should immediately open negotiations looking to the purchase of the Carter plat for park purposes. While the tract is most too small, yet its location, beautiful lawn and inviting shade trees will afford the town something in the shape of a park.

The pleasures and advantages to be derived by all classes of our citizens from the public ownership of even a limited tract of ground in the center of town are manifest to all, and since the estate will probably be disposed of, the town should be the first and most formidable purchaser in the field.

The heirs thought an Edwin Carter Memorial Park a wonderful way for Breckenridge to honor Carter. Saturday, April 7th's newspaper blithely spoke, "Good Morning, Mayor Foote! Are you in favor of the town acquiring the Carter grounds for a public park?" The Edwin Carter Memorial Park did not materialize, even though the proposal "met with a hearty second from ninety-five per cent of the people of Breckenridge; the town needs a park, and the people are in favor of acquiring the Carter tract." A quiet, wooded park in the center of Breckenridge would have been a fine addition to the town.

A Memorial Library was suggested for the "log-cabin museum." Sister's Mustard Seeds organization wanted to establish a library. It had sufficient money to purchase and was interested in the Carter property. The town officials vetoed this.

The Carter property was finally sold. The property on the west side of Ridge Street, five lots, containing the museum, barn, carpenter shop and sheds, was sold to Edward A. Theobald for $500. The tract of ground, east side of Ridge Street, four lots, was sold to George C. Forsythe for $300. Another plot on lower French Street, six lots, brought $50. Carter's camping outfit and the old horse, "Jim," were sold at a private sale. His personal effects were limited to barest necessity—watch, cane, clothing, needful furniture and cooking utensils. He had a small library of carefully selected books—one volume of *Social Etiquette,* four volumes of *Hall's History of Colorado*, books and pamphlets on taxidermy, and an extensive library on *Masonry*. The disposal of these books is unknown.

The biggest item in Carter's estate was his collection of animals and birds. The magnitude of this vast collection is recorded in an inventory, Probate Court Record—No. 18, in Summit County Court House. Forty, 12 x 18 inch pages, in beautiful, clear handwriting are given to list all the items. The appraisement was made by A. M. Rich, J. I. Thomas and L. F. Hilliard and totaled $9,846. The following are a few among the 3300 items of the inventory:

1 Buffalo	$800
2 Buffalo at $400	$800
2 Sow Buffalo at $150	$300
1 Buffalo Calf	$50
1 Elk	$150
1 Grizzly Bear	$150
3 Grizzly Bears at $75	$225
2 Cinnamon Bears at $50	$100
1 Black Bear	$50
1 Deer	$75
3 Wolverines at $20	$60
55 Deer Heads at $15	$825
1 Buffalo Head	$300
1 Buffalo Head	$250
1 Buffalo Head	$100
161 Ptarmigans at $3	$483
2 American Eagles at $20	$40
3 Golden Eagles at $10	$30
Collection of Bird Eggs	$100
Miscellaneous lot of artificial eyes	$.25

One mounted buffalo and one black bear in the Carter Collection, $850, equaled the value of fifteen choice lots with dwelling and other buildings.

When the estate was finally settled $7,117.53 remained to be divided among the heirs. The administrator received a fee of $121.20 for two years of exacting work.

Edwin Carter's body rests in the lonely loveliness of Valley Brook Cemetery, perhaps visited occasionally by his furry and feathered friends from the nearby forest. His gravestone monument, modest and in good taste, is secondary to the museum-monument in Denver's City Park. At the Museum of Natural History an estimated 30 million visitors—school children, seekers of pleasure and knowledge—have passed through the doors to view and study one of the most remarkable exhibits of Natural History in the world. Edwin Carter's famed collection was the nucleus of this magnificent display.

Old-timers in Breckenridge point out the cottage at 111 Ridge Street—"that's the old Carter Museum."

Edwin Carter Museum-Erected 1875-111North Ridge Street,
Breckenridge.

Edwin Carter Museum, Breckenridge, Colorado

Office of Wm. P. Pollock, Summit County Clerk. Date—probably late 1860s or early 1870s. Edwin Carter-third from right. (Note mounted animals in foreground.) Courtesy—Library State Historical Society of Colorado.

INTERIOR VIEW, CARTER'S MUSEUM, BRECKENRIDGE, COLO.

Courtesy—Denver Public Library Western Collection.

Edwin Carter

Interior-Edwin Carter Museum
Courtesy—Summit Historical Society.

Interior-Edwin Carter Museum.
Courtesy—Summit Historical Society.

Buffalo of Edwin Carter's Collection; posed in woods at Breckenridge.
Courtesy—Mrs. H. G. Culbreath (daughter of Banker George Engle).

Elk of Edwin Carter's Collection; posed in woods at Breckenridge.
Courtesy—Mrs. H. G. Culbreath (daughter of Banker George Engle).

FIRST PRIVATE CITIZEN ACCORDED PUBLIC HONORS

Amid costly floral tributes from men whose favors would most likely grace the caskets of the most noted statesmen and public officials, the remains of Professor Edwin Carter, the great naturalist, lay at the state capitol building yesterday from 10 a. m. to 3 p. m.

Edwin Carter's Body Lying In State—Colorado Capitol.
Courtesy—Library State Historical Society of Colorado.

Edwin Carter funeral service, Masonic Hall, Breckenridge.
Courtesy—Mr. Melvin Gaymon.

Know all Men by these Presents, That I, Edwin Carter, of Breckenridge in the County of Summit and State of Colorado, of the first part, for and in consideration of one Dollars, to me in hand paid, at or before the ensealing or delivery of these presents, by George Engle of said place of the second part, the receipt whereof is hereby acknowledged, have bargained and sold, and by these presents do grant and convey unto the said party of the second part his executors, administrators and assigns all my personal property and effects of every kind, name and nature whatsoever including all my museum of animals and birds and all other things therein or belonging or appertaining thereto and everything and property both real and personal

belonging to me and now in my possession at and near said town of Breckenridge to have and to hold the same unto the said party of the second part his executors, administrators and assigns forever. And the said party of the first part does, for himself, his heirs, executors and administrators, covenant and agree to and with the said party of the second part his executors, administrators and assigns, to WARRANT AND DEFEND the sale of said property, goods and chattels, hereby made, unto the said party of the second part, his executors, administrators and assigns, against all and every person or persons whomsoever

IN WITNESS WHEREOF, I have hereunto set my hand and seal this day of June, A.D. 1893.

Signed, Sealed and Delivered in Presence of

W.H. Clark

Edwin Carter [SEAL]

[SEAL]

Administrator's original records of Edwin Carter Estate—George Engle, Administrator. Courtesy—Mrs. H. G. Culbreath (nee Elizabeth Engle, daughter of Banker Engle.)

This agreement made and entered into this 28th. day of May, A. D. 1896, by and between Edwin Carter and William H. Wilkinson, witnesseth:

That, whereas, said parties were some years ago associated with each other as partners in the collection and preparation of specimens for the purpose of establishing a museum, and

Whereas, said parties dissolved their said partnership some sixteen or seventeen years ago, except as to the collection which had been made up to that time, and

Whereas said parties are desirous of making some arrangements concerning the disposition of said collection so made as aforesaid while said parties were partners as aforesaid, said collection being now a part of what is known as " Carter's Museum ", located in the town of Breckenridge, in the county of Summit, in the state of Colorado,

THEREFORE it is agreed by and between said parties hereto that the said Edwin Carter may, and shall have the right to, dispose of said museum including all things belonging to said partnership collection, as he shall see fit, and that when said Edwin Carter disposes of said museum he shall pay to the said William H. Wilkinson the sum of fifteen hundred dollars ($1500) in lawful money of the United States, which said fifteen hundred dollars shall be the consideration in full for the interest of the said William H. Wilkinson in said museum.

If said museum is not disposed of by said Edwin Carter, then the said William H. Wilkinson shall retain such interest therein as the register of said museum shows him to be entitled to.

In witness whereof the said parties have hereunto set their hands and seals the day and year first above written.

A. G. Hooper. Witness   *Edwin Carter*
                                 W. H. Wilkinson

Administrator's original records of Edwin Carter Estate—George Engle, Administrator. Courtesy Mrs. H. G. Culbreath (nee Elizabeth Engle, daughter of Banker Engle.)

Professor Edwin Carter—one year before his death. Photograph by E.C. Peabody. Courtesy—Denver Public Library Western Collection.

Carter's tombstone in Breckenridge Valley Brook Cemetery, secured through the devoted, persistent effort of friend and administrator of Carter's estate, Banker George Engle.

Courtesy—Denver Public Library Western Collection.

Courtesy—Patterson Distributing Co., Denver.
Photograph—F. G. Brandenburg.

EPILOGUE

VALLEY OF DRY STONES

AN ANCIENT PROPHECY FOR OUR DAY

*(Old Testament Prophecy of Ezekiel;
Ezekiel 37:1-5)*

*The hand of the Lord was upon upon me,
and carried me out in the spirit of the Lord,
and set me down in the midst of the valley
which was full of bones,*

*And caused me to pass by them round
about: and, behold, there were many in the
open valley; and, lo, they were very dry.*

*And he said unto me, Son of man, can
these bones live? And I answered, O Lord God,
thou knowest.*

*Again he said unto me, Prophesy upon
these bones, and say unto them, O ye dry bones,
hear the word of the Lord.*

*Thus saith the Lord God unto these bones;
Behold, I will cause breath to enter into you,
and ye shall live.*

The Valley of the Blue said its goodby to
the nineteenth century from the decks of newly-
chartered gold boats. The twentieth century was
hopefully toasted "full speed ahead!" from the
same decks. A new era was beginning which
would write its own brand of history, totally different from the preceding century. Softly Beautiful Valley, once sparkling with rippling water
and verdant with willow, sage, pine and spruce,
would become a valley of dry stones—analogous
to the dry bones of Ezekiel's valley. Those wondering, "can these dry stones live?" answered
their doubts, "only the Lord God knows." Seemingly, it was impossible; dry bones and dry stones
hold little prospect of life. When the gold boats
finished their devastation, "Softly Beautiful" had
become miles of lifeless, bone-gray rock piles.

Gold Boats and the Great Depression ruled
the first half of the twentieth century in Breckenridge. Both left their scars, scabbed and unhealed.
"Gem of the Mountains" lost its luster for a time.
Only a few remained, believing in the permanency and genuineness of the jewel.

A different kind of history is in the making,
setting the stage of the 1960-2000 era. Booms
of 1860 and 1880 are being revived in the present century, perhaps exceeding the former in
liveliness and affluence. In a not-too-distant new
century historians will be seeking light from the
lamps kindled and kept aflame by "pioneers"
of this age. No doubt the twenty-first century will
find today's Breckenridge as quaint and interesting as we find the Blasted Beloved Breckenridge
of 1860-1900.

Ben Stanley Revett—the man largely responsible for transforming the Valley of the Blue into a valley of stones, dredging valleys to rock bottom in search for gold. A remarkable transformation is taking place in the last decades of the twentieth century. Miles of rock piles are being shifted and levelled. On them emerges an airport, dwellings, recreational developments. Vast wealth poured upon the valley of stones far exceeds the gold taken from hills and valleys. Courtesy—*Colorado Magazine*, XXXIX, Oct. 1962, p. 244.

Ben Stanley Revett with a "customer" coming off Farncomb Hill

Gold Boat rock piles, showing airplane landing strip. Small plane coming in for landing—(far left). Picture taken from high plateau above Highway #9.

Planes landed at the rock-pile airport.

Epilogue

(Left:—Belle Turnbull; Right:—Helen Rich)

Two Breckenridge authors made imprint for future historians—Helen Rich and Belle Turnbull. Two decades, 1930s and 1940s, are portrayed in poetry and novel. Belle Turnbull's novel, *The Far Side Of The Hill,* and poetry, under titles of *Gold Boat* and *Ten-Mile Range,* capture life and atmosphere of gold boat decades. Helen Rich's novels, *The Willow Bender* and *The Spring Begins,* bring alive people of the time and delve into intimate life of an arid-appearing existence, far from lifeless beneath the surface. Helen Rich's numerous short stories further reveal Breckenridge life as it was really lived. Draw the curtains from poetry and novel and Breckenridge stands revealed. Courtesy—Mrs. Minnie Thomas.

Jane (Porter) Robertson was Breckenridge's artist of note and recognition. Art was her life and calling. Marriage arrested the pursuit of her career; life then was devoted to being housewife and mother in Pittsburgh, Penna. At the age of 49 she applied for admission to art classes at Carnegie Institute, Pittsburgh. Admission was refused because she was "too old." A second time she was rebuffed "none too gently,"—"we admit only students who are young enough to advance." Through night courses, and every avenue open to her, she pursued her life ambition. After the death of her husband, 1940, she came to live with her sister, Charlotte Porter, in Breckenridge. Before she left Pittsburgh Jane (Porter) Robertson's paintings were exhibited in the august galleries of Andrew Carnegie Institute. Frank S. Dorsay, instructor of drawing at Columbia University, said of Jane Robertson's art: "She has captured the mood and feeling of this beautiful country. Her pastels, above all, are highly successful, and her handling of such a difficult medium is truly superb. Besides her landscape and flower studies her portraits have a universal undercurrent rather than just a momentary appeal. One miniature of a child is especially outstanding. All attests to Mrs. Robertson's versatility as an artist. She is an artist and a person eternally youthful."

Breckenridge Ski Area

Picture: Permission and kindness of Summit County *Journal* and John Topolnicki, Photographer.

Winter sports in the Breckenridge area. Courtesy—Summit County *Journal* and John Topolnicki, Photographer.

Dillon Reservoir - Summer - Ten-Mile Range in background. Courtesy—
John Topolnicki, Photographer.

Dillon Reservoir - winter - Ten-Mile Range in background, showing path
of Masontown snow slide. Courtesy—C. C. Paterson, Photographer.

Epilogue

Type of homes rising during Breckenridge Ski Boom—1970s.

Condominiums—in town and seclusion of woods—are part of Recreational Development of Breckenridge and Blue River Valley.

Breckenridge — "Gem of the Mountains" — 1972.

Cabin on writer's Look-Up Lodge property where much writing of *Blasted Beloved Breckenridge* was done. Cabin originally built by Father John Lewis Dyer to shelter two young prospectors, befriended by the "Snow-Shoe Itinerant." (Snow-Shoe Itinerant, page 335) (Built, Spring 1880, at rear of Father Dyer Church, Breckenridge; when threatened with destruction, moved to Look-Up Lodge and restored.)

NOTES

The author did not follow customary usage of page-by-page footnotes. Many source records were incorporated within the manuscript. In order to keep the historical story from being too "heavy" with documentation many of the newspaper sources were omitted. Suffice to say, most of the items, from 1859 to 1880, came from the files of *Rocky Mountain News*. After 1880 the files of *Summit County Journal* were the primary source. Regretfully, a number of early *Summit County Journal* issues are missing; undoubtedly, they would provide much-desired interest items.

The references, however, are voluminous—far too many to be minutely recorded in a work of this kind. This is not intended to be a history book; instead, it is a book of early Breckenridge-Blue River Valley stories, "loaded" with historically-documented material. Additional pages and cost of printing did not warrant a completely-recorded documentation. Chapter "Notes" contain a few additional interest items and further explanation when deemed necessary.

(*Rocky Mountain News* will be abbreviated RMN; *Summit County Journal*, SCJ).

INTRODUCTION

"Twenty Miles to Hell and Back"—RMN, May 23, 1860. "Breckenridge the most fiendish place"—Report of the Princeton Scientific Expedition. "Some it pays and others not"—RMN, Sept. 22, 1858. "Weather of the Rocky Mountain Region" —Villard's *The Past and Present of the Pike's Peak Gold Regions*. "Outside people coming to live in Buckbush"—*The Spring Begins*, page 4, Helen Rich. Breckenridge—"Gem of the Mountains"—SCJ, Sept. 15, 1887.

Two towns, Naomi and Lakeside, could not be shown on the Planimetric Map. They were down Blue River—north of Dillon. Naomi was described, SCJ, Feb. 21, 1883: "Naomi:—Mouth of Rock Creek, nineteen miles north of Breckenridge. It is the shipping point for the large number of mines discovered and opened in 1881-1882. There is a hotel, and postoffice. Harry Forshay is postmaster." Lakeside was located between Otter Creek and Black Creek and has been swallowed by Green Mountain Reservoir. The census, recorded SCJ, Jan. 30, 1892, listed Naomi 80; Lakeside, 88.

"Dickey" is recorded in *Crowfutt's Knapsack*: "Summit County on the Blue River, junction of the Breckenridge Leadville and Keystone branches of the Union Pacific Railway, six miles north from Breckenridge. Stock-raising and mining in the vicinity." 1885 population of Dickey was 32. (Dickey now submerged by Dillon Reservoir.)

CHAPTER I

Geological information comes from *Geology and Ore Deposits of the Breckenridge District, Colorado*, by Frederick Leslie Ransome, *United States Geological Survey, 1911*. "Lincoln City petrified man"—SCJ, Jan. 5, 1907 (A Glimpse Into History); "Four tribes of Ute Indians"—RMN, Oct. 2, 1879.

"Nah-oon-ka-ra"—Villard, p. 71, 106. "Breckenridge—a proud little place—she rests on a bed of gold"—RMN, Aug. 8, 1872. "Turn back the pages of American History to 1858"—*Mining Industry and Review*, Jan. 6, 1898. "Colonel Fremont, 1843-1844, explored the headwaters of Green and Grand Rivers and the Three Parks"—Villard, page 4.

"Bloody Utahs"—Villard, p. 121. "Incorrigible beggars"—Stegner, Wallace—*Beyond the Hundredth Meridian*, p. 40. "Breckenridge burned to ashes"—Dyer, John Lewis, *Snow-Shoe Itinerant*, p. 329.

"Three wagon loads of elk"—SCJ, Jan. 5, 1907 ("A Glimpse Into History"); "Jack Burns, a load of deer and elk"—SCJ, Sept. 20, 1929 ("The Good Old Days").

CHAPTER II

George Spencer and Breckenridge townsite—*History of Colorado*, Frank Hall, Vol. IV, pp. 327-328. Poznansky and Breckenridge townsite—SCJ, May 12, 1906 ("Some Interesting Breckenridge History"). Spaulding's Account of founding Breckenridge—*History of Colorado*, Vol. IV, pp. 326-327. "Fort Mary B"—*Miners' Record*, July 20, 1861. M. B. Ogden's weather report of first winter—Blue River Diggings—RMN, May 30, 1860. Forest Fires—RMN, June 27, 1860 and July 11, 1860. Silver leads—RMN, Aug. 16, 1860.

CHAPTER III

"William Byers—best statistical writer—closest observer of mining matters in the Territory"—RMN, July 6, 1861. Development of Parkville and Swan Valley—*Miners' Record*, Aug. 17, 24, 1861. Georgia and Humbug Gulches—RMN, Aug. 21, 1861. Lieutenant Roath and the Zouaves—*Miners' Record,* Sept. 14, 1861.

CHAPTER IV

"Composition of the average mining camp"—*Miners' Record*, Sept. 14, 1861. Rev. William Howbert—*Echoes from Peak and Plain*, Beardsley, Isaac. Bishop Talbot—Episcopal Church—*Miners' Record*, Aug. 17, 1861. Catholic Priest tours mountain towns, *Miners' Record*, Sept. 14, 1861. "Blowing the trumpet of Zion"—material largely from *Snow-Shoe Itinerant*, Dyer, John Lewis.

CHAPTER V

Material derived almost entirely from Bayard Taylor's, *Colorado—A Summer Trip*, and William Byers' report to the RMN.

CHAPTER VI

Material for the Marshall Silverthorn story came mostly from Samuel Bowles, *The Switzerland of America*, p. 105; the *Princeton Scientific Report*, p. 8; *Tales of Colorado Pioneers*, by Alice (Polk) Hill, and Agnes (Finding) Miner's stories—*The Story of a Colorado Pioneer and Founding and Early History of Breckenridge, Colorado*.

CHAPTER VII

"Father Dyer—First U. S. Skier"—*Time* Magazine, Jan. 13, 1936, p. 46. Father Dyer's first attempts at skiing—*Snow-Shoe Itinerant*, p. 144. Father Dyer's Skiing Ventures—*Snow-Shoe Itinerant*, pp. 149, 163-165, 172-176. "Inventive minds tried to improve transportation"—SCJ, March 26, 1954.

CHAPTER VIII

Breckenridge—"Spacious wharf and a line of piers"—*Miners' Record*, Aug. 10, 1861. "Dillon Navy Days"—SCJ, July 6, 1956; July 5, 1957; June 13, 1958; June 12, 1959. U. S. Summit County—SCJ, Dec. 9, 1966. "Breckenridge Navy"—*Beyond the Hundredth Meridian*, Stegner, Wallace—(an abridgement of Breckenridge Navy as related pp. 50, 53, 77-82, 200-201.)

CHAPTER X

Breckenridge church attendance—SCJ, October 9, 1909; June 13, 1881; Sept. 26, 1908 ("25 Years Ago—1883").

Methodist Church—*Snow-Shoe Itinerant*, Dyer, pp. 326-344; SCJ, July 21, 1883; April 12, 16, 17, 30, 1886; Nov. 2, 1907.

Catholic Church—purchases bell and builds belfry—SCJ, Aug. 12, 18, 1899; Nov. 11, 1905.

Congregational Church—SCJ, Oct. 27, 28, 1881; Dec. 12, 17, 1881; Summit County Records, Book 41, p. 396.

Episcopal Church—SCJ, July 10, 1886; July 22, 1887; Oct. 29, 1887; June 2, 1888.

CHAPTER XI

Historical items of Breckenridge Schools—SCJ, Nov. 14, 1887; SCJ, Jan. 30, 1931 (Reminiscences—1882); SCJ, Sept. 20, 1929 ("The Good Old Days—1881"); Aug. 16, 1929 ("The Good Old Days—1881"); Clamoring for a new school—SCJ, Jan. 11, 1908.

CHAPTER XII

Historical items of the Summit County Court House—SCJ, Nov. 7, 1908; Feb. 27, 1909; July 31, 1909.

CHAPTER XIV

Broncho Dave references—SCJ, June 8, 1881; Sept. 6, 1881; July 30, 1887; Sept. 8, 1887; Oct. 8, 1887; Nov. 28, 1891; Feb. 27, 1892; Dec. 26, 1908; Jan. 30, 1909; Aug. 13, 1910; May 3, 17, 1929; Dec. 20, 1929.

CHAPTER XV

Argentine—SCJ, May 12, 1886; Oct. 23, 1886; Dyersville—*Snow-Shoe Itinerant*, Dyer, John Lewis, pp. 335-340; SCJ, May 29, 1882; July 14, 1882; April 17, 1885; Nov. 3, 1886; Jan. 3, 1920; Feb. 21, 1920.

CHAPTER XVI

Fireman Hall—Record Book of Pioneer Hook and Ladder Company, No. 1; *Summit County Journal* added many other items of interest and documentation. The unique system of bell taps, calling meetings of the three companies: Hook and Ladder, Independents, and Blue River is recorded SCJ, Feb. 21, 1888.

CHAPTER XVII

After the Silverthorn-Finding plot was acquired in Riverside Cemetery, Sister Ada's body was transferred from the nearby Joseph C. Wilson plot.

CHAPTER XIX

Ed Auge's story of Pug Ryan finds verification in Denver newspaper stories of the time. Pug Ryan was thrilling reading for a number of days.

CHAPTER XX

As in "Pegasus and the Golden Horseshoe," the writer takes poetic license in "Boreas—God of the North Wind." It is only to a limited extent, however; most of the details are factual. Far-reaching happenings are related to counteract the belief, held by many, that the Big Snow of 1898-99 was localized at Breckenridge and nearby area. Accounts of the Silver Plume snow-slide are recorded RMN, Feb. 13, 14, 1899. Denver newspapers gave coverage of the Loren Waldo story.

CHAPTER XXII

The writer chose not to use real names of the people of prominent parts in this story. The one exception is Halverson. Nothing was changed or deleted from this newspaper account.

CHAPTER XXIII

"Tom's Baby" story represents a number of years of researching. The story is told as it unfolded. The search seemed to arrive at an end a number of times, and then something demanded further research. So it continued almost to the last moment before publication. The writer was reconciled to leaving it an unsolved mystery. The most startling discovery came only a few months before publication date. It was a "maddening mystery" to the writer—almost to the very end. Then a happy Addendum closed the story and the search.

CHAPTER XXIV

The visitor to Denver Museum of Natural History moves in amazement and delight from one exhibit to another in the magnificent display of wonders of nature, wild-life of Colorado and the world, and the wealth of minerals preserved for posterity within the walls of this institution. If one is familiar with the story of Edwin Carter and the Breckenridge Museum, he has the added pleasure of feeling the presence of the mild, gentle-mannered Carter accompanying him in the corridors and alcoves. It was Carter's dream; it was his gift to the future. Carter's collection of Rocky Mountain fauna was the nucleus of the museum.

Equally significant is the Campion Gold Collection of Denver Museum of Natural History. Its Farncomb Hill crystallized gold is unequalled in beauty, size of specimens and number of specimens. This, too, brings credit to Breckenridge, for here this glorious gold was found. Two of the major attractions of Denver Museum of Natural History came from Breckenridge. Breckenridge has reason to be proud.

BIBLIOGRAPHY

BOOKS

Amory, Cleveland, & Others
American Heritage Cookbook and Illustrated History of American Eating and Drinking
American Heritage Publishing Company—New York—1964

Beardsley, Isaac Haight
Echoes From Peak and Plain
Cincinnati: Curtis & Jennings
New York: Eaton & Mains
1898

Bowles, Samuel
The Switzerland of America—A Summer Vacation in the Parks and Mountains of Colorado
S. Bowles & Company—New York—1869

Dyer, John Lewis
The Snow-Shoe Itinerant
Cranston & Stowe, Cincinnati—1891

Hall, Frank
History of the State of Colorado—Vol. IV
The Blakely Printing Company, Chicago, 1895

Harper, Frank
World Ski Book
Longmans, Green & Company, Inc.
New York-London-Toronto 1949

Hill, Alice (Polk)
Colorado Pioneers in Picture and Story
Brock-Haffner Press, Denver, 1915

Hill, Alice (Polk)
Tales of the Colorado Pioneers
Pierson & Gardner, Denver, 1884

Hurley, Thomas Jefferson
Famous Gold Nuggets of the World
American Institute of Mining Engineers and American Geographical Society
1900

Gaarden, John
Gold Nuggets of the World
Gaarden Publishing Company
Hollywood, California
1940

Rich, Helen
The Spring Begins
Simon and Schuster
New York, 1947

Smiley, J. C.
History of Denver
Times-Sun Publishing Company, Denver, 1902

Stegner, Wallace
Beyond The Hundredth Meridian
The Riverside Press, Cambridge, Houghton Mifflin Company, Boston, 1954

Taylor, Bayard
Colorado—A Summer Trip
G. P. Putnam and Son, New York, 1867

Vickers, W. B.
History of the City of Denver
O. L. Baskin & Company, Chicago, 1880

Villard, Henry
The Past and Present of the Pike's Peak Gold Regions
Humphrey Milford Oxford University Press, London, 1860,
Reprint with Introduction and Notes, By Leroy R. Hafen, Secretary, The
Colorado Historical Society, Princeton University Press, 1932

White, T. and Iglehard, W.
The World's Columbian Exposition, Chicago, 1893

DOCUMENTS

Commonwealth of Australia, Department of National Development,
Bureau of Mineral Resources, Geology and Geophysics,
Canberra, Australia, 1970

Geology and Ore Deposits of the Breckenridge District, Colorado.
By Frederick Leslie Ransome. (Department of the Interior—United
States Geological Survey—Washington, Government Printing Office, 1911)

Libbey, William, Jr., and McDonald, W. W.
*Topographic, Hypsometric and Meterologic Report of the Princeton
Scientific Expedition,* (Diary of the Report) 1877

National Archives and Record Service
State of California, Department of Conservation—Division of Mines
and Geology—Second Report of the State Mineralogist, 1882

State of Montana—Bureau of Mines and Geology

State of Nevada, Bureau of Mines—McKay School of Mines, University
of Nevada

State of North Carolina, Department of Conservation and Development,
Bulletin #38, *Gold Deposits in North Carolina*—Historical Notes on
Gold Mining in North Carolina

U. S. Department of Commerce—Bureau of the Census of 1880

NEWSPAPER SERIES

Auge, Ed, *History of Breckenridge Mining District*
Summit County Journal, October 15, 1937 to January 28, 1938

Auge, Ed, *The Big Snow Blockade During the Winter of 1898-99*
Summit County Journal, March 29, 1935

Miner, Agnes F., *The Story of a Colorado Pioneer*
Summit County Journal, September 7,14,21, 1951

Peabody, E. C., *Did Tom Wintermute Take Fabulous Tom's Baby East?*
Summit County Journal, April 29, 1955

Peabody, E. C., *Personal Account of the Big Snow*
Summit County Journal, March 26, 1954 to April 30, 1954

Thar's Gold In Them Thar' Hills
Summit County Journal, December 24, 1954 to April 15, 1955

CORRESPONDENCE

Capra, Al, Prosecuting Attorney—Archie Willson's fake gold "Tom's Baby"

Hornung, Fr. Francis, Holy Cross Abbey, Canon City, Colorado—
Breckenridge Catholicism

Jean Marie, Mother, O.S.B., Prioress St. Scholastica Convent, Chicago
Breckenridge St. Gertrude's School and St. Joseph's Hospital

NEWSPAPERS

Breckenridge Bulletin

Canon City Record

Daily Alta, California

Denver Republican

Denver Times

Miners' Record

New York Times

Rocky Mountain News

Summit County Journal (Daily)

Summit County Journal (Weekly)

The Denver Post

Western Mountaineer (Golden)

MAGAZINES

Colorado Magazine Vol. XL, No. 1, January, 1963

Mining Industry

Mining Industry and Review

Mining Industry and Tradesman

Mining Reporter

Proceedings of the Colorado Museum of Natural History, Vol. XVII, No. 1,

March 1, 1938, *The Colorado Museum of Natural History—An Historical Sketch,*
By Charles H. Hanington
Time Magazine

PRIVATE COLLECTIONS

Rich, Helen, (Files) *Founding and Early History of Breckenridge,*

By Agnes F. Miner

Rich, Helen, (Files)—"Tom's Baby" items.

Slattery, Fr. John, Research papers on early Breckenridge Catholicism

LEGAL RECORDS

Denver Probate Court Records

Summit County Clerk Records

Summit County Probate Court Records

SPECIAL SOURCES

Campion, John F., Papers—Released by Colorado University Norlin Library, Western History, January, 1972

Carter, Edwin, Estate Papers, George Engle, Administrator—Courtesy Mrs. H. G. Culbreath

Parish Records—St. John the Baptist Episcopal Church, Breckenridge

Pioneer Hook and Ladder Company, Secretary's Record—Courtesy Mrs. James Vasilka

INDEX

Acton, Chet, 203, 204
Adams, Samuel, 80-83
Alaska's Nugget, 269
Algier, Rev. C. M. (Catholic), 106
Alma, Colo., 27, 104, 185, 193, 207, 240
American Gulch, 22, 23, 24, 26, 29, 43, 252, 253
American Heritage Cookbook, 256
Anaphrodisiac, 4, 237
Angels Rest, 151, 156-157
Antrim, Rev. J. A. (Episcopal), 108
Arbogast Building, 111
Arbogast, Dr., 139
Argentine. See Conger's Camp
Argentine (Decatur), 153
Argentine City, 153
Arlington House, 222
Arps, Louisa (Mrs. Elwyn), 245, 286
A. T. Lewis & Son (Denver), 278
Auge, Ed, 152, 201, 202, 203, 204, 206
Auraria, 5, 6, 26

Bailey, John (Tink), 79
Balaklava, 52, 53
Barker, Bishop W. M. (Episcopal), 111
Beardsley, Isaac H., 97, 193
Benedictine Sisters, 104, 105, 125, 139, 140
Berry, Bill, 71
Bickford, Rev. W. F. (Congregational), 106, 107
Bigelow, Mrs. Mary, 17
Billingsley, Brother (Denver clergyman), 30, 31
Black Hawk, Colo., 303, 304
Blockade (Snow, 1898-1899), 206-210, 212
Blue Goose, 240
Blue River, 28, 49, 50, 51, 68, 79, 80, 83, 143, 146, 151, 219
Blue River Company, 219
Blue River Hose Company, 168
Blue River Mines, 20, 21, 22, 23, 68
Blue River Mission, 42, 44, 49, 67, 68, 98

Blue River Valley
  arrival of iron horse in, 103
  Bayard Taylor's report of, 50, 51
  Braddock's Station in, 146
  early setlement of, 15-24
  Father Dyer and, 31, 42, 44, 68, 98
  goldboats in, 219
  Indian name of, 4
  opening of, 97
  Pegasus and, 25
  Rev. William Howbert enters, 41
  Silverthorn, Minehost of, 61
  today's charm of, 7
  transformation of, 6
  upper section of, 3, 49
  William Byers and, 26-29, 68-69
Boigegrain, Rev. Walter J. (Methodist), 193
Boreas (North Wind), 205-211
Boreas Pass, 41, 61, 91, 97, 151, 207, 210
  road over, 151
  station at, 145, 207, 210, 305
Bowles, Samuel, Switzerland of America, 59
Boyd, Dr. E. H. (also given, P.H.), 17, 18
Braddock, David, 25, 143-147
Braddock, Mattie, 145
Braddockville (Braddocks, Braddock), 25, 26, 143-144, 145, 146, 147
Brandt, Postulant Minnie, 105
Breckenridge Bi-Metallic, 92
Breckenridge Bulletin, 91, 100, 101, 106, 111, 140, 178, 204, 225, 240
Breckenridge Daily Journal, 87, 88, 89, 90, 91, 92
Breckenridge Democrat, 267
Breckenridge Mining District, 26
Breckinridge, John Cabell, 16, 52
Breckinridge, Robert J., 52
Brewer, Ed, 201, 202, 203, 204
Brockman, Jack (attorney), 284, 286
Brown, F. F. (sheriff), 189
Brown, Frank Jr., 80
Brown's Gulch, 23

Bryant, Dick (also given, Dick Bryan), 202, 203, 204
Buckskin Joe (early mining camp), 6, 29, 42, 53, 68, 98
Buffalo, 4, 6, 60, 304, 315
Buffalo Flats, 28, 52
Bullock (Diamond Blackie), 285, 286
Bullock-Webster, Phyllis (Campion), 243
Byers, William N., 17, 26-29, 50, 51, 52, 53, 59, 68, 69, 87
Byrne, Rev. Francis (Episcopal), 109

Cahill, Rev. Thomas M. (Catholic), 103, 106
California Gulch, 42, 68, 70, 303, 304.
  See also Leadville
Calithumpians, 93, 222
Calling cards, 222
Camp Downing, 31
Campion, John F., 243, 244, 245, 257, 258, 259, 295, 303, 307, 308, 309, 310, 311, 314
  Carter correspondence of, 307, 308
  gold collection of, 243, 244, 245, 259, 283, 284, 285, 293, 294, 295
  mining interests of, 244
  papers of, 294
Candell and Thompson (helped by Father Dyer), 153, 154
Capra, Al (attorney), 277, 284
Carlson, Allie, 202
Carlson, Gus, 203
Carpenter, Col. Mason B., 251, 252, 253, 254, 257, 258-259, 293
Carrigan, Rev. J. P. (Catholic), 104
Carson Hill Nugget (California), 269
Carter Avenue, 304
Carter Edwin, 178, 233, 303-315, 338
  correspondence of, 306
  estate of, 306, 313, 314, 315

Carter Museum, 244, 303-313, 315
Carter Museum-Library Ass., 308,
    311, 312, 313
Carter, Theodore (brother), 310
Casto, J., 18
Cathedral of St. John the
    Evangelist (Denver), 109
Catholic Church, 41, 97, 102-106
Central City, Colo., 42
Central Park (Breckenridge), 255
Chapin House, 30
Chapman, Mrs. B. M., 111
Chapuis, Rev. James E. (Catholic),
    Introd. XVI, 104, 105, 123, 124,
    125
Cherry Creek, 5, 6, 26
Chicago *Record,* 303
Chihuahua, 151, 168
Chipperfield, Rev. George P.
    (Congregational), 106
Chinese laborers, 224
Chivington, Rev. John M.
    (Methodist), 41
Christian Advocate, 43, 176
Christian Science Church, 111-112
Church Bell, The, 185, 186, 187,
    188, 190, 191, 194
City Park (Denver), 239, 306, 307,
    310, 315
Clinton, J. J. (Frisco Hotel), 144
Clisbee, Professor (dancing
    master), 209
Coffman, Rev. J. F. (Methodist),
    99
Colcord, Mr. and Mrs. A. B., 225
Collingwood, Ed J., 244, 305
Colorado House, 220
Colorado Mining Exchange
    Building, 246
Colorado Pioneers, 58
Colorado State Historical Society,
    27, 244, 245, 259
Colorado (Ute Chief), 51
Columbian Exposition, 1892-1893,
    189, 190, 243, 244, 246
Como, Colo., 104, 151, 152, 156,
    207, 208, 210, 211, 212
Como *Record,* 98, 101, 188
Conger, Col. S. P., 151, 152
Conger, Mrs. Diantha (S.P.),
    152, 153
Conger's Camp (Argentine),
    151-153, 156, 168
Congregational Church, 106-108,
    109, 164
Conrad, Ernest, 202, 204

Continental Divide, Introd. XIII,
    3, 6,
Corduroy, 221
Court House, 129-131
    dedication of, 131
    laying cornerstone of, 130
    location of, 129
Cowell, Dave, 201
Craig, James, 211
Cramer, F. C., 151
Crimean War, 52, 53
Cripple Creek, Colo., 177, 202,
    257
Crowfutts' Knapsack, 335
"Cucumber" (early miner), 17
Cucumber Creek and Gulch,
    17, 255
Culbreath, Mrs. H. G., 225
    See also Engle, Elizabeth
Curator of Geology, *See* Murphy,
    Jack
Currigan, Martin D., 305, 309

Dave's Broncho Stage Line, 143
Decatur, 151, 168
Delaware Flats, 24, 25, 28, 29, 43,
    45, 49, 51, 143
Delaware Gulch, 28
Denver, 7, 16, 20, 27, 59, 93, 175,
    187, 188, 210, 212, 239, 240,
    256, 258.
    Alfred J. Ware home at, 257
    blizzard at, 208
    business places of, 277, 278
    Carter Museum to, 303, 304,
        306-314
    churches in, 190
    early settlement of, 5, 6, 19, 21,
    26, 29, 30, 31, 49, 50, 60
    flesh pots of, 207
    influential citizens of, 305
    music circles of, 53
    postoffice of, 18
    Probate Court records at, 259
    Silverthorn, respected citizen of,
        58
    train to Leadville from, 202
    Trinity Church of, 191, 194
    Wintermute accident at, 279
    World Conclave of Knights
        Templar at, 246
Denver and Rio Grande Western
    Railroad, 145
Denver and South Park Railroad,
    144, 145, 151, 152, 252, 255

Denver City Park Museum of
    Natural History, 244, 245, 259,
    283, 285, 286, 293, 295, 303,
    306, 307, 314
Denver Hotel (Breckenridge), 201,
    203, 204, 256, 305
Denver National Bank, 313, 314
Denver *Post,* 244, 277, 285
Denver *Republican,* 192, 244, 252
Denver *Times,* 203
Destefano, Dominic, 211
Detweiler, Jerry, 202
Dewers, M. J. B., 190, 223
Diantha Lode, 151, 152
Dickey, 335
*Dictionary of Mining, Minerals and
    Related Terms,* 284
Dierks, John, 166
Dillon, Colo., (old Dillon), 49, 79,
    100, 145, 151, 168
Dillon *Enterprise,* 87, 90, 91, 92,
    187, 188, 224
Dillon Navy Days, 79-80
Dillon Reservoir, 3, 49, 80
Ditmer, Joanne, Introd. XVI
Douglas, Stephen, 16
Dye, Rev. William M.
    (Methodist), 101
Dyer, Elias (son of Father
    Dyer), 42
Dyer, Rev. John Lewis (Father
    Dyer),
    beginning of Blue River ministry
        by, 42-45
    Breckenridge church and, 98, 99,
        100, 101, 102, 167, 185, 221
    Brother Passmore compared
        with, 186
    comments on Indian uprising
        by, 7
    couple united in marriage
        by, 144, 222
    Dyersville and, 153-155, 157
    1880 boom described by, 255
    fire bell and, 164
    Jerry Krigbaum and, 156
    ministry in the "true riches"
        of, 31
    skiing and, 67-69, 70, 72
    town lot owned by, 256
Dyerville (Dyersville), 100, 151,
    153, 155, 156, 157

Eagle River *Shaft,* 87
Elder, Dave, 71
Eldorado West, 17, 26

Electricity (in Breckenridge), 110
Ellsworth's Chicago Zouaves,
    See Zouaves
Engle, Elizabeth (Mrs. H. G.
    Culbreath), 225
Engle, George, 94, 306, 310
    administrator of Carter Estate,
    306, 312-315
Engle, Peter, 221
Enterline King Store, 129
Episcopal Church, 92, 108-111,
    164, 176, 179
Etzler, Bob, 202
Evangelical United Brethren
    Church, 98
Evans, George H. (British
    engineer), 225
Evans, Gov. John, 191
Excelsior Gulch, 29

Fairmount Cemetery (Denver),
    53, 93
Fairplay, Colo., 42, 59, 185
Fake Tom's Baby, 277
Farncomb Hill, 26, 245, 246, 251,
    252, 253, 256, 257, 258, 259,
    267, 269, 270, 283, 284, 285,
    293, 294
    gold of, 245, 257, 270, 283,
    284, 285
Farnham, 151, 155, 156
Field and Farm magazine, 146
Figgins, J. D., 285
Financial Panic of 1857,
    5, 42, 58
Fincher, Jonathan C., 87-94,
    188, 192, 194
    See also "Ye Editor"
Fincher, Mrs. J. C., 93
Finding, Ada (Sister), 175, 176,
    177, 179
Finding, Agnes (Aggie), 139, 175,
    176, 177
    See also Miner, Agnes (Finding)
Finding, Antoinette (Tonnie),
    175, 177
Finding, Charles, 57, 61, 175,
    176, 223
Finding, Martha (Silverthorn)
    (Mrs. Charles), 57, 58, 60,
    175, 176
Fire bell, 164, 168, 169
Fire siren, 168-169
Fireman's Ball, 168, 222
Fireman's Hall, 102, 104, 108, 112,
    122, 163-169, 185, 209, 221

Fires, destructive, 22, 23, 163
First improvement, 15
Fish, Erland F., 219
Fishing, 6
Fletcher, Donald, 163
Fletcher, Eli, 72, 144, 156, 207
Fletcher, Will, 207
Floyd, Prof. A. J., 121
Foote, Robert, 201, 202, 203, 204
Ford, Barney, 157, 223, 224
Fort Mary B (Mabery, Maribeh),
    15, 17, 18, 19, 20, 21, 22, 24,
    68, 225
Foss, Bishop, 192
Four Seasons Development
    Center, 83
French Creek, 3
French Gulch, 17, 19, 22, 26, 31,
    42, 43
Frisco, Colo., 99, 121, 144, 145,
    151, 168, 223, 225
Fryer, James, 155
Fuller Placer, 251
Fulton, Carl, 202
    father of, 206

Galena Gulch, 23, 24, 28, 43, 143
Galway, Rev. D. W. (Episcopal),
    111, 176
Gambling Law of 1866, 188
Ganong, Earl, 79, 80
Gaymon, Oren K., 90, 91, 92, 223
Gaymon, Mrs. O. K., 177, 224, 225
Gayosa Hall, 29, 30
Geiger, Eusebuis, O. S. B., 104
Georgetown, Colo., 211, 304
Georgia Gulch, 26, 29, 30, 31, 42,
    43, 45, 60, 61, 98
German Prince and Party, 225
Gertsgrasser, Willi, 79
Gibbons, Rev. William C.
    (Congregational), 107, 108
Gibson Gulch, 43
Gibson Hill, 97
Gold, 16, 17, 18, 19, 67
Goldboat, Introd. XV, 83, 219
Gold Flake Lode, (Mine) (Vein),
    253, 259, 267, 269, 284, 295
Gold Hill, 28
Gold Run, 21, 26, 28, 31, 41, 43,
    67, 97
Goldfield, 240
Goldpan Shops, 225
Graff's Opera House (Frisco),
    144, 278

G. A. R. Hall, 102, 108, 110, 124,
    130, 168, 201, 209, 222, 279
Griswold, Don and Jean, 153
Groves, Jerry, 256, 257
Groves, Lizzie, 256, 257, 295
    See also Ware, Elizabeth
    (Groves)
Groves, Tom, 251, 252, 253, 254,
    256-257, 258, 259, 293, 294, 295
Guards, United Bank of
    Denver, 295
Guest List of Carter Museum
    Notable Visitors, 305
Gutmann, Rhabanus, O. S. B., 104

Half-Way Gulch, 151, 210, 212
Hall, Frank, *History of Colorado,*
    16, 17, 68
Halverson, Carl, 240-241
Hamburg steak, 221
Hanash, Ed, 253
Hardy, Charles E., 90, 92
Hartman, J. H. and Bros., 210, 211
Hartman, John, 253
Haydee, M'lle. (entertainer), 29, 30
Henderson, Walter, 72
High Tor Lodge, 147
Hill, Alice Polk, *Tales of Colorado
    Pioneers,* 59
Hilliard, L. F., 224, 245, 252
Hilliard, Mrs. L. F., 224
*History of the Breckenridge Mining
    District,* 152
Hodder, Rev. Charles W.
    (Episcopal), 109, 110, 111, 185
Holtermann's Conglomerate
    (Australia), 269
Holy Cross Abbey (Canon City),
    102, 104, 125
Hook and Ladder Company, 164,
    167, 168
Hoosier Pass, Introd XIII, 3, 4
Hornung, Father Francis, 102,
    104, 125
Hospitals, 139-142
Howbert, Rev. William
    (Methodist), 41, 97
Huber, Mother Luitgard, 124
Humbug Gulch, 22, 23, 24, 26,
    29, 30, 304
Huntress, Deacon M. H., 225
Hurley, Thomas J., *Famous Gold
    Nuggets of the World,*
    268, 269, 285
Hyacinthus, 205, 211

Illinois Gulch, 27
Independent (Fort Independence), 15, 16, 18, 21
Independent's Company, 167, 168
Indiana Gulch, 91, 100, 151-157
Inside Detective magazine, 284
Iowa Gulch, 28

Jander, Gus, 222
Jefferson Territory, 19, 20
Jones Fort, 18, 19
Jones Mill, 255
Jones, Sam, 202
Jones, Mrs. Samuel W., 176, 177, 179
Jones, S. G., 18, 19

Kadrinka, Henri, 79
Kaiser, Christ (Chris), 92, 209, 222
Keables, A. E. and Hattie, 140
Kehler, Father (Denver Clergyman), 30, 31
King, Ralph H., 284
Kiowa Tribe of Redmen, 279
Kirschbaum, Walter, 79
Knorr, W. P., 201, 203
Kobish, John, 277
Kokomo, 87, 100, 145, 168, 202, 203, 204
Krigbaum, Jerry, 155, 156-157

Lakeside, 335
Langrishe and Daugherty, 29, 30
Leadville (California Gulch), 87, 88, 124, 145, 192, 193, 194, 203, 244
Leadville *Democrat*, 187
Leadville *Herald-Democrat*, 237
Leadville *Journal*, 90
Levy, Charles, 201-202
Ley, Father, 104
Lincoln, Abraham, 16
Lincoln City (Lincoln), 4, 26, 43, 44, 68, 100, 146, 151, 168, 220
Lodges, 222
Lytton, Harry (Litten), 251, 252, 253, 256, 267, 277, 293

McClaine, C. E., 285
McCourt, Elizabeth (Baby Doe), 106
McCourt, Rev. J. C. (Catholic), 106
McDowell, Chancellor, 191

Machebeuf, Bishop Joseph P. (Catholic), 102, 103, 104, 124
McIntyre, Dr. 191
McNulty's Gulch Placer, 251
Mahon, John, 71
Manley, Dick, 202, 203, 204
Mannerchor, 221
Mardi Gras, 208, 209
Marranzino, Pasquale, 245
Masons, 130
    annual ball of, 222
    Breckenridge Lodge #47 of, 304, 311, 312
    hall of, 29
    monument of, 45
    Parksville Lodge of, 45, 98, 304
Masontown, 140
Mastodon (Antediluvian relic), 4
Matz, Bishop Nicholas C. (Catholic), 105, 106, 124
Mayo Gulch, 43
Meeker Massacre, 7
Mercer, Rev. Richard (Episcopal), 111
Merkle, William, 139
Methodist Church, 49, 98-102
    Annual Conference of, 191, 192
    bell of, 185, 186, 187
    Community Christmas Tree-Program of, 223
    construction of Fireman's Hall and, 164
    description of the Breckenridge, 112
    early Breckenridge Sunday services schedule of, 106
    Father Dyer, 44
    fire in, 164
    first Blue River services of, 41, 97
    Judicial Confernce of, 193
    nomenclature of, 98
    Sister's Mustard Seeds gift to, 179
    social issues of, 190
    Sunday School class of, 176
    use of fire bell by, 167
Middle Park, 50, 52
Miner, Agnes (Finding), 60, 61, 175
Miners and Prospectors Ass., 238
Miner's Hospital, 139
Miners Protective Ass., 139, 238
Miners' *Record*, 15, 17, 26, 27, 29, 30, 59, 79, 87, 220
Mining Congress, 246
Mining Industry, 253, 256, 257, 258, 267

Mining Industry and Review, 284, 293
Mining Reporter magazine, 294
Minnie's House, 240
Moffat, D. H., 309, 313
Montana's Nugget, 269
Montezuma, Colo, 100, 104, 145, 168
Montezuma *Millrun*, 87, 91
Mosquito Range and Pass, 68
Mount Argentine, 151
Mount Baldy, 145
Murphy, Jack (Curator of Geology), 283, 293, 295

Naomi, 335
Nashold, E., 107, 122, 165, 167
National Archives and Records Service, 16, 153
National Editorial Ass., 89
New Year's Eve Ball, 168
New York *Times*, 208, 209
Nigger Hill (now known as Ford Hill), 106
Norlin Library, University of Colo., (Western History), 294

Occidental Hotel, 209
Ogden, M. B., 20-21
Orithyia (nymph), 205
Oro Mine, 201
Osceola Nugget (Nevada), 269
Ouray (Ute Chief), 7

Paige City, 25
Painsett, J., 211
Painsett, Thomas, 207-208, 211
Paris, Roger, 79
Park City (Parkville), 29, 30, 45, 61, 98, 129
Passmore, Rev. Florida (Methodist), 92, 101, 185, 186, 188, 189-194
"Patch," The, 27
Patriotic Order of the Sons of America, 58
Peabody, E. C., 71, 206, 209, 277-278
Peabody, Mrs., 209
Peck, Dean A. C., 192
Petrified giant, 4
Pettenes (early news correspondent), 30
Phillips, Commissioner A. W., 131
Phipps, Allan, 293
Pike's Peak Gold Rush, 5-6

Placer mining, 17
Planimetric map, 335
Pollack, William P., 220
Pollock (Pollard), 15, 16
Powell, Major John Wesley, 7, 80
Poznansky, Felix, 15-16
Prentiss, Rev. (Episcopal), 108
Presbyterian Church, 102
Preston (early mining camp), 145
Preston, Captain, 220
Princeton Scientific Expedition,
    Introd. XIII, 59
Professional hunter, 6
Ptarmigan collection, 304
Public schools, 121-123
Pug Ryan (Louis A. Scott),
    201-204

Ralston, George, 201, 203, 204
Ransome, Frederick Leslie, 335
Red-Wing *Republican*, 89
Reed, Myron W., 193
Revett, Ben Stanley, 83, 219, 223,
    225, 294, 295, 308.
    correspondence of, 295, 308-310
    dredgeboats of, 83, 325
Revival and Temperance
    Meetings, 101-102
Rich, Helen, Introd. XV
Richards, S. T., 207
Rifle Circuit (Methodist
    Church), 193
Riverside Cemetery (Denver),
    57, 176
Roath, Lt. W. T., 31
Roberts, Hon. Caesar A., 131
Robinson (early mining camp),
    87, 100, 104, 168, 225
Robinson, Father (Catholic), 106
Robinson *Tribune*, 87
Rocky Mountain News, 18, 19, 20,
    23, 24, 26, 29, 30, 43, 50, 57,
    58, 68, 79, 87, 191, 192, 193,
    208, 245, 246, 252
Rogers, Mayor (Denver), 306
Routt, Gov., 305
Ruff, Eli, 210
Russell, Green, 5, 18
Ryman, Richard, 79

Saint Gertrude's Select School
    (Academy), 104, 123-125, 140
Saint Joseph Hospital, 104, 139
Saint Scholastica Academy
    (Canon City), 125
Saloon Law, 186-187

Salt, 21
Salt Lick (near Dillon, 304, 309
Salt Valley (Valle Salade), 3
Scott, Walter (State Director of
    Mines), 245
*Second Report of the State
    Minerologist* (Calif)., 269
Seyball, Sutton and Company, 152
Shannon, Rev. J. R.,
    (Methodist), 185
Sharp, Verna, *A History of
    Montezuma, Saints John, and
    Argentine*, 153

Silver Lode, 23, 24
Silver Plume, Colo., 211, 221
Silver Plume Eleven Italians
    (snowslide victims), 211
Silverthorn Flats, 61
Silverthorn, Judge Marshall,
    Introd. XIII, 4, 41, 53, 57, 59,
    60, 68, 81, 163
    hotel of, 52, 58, 59, 60, 61, 68,
    97   129, 164, 220
    Mrs. Silverthorn, wife of, 52, 58,
    59, 60, 61, 81
    Mr. and Mrs., 52, 58, 97

Silverthorne (Silverthorn), 57, 61
Sis Orinda, 224
Sister's Mustard Seeds, 109,
    175-179
Skiing (popularly known as "snow-
    shoeing"), 67-68

    Breckenridge Lincoln Avenue
        for, 71
    Father Dyer a novice at, 67
    Father Dyer hailed United States'
        first at, 67
    Father Dyer not United States'
        first at, 68
    Father Dyer's harrowing
        adventures when, 70
    Father Dyer's mail-carrying
        by, 68
    First winter travelling in Blue
        River Valley by, 68
    Gold-Rush miners fostered birth
        of American, 71
    Invention attempts (snow-bikes,
        snow-mobiles) to make
        easier, 71-72
    Skis made locally for, 72
    "Snow-Shoe Thompson's" Sierra
        Mountains mail-carrying by,
        69-70

William Byers' (*Rocky Mountain
    News* editor), first attempt
    at, 68-69
Smiley, J. C., 243
Smith, William A., 19, 20, 22, 23,
    24, 68
Snake River, 3, 50, 51
Snow-Shoe Thompson, 69-70
Snow-Shoeing (*See* Skiing)
Snowden, Rev. Chauncey E.
    (Episcopal), 111, 131
Snowshoes (Skiis), 17, 19
South Park, 3, 7, 41, 42, 44, 208
South Park Mining Camps, 27
Spalding, Bishop (Episcopal),
    108, 110
Spaulding, Ruben J. (Spalding),
    15, 16, 17, 18, 21, 24
Spaulding District, 15
Spencer, Gen, George E., 15, 16, 21
State Historical Society of Colorado.
    See Colorado State Historical
    Society
Stegner, Wallace, 7
Stewart, Rev. John
    (Episcopal), 111
Stratton, W. S. (Cripple Creek),
    177, 178
Summit County
    Blue River Mission of, 42, 67
    Braddock's crop experiments
        in, 146
    commissioned ship named for, 80
    consolidated school of, 121
    Father Dyer's ministry in, 100
    Fincher's newspaper work in,
        88, 89, 90
    first newspaper published in, 87
    first organized river boat races
        of, 79
    gold boats of, 83, 219
    gold exhibit from, 244, 246
    Loren Waldo's working in, 210
    mining interests of, 258, 259
    resident ministers in, 101
    royal visit to, 225
    Silverthorn and, 58, 61
    size of, 129
    snow blockade of, 207
    theatrical performances in
        early, 44
Summit County *Democrat*, 90
Summit County *Journal*, 87, 88, 89,
    92, 98, 101, 109
Summit County *Leader*, 87, 89,
    90, 106

Summit County Mining Exchange, 140
Sumner, Jack (mountain guide and trader), 50, 51
Sunderling, George, (snow victim), 206
Sutherland, Alexander, 52, 53
Sutton, Charlie-Mary, 140
Swan City (Swan), 143, 144, 145
Swan River, 3, 21, 22, 23, 51, 67, 83, 143
Swan River Valley, 4, 24, 26, 29, 31, 44, 143, 144, 168
Swedish Hoting Ski, 72
Swisher, James W., 88, 91, 131, 192

Tabor, H. A. W., 70, 106, 246
Talbot, Bishop (Episcopal), 41, 108
Tarryall, South Park, 15, 18, 22, 26, 41, 68, 87, 108
Taylor, Bayard, 49-52, 237, 241
Temperance drink, 145
Ten Mile Creek (River), 3, 21, 50, 145
Ten Mile *News*, 87
Teutonia Leiderkranz, 222
Thatcher, J. A., 313, 314
Theobald, Mr. and Mrs. Robert A., 140
Thomas, Gov., 311
Time Magazine, 67
Tom's Baby (Maddening Mystery), 243-295
Tonapah Shops, 219
Town Company, 99
Town Hall Center (Civic Center), 169
Turnbull, Belle, Introd. XV
Tuttle, G. E., 100

United Bank of Denver, 245, 286, 293, 295
U. S. Geological Survey, 1911, 244, 267
U. S. Nuggets, 268-269
USS Summit County, Colorado, 80
Ute Indians, 4, 6, 7, 16, 21, 22

Valle Salade. *See* Salt Valley
Valley Brook Cemetery, 206, 238, 255, 279, 304, 311, 312, 314, 315
Van Cott, Mrs., 101, 102

Van Nostrand, Bessie (Ware), 293. *See also* Ware, Bessie (Van Nostrand)
Vegetable gardening, 23, 146
Victoria, 294, 295. *See also* Wapiti
Victoria Company, 254
Victoria property, 267
Villard, Henry, *The Past and Present of the Pike's Peak Gold Regions,* 6, 49

Waldo, Loren, 210, 211, 212
Waldo, Minnie (Volkart), 210, 211, 212
Waldo, Nathan (father), 211
Walker, Charlie, 309, 310, 311
Wallpaper, 221
Wapiti (Victoria), 26, 244, 257, 294
Ware and Groves Mining Claim, 257
Ware, Bessie E. (Van Nostrand), 255, 256, 257, 258, 259, 293
Ware, Col. A. J., 251, 252, 253, 254, 293, 294
Ware, Elizabeth (Groves), 256, 257, 258. *See also* Groves, Lizzie
Ware, Harry C., 257, 258
Ware-Carpenter Concentrator, 294
Ware-Carpenter property, 253, 254
Warren, Bishop (Methodist), 192
Warrior's Mark, 100, 151, 153, 154, 155, 156
Washington hand press, 89
Watson's Warm Stove Mine, 223
Weaver, Balce, 17, 29
"Welcome Stranger" (Australia), 245, 269-270
Wesley, John (Aldersgate experience), 98
"West Breckenridge," 255, 256
Westerman, C. L., 131, 143, 305
Westerman, Clara, 105
Weurfmansdobler, Xavier, 79
Wheeler, 145, 151, 168
Wheeler, John H., 268
White, Miss L. M. (revivalist), 102
White, T. and Igleheard, W., 244
Whitney, Sumner, 202, 204
Wildlife, 4, 6, 18
Wilkinson, William H., 306, 307, 313, 314
Williams, Mrs. Mary (Hilliard), 245

Willson, Archie V., 277, 283, 284, 294
Wilson, Matilda (Silverthorn) (Mrs. Joseph), 57, 58, 60
Wilson, Mrs. Oral K. ("Frankie" Gore), 245
Wilson Smelter, 255
Wintermute, Mrs. Tom (Clara Remine), 109, 277-279
Wintermute, Tom, 277-279, 283
Woman's Club, 168-169
World Conclave of Knights Templar, 246
World's Fair Breckenridge Gold Exhibit, 295
World's Largest Nugget (Australia), 269-270
Wynkoop, Editor, 293, 294

"Ye Editor," 87-94, 294
  civic projects prodded by, 221
  comments on Broncho Dave by, 144, 145, 146
  comments on Chinese laborers by, 224
  comments on Fireman's Hall by, 165, 167, 168
  comments on Rev. Passmore by, 187, 188-189, 194
  social distress of, 223
  See also Fincher, Jonathan C.
Yuba Dam Flats (U-B Dam) (U-Be Dam), 139
Yust, Henry, 221

Zouaves, 31